The **Rough Guide** to

New Orleans

written and researched by

Samantha Cook

ROUGH
GUIDES

www.roughguides.com

Contents

Big Easy cuisine
colour section
following p.48

Mardi Gras colour
section following p.176

Colour maps following
p.264

◀◀ Steamboat on the Mississippi River ◀ Mardi Gras Indian

Introduction to
New Orleans

As it enters its fifth century, New Orleans remains proudly apart from the rest of the United States. The product of a dizzying jumble of cultures and influences, it's a place where people dance at funerals and hold parties during hurricanes, where some of the world's finest musicians make ends meet busking on street corners, and fabulous Creole cuisine is dished up in hole-in-the-wall dives.

There's a wistfulness here too, along with its famed *joie de vivre* – not only in the ghostly devastation of the flood-wracked **Ninth Ward**, but also in the peeling facades of the old **French Quarter**, in its filigree cast-iron balconies overgrown with ferns and fragrant jasmine, and in the cemeteries lined with crumbling above-ground marble tombs. New Orleans' melancholy beauty – along with its ebullient spirit – has always come with an awareness of the fragility of life, due at least in part to its perilous geography.

Founded by the French in 1718 on the swampy flood plain of the lower Mississippi River, and today spreading back as far as the enormous Lake Pontchartrain, New Orleans is almost entirely surrounded by **water**, which since its earliest days has both isolated it from the interior and connected it to the outside world. By the time the Americans bought it, in the Louisiana Purchase of 1803, this was a cosmopolitan city whose ethnically diverse population had mingled to create a distinctive **Creole** culture. In the nineteenth century its importance as a port brought in the smugglers, gamblers, prostitutes and pirates that gave it the decadent "**sin city**" notoriety that it still has today. Ever since then visitors, among them an inordinate number of artists, writers and sundry bohemians, have poured in to see what the fuss was about; many found themselves staying, unable to shake this dreamy, steamy place out of their system.

After the Civil War, which brought the city to its knees, New Orleans trailed financially in the wake of its more dynamic Southern rivals. The economy soon became dependent on **tourism**, with millions of visitors seduced by the allure of its authentic **jazz**, fine **food**, vibrant **festivals** and free-flowing **alcohol**. Perversely, New Orleans' second-league status, in commercial terms, has long protected it from the modernization that ripped out the old hearts of wealthier cities, and allowed it to hold on to its distinctive character. Being poor, however, is not always easy. Even before Katrina, there was a side to the city that the tourist literature chose determinedly to ignore: just footsteps away from the feted French Quarter and Garden District – themselves touched by decrepi-

▲ Jackson Square

tude and decay – lay woefully neglected housing projects and poverty-scarred neighbourhoods that, since the floods, have yet to fully recover.

New Orleans, however, will never give up on itself. A city defined by tradition, ceremony and ritual – from the devout celebration of Catholic saints' days and the offerings left at **voodoo** shrines, to the **Second Line parades** in which umbrella-twirling dancers and blasting brass bands lead crowds of thousands through poor black neighbourhoods just as they have since the 1890s – much of its vitality and sheer panache comes from a heartfelt belief that what has gone before is worth keeping. As anyone who has witnessed a **jazz funeral** knows, mourning in New Orleans can also be joyful; the memory of what is lost sustains those who remain.

Spread across a patchwork of distinctive **neighbourhoods**, New Orleans has always felt surprisingly small – even before some of those neighbourhoods were wiped out by the floods. Simple to get around and easy to get to know, it's one of the best places in the US to kick back and unwind for a few days. Above all, it is less a city of major sights than of **sensual pleasures**. Many of its most lingering delights come after dark, when the streets fill with people eating in the hundreds of restaurants, drinking at its venerable bars, and enjoying a live music scene to rival any in the world. With its subtropical climate, Latin-influenced architecture and black majority population, its voodoo worshippers, street culture and long-held carnival traditions, New Orleans is often called the northernmost Caribbean city. Sybaritic vices are relished here – no more so than during the many festivals, especially, of course, the world-famous **Mardi Gras**, when real life is put on hold as businessmen and bus-boys alike

Visiting New Orleans post-Katrina

It has been horribly clear, since the events of August 2005, that there's a lot more to the Big Easy than its image as a nonstop party town. And while this very special place has lost none of its power to beguile, **visiting New Orleans after the floods** still requires sensitivity and compassion. Even at the best of times this was a contradictory city, repeatedly striking you with the stark divisions between rich and poor (and, more explicitly, between white and black); years after Katrina, with the emotional and physical scars still running deep, those contradictions remain, writ large. While you can party in the French Quarter and the Faubourg Marigny till the early hours, dancing to great jazz and gorging on delicious Creole food, just ten minutes away entire neighbourhoods struggle to rebuild, blanketed, despite the immense efforts of their pioneering returnees, by a ghostly silence.

That's not to say that enjoying life is inappropriate in today's New Orleans – while it was dealt a crippling blow, let down not only by nature but also by federal and local governments, the vitality, courage and sheer stubborn loyalty of its citizens remain strong. The city is still rebuilding, not only its communities but its culture, and needs the support of visitors more than ever. Whether that support takes the shape of dancing in the streets to a noisy brass band or donning overalls and helping rebuild the Ninth Ward, it will be repaid to you tenfold.

are swept along by an increasingly frenzied season of parties, street parades and masquerade balls.

Whatever time of year you come, you'll slip easily into the indolent way of life, rejecting an itinerary of museum-hopping in favour of a stroll around the **French Quarter**, where the quirky street life and elegant crumbling buildings provide feasts for the eye; a leisurely steamboat cruise on the **Mississippi River**; or simply a long cool drink in a hidden courtyard. Perhaps the most taxing thing you'll do is head out on the slow-moving old streetcar to the **Garden District**, where dark green shrubs weighed down by fat magnolia blossoms squat in the shadow of centuries-old live oaks tangled with ragged grey streamers of Spanish moss. Wherever you find yourself, you will soon come to know that this beautiful and beleaguered place – and every person

▲ Street parade

who calls it home – matters. That the world nearly lost New Orleans is a tragedy. That it didn't is testament to its people. The mélange of cultures and races that built the city still gives it its heart; not "easy," exactly, but quite unlike anywhere else in the world.

Where to go

Most tourists head first for the battered old **French Quarter** (or Vieux Carré), the compact, thirteen-block-wide site of the original grid settlement. Centering on lively Jackson Square and bordering the Mississippi, the Quarter's combination of Creole architecture, fabulous restaurants and eccentric street life proves irresistible. Downriver, oak-shaded Esplanade Avenue, lined with crumbling Italianate mansions, separates the Quarter from the funky **Faubourg Marigny**, a low-rent district of ramshackle Creole cottages. Though predominantly residential, the Faubourg features a handful of excellent bars, clubs and restaurants, especially along Frenchmen Street, which shoots off at an angle from Esplanade. There's another rash of good bars and restaurants in the neighbouring **Bywater**. A residential area of brightly painted shotgun houses, warehouses and storage lots, there's little to actually see here, but as the focus of a hip arts scene, it's a prime place to hang out. The Quarter's lakeside boundary, North Rampart Street, separates it from the historic African-American neighbourhood of **Tremé**. Music permeates everything here, from the brass bands playing festivals at Louis Armstrong Park and in a handful of neighbourhood jazz clubs, to the lively Second Line parades.

On the other side of the Quarter, across **Canal Street**, the **CBD** (Central Business District), bounded by the river and I-10 (Claiborne Avenue), spreads upriver to the elevated Pontchartrain Expressway. This was the early "American sector", settled by Anglo-Americans after the Louisiana Purchase in 1803. Today, dominated by offices, hotels and banks, it also incorporates the **Warehouse District**, studded with galleries and museums and, towards the lake, the gargantuan **Superdome**. It's an easy journey upriver from the CBD to the rarefied **Garden District**, an area of gorgeous old mansions covering the thirteen or so blocks between Jackson and Louisiana avenues. Don't confuse it with the **Lower Garden District**; creeping between the expressway and Jackson, this is quite a different creature, its run-down old houses home to a mixed population of young creatives and old-timers. The best way to get to the Garden District is on the historic streetcar along toney **St Charles Avenue**, the district's lakeside boundary; you can also approach it from **Magazine Street**, a six-mile stretch of galleries, restaurants and antique stores that runs parallel to St Charles riverside. Entering the Garden District you're officially **uptown**, which spreads upriver to encompass **Audubon Park and Zoo**, Loyola and Tulane **universities** and, where the streetcar takes a sharp turn inland, the studenty **Riverbend** district. If you're here for Jazz Fest or Voodoo Fest, you'll be spending a lot of time in **Mid-City**, the huge sweep of land fanning out beyond Tremé and the CBD up to Lake Pontchartrain. Esplanade Avenue slices through the heart of the district, passing the Fair Grounds racetrack, site of the festivals, before ending up at **City Park** with its impressive Museum of Art.

Though New Orleans has enough to keep you in its thrall for a few laid-back days, it also offers a couple of intriguing **side-trips**. Hire a car and you can head out to the alligator-infested **swamps** that soak the land south of the city and be back in time for a slap-up feed. If you fancy spending a night away, on the other hand, check out the restored **plantation homes** along the River Road, many of which offer luxurious and reasonably priced B&B rooms. Anyone in town in October or April, meanwhile, should head out to see the extraordinary **Angola Prison Rodeo** – a long, lonely drive, but one that rewards you with an unsettling, bizarrely compelling experience.

Napoleon House

When to go

New Orleans has a subtropical **climate**, with warm temperatures, high humidity and heavy rainfall. The peak **tourist seasons** are Mardi Gras – which starts on Twelfth Night and builds up in intensity until Mardi Gras itself, the day before Ash Wednesday – and Jazz Fest, which spreads across a fortnight at the end of April and the start of May. Both, along with the increasingly popular French Quarter Festival, occur in **spring**, which is a pleasant, sunny time to visit. However, the humidity is already building up by then, and Jazz Fest especially can be plagued by heavy rain.

The torpid months between June and September, when the blistering heat and intense humidity prove debilitating, count as **off-season**; prices tend to be lower and crowds thinner at this time. From May to November the city is at risk from the **hurricanes** that sweep through the Gulf of Mexico.

▲ Lafitte's Blacksmith Shop

Climate-wise, **autumn** is one of the best times to visit: October especially tends to be sunny, warm and relatively dry, though the nights can be chilly. Even **winter** days don't usually get too cold; the nights, however, are another matter, cursed by the bone-bitingly damp air that creeps in from the river.

New Orleans' climate

	Jan	Feb	Mar	Apr	May	Jun	Jul	Aug	Sep	Oct	Nov	Dec
Average daily temperatures (°C)												
Max/min	20/6	18/7	21/11	26/15	29/18	32/21	33/23	32/21	30/21	26/15	21/10	17/7
Average daily temperatures (°F)												
Max/min	69/43	65/45	71/52	79/59	85/65	90/71	91/74	90/71	87/70	79/59	70/50	64/45
Average monthly rainfall (mm)												
	126	133	120	114	129	118	171	153	149	67	103	134

things not to miss

It's not possible to see everything that New Orleans has to offer in one trip – and we don't suggest you try. What follows is a selective taste of the city's highlights, from its street parades and world-famous festivals to its quirky bars and intriguing museums. They're arranged in four colour-coded categories to help you find the very best things to see, do, eat and experience. All highlights have a page reference to take you straight into the Guide, where you can find out more.

01 The French Quarter Page **31** • The spiritual heart of the city – its gorgeous lacy balconies captured on countless postcards – is where New Orleans all began. That it still manages to captivate all who come here is testament to its history, its spirit, and its haunting, faded beauty.

02 **Mother-in-Law Lounge** Page **150** • Hang out in this Tremé lounge to pay respects to "Emperor of the World" R&B star Ernie K-Doe and his wife Antoinette. They may have both passed on, but New Orleans will not let them die.

04 **Kermit Ruffins** Page **157** • Whether at his legendary Thursday night gigs at *Vaughan's*, at a festival, or cooking up barbecue at a Tremé bar, the hardest-working musician in town all but defines the spirit and joy of the city.

03 **Steamboating on the Mississippi** Page **57** • Sit back and enjoy the cool river breezes as the lovely old Natchez steamboat – calliope and all – churns its way through the Big Muddy, providing great views and a true sense of the river's awesome power.

05 **Louisiana Music Factory** Page **195** • Splendid French Quarter music store, with regular live gigs, that marks ground zero for anyone interested in New Orleans and roots music.

06 **Garden District** Page **84** • In marked contrast to the hustle and buzz of the French Quarter, the grand old Garden District is a peaceful oasis lined with wonderful old piles and lush, jungly gardens.

07 **Mardi Gras Indians** Page **166** • Witnessing the Indians showing off their meticulously hand-sewn suits, and competing with each other in song and dance, is a rare and sacred experience.

09 Volunteering in the Ninth Ward Page **104** • Though the flood-devastated Ninth Ward still has an enormous way to go, the commitment shown by the volunteers who have helped rebuild it is a heartening sign that its streets will ring with life once more.

10 Frenchmen Street Pages **148**, **157** & **160** • There is always something going on in the bars and clubs of Frenchmen Street, the city's hippest nightlife stretch, from tea dances to brass band blowouts to electro DJs and swing nights.

08 NOMA Sculpture Garden Page **98** • A peaceful garden attached to the superb art museum in City Park, its sculptures – from artists including Louise Bourgeois and Henry Moore – seem to grow out of the lush, fertile land.

11 Ogden Museum of Southern Art Page **80** • New Orleans' classiest museum, offering a cornucopia of work that defines this evocative, distinctive and otherworldy region.

12 **Preservation Hall** Page **156** • Trad jazz at its joyful best, played in a battered old venue that's been here for generations.

14 **Trashy Diva** Page **189** •
Feminine, elegant and utterly gorgeous, Trashy Diva's own-line frocks combine *A Streetcar Named Desire* decadence with old-school Hollywood glamour to create something totally New Orleans.

13 **Second Lines** Page **68** •
New Orleans marks anything of any significance with a street parade led by brass bands – the ragtag Second Liners who follow, dancing in the streets, are integral. Feel free to join in – that's the whole point.

15

16 **Backstreet Cultural Museum** Page **66** • Tremé's love letter to New Orleans street culture, from its Second Line parades to its Mardi Gras Indians to its jazz funerals.

15 **Festivals** Page **175** • With its European, Caribbean and African roots, New Orleans is a superb festival city. Marching bands, masking, music and food abound, as do the crazy street parades that just shout for you to join in.

17 **Mid-city Lanes Rock'n'Bowl** Page **162** • Authentic swamp pop and zydeco, bowling lanes and cold beer: it's an irresistible, only-in-New Orleans combination.

Basics

Basics

Getting there

Driving to New Orleans, while convenient and easy enough, is not necessarily the best option unless you are on a road trip – you won't be using a car much during your stay, and, in the French Quarter at least, it costs a lot to park. You can get to the city by train or bus, but most people arrive by air. Air fares to New Orleans fluctuate depending on the big events, and will increase around Mardi Gras and Jazz Fest, for example. Flying on weekends, whatever time of year, usually adds a premium to the cost; price ranges quoted below assume midweek travel. As there are no direct, non-stop flights from the UK, Ireland, Australia, New Zealand or South Africa to New Orleans, overseas travellers will have to fly into some other US city, and pick up a connecting flight from there. For details of entry requirements for overseas visitors, see p.27.

Flights from the US and Canada

New Orleans is served by a number of domestic **airlines**, including American, Continental, Delta, Jetblue, Northwest, Southwest, United and US Airways. It's usually possible to find round-trip fares for around $200 from New York, $275 from Los Angeles, and Can$500 from Toronto.

Flights from the UK and Ireland

No UK airline serves New Orleans, so it works out cheapest to fly with a US carrier. Typical routings include travelling via New York's JFK airport with Delta; via Chicago or Washington DC with United; or via Houston with Continental. Thanks to the time change, it's perfectly possible to fly out of London in the morning and reach New Orleans that same day; the return journey, however, will almost certainly involve an overnight flight. Typical round-trip fares range from around £400.

From **Ireland**, Aer Lingus flies from Dublin or Shannon to Boston, Chicago, New York, Orlando, and Washington, and Delta from Dublin and Shannon to Atlanta and New York. Alternatively, you can fly to London and take your pick of transatlantic routes.

Flights from Australia, New Zealand and South Africa

There are **no direct flights** from Australia or New Zealand or South Africa to New Orleans, so you'll have to fly to one of the main US gateway airports and pick up onward connections from there. The cheapest route, and the one with the most frequent services from **Australia** and **New Zealand**, is to Los Angeles, which also has plenty of onward flights to New Orleans. Air New Zealand and Qantas/American fly to LA at least twice daily, while United flies once a day; other airlines that serve LA include Japan Airlines and Singapore Airlines. From **South Africa**, by far the cheapest route is usually to fly with Virgin Atlantic from Johannesburg to London, and then from London to the US.

Trains

Three **Amtrak** routes (☎1-800/872-7245; ⊛www.amtrak.com) stop in New Orleans. The daily **City of New Orleans** leaves Chicago and travels via Memphis and Jackson, Mississippi, arriving in New Orleans at around 3.30pm; the full single fare from Chicago is $110, and the journey time around twenty hours. The **Crescent** also runs daily, starting in New York City and stopping in Philadelphia, Baltimore, Washington DC, and Atlanta before finishing its journey at New Orleans some 29 hours later, at around 7.30pm; to travel the entire route costs around $130 one-way. New Orleans is also a stop on the **Sunset Limited**, which runs three times a week; it sets off from LA on Sundays, Wednesdays and Fridays, with stops in Palm Springs,

Six steps to a better kind of travel

At Rough Guides we are passionately committed to travel. We feel strongly that only through travelling do we truly come to understand the world we live in and the people we share it with – plus tourism has brought a great deal of **benefit** to developing economies around the world over the last few decades. But the extraordinary growth in tourism has also damaged some places irreparably, and of course **climate change** is exacerbated by most forms of transport, especially flying. This means that now more than ever it's important to **travel thoughtfully** and **responsibly**, with respect for the cultures you're visiting – not only to derive the most benefit from your trip but also to preserve the best bits of the planet for everyone to enjoy. At Rough Guides we feel there are six main areas in which you can make a difference:

- Consider what you're contributing to the **local economy**, and how much the services you use do the same, whether it's through employing local workers and guides or sourcing locally grown produce and local services.
- Consider the **environment** on holiday as well as at home. Water is scarce in many developing destinations, and the biodiversity of local flora and fauna can be adversely affected by tourism. Try to patronize businesses that take account of this.
- Travel with a purpose, not just to tick off experiences. Consider **spending longer** in a place, and getting to know it and its people.
- Give thought to how often you **fly**. Try to avoid short hops by air and more harmful night flights.
- Consider **alternatives to flying**, travelling instead by bus, train, boat and even by bike or on foot where possible.
- Make your trips "**climate neutral**" via a reputable carbon offset scheme. All Rough Guide flights are offset, and every year we donate money to a variety of charities devoted to combating the effects of climate change.

Tucson, San Antonio and Houston, and arrives just under 48 hours later (at around 3pm) in New Orleans on Tuesdays, Fridays and Sundays. The full single fare from LA is around $300. Amtrak offers a range of passes that can cut costs; check their website for details.

Buses

New Orleans is also served by **Greyhound** buses, which are the cheapest, though not the most convenient way to get to town, with a range of fares and online deals available via their website (℡1-800/229-9424; ⊛www.greyhound.com).

Airlines and online search engines

Aer Lingus ⊛www.aerlingus.com.
Air New Zealand ⊛www.airnz.co.nz.
American Airlines ⊛www.aa.com.
Cheapo Air ⊛www.cheapoair.com.
Continental Airlines ⊛www.continental.com.
Delta ⊛www.delta.com.
JAL (Japan Airlines) ⊛www.jal.com.

Jetblue ⊛www.jetblue.com.
Kayak ⊛www.kayak.com.
Northwest ⊛www.nwa.com.
One Travel ⊛www.onetravel.com.
Orbitz ⊛www.orbitz.com.
Qantas Airways ⊛www.qantas.com.
Singapore Airlines ⊛www.singaporeair.com.
Southwest ⊛www.southwest.com.
United Airlines ⊛www.united.com.
US Airways ⊛www.usairways.com.
Virgin Atlantic ⊛www.virgin-atlantic.com.

Agents and operators

North South Travel UK ℡01245/608 291, ⊛www.northsouthtravel.co.uk. Friendly, competitive travel agency, offering discounted fares worldwide. Profits are used to support projects in the developing world, especially the promotion of sustainable tourism.
STA Travel US ℡1-800/781-4040, UK ℡0871/2300 040, Australia ℡134 782, New Zealand ℡0800/474 400, South Africa ℡0861/781 781; ⊛www.statravel.com. Worldwide specialists in independent travel; also student IDs, travel insurance, car rental, rail passes, and more. Good discounts for students and under-26s.

Trailfinders UK ☎0845/058 5858, Ireland ☎01/677 7888, Australia ☎1300/780 212; 🌐www.trailfinders.com. One of the best-informed and most efficient agents for independent travellers. Travel CUTS Canada ☎1-866/246-9762, US ☎1-800/592-2887; 🌐www.travelcuts.com. Canadian youth and student travel firm. USIT Ireland ☎01/602 1906, Northern Ireland ☎028/9032 7111; 🌐www.usit.ie. Ireland's main student and youth travel specialists.

Arrival

Millions of visitors arrive in New Orleans each year, most of them on one of the many domestic flights from the major US hubs. Note that the bus and train stations are next to each other in a sketchy part of town.

By air

Louis Armstrong New Orleans International Airport (MSY; 🌐ww.flymsy.com), some eighteen miles northwest of downtown on I-10, is relatively small and easy to navigate, with an **information booth** (daily 8am–6pm) in the baggage claim area, along with hotel courtesy phones.

The best way to get into town is by **taxi**. Flat-rate fares to downtown – a twenty- to thirty-minute journey – are $33 for up to two people, or $14 each for three or more. Simply join the line outside baggage claim and wait for the controller to usher you into a cab. If you're travelling alone, it's cheaper to take the **airport shuttle** (every 10min; $20 one-way to downtown hotels, $38 round-trip; ☎522-3500, 🌐www.airport shuttleneworleans.com), but because it stops frequently to drop people off, the journey can take as long as an hour. One-way and return tickets are available from 8am to 11pm in the baggage claim area; outside those times you can buy a ticket (one-way only) from the driver.

By car

New Orleans is traversed by **I-10**, which runs east–west between Florida and California.

You can get onto it from I-59 (east of the city) and I-55 (west). Taking I-12, which runs east–west north of Lake Pontchartrain, hooks you up with the **Lake Pontchartrain Causeway** – at 23 miles, the longest bridge in the world – which enters the city from the northwest and connects with I-10.

Approaching from either direction on I-10 you're confronted with the usual bewildering choice of lanes and lack of signs: make sure not to stray onto I-610, which bypasses downtown altogether. For the **CBD** take exit 234C, following signs for the Superdome; for the **French Quarter** take 235B, following signs for Vieux Carré, and for the **Garden District** take the St Charles Street exit.

By bus or train

The Union Passenger Terminal, 1001 Loyola Ave, near the Superdome, serves **Greyhound** buses (station usually open daily 7am–9.15am, 11am–1pm & 2.30–4.30pm; ☎525-6075 station info only) and **Amtrak** trains (station open daily 24hr; ticket office daily 5.45am–11pm). This area, in the no-man's-land beneath the elevated Pontchartrain Expressway, is not great; book a **cab** in advance to take you to your lodgings. United Cabs is the best firm (☎522-9771).

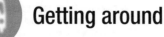

Getting around

Though New Orleans' most-visited neighbourhoods are a dream to walk around – the French Quarter and Garden District, in particular, are best enjoyed by a leisurely stroll – getting from one to another is not always easy on foot. Sadly the streetcar named Desire that inspired Tennessee Williams is long defunct, but streetcars do still run along the river, up Canal Street, and along St Charles Avenue. They're useful, but with the exception of these and a couple of buses you'll get little mileage out of the city's public transport system. To make the most of your time, budget for quite a few taxi rides, and always count on taking a cab if you're travelling anywhere outside the French Quarter at night. For more on staying safe when walking around New Orleans, see p.26.

Buses and streetcars

The **Regional Transit Authority** (RTA) runs a network of buses and streetcars (all $1.25, exact fare required, 25c for transfers; ☎248-3900, ⓦwww.norta.com); **routes** are numbered and named. The most useful **buses** include "Magazine" (#11), which runs along Magazine Street between Canal Street in the CBD and Audubon Park uptown, and "Jackson-Esplanade" (#91), from Rampart Street on the edge of the Quarter up Esplanade Avenue to City Park.

You're far more likely, however, to use the handsome and historic sage green **St Charles streetcar**, which rumbles a thirteen-mile loop from Canal Street at Carondelet, along the "neutral ground" (median) of St Charles Avenue in the Garden District, past Audubon Park and the Riverbend, to Carrollton uptown. The cars (#12) trundle along at an average speed of 9mph; it takes about 45 minutes for a full one-way trip. Services taper off considerably after dark, when you're better taking a cab than hanging around in an unfamiliar neigh-bourhood. For the **history** of the St Charles streetcar, see p.83.

There is also a **Riverfront streetcar** (#2; 7am–10pm, every 15–35min) line, with red trolleys running the two short miles between Esplanade Avenue and the Convention Center. More useful are the two **Canal Street streetcars**, and in particular the **City Park** service (#48, "City Park/Museum"; 7am–1am, every 35min on average), which starts by Harrah's casino on Canal Street,

turning off at Carrollton Avenue and heading to City Park. The **Carrollton Avenue** line (#47, "Cemeteries"; 5am–1am, every 35min on average) travels the length of Canal Street to where it meets City Park Avenue; if you're heading to City Park, make sure to get off at Carrollton Avenue and transfer onto the #48 trolley.

VisiTOUR passes, which provide unlimited rides for a set number of days can be used on the bus and the streetcar ($5 for one day, $12 for three, or $20 for five). The RTA website lists the various banks, hotels and grocery stores that sell the pass; note that the three-day pass is most widely sold.

Incidentally, though it is **legal to drink** a cocktail on the streets of New Orleans (see p.145), you can't carry it – or any drink – onto the bus or streetcar. Nor can you eat or smoke on board.

Taxis

The most convenient way of travelling any distance in New Orleans, especially after dark, is by **taxi**. **United** is by far the best firm, with the most reliable drivers and the safest cars. You can call them (☎522-9771), hail them from the street (try along Canal or Decatur), or pick them up in the French Quarter outside the Omni Royal Orleans Hotel on St Louis Street at Chartres, or the Bourbon-Orleans on Orleans Street.

Driving

It's not a particularly good idea to **drive** in New Orleans, especially around the French

Getting your bearings in New Orleans

One of New Orleans' many nicknames is "the Crescent City", because of the way it nestles between the southern shore of Lake Pontchartrain and a dramatic horseshoe bend in the Mississippi River. This unique location makes the city's layout confusing, with streets curving to follow the river and shooting off at odd angles to head inland. In the face of such dizzying geography, compass points are of little use – locals refer instead to **lakeside** (toward the lake) and **riverside** (toward the river), and, using Canal Street as the dividing line, **uptown** (or upriver) and **downtown** (downriver). In a sense, everything begins at **Canal Street**, the broad thoroughfare that sweeps in one dead straight line from the river up to the lake. Streets crossing Canal, which in the 1800s divided the old Creole city from the new American suburbs, change their names on either side of it – thus Royal Street in the French Quarter becomes St Charles uptown, Bourbon becomes Carondelet and so on, while downriver of Canal Street any street name prefixed with "North" simply swaps it for "South" uptown. Building numbers also restart at 100 on either side of Canal.

Quarter, where sections of the narrow, one-way streets are regularly closed off to create pedestrianized enclaves, plodding mule-drawn buggies cause traffic snarl-ups and parking, except in expensive lots, is all but impossible. Citywide, the brutal **parking** restrictions are something of a local joke, with a host of impenetrable regulations that lead to regular impounds and steep fines. If your car is towed, call ☎525-0088 or log onto ⊛www.cityofno.com. The pound is at 400 N Claiborne Ave.

You may, however, want to **rent a car** to head out of the city. Though all the major chains have booths at the airport, it may be cheaper to arrange rental from a downtown branch. Be aware that rates vary widely according to season, the day of the week and special deals.

Cycling

Cycling is a quick and cheap way of getting from one neighbourhood to another, though the faint of heart may want to avoid the cut-throat drivers on the main roads. However, for anyone who wants to join a Second Line in the depths of the back streets, say, or simply to nip between the Quarter and Bywater, a bike can be really useful – most Faubourg and Bywater residents get around on two wheels. To **rent a bike**, try **Bicycle Michael's**, in Faubourg Marigny at 622 Frenchmen St, which has road and mountain bikes (hourly $10, daily $25, five days $100, weekly $130), along

with baskets and helmets (Mon, Tues & Thurs–Sat 10am–7pm, Sun 10am–5pm; ☎945-9505; ⊛bicyclemichaels.com). Based in the Bywater, **Confederacy of Cruisers** (☎400-5468, ⊛confederacyofcruisers.com), charges similar rates, though only by the day or the week, and will drop off a bike and pick it up again from your hotel. They also offer good bike tours (see p.24).

Sightseeing tours

Tours of New Orleans range from overpriced whistle-stop jaunts in air-conditioned buses to tongue-in-cheek moonlit ghost-hunts. Walking or cycling tours are the best way to see the city, providing intimate insights into gorgeous hidden courtyards and fine architectural details – in summer, though, remember that the heat and humidity can be debilitating. The list below features the best options; the Welcome Center on Jackson Square (see p.28) has leaflets detailing others. Some of the tour operators listed below can also take you to the River Road plantations (see p.204).

Many visitors take a narrated trot through the Quarter, and sometimes the Faubourg in one of the **mule-drawn carriages** that wait in line behind Jackson Square on Decatur Street. These can be fun, especially as the sun sets, though in most cases you should take the "historic" running commentary with a pinch of salt – and the sight of the mules, decked out in funny hats, puts some people off. Rates are generally negotiable; expect to pay around $13–16 per person for a trip of between thirty and forty-five minutes.

One lazy way to while away a steamy afternoon is to take a **cruise** along the Mississippi. For details of the Natchez steamboat, which offers narrated river cruises with a live jazz band, see p.56.

Walking and cycling tours

Confederacy of Cruisers ☎ 400-5468, ⊛ confederacyofcruisers.com. Call to arrange a time; 3hr; $45. If you want to get a feel for the neighbourhoods of New Orleans, its street culture and its quirks, join the small-group (min 2, max 8) cycle tours offered by this laid-back, one-man operation. Jeff Shyman provides an informative overview and lots of juicy anecdotes as you ride through the Faubourg and the Bywater, St. Roch and Tremé, stopping off for the best street food along the way and more than likely taking a drink at *Ernie K-Doe's Mother In Law Lounge* (see p.150). You can also rent bikes by the day or the week (see p.23).

Friends of the Cabildo ☎ 523-3939. Tues–Sun 10am & 1.30pm; 2hr; $15; no reservations required; arrive 15min before the tour starts. Reliable historical overviews, concentrating on the French Quarter. Tours set off from the shop at the 1850 House, 523 St Ann St on Jackson Square.

Historic New Orleans Walking Tours ☎ 947-2120, ⊛ www.tourneworleans.com. A range of lively tours, among them a "Hurricane/Rebirth" option which buses you out to areas not covered by other tours, including the Ninth Ward (daily 1.30pm; 3hr; $40; meet at *CC's Community Coffeehouse*, 505 Decatur St); a jazz tour (Sat & Sun 2.30pm; 2hr; $20; meet at the *Café Beignet*, 311 Bourbon St); a "Cemetery and Voodoo" tour, covering St Louis No. 1 cemetery, Congo Square, priestess Marie Laveau's home and a voodoo temple (Mon–Sat 10am & 1pm, Sun 10am; 2hr; $20; meet at *Café Beignet*, 334 Royal St), and the anecdotal "Garden District and Cemetery" tour, which also emphasizes architecture and plant life (daily 11am & 1.45pm; 2hr; $20; meet at the Garden District Bookshop in The Rink mall at Washington and Prytania). There's also a rather tongue-in-cheek "Haunted French Quarter" option (nightly 7.30pm; $20; meet at *Bourbon-Oh!* in the *Bourbon-Orleans* hotel at Bourbon St and Orleans). None but the Hurricane tour requires reservations, though you can book online. Otherwise, simply arrive at the relevant meeting point 15min before the scheduled departure time.

Jean Lafitte National Historical Park Service ☎ 589-2636. Daily 9.30am; 45min; free. Led by National Park rangers, these daily tours offer scholarly and accessible overviews of the Quarter and the role of the Mississippi River in the development of the city. Space is limited, and it's first-come, first-served, so turn up at 9am at the visitor center, 419 Decatur St, to collect your ticket. For more on this exemplary visitor centre, see p.41.

New Orleans Ghost & Vampire Tour ☎ 861-2727, ⊛ www.neworleansghosttour.com. New Orleans offers an inordinate number of tours dealing in magic, voodoo, vampires and ghosts. Among the high-camp, the overpriced and the just plain silly, these French Quarter tours – featuring magic tricks and "psychic demonstrations" – are an entertaining option. Ghost tours leave from Rev Zombie's Voodoo Shop, 723 St Peter St in the French Quarter (daily 6pm & 8pm; around 2hr; $20); vampire tours from St Louis Cathedral on Jackson Square (daily 8.30pm; around 2hr; $20). Make reservations via the website.

Save Our Cemeteries ☎ 525-3377, ⊛ www .saveourcemeteries.org. Non-profit restoration organization that leads fascinating tours around two of New Orleans' above-ground cemeteries (see p.106): Lafayette #1 in the Garden District (Mon, Wed, Fri & Sat 10.30am; 1hr; $10; meet at the Washington Avenue Gate, 1400 block of Washington Ave), and St Louis #1, across Rampart Street from the French Quarter (Fri, Sat & Sun 10am; 1hr; $12; meet at the Basin Street Station Visitor Center, 501 Basin St). No reservations are required, but call to double-check that tours are running.

Swamp tours

In many ways, the popular fantasy of the misty, mysterious **Louisiana swamp** as an eerie place, flickering with ghostly grey Spanish moss, is not so very far from the truth. New Orleans' local swamps – many of them protected wilderness areas just thirty minutes' drive from downtown – are other-worldly enclaves, brought to life by informed guides eager to share their knowledge of local flora and fauna. The closer you get to the coast, however, to tour the Barataria swamp, for example, you will inevitably come face to face with some harsh realities. Louisiana's coastal wetlands are eroding at a horrifying rate (see p.211) and even despite valiant restoration efforts, these swamps – and the communities that exist around them – are under intense pressure. Tour guides emphasize the difficulties faced by the wetland communities while pointing out the swamps' beauty and ecological importance.

Bear in mind too that although the swamp ecosystem supports a wide range of **wildlife**, including bald eagles, deer, snapping turtles, bears, alligators and bobcats, what you actually get to see will depend upon the season and sheer luck. Wildlife is most visible in April and May and September to November. Your best chances of seeing an **alligator**, however, are in the summer, when they bask sleepily in the sun. Whatever time of the year you come, bring a hat, sunscreen and – most importantly – bug repellent.

In addition to the operators listed below, *Historic New Orleans Walking Tours* (see p.24) offer a tour of the Barataria-Terrebonne estuary, picking up from *La Boucherie* coffee house at 339 Chartres St (daily 8.30am; 4hr; $49 adults/$30 children; reservations essential. If you prefer to explore the swamps **independently**, turn to the account of the Barataria Preserve in "Out of the city", p.210.

Dr Wagner's Honey Island Swamp Tours ☎985/641-1769, ⊛www.honeyislandswamp.com. Based outside suburban Slidell, north of Lake Pontchartrain, these tours use small boats to venture onto the delta of the Pearl River, a wilderness occupied by raccoons, nutrias, bobcats, black bears, and alligators, as well as ibis, great blue herons, and snowy egrets (2hr; $23 adults, $15 children, plus $22/$17 for transport from downtown). Reservations required.

Louisiana Swamp Tours ☎689-3599, ⊛www .louisianaswamp.com. This tour company, on Hwy-301, south of the Lafitte National Park visitor center (see p.212), offers a number of tours, including daily boat trips through the nearby Barataria swamps (with transportation 8am, 10.20am, 12.30pm & 3pm; $49, children $25; without transportation 9.30am, 12.10pm, 2.10pm, 4.15pm; $29, children $15). They also offer a plantation-swamp combination, visiting either Oak Alley (see p.208) or Laura (see p.206), with transportation included (pick up 8.30am, return 4.45pm; $89, children $58). Reservations essential.

The media

There's no better way to get a sense of what drives this quirky city than by reading its papers. The news daily is the *Times-Picayune* (⊛www.nola.com) which costs 50¢, $1.50 on Sunday. Heavily focused on local stories, it has some strong columnists, and on Friday it includes an entertainment supplement, *Lagniappe* (another Creole term, meaning a little extra, a treat) – though the music listings, arranged first by venue and then by date, aren't all that user-friendly.

Free papers

New Orleans also has a host of good **free papers**, available from cafés, bars and stores. The superb weekly **Gambit** (⊛www .bestofneworleans.com), published on Tuesdays, leans slightly more to the left than the *Times-Picayune*, with lively editorials, local news, excellent entertainment listings and food features. Online, its **blog** pages (⊛blogofneworleans.com) provide unrivalled insights into all the latest in music, street culture and local politics. The student-focused monthly **Where Y'at** (⊛www .whereyat.net) is worth a look for feature articles and record reviews, but star among

the city's publications, however, has to be **Offbeat** (⊛www.offbeat.com), a very good **music monthly** filled with news, features, reviews and extensive listings. Though it's essential for anyone interested in the live music scene, by the end of the month the listings can be less reliable, so call venues to check, or listen to the nightlife schedules announced every two hours on the splendid radio station WWOZ (see p.26). **Antigravity** (⊛antigravitymagazine.com), which is published monthly and can be picked up free at bars and restaurants throughout the Lower Quarter, the Faubourg and Bywater, is the most alternative of the free listings papers, with a heavy emphasis on all things indie, fringe and avant garde, and some good feature articles. *Ambush* (Ⓦwww .ambushmag.com), published every other Tuesday, is New Orleans' major **gay** listings paper, available free from clubs, bars, cafés, and record stores.

Radio

You're not likely to be spending much time in front of the TV in New Orleans, but anyone with even the slightest interest in local music will want to tune into the fabulous, nonprofit radio station **WWOZ** (90.7FM). Playing roots New Orleans music – R&B, blues, brass, jazz, funk, gospel – along with world music, Cajun and old-time country, it also features jam sessions, interviews, poetry and ticket competitions. You can hear it **online** at Ⓦwww.wwoz.org. There's more New Orleans music on Sunday evenings (6–8pm), when local **NPR station** WWNO (89.9FM) airs *American Routes*, which covers the history of American music from a local angle (Ⓦwww.americanroutes.org).

Crime and personal safety

New Orleans' high crime rate should be taken seriously. While it's true that most gun crimes occur in neighbourhoods where tourists would simply never go, other random incidents, including the 2009 Mardi Gras shooting – in which seven members of the public, including a baby, were injured as they watched a daytime parade along swanky St Charles Avenue – provide reality checks for visitors who think they are untouchable.

In a city where widespread poverty, desperate neglect, and attendant drug problems are rife, no one can ignore the tension that can bubble up anywhere, any time. Simply crossing the street can take you from a familiar environment into a bleak, potentially threatening neighbourhood, where tourists tripping around with cameras and wallets full of dollars are easy prey. All that said, visitors who use a modicum of common sense will probably be faced with nothing more threatening than the gangs of young gutter punks and local school kids who beg and hustle tourists in the French Quarter.

However, you do need to keep your wits about you. While it's safe enough to walk around the **French Quarter** during the day, you should be on your guard – especially if you're on your own – when wandering the quieter streets on its fringes after dark. Though you're not necessarily in any danger when approaching **Rampart Street**, the border with the underprivileged neighbourhood of Tremé, it can feel intimidating until you get your bearings, and **Louis Armstrong Park** should certainly be avoided at night. Similarly in the **Faubourg Marigny**, heavily trafficked Frenchmen Street is safe, but the surrounding streets can feel very quiet indeed after dark. The **Garden District**, also, is safe enough during the day, though at night – when in any case there's little reason to be wandering around – you should be on your guard. Parts of the **Lower Garden District**, including some run-down stretches on and around lower Magazine Street, and whole swathes of the flood-scarred **Mid-City** can feel menacing at any time, though again this can be due to unfamiliarity more than anything else.

Wherever you are, if you feel nervous, trust your instincts, turn back, or call a **taxi**. And *always* take a cab when travelling any distance outside the Quarter at night.

Travel essentials

Area code

New Orleans' area code is ☎504.

Costs

Accommodation in New Orleans is expensive by US standards (see p.115), but eating out, on the other hand, is relatively inexpensive – especially given the high quality. Seeing live music can also be very cheap, with many places having no cover whatsoever. There is no need to rent a car, either, but you should budget for taxi rides after dark (see p.22).

Electricity

Electricity runs on 110V AC. American plugs are two-pronged.

Entry requirements

Under the visa waiver scheme, passport-holders from Britain, Ireland, Australia, New Zealand, and most European countries do not require visas for trips to the US, as long as they stay less than ninety days, and have an onward or return ticket. However, anyone planning to visit the US using the visa waiver scheme is required to apply for travel authorization in advance, online. It's a very quick and straightforward process, via the website ⓦwww.cbp.gov/xp/cgov/travel/. Fail to do so, however, and you may well be denied entry. In addition, your passport must be machine-readable, with a barcode-style number. All children need to have their own individual passports. Holders of older non-readable passports should either obtain new ones or apply for visas prior to travel. Prospective visitors from parts of the world not mentioned above need a valid passport and a nonimmigrant visitor's visa. How you'll obtain a visa depends on what country you're in and your status when you apply, so call the nearest US embassy or consulate. For full details visit ⓦhttp://travel.state.gov.

US embassies and consulates abroad

Australia MLC Centre, Level 59, 19–29 Martin Place, Sydney ☎02/9373 9200, ⓦusembassy-australia.state.gov
Ireland 42 Elgin Rd, Ballsbridge, Dublin ☎01/668 8777, ⓦdublin.usembassy.gov
New Zealand 29 Fitzherbert Terrace, Thorndon, Wellington ☎04/462 6000, ⓦnewzealand.usembassy.gov
South Africa 877 Pretorius St, Arcadia, Pretoria ☎12/431-4000, ⓦsouthafrica.usembassy.gov
UK 24 Grosvenor Square, London W1A 1AE ☎020/7499 9000, ⓦwww.usembassy.org.uk; 3 Regent Terrace, Edinburgh EH7 5BW ☎0131/556 8315, ⓦwww.usembassy.org.uk/scotland; Danesfort House, 223 Stranmillis Rd, Belfast BT9 5GR ☎028/9038 6100, ⓦwww.usembassy.org.uk/nireland

Internet

Bastille Internet Café, in the French Quarter at 605 Toulouse St at Chartres (Mon–Sat 10am–8pm; ☎581-1150) offers cable internet access on their computers at a rate of $2.75 for 15min, $4.75 for 30min, and $7.75 for 60min; bringing your own cuts costs down to $2.75 for 30min and $4 for 60min. They also have CD-burning, scanning and printing services. A number of bars and coffee houses offer free **wi-fi**: in the French Quarter head to *La Boucherie* (see p.140), *CC's Community Coffeehouse* (see p.140) and *Pravda* (see p.148); in the Faubourg, *Rose Nicaud* (see p.142); in the Bywater, *Sound Café* (see p.142); in Mid-City, *CC's* (see p.142); and uptown, the *Oak Street Café* (see p.137) and *Rue de la Course* (see p.141).

Money

Most of New Orleans' banks, and many of its bars, have ATMs; most accept bank cards linked to the Cirrus or Plus systems, for a fee of between $2 and, occasionally, $4 per transaction. Overseas travellers may need to inform their bank if they wish to draw out money when they are in the USA; check with your bank beforehand.

Pharmacies

There's a 24-hour drive-through pharmacy in the Walgreens at 1801 St Charles Ave at Felicity (☎561-8458), and Walgreens with pharmacies in the French Quarter at 619 Decatur St at Wilkinson Row (store daily 8am–10pm; pharmacy Mon–Fri 9am–7pm, Sat 9am–5pm, Sun 10am–5pm; ☎525-7263) and on 900 Canal St at Baronne (store daily 7am–midnight; pharmacy Mon–Fri 8am–8pm, Sat 9am–6pm, Sun 10am–6pm; ☎568-1271). You can also get over-the-counter drugs in the French Quarter at the Walgreens at 134 Royal St at Iberville (daily 9am–6pm; ☎525-2180), Rouses at 701 Royal St at St Peter (daily 7am–1am; ☎523-1353) and at the lovely old-fashioned Royal Pharmacy, 1101 Royal St at Ursulines (☎523-5401).

Phone cards

Semans House, 115 Royal St at Canal (☎529-6000), sells cheap national and international phone cards.

Photography

As a rule you should avoid the cowboy outfits along Canal Street, but Canal Camera Center 615 Canal at Chartres (☎525-6865) is one of the more reputable, selling useful things like camera batteries and film for your movie camera.

Police

There's a police station at 334 Royal St in the French Quarter. In emergencies call ☎911.

Post office

The main post office is in the CBD at 701 Loyola Ave at Girod (Mon & Wed–Fri 7am–8pm, Sat 8am–5pm; ☎589-1706). An equivalent service, along with fax, photocopying, FedEx, phonecards and the like, is offered by French Quarter Postal Emporium, 1000 Bourbon St at St Philip (Mon–Fri 9am–6pm, Sat 10am–3pm; ☎525-6651, ☼www.frenchquarterpostal.com) and Royal

Mail, 828 Royal St at Dumaine (Mon–Fri 9am–5pm, Sat 10am–4pm; ☎522-8523).

Tax

New Orleans' sales tax is 9 percent, or 11–13 percent on hotel bills, depending on the size of the hotel. For international visitors, the Louisiana Tax-Free Shopping (LTFS; ☼www .louisianataxfree.com) scheme reimburses the tax on all goods that you can take out of the country. Most participating businesses display a sticker; it's worth asking if you don't see one. Show your passport and they'll give you a voucher, redeemable – with the sales receipt – at the LTFS booths at the airport (Mon–Fri 8.30am–4.30pm, Sat & Sun 9am–1pm; ☎467-0723) and on the second level of the Riverfront Marketplace mall (Mon–Sat 9.30am–4.30pm, Sun 10am–4.30pm; ☎568-3605). Refunds of less than $500 are given out in cash on the spot; higher sums will be mailed. There's a small handling fee.

Time

New Orleans is on Central Standard Time, six hours behind Greenwich Mean Time. Daylight-Saving Time, when clocks go forward an hour, runs from the first Sunday in April to the last Sunday in October.

Tipping

Wait staff in restaurants expect tips of around 17.5 percent, higher if you've had particularly good service. Bar staff should get 15 percent, or a dollar per round, whichever is higher; taxi drivers 15 percent; hotel porters about $1 per piece of baggage; and housekeeping staff $1 per night.

Tourist information

For official information put out by the tourist board before you leave home, check ☼www .neworleansonline.com, which features a directory of restaurants and hotels, articles on culture, music, and activities, plus online-only accommodation deals and downloadable discount coupons. Once you've arrived, you can speak to helpful attendants and pick up self-guided walking tours, free maps, and more discount vouchers at the Welcome Center on Jackson Square at 529 St Ann St in the Quarter (daily 9am–5pm; ☎566-5031).

The City

The City

The French Quarter

he heartbreakingly beautiful **French Quarter** – or Vieux Carré ("old square") – is where New Orleans all began. Today, despite rampant gentrification and the shameless condo-ization of many of its loveliest buildings, despite the tacky T-shirt shops and the trashy bars that fill its tumbledown cottages, it's still the spiritual core of the city; its fanciful cast-iron balconies, lush hidden courtyards and time-stained stucco buildings exert the same haunting fascination today as they have for nearly three hundred years. Don't be misled by its name into expecting some sort of *petit Paris* – largely the creation of French Creoles, the battered, bohemian Quarter has always had more of the feel of a seductive Caribbean port than a European metropolis. It doesn't even look particularly French, as its architecture is predominantly Spanish colonial – most of the buildings of the French city burned in two major fires in 1788 and 1794.

The Quarter covers a compact **grid** – unchanged since it was laid out by military engineer Adrien de Pauger in 1721 – bounded by the Mississippi River, Rampart Street, Canal Street and Esplanade Avenue. Its hub is Europeanate **Jackson Square**, facing the river. Upriver, the **Upper Quarter** sees most of the **commercial activity**, concentrated in the blocks between brash Decatur and Bourbon streets. Here, as in the days of the Creole city, the gorgeous old buildings hold offices, shops, galleries, restaurants and bars on the lower floors, with apartments on the upper storeys. In the streets beyond Bourbon, up toward Rampart Street, and in those of the **Lower Quarter**, downriver from Jackson Square, things become more peaceful. These are quiet, predominantly **residential** neighbourhoods, home to much of the Quarter's **gay** community.

While there's no shortage of formal **attractions** – the Presbytère, Cabildo and Historic New Orleans Collection museums, to name but a few – you could easily spend an entire week simply wandering the streets, absorbing the Quarter's melange of sounds, sights and smells. Early morning, when the city is washed in pearly light from the Mississippi, is a good time to explore, as sleepy locals wake up with strong coffee in neighbourhood patisseries, stores crank open their shutters and streetwise brass bands set up to blast the roofs off Jackson Square.

The best French Quarter **walking tours** are detailed on p.24.

Some history

Despite inauspicious beginnings as a miserable colonial outpost built on an unprepossessing swamp, the French – then Spanish – city thrived thanks to its location near the mouth of the Mississippi River. Well into the nineteenth century, when, following the Louisiana Purchase, the new, Anglo-American Faubourg St Mary mushroomed around it, the Vieux Carré held its own, becoming the **first municipality** of a divided city (see p.221). Though New Orleans' **antebellum** "golden era" marked the ascendancy of the American sector, planters, bankers and lawyers continued to build homes in the old Creole quarter, entertaining in its famed theatres and ballrooms. During this period a third of the French Quarter was owned by **free people of colour**, wealthy francophones – many of them slave-owners from the West Indies – a significant number of whom sent their children to Paris to be educated.

After the **Civil War**, the district took a downturn, its old buildings used as tenements to house poor Italian and black families, or torn down to make room for new developments along the river and behind Canal Street. Things improved in the 1920s, however, when a colony of **artists**, including writers Sherwood Anderson and William Faulkner, drifted to the Quarter; it was partly their fascination with its architecture and rich cultural history that led in the 1930s to the formation of the **Vieux Carré Commission** – whose remit was to preserve the district's "quaint and distinctive character" – and a restoration programme undertaken by Roosevelt's Works Progress Administration (WPA). Since then, the Quarter has been both a refuge for bohemians and something of a battleground for preservationists – the hardest fight yet being against a 1946 proposal to build a highway right through it, which was only definitively defeated in the 1970s. However, as the mounting number of themed restaurants, condo developments and fast-food outlets reveals, the Commission's authority does not extend to vetting either what buildings are used for, or what is done to their interiors. There is genuine concern that as skyrocketing rents squeeze out longtime locals and pump in well-heeled out-of-towners – those who can afford to pay premium rates for a bijou condo with a cast-iron balcony – this historically evolving, vibrant neighbourhood could well transmogrify into a lifeless theme park.

For now, however, and against all the odds, the Quarter battles on, as vital and full of heart as ever. Its lopsided buildings, many of them buckling and rotting in the perpetual damp, still emanate a ghostly beauty, accentuated by the tiny aesthetic details – a string of Christmas-tree lights, a little cast-iron chair, voluptuous green ferns – added by residents too besotted by the place to let it die.

Jackson Square

Ever since its earliest incarnation as the Place d'Armes, a dusty parade ground used for public meetings and executions, **Jackson Square** has been at the heart of the French Quarter. Its spruce appearance today owes much to the **Baroness Pontalba**, who in 1851 revamped the drill ground into a landscaped park and renamed it for Andrew Jackson, hero of the Battle of New Orleans (see p.61), who went on to become the US president.

A welcome open space in the congested French Quarter, the square is bathed in the light from the Mississippi, "a worldly sort of light", as Mark Twain put it, that still today renders it "brilliant". And with its iron benches, neat lawns, tinkling fountain and blaze of flowerbeds, it somehow manages to stay tranquil, despite the streams of photo-snapping tourists, overexcited school groups, bus-boys on their breaks and the odd crashed-out casualty. Presiding over them all, an **equestrian statue** – the first in the nation, constructed by Clark Mills in 1856 – shows Jackson in uncharacteristically jaunty mode, waving his hat. It's a sculptural masterpiece, with the mighty horse, rearing on its hind legs, perfectly balanced on the plinth. The hectoring inscription, "The Union Must and Shall be Preserved", was pointedly added by General "Beast" Butler (see p.79) during the Civil War occupation.

St Peter, Chartres and St Ann streets are pedestrianized where they border the square. In this enclave you'll find some of the city's major sights: the chic **Pontalba Buildings**, their street-level rooms taken up by shops and restaurants (and a tourist

▲ Jackson Square

information centre, see p.28); **St Louis Cathedral**; and, flanking the cathedral like stout bodyguards, the **Cabildo** and **Presbytère** museums. During the day, everyone passes by at some time or another, weaving their way through the tangle of artists, Lucky Dog hotdog vendors, rainbow-clad tarot-readers, magicians, shambolic jazz bands and blues musicians. At night it's quieter, with just a few itinerant waifs and strays lingering in the shadows cast by the stately, floodlit buildings.

St Louis Cathedral

A postcard-perfect backdrop for the Andrew Jackson statue, **St Louis Cathedral** (daily 7.30am–6.30pm; free; ⓦ www.stlouiscathedral.org), commanding the square across Chartres Street, is the oldest continuously active cathedral in the United States, and the third church on this spot. Its construction in 1794 – the second church had been destroyed by the fire of 1788 – was funded, along with the Cabildo and the overhaul of the Presbytère, by the philanthropist Don Almonester. In 1850, while Almonester's daughter, the formidable Baroness Pontalba, was busy sprucing up the square around it (see box, p.36), it was enlarged and remodelled by eminent architect J.N.B. de Pouilly. Dominated by three tall slate steeples, the dove-grey facade, which marries a Greek Revival symmetry with copious French arches, is oddly two-dimensional, like some elaborate stage prop for the lively street theatre below.

Though the cathedral has always been central to the life of this very Catholic city – Andrew Jackson laid his sword on the altar in thanks for victory at the Battle of New Orleans; voodoo queen Marie Laveau (see p.52) was baptized and married here – the **interior**, an unexceptional assemblage of murals, sculpture and stained glass, is modest. Highlights include Don Almonester's marble tomb, inscribed with a list of his many bequests, and an overblown tabernacle brimming with cherubs.

Flanking the cathedral, two narrow flagstoned lanes link Jackson Square to Royal Street. Downriver, **Père Antoine Alley** is named for the beloved Capuchin priest

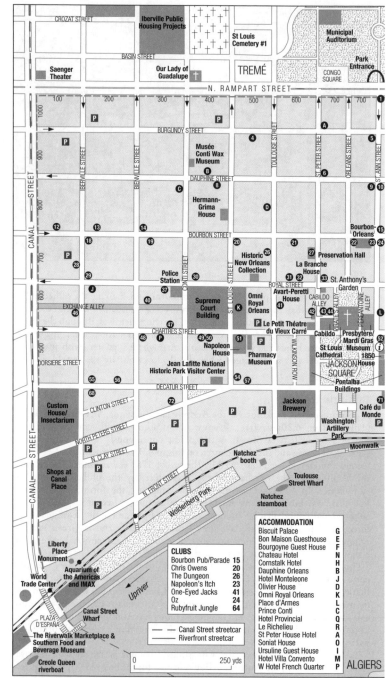

CROZAT STREET

Iberville Public Housing Projects

St Louis Cemetery #1

Municipal Auditorium

Park Entrance

Saenger Theater

BASIN STREET

Our Lady of Guadalupe

TREMÉ

CONGO SQUARE

N. RAMPART STREET

100 200 300 400 500 600 700 700

BURGUNDY STREET

Musée Conti Wax Museum

DAUPHINE STREET

Hermann-Grima House

BOURBON STREET

Historic New Orleans Collection

Preservation Hall

La Branche House

St. Anthony's Garden

Police Station

ROYAL STREET

Avart-Peretti House

CABILDO ALLEY

EXCHANGE ALLEY

Supreme Court Building

Omni Royal Orleans

Le Petit Théatre du Vieux Carré

CHARTRES STREET

Napoleon House

Pharmacy Museum

Jean Lafitte National Historic Park Visitor Center

DORSIERE STREET

Cabildo

Presbytère/ Mardi Gras

St Louis Museum

Cathedral

1850 House

JACKSON SQUARE

Pontalba Buildings

DECATUR STREET

Custom House/ Insectarium

CLINTON STREET

Jackson Brewery

Café du Monde

Washington Artillery Park

NORTH PETERS STREET

N. CLAY STREET

Shops at Canal Place

Natchez booth

Moonwalk

Toulouse Street Wharf

Natchez steamboat

N. FRONT STREET

Woldenberg Park

Liberty Place Monument

Aquarium of the Americas and IMAX

World Trade Center

Upriver

PLAZA D'ESPAÑA

Canal Street Wharf

The Riverwalk Marketplace & Southern Food and Beverage Museum

Creole Queen riverboat

CLUBS
Bourbon Pub/Parade	15
Chris Owens	20
The Dungeon	26
Napoleon's Itch	23
One-Eyed Jacks	41
Oz	24
Rubyfruit Jungle	64

— — Canal Street streetcar
——— Riverfront streetcar

0   250 yds

ACCOMMODATION
Biscuit Palace	G
Bon Maison Guesthouse	E
Bourgoyne Guest House	F
Chateau Hotel	N
Cornstalk Hotel	H
Dauphine Orleans	B
Hotel Monteleone	J
Olivier House	D
Omni Royal Orleans	K
Place d'Armes	L
Prince Conti	C
Hotel Provincial	Q
Le Richelieu	R
St Peter House Hotel	A
Soniat House	O
Ursuline Guest House	I
Hotel Villa Convento	M
W Hotel French Quarter	P

ALGIERS

Algiers

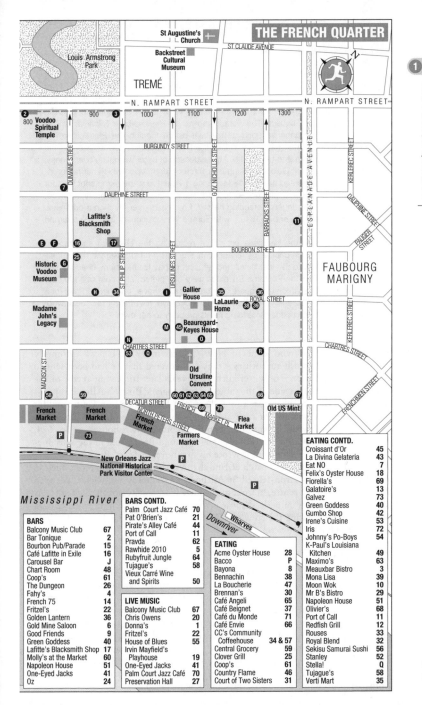

THE FRENCH QUARTER

St Augustine's Church
Backstreet Cultural Museum
TREMÉ
Louis Armstrong Park
ST CLAUDE AVENUE

N. RAMPART STREET

800 | 900 | 1000 | 1100 | 1200 | 1300

2 Voodoo Spiritual Temple

BURGUNDY STREET

DAUPHINE STREET

Lafitte's Blacksmith Shop

BOURBON STREET

Historic Voodoo Museum

FAUBOURG MARIGNY

Madame John's Legacy

Gallier House
LaLaurie Home
ROYAL STREET
Beauregard-Keyes House

CHARTRES STREET

Old Ursuline Convent

DECATUR STREET
NORTH PETERS STREET
FRENCH MARKET PL

French Market
French Market
French Market
Flea Market
Farmers Market
Old US Mint

New Orleans Jazz National Historical Park Visitor Center

Mississippi River

Downriver — Wharves

BARS

Balcony Music Club	67
Bar Tonique	2
Bourbon Pub/Parade	15
Café Lafitte in Exile	16
Carousel Bar	J
Chart Room	48
Coop's	61
The Dungeon	26
Fahy's	4
French 75	14
Fritzel's	22
Golden Lantern	36
Gold Mine Saloon	6
Good Friends	9
Green Goddess	40
Lafitte's Blacksmith Shop	17
Molly's at the Market	60
Napoleon House	51
One-Eyed Jacks	41
Oz	24

BARS CONTD.

Palm Court Jazz Café	70
Pat O'Brien's	21
Pirate's Alley Café	44
Port of Call	11
Pravda	62
Rawhide 2010	5
Rubyfruit Jungle	64
Tujague's	58
Vieux Carré Wine and Spirits	50

LIVE MUSIC

Balcony Music Club	67
Chris Owens	20
Donna's	1
Fritzel's	22
House of Blues	55
Irvin Mayfield's Playhouse	19
One-Eyed Jacks	41
Palm Court Jazz Café	70
Preservation Hall	27

EATING

Acme Oyster House	28
Bacco	P
Bayona	8
Bennachin	38
La Boucherie	47
Brennan's	30
Café Angeli	65
Café Beignet	37
Café du Monde	71
Café Envie	66
CC's Community Coffeehouse	34 & 57
Central Grocery	59
Clover Grill	25
Coop's	61
Country Flame	46
Court of Two Sisters	31

EATING CONTD.

Croissant d'Or	45
La Divina Gelateria	43
Eat NO	7
Felix's Oyster House	18
Fiorella's	69
Galatoire's	13
Galvez	73
Green Goddess	40
Gumbo Shop	42
Irene's Cuisine	53
Iris	72
Johnny's Po-Boys	54
K-Paul's Louisiana Kitchen	49
Maximo's	63
Meauxbar Bistro	3
Mona Lisa	39
Moon Wok	10
Mr B's Bistro	29
Napoleon House	51
Olivier's	68
Port of Call	11
Redfish Grill	12
Rouses	33
Royal Blend	32
Sekisu Samurai Sushi	56
Stanley	52
Stella!	Q
Tujague's	58
Verti Mart	35

1

The Baroness

Jackson Square, and the smart red buildings that flank it, are the result of a melodrama of murder and money starring the wilful **Baroness Pontalba**, known in New Orleans simply as "the Baroness". Born Micaëla Almonester in 1795, the daughter of Don Andrés Almonester – who came to New Orleans from Spain in 1769 as a clerk and went on to become one of the city's richest and most influential philanthropists – at the age of 16 she was married in St Louis Cathedral to Célestin Pontalba, a distant cousin. The couple moved to Paris, where Micaëla, whose considerable inheritance included all the real estate fringing the Place d'Armes, became convinced that her father-in-law, the Baron Pontalba, had engineered the wedding in order to get to her wealth. After a decade of bitter wrangling over money, Micaëla eventually left Célestin, taking their three children, upon which her father-in-law promptly disinherited them. In 1834, during a violent row, the baron shot her four times in the chest, and proceeded to kill himself. Micaëla miraculously survived, though she lost two fingers defending herself. Four years later, by then a baroness, she divorced Célestin, and in 1849 – with Europe in revolutionary turmoil – returned to New Orleans.

Back in the city, the baroness set about recreating the elegance she had so admired in the French capital. By all accounts she was a harsh taskmistress, supervising construction to the last detail and refusing to pay for the many changes she demanded. In 1851 the Pontalba Buildings were completed, at a cost of $300,000, and renovations began on the square. The baroness, however, returned to Paris for a reconciliation with Célestin. Seriously ill, he handed over his affairs to Micaëla, who, in an ironic twist, succeeded in adding all his property to her own.

Antonio de Sedella, who came to New Orleans in 1779. He was promptly banished by the Spanish authorities – they'd discovered that he had been sent to enforce the Inquisition – only to return a few years later to become rector of the cathedral. On the other side of the cathedral, photogenic **Pirate's Alley** is supposedly built on the site where Andrew Jackson met local pirate Jean Lafitte and his band of buccaneers to ask for their aid in fighting the Battle of New Orleans in 1815. It's a lovely spot, lined with vibrantly coloured town houses; at no. 624, Faulkner House Books (see p.188) occupies a ground-floor room in the sunshine-yellow building where the author wrote his first novel, *Soldiers' Pay*, in 1927.

Behind the cathedral, on a patch of land that was the scene of numerous duels in the 1800s, the pretty, iron-fenced **St Anthony's Garden** is sandwiched between the two alleys. In the centre, in front of the huge marble statue of the Sacred Heart of Jesus, which casts an eerie shadow across the cathedral wall after dark, is an obelisk commemorating the crew of a French ship who in 1857 all died of yellow fever in the Gulf of Mexico.

The Cabildo

On the upriver side of the cathedral, the Hispanic **Cabildo** (Tues–Sun 10am–4.30pm; $6) was built as the Casa Capitular, seat of the Spanish colonial government (the "Very Illustrious Cabildo"). Today, it is home to an outstanding, people-oriented history museum. The building – which cuts an impressive dash with its columned arcade, fan windows and fine wrought-iron balconies – is another legacy of the philanthropist Don Almonester, who, after the original building burned in the fire of 1788, offered to remodel it in the grand style of the home country. Historically, the Cabildo is hugely significant – not least for being where the Spanish colony was transferred back to France in 1803, and three weeks later, under the terms of the **Louisiana Purchase**, was sold to the United States (see p.219).

The **museum** ably picks its way through the complex tangle of cultures, classes and races that binds together Louisiana's history. Crammed with well-captioned artefacts, it sets off with the Native Americans and winds up with the demise of Reconstruction – rather than attempting to see the whole place, it's best to concentrate on a few sections that particularly interest you. It certainly pulls no punches – in keeping with the city's uncommon fascination with matters morbid, there's a gloomy section devoted to disease, death and mourning, while another displays the venom with which the White League-dominated Mardi Gras krewes (carnival clubs) resisted Reconstruction, barely masking their hatred in racist, themed parades. A series of designs shows Union generals portrayed as insects and vermin and newly liberated slaves as simian fools. **Black history** is well represented throughout, with as much emphasis on the free people of colour as on the city's role as the major slave-trading centre of the South. Bills of sale show slaves priced for as much as $1350 each, while a worn-smooth auction block stands in front of an enlarged 1860 engraving depicting the markets held in the old *St Louis Hotel* (see p.47).

You can also see the haunting bronze **death mask of Napoleon**, made and brought to New Orleans by the exiled emperor's doctor, Francesco Antommarchi, who displayed it in his office on Royal Street for thirteen years before donating it to the city in 1834. On the second floor is the reconstructed **Sala Capitular**, where, in 1803, the city of New Orleans – having been handed over just three weeks earlier from Spain to France – was sold by a cash-strapped Napoleon to the United States under the terms of the Louisiana Purchase (see p.219). In 1892 the historic "separate but equal" **Plessy vs Ferguson** case (see p.222), which legalized segregation throughout the South, was first argued in this room.

If you've got time, head back to the lobby and nip through the side door into the old **Arsenal**, where they host temporary exhibits on subjects of local interest – from the coffee trade to the golden age of the Mississippi to Louisiana's place in rock'n'roll history.

The Presbytère Mardi Gras museum

Forming a matching pair with the Cabildo, the **Presbytère** (Tues–Sun 10am–4.30pm; $6), on the downriver side of the cathedral, was designed in 1791 as a rectory. It was never used as such, however; the death of Don Almonester, its chief benefactor, put construction on hold, and it was not completed until 1813, when it went on to serve as a courthouse. Today it's an exceptionally good **Mardi Gras museum**, which, by covering carnival from every conceivable angle offers a penetrating look into the culture and history of the city, and, even better, a sense of what makes the place tick. For visitors out to get drunk on Bourbon Street and catch a few beads, Mardi Gras won't disappoint. For New Orleanians, however, this arcane, complex melding of African, Creole and European carnival traditions, mixed up with the city's very particular racial, cultural and social dynamics, is a sacred ritual. And while nothing can compare with being in town for the real thing (see colour section and pp.163–174), a visit to the museum is (almost) second best.

Upon entering, you're heralded by a jubilant soundtrack into a darkened room where noisy videos of parades and street revels share space with seemingly incongruous objects – a decorated coconut, a toy coin, a stepladder – that give a taste of what's to come. Beyond the next section, which deals with **carnival's roots** in Europe and Africa and is illustrated with European carnival posters and vintage masks, much of the ground floor is concerned with **official carnival**. Here you can see close-up the extraordinary **costumes** worn at private balls and in the formal parades – jewel-encrusted sceptres, crowns and gauntlets, velvet and ermine cloaks heavy with gems and beads, and plumed, sparkling headgear fit for a fairytale king. Some of the most dazzling exhibits date from the 1870s to 1890s, the golden age of **carnival artistry**, when old-line krewes Comus, Rex, Proteus and Momus dominated the scene. As much creativity went into the invitations, with their arcane wording and bizarre imagery, as into the designs for parade floats and costumes – even the cue sheets for the elaborate tableaux vivants staged at the private balls are works of art. A glass case displays the popular newspaper illustrations that recreated these formal extravaganzas for the commoners, while a video offers a privileged glimpse into today's private balls, from old-krewe debs, graciously waving diamond-studded sceptres at their court, to tuxedoed businessmen in weird masks waltzing with ball-gowned beauties.

The ugly side of this pomp and pageantry – the explicit white supremacist message in many of the satirical Reconstruction parades, for example (covered superbly in the Cabildo, see p.37), is alluded to; a lot of space is also given to **Zulu**, the hugely popular black-dominated krewe whose members parade in black faces and grass skirts. Created by a black fraternal organization in 1909, and inspired by a vaudeville skit, Zulu began as a parody of white Mardi Gras but has grown to become a mainstay of official carnival even while maintaining its transgressive chutzpah. The jaw-dropping costumes of regular characters like Mr Big Stuff and the Big Shot of Africa are on display, revealing influences as diverse as Haiti (sequins) and Mardi Gras Indians (feathers), and increasing in size and flamboyance with each passing year.

On the second floor, **unofficial carnival** is covered in equal detail, with lots of good stuff on the **Mardi Gras Indians** (see p.166), including footage of a Sunday evening Indian practice, and fine examples of the spectacular feather-and-bead "suits" that are painstakingly hand-sewn by each Indian, with help of friends and family, for as much as a full year before being paraded on Mardi Gras day. In these you can trace various trends in designs and styles: loosely, the downtown "gangs" prefer abstract African designs, sequins and big, sculptural elements, while those from uptown tend towards intricate beadwork, rhinestones and Wild West motifs.

Another case holds costumes worn by lesser-known black carnival groups. The **Skeletons**, or "Skull and Bone Gangs", originated in the early nineteenth century; today, wearing tatty black suits painted to resemble human skeletons and aprons bearing gruesome messages, some of them sporting massive papier-mache skulls or carrying butchers' bones, they come out in Tremé at dawn on Mardi Gras morning, drumming and hollering, to "wake the day", scare the children, and herald the imminent arrival of the Indians. The **Baby Dolls** – sassy groups of black women who, starting around 1912, would flounce through town on Mardi Gras day in big pink bonnets, short skirts and satin bloomers – had all but disappeared by the end of the twentieth century; in the last decade they have seen a resurgence, started by descendants of the original Baby Dolls and spearheaded by

Lucky Dogs

New Orleans' preposterous **Lucky Dogs** carts, shaped like giant hot-dogs and pushed by salty old gents in candy-striped uniforms, are as much a feature of the French Quarter landscape as its fine filigree balconies. Featured in John Kennedy Toole's quintessential New Orleans tragi-comedy *A Confederacy of Dunces*, in which pompous and repulsive anti-hero Ignatius J. Reilly wreaks havoc through his insalubrious and surreal city, they, and their attendants, have become New Orleans icons. In truth, though, the "dogs" themselves are nothing to write home about.

Tremé matriarch Antoinette K-Doe (see p.150). Since K-Doe's death, the tradition has been upheld by various young white hipsters; few black women dress as Baby Dolls today. The section on **gay** Mardi Gras – a cornucopia of fantastic outfits – climaxes in a video of the notorious Bourbon Street awards, where gaggles of glamorous drag queens stagger under colossal get-ups as they compete for the prestigious best costume prize.

The room on **Cajun Mardi Gras** reveals the anarchic-seeming celebrations of rural Louisiana to be just as stylized, if not more so, than their urban counterparts. Ancient rituals dominate the Cajun display of misrule, with ragged costumers – loosely taking on the roles of tricksters, thieves, outlaws, fools and beggars, with a capitaine to keep them all in order – staging drunken mock battles on horses and riding from house to house singing for their supper and begging for chickens and cash. Among the artefacts, photos and videos, highlights include vaguely disturbing Cajun Mardi Gras costumes, with their medieval-style capuchin hats, Spanish-moss wigs and impassive full-face mesh masks. Watch out for the startling life-sized video screen disguised as a porch door, behind which mischievous, costumed figures jump out at you begging, clucking and jeering in nasal French – an experience every bit as unsettling as carnival itself.

It would take several days to see this fantastic museum in its entirety – there are exhibits on "throws" (see p.171), trash collection, float building, music and so on – but be sure you leave time to play **dress-up**: there's a jumble of carnival outfits by the exit that you can try on. You leave through the gift shop, which though mostly pretty tacky is worth a look for its quirky and vintage carnival **postcards**.

The Pontalba Buildings

A brace of imposing red-brick terraces elegantly book-ending the square, the three-story **Pontalba Buildings** were commissioned in 1850 by the Baroness Pontalba (see p.36). Having returned from France in 1849 to find her real estate palling in comparison to the American sector across Canal Street, she sought to replace the shabby buildings around the Place d'Armes with elegant colonnaded structures resembling those she'd admired in Paris. The original **architect**, James Gallier Sr – whom the baroness eventually sacked because of their endless squabbling – was responsible for many of the buildings' Greek Revival elements, but the large courtyards at the back, and the arrangement of commercial units on the ground floor with living spaces above, are typically Creole. These were not, as is commonly claimed, the first apartment buildings in the United States, but they were innovative in their use of mass-produced materials and, in particular, of **cast iron** – the iron was cast in New York, the red brick pressed in Baltimore, and the plate glass and slate roof tiles came from England. The stunning visual effect of the wide galleries and balconies, their decorative curlicues centering on cartouches inscribed with the initials A&P – Almonester and Pontalba – sparked off a city-wide fad for lacy cast iron, which came to replace the plainer, hand-wrought iron fashioned locally by African slaves.

As the Quarter declined after the Civil War, the apartments lost their exclusivity, and by the end of the nineteenth century they had become tenements. In the 1920s, Sherwood Anderson, who along with William Faulkner, spearheaded the influx of writers into the Quarter, hosted important literary salons in his apartment here, and by the 1930s, restored by the WPA, they regained their former prestige. Today they are some of the city's most desirable places to live, with stores and restaurants, along with the **Welcome Center** (see p.28), on the ground floors.

French Quarter architecture

While the French Quarter streets are as straight as a die, its **architecture** is a fabulous jumble of shapes and sizes, colours, styles and states of repair. Most of it dates from after the two great **fires** of 1788 and 1794, when Spanish Governor Carondelet ordained that all new buildings should be made of brick, plaster and stucco, with tiled roofs. That said, the streetscape is far from purely Spanish. Most structures marry French and Spanish colonial elements, and many reveal Caribbean influences. Others, most of them dating from the antebellum era, meld Anglo-American and Creole styles.

Many of the vernacular buildings are one-storey **Creole cottages**, and multistorey **Creole townhouses**, both of which are built about a foot off the ground, above a closed ventilated area known as a "crawl space", and with a high gabled roof. The interiors were designed without a hall, with four rooms in a checkerboard square; doors, indistinguishable from the outside from the shuttered ceiling-to-floor windows, open straight from the street into the living quarters. Outside areas held slave quarters, kitchens, outhouses and **garconnières**, where the sons of the house would take up residence after reaching adolescence. Planters from the **West Indies** brought the notion of building houses on pillars, protecting them from waterlogging, and added porches – known as galleries – to shield against the sun and rain. The ground floor was used for storage, with living space above and, during good weather, out on the gallery. Hot air inside the house could rise and escape through tall dormer windows, set in steep pitched roofs.

Under the Spanish, louvred shutters replaced heavier battened ones, and fine iron balconies were wrought by African craftsmen. Though they rarely stood higher than two storeys, the public buildings especially became heavier-looking and more obviously Mediterranean in style. **Courtyards** were designed now as extra living areas, where residents cultivated lush tropical plants, along with potent flowers, spices and herbs to mask the odours from the street.

As the nineteenth century drew on, **Anglo-American** incomers tended to settle on the other side of Canal Street in what is now the CBD, but their influence was still felt in the Quarter, where a number of buildings were designed in simply elegant Federal or Greek Revival styles. With a concern for privacy alien to the Creoles, Americans built their homes with enclosed hallways and indoor toilets.

The ornate **cast iron** so associated with the Quarter didn't come in till the 1840s, when improved communications and technologies meant that it could be bought in bulk from the industrializing north. Inspired by Baroness Pontalba's apartment buildings on Jackson Square (see p.39), a fad developed for filigree balconies and fences, curly brackets and fluted columns, which were added to old buildings and incorporated into new ones. At the same time, large two- or three-storey **galleries** were tacked onto the front of buildings, supported by narrow pillars, or **colonnettes**. Extending over the sidewalk, the galleries provided shade and shelter for pedestrians and more living space for residents. In the late 1800s, **shotgun houses** emerged in force: composed of a single row of rooms opening onto each other, with no hallway, they're supposedly named for the fact that you could, in theory, shoot a bullet from the front door to the back without it hitting anything. Other historians argue that they bear a resemblance to West African homes, and that the name may come from the Yoruba word for house, "togun". Long, narrow clapboard structures, shotguns are most notable for the decorative wooden gingerbread details that early owners ordered from catalogues and stuck to the fronts.

For a **glossary** of architectural terms, see p.245.

Avart-Peretti House

Built by J.N.B de Pouilly, the eminent local architect who also worked on St Louis Cathedral and Tremé's St Augustine's Church (see p.68), the 1842 **Avart-Peretti**

townhouse, just off Jackson Square at 632 St Peter St, was where Tennessee Williams wrote much of *A Streetcar Named Desire*. The Mississippi native, who said "If I can be said to have a home it is in the French Quarter, which has provided me with more material than any other part of the country," lived here during the winter of 1946-47, making final revisions to his manuscript *The Poker Night*. Working on his balcony to the accompaniment of "that rattletrap of a streetcar that bangs up one old street and down another" inspired him to rename and finish his work in progress, relocating it to New Orleans. Sadly, the streetcar itself, which ran through the Quarter to Desire Street in the Faubourg Marigny, stopped running in 1948.

Decatur Street

When the French Quarter was laid out in 1721, **Decatur Street** (pronounced "deKAYder"), then known as Levee Street, abutted the Mississippi. Today, the land that separates it from the water – four whole blocks of it at the Canal Street end – has all been dumped by the dramatically shifting river. A broad, busy thoroughfare, noisy with traffic and lined with cheap-and-cheerful tourist shops, bars and restaurants, Decatur becomes more countercultural as you head downriver beyond Ursulines Street and the touristy **French Market**. Here, in **Lower Decatur** – the haunt of gutter punks and dirty-footed would-be hobos, busking and sipping macchiatos – a string of dive bars, cheap restaurants and thrift stores leads you toward the funky **Faubourg Marigny**.

Jean Lafitte National Historical Park Visitor Center

Something of an anomaly among Upper Decatur's brassy T-shirt shops and theme restaurants, the elegant **Jean Lafitte National Historical Park Visitor Center**, 419 Decatur St (daily 9am–5pm; free; Ⓦ www.nps.gov/jela), is easy to miss; the entrance is around the back, tucked away beyond a broad carriageway and large, tranquil courtyard. This is a shame: quite apart from being a starting point for excellent French Quarter **walking tours** (see p.24), as a free one-room introduction to Louisiana's delta region and to the city itself the place can't be bettered.

Illustrated panels and detailed timelines cover subjects as varied as local architecture, cultural and spiritual traditions, festivals, cuisine and ecology – Katrina is represented via a small board of yellowing newspaper clippings. You can skip the twelve-minute movie with its overblown commentary and head instead for the **listening stations**, where Louisiana natives expound, in a variety of accents, on the meaning of all those unique phrases and expressions such as gumbo, *fais-do-do* and, in the words of the song, "Iko Iko". **Touch-screen monitors** show videos on jazz, brass bands, gospel, R&B, Cajun and zydeco, with rousing classic footage of Louis Armstrong, Mahalia Jackson and Professor Longhair, among others. During busy times, like Mardi Gras and Jazz Fest, rangers hold lively afternoon talks on subjects as varied as the river, women in New Orleans, or cast versus wrought iron – check the monthly schedules online or at the information desk. There's also a small **bookshop**, particularly strong on titles dealing with the early history of the city.

The **Jean Lafitte National Historical Park**, which preserves natural and historic sites of interest in the Mississippi Delta, is scattered throughout southern Louisiana. Other sites include the **Chalmette Battlefield** (see p.61) and the Barataria Preserve (see p.210).

The French Market, Farmers Market and Flea Market

Spanning the five or so riverside blocks downriver from Jackson Square, the low, red **French Market** (Ⓦ www.frenchmarket.org) buildings are said to stand on the site of a Choctaw trading area. There has certainly been an active market here, in one form or another, since the 1720s; nineteenth-century visitors marvelled at the exotic, chaotic jumble of Native Americans, Africans and Creoles, Sicilians, Chinese and Hindus, farmers and fishermen, adventurers and shysters, fast-talking in every language imaginable, trading fragrant herbs, mysterious wild birds and even alligators. Naturalist John James Audubon, shopping in 1821 for fowl to use as studies for his Birds of America, called it "the dirtiest place in all the cities of the United States".

The colonnaded arcades – much reworked and restored since the first was built in 1813 – are more sanitized now, their speciality stores teeming with tourists snapping up T-shirts, cookbooks, beads, masks and pralines, while musicians play jazz outside crowded cafés. Despite the relentless commercialization, there are some good finds to be had among the tourist tat, and the 24-hour **Café du Monde**, traditionally *the* place to snack on *beignets* and café au lait (see p.140), is a must. Come very early, or very late, and you can almost imagine yourself back at the old French Market coffee stands, where dockers, farmers, businessmen and society ladies would gather at the marble-topped tables to drink steaming, strong coffee before hurrying on with their affairs.

Heading downriver brings you to the **Farmers Market** at the 1100 block of N Peters Street. Depending on season, you'll find mountains of fresh pumpkins, sugarcane, Creole tomatoes, shrimp, sausages, and crabs sold around the clock, along with herbs, spices, coffee, hot sauce, and the like. Even if you're not buying, it's a great spot to fill up on fresh, inexpensive Creole cuisine served at bustling food counters. Next door, the so-called **flea market**, which occupies the 1200 block of N Peters Street, is in fact the domain of ugly ceramic Mardi Gras masks, T-shirts and designer rip-offs; for vintage curiosities, you'd do better to head to the cavernous thrift and rummage stores across the way on Decatur.

French Market Place, the innocuous alley that runs alongside the farmers and flea markets, was, in the second half of the nineteenth century, **Gallatin Street**, the dingiest, deadliest block in New Orleans. Blind-drunk sailors and swaggering young blades would enter this cesspit of brothels, barrel-houses and dark gambling dens at their peril, many of them never to be seen again. Even policemen refused to set foot near the place, fearing encounters with garroters, murderous prostitutes and knife-wielding pimps. There's little to show for all this derring-do today: just the market stalls on one side and the shabby back end of the Decatur shops on the other. During Mardi Gras, this is the site of one of the city's best mask markets, and it also provides a good open stage for regular music events (check ⓦwww .frenchmarket.org for details).

For more on **shopping** in the French Market, see p.184.

New Orleans Jazz National Historical Park Visitor Center

Tucked away between the French Market and the river at 916 N Peters St, the **New Orleans Jazz National Historical Park Visitor Center** (Tues–Sat 10am–5pm; free; ⓦwww.nps/gov/jazz) is a must for any music fan. Though the park itself (due to be located in Louis Armstrong Park) is as yet a twinkle in its planners' eyes, the events staged here are always top-notch, from masterclasses, ranger talks and workshops to short **concerts** from the very best local and visiting musicians. The light, airy room is a great place to hear music, with good acoustics and an intimate scale; in addition to jazz bands trad and modern, religious groups, barrelhouse piano professors and brass bands take the stage to define jazz in the broadest of terms. Check out too the rare photographs, information sheets (including a selection of self-guided jazz walking tour brochures), and the **bookstore**, which is, of course, packed with music titles and CDs.

For reviews of New Orleans' best **jazz clubs**, see pp.154–158.

Old US Mint/Jazz Museum

Continuing downriver, you'll come to **Esplanade Avenue**, a romantic, oak-shaded boulevard lined with decaying Creole mansions that forms the boundary between the Quarter and the Faubourg Marigny. Pre-Katrina, the **Old US Mint** (Tues–Sun 10am–4.30pm; $6), the rust-coloured Greek Revival hulk on the 400 block near the river, housed a fascinating **jazz museum** – featuring old instruments, sheet music, photos, and personal effects – that has yet, despite all best intentions, to re-open. In the meantime, the Mint hosts small touring shows of local interest (recent highlights have included a Napoleon exhibition, another of African-American photography, and displays on early jazz).

The building itself is of some interest; from 1838 to 1909 – with a break during the Civil War and Reconstruction – $300 million worth of currency was churned out here, including, for a year or so, Confederate gold coins. It was also on this spot in 1862, at the outset of the city's occupation by Union troops, that William Mumford, riverboat gambler and Confederate patriot, tore down the star-spangled banner from the flagpole and dragged it through the streets – a crime for which Union General "Beast" Butler (see p.79) hanged him from the peristyle.

Chartres Street

Chopped in half by Jackson Square, **Chartres Street** (pronounced "Charders") is quieter and more characterful than Decatur, its appealing mix of bars and offbeat shops geared as much to locals as to tourists. It was here, in a building on the corner with Toulouse Street, that the **great fire** of Good Friday 1788 broke out, after a candle in a small household shrine set light to a curtain. The family, along with most of the city's population, was at church, leaving the conflagration to rage unabated and 856 buildings, including St Louis Cathedral, to be destroyed in its wake.

The Napoleon House

Now a hugely atmospheric bar and restaurant (see p.129), the **Napoleon House**, 500 Chartres St, is in fact made up of two houses. The original, 1797 building is a two-storey structure on St Louis; the elegant three-storey building on Chartres was added in 1814. With its weatherbeaten stucco walls, heavy battened wooden shutters and cupola, it's one of the loveliest buildings in the Quarter, and even more so inside – make sure to spend time in its historic, shadowy bar or lush courtyard, sipping a Pimm's Cup and snacking on fine muffulettas (see p.247).

The main house was built for Mayor Nicholas Girod, who, so the story goes, volunteered to host the exiled French emperor in the New World. Sometimes the story goes even further, claiming that, with the help of pirates Jean Lafitte and Dominique You, Girod sent a boat, the *Seraphin*, to rescue Napoleon from the island of St Helena – unaware that he had died three days before it set sail.

Historical Pharmacy Museum

The quirky **Historical Pharmacy Museum**, 514 Chartres St (in theory Tues–Sat 10am–5pm, but hours change, so check website; $5; ⓦ www.hnoc.org), offers fascinating insights into the history of medicine. Lining the walls of the 1820s apothecary – in a Creole-American townhouse designed by J.N.B. de Pouilly, who also remodelled St Louis Cathedral – huge rosewood cabinets are filled with ancient glass jars crammed with herbs, froufrou china containers advertising Creole miracle cures, old medical books and ledgers, and terrifying surgical implements. Indeed, the whole place delights in dwelling on the gorier side of medical history. There's plenty of gruesome detail on the **epidemics** that ravaged the city in the nineteenth century, particularly yellow fever, or "black vomit", for which

▲ The Napoleon House

the purging, bleeding and blistering tried by doctors did nothing to prevent it felling one tenth of the population in one year alone.

Look out for the 1850s **trephination drill**, a savage saw-toothed corkscrew that was bored into the skull in the belief that it might cure a headache, and the scary-looking **scarefier**, a nineteenth-century blood-letting apparatus with twelve razor-sharp blades. Perhaps worst of all is the present-day **leech mobile home**, a jar of water filled with fat, lurking leeches, just waiting to suck on the tissue of cosmetic or reconstructive surgery patients. A voodoo cabinet reveals the *gris-gris* – charms, or spells, sold under the counter in many nineteenth-century New Orleans pharmacies – to have been nothing more mysterious than essential oils. Other voodoo remedies – for syphilis, say, or mastitis (mouldy bread soaked in milk, and sheep-manure tea, respectively) were less pleasant.

Climbing the winding stairs past the pretty courtyard brings you to the **entresol**. This shallow storage area, invisible from the outside of the building, is a typical feature of Creole townhouses, sandwiched between the ground-floor commercial area and the private living space above. Upstairs, along with an intriguing collection of vintage spectacles from around the world, the museum is mostly devoted to **women's medicine**, with jars of herbs and roots (complete with details of their dismal side effects), barbaric gynecological speculums and a recreated nineteenth-century home-birthing area. Potted histories chart the course of common drugs like morphine and opium – used in the 1800s by 65 percent of women aged 25 to 55 to cure everything from PMS to "hysteria". There's also an account of Lily the Pink, one Lydia Pinkham, whose wildly popular cure for female weakness (which, in the words of the song, did indeed prove to be "most efficacious, in every case") was found in 1906 to be made almost entirely of pure alcohol.

Incidentally, the heady **fragrance** in the museum courtyard comes from its sweet olive tree, cultivated in many New Orleans gardens; you can buy it in perfume form at the nearby Hové Parfumeur (see p.187).

Le Petit Théâtre du Vieux Carré

In a handsome Spanish Colonial building on the corner of Chartres Street and Jackson Square, **Le Petit Théâtre du Vieux Carré** has been home since 1922 to the nation's longest-running community theatre group, the Drawing Room Players. It's a pretty, intimate setting for middle-of-the-road musicals, comedies and drama, and a suitably historic venue for the annual Tennessee Williams Literary Festival (see p.179).

The Beauregard-Keyes House

A raised 1826 Creole cottage at 1113 Chartres St, the **Beauregard-Keyes House** (hourly tours Mon–Sat 10am–3pm; $5) owes the first part of its name to Confederate **General Pierre Beauregard**, who ordered the first shot of the Civil War at Fort Sumter and remained a hero in the South long after the war was lost. He lodged here for a couple of years during Reconstruction in his new capacity as a railroad president. After narrowly escaping being demolished to make way for a macaroni factory in the 1920s, the house was bought in the 1940s by popular novelist **Frances Parkinson Keyes**, who made it her winter home and wrote many of her New Orleans-based titles here. Perhaps unsurprisingly, tour guides tend to skim over the years in between, when the French Quarter had declined into a slum, populated mostly by the poor Italians who came to the city in the 1890s. In the early 1900s the house was home to one Corrado Giacona, a Sicilian who sold liquor from the downstairs rooms and refused to pay off the local mob. When four men broke in, intending to make him an offer he couldn't refuse, Giacona was armed and ready; he killed three and critically injured the fourth. Just a typical night in the pre-Vieux Carré Commission French Quarter – or Latin Quarter, as it was then known.

Nothing remains from Gicacona's inauspicious residence in the house, which today is at pains to present itself as an eminently genteel place. It works best as a museum of **decorative arts**, showcasing a wide range of fine old furniture, from Beauregard's rosewood armoires to Keyes' New England-made pieces. Oil paintings include a likeness of the general's daughter Laurie, wearing a bracelet of brass buttons that he sent her from battle. Beyond the pretty hidden courtyard, the back rooms look much as they did in Keyes' day, when she set up a study in the old slave quarters; hand-written drafts of her work lie on her desk. While travelling around the world as editor of *Good Housekeeping* magazine, hobnobbing, according to photos on display, with everyone from Mussolini to the Duchess of Windsor, Keyes accumulated an extensive **doll collection**, some of which is on display in the carriage house, along with decorative porcelain *veilleuses* (nightlights) from Europe.

Tours end up in the funny little **gift shop**, which stocks secondhand copies of Keyes' titles (now out of print), including *Dinner at Antoine's*, which sold more than two million, and *Madame Castel's Lodger*, a romance about the house's Beauregard period; you can get them more cheaply, however, in local used bookstores. Before you leave, make sure to stop by the peaceful walled **garden**.

The Old Ursuline Convent

Built between 1745 and 1750, the tranquil **Old Ursuline Convent**, 1112 Chartres St (Mon–Sat 10am–4pm; $5), is the only intact French colonial structure in the city, and quite possibly the oldest building in the Mississippi valley. The first Ursuline nuns – twelve of them – arrived in town after a five-month-long sea voyage from France in 1727, invited by Sieur de Bienville to establish a hospital for his soldiers. Their importance to the early settlement was incalculable: in 1729 they established an orphanage for the children of colonists killed in the Indian rebellion at Fort Rosalie (now Natchez, Mississippi); they also taught (segregated) classes for young Creole, African and Native American girls. Since 1824, when the nuns moved to a new site, the imposing, dove-grey building – typically French-Canadian, with its tall casement windows and steeply pitched roof – has served variously as a school, the seat of the state legislature, and the archbishopric. Guides on the Quarter's many ghost tours insist it is haunted by ghosts of the French **casket girls**, respectable white virgins shipped over in the early days of the colony, who were kept here by the nuns before being sold off as wives – an attempt by Bienville to discourage his French soldiers from coupling with Indian or African women.

Inside, the hushed rooms are lined with wordy old information panels explaining the history of the convent and the gruelling existence of the nuns who lived here. The mishmash of religious paraphernalia includes minor icons and statues from the nuns' original Ursuline convent in France, but the main interest is in the time-worn rooms themselves. You can also see the glass jars, pestles and mortars used by Mother St Francis Xavier Herbert, who dispensed herbal cures from the convent and is reckoned to have been the first female pharmacist in the US; the delightfully peaceful herb garden at the back of the convent is now maintained by Chef Scott Boswell for his two renowned restaurants *Stella!* (see p.130) and *Stanley* (see p.129).

In the 1846 **St Mary's chapel** next door, a Baroque marble altar displays an overwrought scene of the Revelation and the Virgin Mary, who pops up again on the stained-glass windows; to the right of the altar, she's shown above a foggy view of the Battle of New Orleans.

Royal Street

Elegant **Royal Street** was the main commercial thoroughfare of the Creole city, inhabited by the wealthiest sugar planters and lined with the finest shops. Despite being one of the most touristed routes through the Quarter, it's still a dignified old place, lined with landmark buildings, antique stores and toney art galleries. Its fabulous cast-iron **balconies**, the cream of the Quarter's crop, create a stunning streetscape familiar from countless movies, coffee-table books and postcards. Upper Royal Street, which is occasionally closed off to cars, is also a favourite stretch for **buskers**, from ragamuffin spasm bands plucking banjos and playing fiddle to chunky sousaphone players blasting out New Orleans carnival music.

Exchange Alley

Exchange Alley, the pedestrianized lane running parallel to Royal Street between Canal and Conti, was originally intended to lead all the way to the Cabildo. It never got further than the *St Louis Hotel*, however – making a convenient conduit from the American sector straight into the hotel's slave exchange (see opposite).

In the 1800s this was the "street of the **fencing masters**", inhabited almost exclusively by skilled teachers who trained young men in the art of duelling. Duels, or *affaires d'honneur*, had long been part of the fabric of the French and Spanish colony, fought with rapiers by proud young Creoles and settled at "first blood". In the nineteenth century, however, as the city Americanized and rifles became the weapons of choice, the duels became contests to the death.

Exchange Alley cuts across **Bienville** and **Iberville streets**, parallel to Canal, where despite the occasional new development, the sleazy, pre-preservation Quarter is revealed in all its dingy glory in the shabby buildings and lots, 1950s neon and dim, dank girlie bars.

The Supreme Court Building

In 1910, when the Quarter was at its most run-down and the Vieux Carré Commission barely dreamed of, an entire block, bounded by Royal, St Louis, Chartres, and Conti, was demolished to make way for a colossal new courthouse. Abandoned in the 1950s in favour of more modern premises in the Central Business District, the Beaux Arts behemoth was finally restored in 2004 to house the **Louisiana Supreme Court**. Though the sheer scale of the place makes it an incongruous sight in the narrow streets of the Quarter, its glossy, veined marble facade, gleaming behind huge green palms, makes it an undeniably handsome one.

Omni Royal Orleans Hotel

At the corner of Royal and St Louis, the swanky **Omni Royal Orleans Hotel** stands on the site of the famed **St Louis Hotel**, designed in 1838 by J.N.B. de Pouilly. With its copper dome, colossal spiral staircase and opulent frescoes, the *St Louis* was at the heart of Creole high society, hosting the grandest balls and, in its columned, marble rotunda, holding the city's largest **slave exchange**. To encourage traders to stay the full three hours between noon and 3pm, when auctioneering took place, management offered them a free lunch at the bar – a canny promotion that spread like wildfire through taverns around the nation until the onset of Prohibition.

The hotel's **demise** began with the Civil War. During the city's shambolic Reconstruction period it housed the State Capitol, but was abandoned in 1898 and left to decay for years. Visitors could pay a small fee to tour the ruins – in 1912, British author John Galsworthy was struck by his encounter with a wounded horse, stumbling alone through the broken marble. A hurricane blasted off the roof in 1915, and the wrecked building was finally demolished a year later, to be replaced in 1960 with the *Omni Royal*. At the back of the hotel, on Chartres Street, you can still make out the shadow of the word "exchange", painted on blocks of stone taken from the original building.

For a **review** of the hotel itself, see p.117.

The Historic New Orleans Collection

The bulk of the superb **Historic New Orleans Collection** (Tues–Sat 9.30am–4.30pm, Sun 10.30am–4.30pm; ⓦwww.hnoc.org) is in the 1792 **Merieult House**, standing proud among the neighbouring antique stores and chi-chi art galleries at 533 Royal St. In 1938, General Kemper and Mrs Leila Williams, wealthy cypress-mill owners who struck oil on their property, bought and restored the building – one of the few survivors of the 1794 fire – along with a neighbouring structure around the corner on Toulouse Street. Entry to the excellent **temporary exhibitions** in the street-front room of the Merieult House is free (past exhibits have covered Mardi Gras, maps, the cotton trade and jazz), but to see the best of the collection, you'll need to take a **guided tour** (10am, 11am, 2pm & 3pm; $5), which might cover the **Louisiana History galleries** upstairs, or the **Williams' home** on Toulouse, depending on the preferences of the group and the enthusiasms of your tour guide. They also offer a tour of the HNOC's lovely **architecture and courtyards**.

The **history galleries** on the top floor of the Merieult House hold a fascinating treasure-trove of old maps, drawings, architectural plans, documents relating to the Louisiana Purchase, furniture, decorative arts and paintings. Eleven galleries, organized chronologically, span the years from French settlement up the twentieth century, ending with some charmingly low-key early Jazz Fest posters. Though there is far more to see than can be taken in on one 45-minute tour, **highlights** include the only known portrait of Bienville painted from life and two revealing portraits of Andrew Jackson – furrow-browed and quizzical in 1819, and far more world-weary 21 years later, after his stint as the seventh US president. Look out, too, for the 1720 engraving that portrays the colony as a land of milk and honey peopled with beaming natives – an early publicity poster put out by John Law's Company of the West (see p.217) to attract settlers from Europe to what was, in reality, an unprepossessing, disease-ravaged swamp. In contrast, an 1803 engraving showing the view from Bernard de Marigny's plantation (today's Faubourg Marigny; see p.99) reveals a vast expanse of open lots and unpromising swamp. Among artefacts from the antebellum era you can see decorative broadsheets from the Creole Salle d'Orleans ballroom and the St Charles Theater, its equivalent in the American sector; a brace of duelling pistols; and designs for elaborate Mardi Gras floats.

For anyone interested in design and decorative arts, the 1889 **Williams Residence**, 718 Toulouse St (reached via the Merieult House), is a must. The Williamses were prominent citizens – as a young deb during Mardi Gras 1936 Leila reigned as Comus' Queen, while Kemper was Comus in 1953 – and a widely travelled pair, who filled their house with unusual, exotic objects. Treasures include a stool fashioned out of a column from a ruined plantation, lamps made from samovars and antique Chinese burial art, and a host of antique maps.

The gift **shop** sells excellent books, reproductions of old prints and maps, and a good range of unusual postcards; see p.187.

La Branche House

The **La Branche House**, towering graciously over the corner at 700 Royal St, encapsulates all that people imagine the French Quarter to be. Its gorgeous cast-iron balconies and galleries, added a decade after the house was built, form a fanciful, filigree cage around the relatively plain, Greek Revival structure – the apotheosis of the style that the city went mad for in the 1850s. Incidentally, the La Branche family originally came from Germany; in New Orleans their name, Zweig, meaning "twig", was Gallicized, a common fate for many non-French surnames.

▲ Creole houses in the French Quarter

Big Easy cuisine

New Orleans is one of the world's great foodie cities. Locals live to eat and love to eat out, and you can feast on its distinctive Creole cuisine anywhere from ravishing old-world dining rooms to homey neighbourhood dives that have seen better days. Food, as so much else here, is not only drenched with tradition and history but also celebration, joy, and excess. Eating out in New Orleans is a ritual to take seriously and to relish: it will fill your heart and feed your soul.

Gumbo ▲

Po-boy ▼

Creole cooking

New Orleans cooking, commonly defined as **Creole**, is a spicy, substantial – and usually very fattening – blend of French, Spanish, African, Caribbean, Italian and Cajun cuisines, mixed up with a host of other influences including Native American and German. It tends to be rich and fragrant, using heaps of herbs, peppers, garlic and onion, but rarely, despite the common misconception, will it taste fiery. Some of the simpler dishes, like **red beans and rice** (traditionally served on a Monday, using the meat leftovers from the weekend), reveal a strong West Indies influence, while others are more French, cooked with long-simmered sauces based on a **roux** (fat and flour heated together) and herby stocks. You'll often get surprising twinnings – oysters and tasso, say, or crabmeat and veal – and many dishes are served **étouffé**, literally "smothered" in a tasty Creole sauce (a roux with tomato, onion and spices), on a bed of rice. The mainstays of most menus – **gumbo**, **jambalaya**, **po-boys**, **muffulettas** – will become old friends after a day or two. We've defined some of the more unfamiliar terms on p.246, but in a nutshell a gumbo is a stew, jambalaya is a rice dish, and po-boys and muffulettas are sandwiches overstuffed with seafood, meat, and just about anything else at hand.

Note that **Black Creole** restaurants offer a New Orleans take on Southern soul food – you won't find chitlins here, but you will find gumbo – and that Creole food is not the same as **Cajun** food, its one-pot country cousin. What passes for Cajun food in the city is often a modern, Creolized hybrid: the "blackened" dishes, for example, slathered in butter and hot spices, made famous by Cajun chef Paul Prudhomme in the 1980s.

Seafood

Seafood is abundant and usually inexpensive – hardly surprising when you consider the city is almost entirely surrounded by water. **Shrimp** is a mainstay on many menus – "barbecue shrimp", which bears little relation to barbecue as the rest of the world thinks of it, instead sees the tasty jumbo crustaceans served in a hot, garlicky and buttery sauce (you'll be glad of the paper bib that many restaurants provide when you order them) – while **softshell crabs** add their delicate flavour to everything from gumbos to po-boys. You'll also get famously good raw **oysters**, shucked and slurped along marble-topped counters all around the city; they're served deep-fried in po-boys, char-grilled with piquant cheese, plump and briny in gumbos, embellished with fancy sauces in dishes like Oysters Rockefeller or Sardou, or simply raw with a dash of horseradish and a very cold martini. Though their production is under serious threat from wetland erosion, they're still very much in evidence in New Orleans, and in season from September to April.

Once looked down on as "trash" food, **crawfish**, or mudbugs, are a firm local favourite. Closely resembling langoustines, they're served in everything from omelettes to bisques, and often in an étouffé, smothered in a delicious tomato-rich sauce. To enjoy them as the locals do, however, get yourself invited to a **crawfish boil**, where they are simply boiled, in vast quantities, with corn cobs, lemons and bay leaves, in a spicy Tabasco-infused stock. Though you can get them any time from December through to July, they're most plentiful between March and May – crawfish boil season. To eat them, tug off the overlarge head, pinch the tail and suck out the juicy, very delicious flesh.

▲ Barbecue shrimp

▼ Oysters

▼ Crawfish

Green Goddess ▲

Cochon ▼

Don't-miss dining

For the most satisfying and distinctive New Orleans dining experiences, make sure to try the following dishes or local cuisines. You'll find them all over the city, but these are the places that do them best. For more on the city's signature dishes, and where to eat them, see p.123.

▶▶ **Barbecue shrimp** *Green Goddess* (see p.127), *Liuzza's by the Track* (see p.138), *Mr B's* (see p.128), *Pascal's Manale* (see p.137).

▶▶ **Black Creole** *Café Reconcile* (see p.134), *Dooky Chase's* (see p.138), *Lil' Dizzy's* (see p.130), *Ms Hyster's Barbecue* (see p.135), *Olivier's* (see p.129), *Willie Mae's* (see p.139).

▶▶ **Cajun** *Cochon* (see p.133), *K-Paul's* (see p.128).

▶▶ **Classic Creole** *Commander's Palace* (see p.134), *Galatoire's* (see p.126), *Tujague's* (see p.130).

▶▶ **Contemporary Creole** *Brigtsen's* (see p.136), *Jacques Imo's* (see p.137), *Mr B's* (see p.128), *Palace Café* (see p.134), *Ralph's on the Park* (see p.139).

▶▶ **Gumbo** *Bayona* (see p.124), *Dooky Chase's* (see p.138), *Gumbo Shop* (see p.127), *K-Paul's* (see p.128), *Lil' Dizzy's* (see p.130), *Mandina's* (see p.138), *Olivier's* (see p.129).

▶▶ **Jambalaya** *Coop's* (see p.125).

▶▶ **Muffulettas** *Central Grocery* (see p.143), *Napoleon House* (see p.129).

▶▶ **Oysters** *Acme* (see p.124), *Casamento's* (see p.136), *Felix's* (see p.126).

▶▶ **Po-boys** *Domilise's* (see p.136), *Guy's* (see p.137), *Johnny's* (see p.128), *Mother's* (see p.133), *Parkway Bakery* (see p.138).

▶▶ **New Orleans Southern** *Boucherie* (see p.135), *Dick and Jenny's* (see p.136), *Elizabeth's* (see p.131), *Jacques Imo's* (see p.137).

Madame John's Legacy

A rare example of the French Quarter's early, West Indies-style architecture (see p.40), **Madame John's Legacy**, just off Royal Street at 628 Dumaine St (Tues–Sun 10am–4.30pm; free), was rebuilt after the fire of 1788 as an exact replica of the 1730 house that had previously stood on the site. It was constructed using the *briquete entre poteaux* technique, in which soft red brick is set between steadying, hand-hewn cypress beams, and raised off the ground on stucco-covered brick pillars. The distinctive, deep wraparound gallery provided extra living space, cooler and airier than the indoor rooms.

Today it stands flush with the street; in the days of the French colony it would have been surrounded by far more land. Gates at the side open onto the wide carriageway that leads around the back, past the kitchen and *garconnière*. Inside, a small interpretative exhibition details the house's various inhabitants and changes in fortune; ironically, the lack of artefacts in these empty, silent rooms endows the place with an enormous sense of atmosphere, allowing you to appreciate the structure itself.

Incidentally, there never was a real Madame John – the name was given to the house by nineteenth-century author George Washington Cable (see p.227) in his tragic short story *'Tite Poulette*, and it simply stuck, attracting at the time hundreds of book-loving tourists to the city and spawning a nice line in Madame John souvenirs.

Back on Royal Street, look out for the cast-iron **cornstalk fence** fronting the *Cornstalk Hotel*, 915 Royal St (see p.116). Bought from a catalogue in the 1850s, at the peak of the city's craze for cast iron, the elaborate tangle of brightly painted cornstalks entwined with morning glories has a twin in the Garden District (see p.87), and has become something of a local landmark.

Gallier House

The handsome **Gallier House**, 1132 Royal St (Mon & Fri hourly tours 10am–2pm, Sat hourly tours noon–3pm; $10 or $18 with the Hermann-Grima House, see p.51; Ⓦwww.hgghh.org) – reputedly Anne Rice's inspiration for Louis and Lestat's dwelling in her novel *Interview with the Vampire* – is a fascinating little place, built in 1857. Designed for himself and his family by James Gallier Jr, a leading architect like his father before him, it's in many ways a typical Creole structure, with a large carriageway leading to a courtyard. Gallier also, however, incorporated a number of Americanized elements, such as the enclosed hall and indoor bathroom. Innovations included a cooling system and a flushing toilet, while the filigree cast-iron galleries would have been the last word in chic.

Tours of the house, focusing on social history rather than fine furniture, are some of the liveliest in the Quarter. The place is set up to recreate the cluttered style of the antebellum era, when the citywide fashion for fancy decoration had to be balanced with the practicalities of living in a swampy climate: fine oil paintings and hand-carved closets stand tilted away from the walls, to avoid being blighted by mildew. In summer – when wealthy Quarterites would have fled the unbearably hot, disease-ridden city for their plantations, or Europe – the house adopts "summer dress": the furniture is swathed in gauze, and the carpets replaced with straw matting.

Though city slaves – valets, repairmen, cooks and nannies – were regarded as being better off than field labourers, who did the back-breaking work of the plantations, life was by no means easy, as a quick wander around the **slave quarters** reveals. These small rooms were minimally furnished with old or broken furniture from the main house, and because slave skins were thought to be "tough", were free of mosquito netting.

The LaLaurie Home

If the hokey night-time ghost tours are to be believed, the French Quarter has many **haunted houses**; the most famous, the French Empire **LaLaurie Home**, lurks at 1140 Royal St on the corner with Gov Nicholls. In the nineteenth century this gloomy grey and black pile belonged to the LaLauries, a doctor and his socialite wife Delphine, who, although seen wielding a whip as she chased a slave girl through the house to the roof, was merely fined when the child fell to her death. Whispers about the couple's cruelty were horribly verified when neighbours rushed in after a fire in 1834 – believed to have been started intentionally by the shackled cook – to find seven emaciated slaves locked in the attic. There they saw men, women and children choked by neck braces, some with broken limbs; one had a worm-filled hole gouged out of his cheek. The doctor's protestation that this torture chamber was, in fact, an "experiment" was met with vitriol; the next day the pair escaped the baying mob outside their home and fled to France. Since then, many claim to have heard ghostly moans from the building at night; some say they have seen a girl stumble across the balcony.

During Reconstruction the building housed a desegregated girls' school, a hopeful venture that ended in December 1874 when the **White League** militia, a group of ex-Confederates committed to destroying the new Reconstruction government (see p.74), stormed in and evicted by force any of the pupils they believed to have African blood.

The LaLaurie Home's more recent history is no cheerier. In November 2009, actor and would-be property magnate **Nicolas Cage**, who bought the building for $3.5million in 2006, lost it to foreclosure in lieu of unpaid taxes.

Bourbon Street

Though you'd never guess it from the hype, there are two faces to world-renowned **Bourbon Street**. The tawdry, touristy, booze-swilled stretch spans the seven blocks from Canal to St Ann: a frat-pack cacophony of daiquiri laundromats, novelty shops, "big-ass beer" stalls and tired girlie bars offering "French-style" entertainment. This self-contained enclave is best experienced after dark, when a couple – though by no means all – of its **bars** and **clubs** are worth a look, and the sheer mayhem takes on a bacchanalian fascination of its own. When the attraction of fighting your way through crowds of weekending drunks starts to pall, however, it's easy to dip out again into the quieter parallel streets to regain some sort of sanity. If you manage to make it as far as St Ann, you come to a kind of crossroads, marked by the rambunctious **gay** clubs *Oz* and *Parade* (see p.199). Beyond here, Bourbon transforms into an appealing, predominantly gay, residential area, scattered with neighbourhood bars, old-fashioned local stores and casual restaurants.

Ironically, given its reputation, the street's name has nothing to do with booze. One of the first roads laid out by the city's planner Adrien de Pauger in 1721, Bourbon was named for the royal family of France, and until the 1920s it was a desirable, and largely respectable, residential enclave. After the closure of Storyville (see p.65), however, when many of the red light district's establishments shifted down into the Upper Quarter, the existing jazz clubs and restaurants that lined Upper Iberville and Bienville relocated to Bourbon, changing its character from residential to commercial. World War II brought a rash of strip clubs, cabarets and bars – catering to soldiers passing through the port – that eventually came to dominate.

Hermann-Grima House

Half a block above Bourbon Street at 820 St Louis, the 1832 **Hermann–Grima House** (Mon & Fri hourly tours 10am–2pm, Sat hourly tours noon–3pm; $10 or $18 with the Gallier House, see p.49; ⓦwww.hgghh.org) illustrates the lifestyle of two middle-class Creole families in antebellum New Orleans. Though in many ways a typically elegant, Federal mansion, with a number of characteristic American features – including the central hall – the house's loggia and outside kitchen whisper of a lingering Creole sensibility. It was built for Samuel Hermann, a German-Jewish cotton and slave trader, who, following nationwide economic panic in 1837 was forced to sell it in 1844 to Judge Felix Grima. The Grimas lived here until the 1920s, after which it became a women's hostel.

Though standard **tours** tend to skimp on contextual detail in favour of dwelling reverentially on replica antiques, they do at least give you time to wander around the rooms rather than trooping you past a succession of cordoned-off set pieces. Much of the furniture was made by prominent local craftsman Prudent Mallard; note especially the ornate bed with its characteristic egg motif, a visual pun on his surname. Occasional special tours cover social themes in more detail: if you visit between mid-October and early November, for example, don't be surprised to see a black wreath hanging on the front door. Timed to coincide with All Saints' and All Souls' Days (see p.107), the house adopts traditional mourning dress, with draped mirrors and a coffin stand set up in the parlour. In addition, Creole **cookery demonstrations** are held in the kitchen every Thursday from October to May.

Bourbon-Orleans Hotel

The **Bourbon-Orleans Hotel**, on the corner of those two streets, stands on the site of the old **Salle d'Orleans** ballroom, which in the antebellum era was the grandest venue for the city's much mythologized **quadroon balls**. Usually romanticized as glittering occasions where dashing white men had their hearts stolen by beautiful, dusky "quadroon" girls (one-quarter black, usually born to a white father and mulatto mother), the reality of the balls was less glamorous. Put simply, these were dances where wealthy white planters and merchants were able to consort with poorer, mixed-race girls chaperoned by their mothers. Little would usually come of the encounters, but occasionally, under a formalized system known as **plaçage**, arrangements would be made whereby the girls would be taken as mistresses, supported by their white men. A lucky few were set up in homes of their own, raising the children of their paramour, who would usually also be supporting a "respectable" white family. The *Salle d'Orleans* closed at the onset of the Civil War, was reborn as a convent, and finally became a fancy hotel in the 1960s.

The Historic Voodoo Museum

A mesmerizing, if muffled, soundtrack of drumming and chanting introduces the intriguing little **Historic Voodoo Museum**, between Bourbon and Royal at 724 Dumaine St (daily 10am–6pm; $7; ⓦvoodoomuseum.com). A ragbag collection of shrines, ceremonial objects, portraits and *gris-gris* (spells or potions), the museum aims to debunk the myths that surround this misunderstood spiritual practice – an intention undermined somewhat by the self-consciously spooky atmosphere, not to mention its resident skeleton (representing Baron Samedi, gatekeeper between this world and the next), crumbling rat heads and desiccated bats. They also offer readings, rituals, and city tours. See p.52 for more on the **history of voodoo** in New Orleans.

Voodoo in New Orleans

Voodoo, still a significant presence in New Orleans, was brought to the city by African slaves via the French colonies of the Caribbean, where tribal beliefs were mixed with Catholicism, the official religion of the colonies, to create a cult based on spirit-worship. French and, later, Spanish authorities tried to suppress the religion (voodoo-worshippers had played an active role in organizing the slave revolts in Haiti), but it continued to flourish among the city's black population, especially after 1809 when the ban was lifted on importation of slaves from the Caribbean. Under American rule, the weekly slave gatherings at **Congo Square** (see p.218), which included ritual ceremonies, turned into a tourist attraction for whites, fuelled by sensationalized reports of hypnotized white women dancing naked to the throbbing drum beats.

Unlike in the West Indies, where the religion was dominated by male priests, New Orleans had many voodoo priestesses. The most famous was **Marie Laveau**, a hairdresser of African, white and Native American blood. Using shrewd marketing sense and inside knowledge of the lives of her clients, she prepared spells, or **gris-gris** (pronounced gree-gree) for wealthy Creoles and Americans, as well as Africans, and charged admission fees for public ceremonies at Congo Square and along Bayou St John (see p.92). Laveau died in 1881, after which another Marie, believed to be her daughter, continued to practice under her name. The legend of both Maries lives on, and their crumbling **tombs** are popular tourist attractions (see p.108 & p.110).

Nowadays voodoo is big business in the French Quarter, with hokey psychic readers setting up in Jackson Square, "voodoo tours" doing the rounds after dark and countless gift shops selling tacky paraphernalia and ersatz gris-gris. If you've got a serious interest in the religion, head for the **Voodoo Spiritual Temple**, 828 N Rampart St (Ⓦwww.voodoospiritualtemple.org), where the charismatic Priestess Miriam holds services, and offers tours and consultations.

Lafitte's Blacksmith Shop

The alarmingly tumbledown **Lafitte's Blacksmith Shop**, 941 Bourbon St at St Philip – also a popular little bar (see p.147) – is one of the oldest buildings in the Quarter. Built around 1781, it's a typical early cottage, with a steeply pitched roof (the dormers were a later addition), and blotches of stucco on the walls have crumbled off to reveal its *briquete entre poteaux* construction (see p.245).

According to legend, the shop was used as a cover for pirate brothers Jean and Pierre **Lafitte**, leaders of the "Baratarians", a thousand-strong band of smugglers who hid out in the Barataria swamps at the mouth of the Mississippi. Though the importation of slaves was outlawed in 1804, there was such a high demand for labour in the thriving colony that illegal slave smuggling was a lucrative racket, and it was in murky little cottages like these that plans were hatched and raids were plotted.

For more on the **Barataria swamps**, see p.210.

Above Bourbon Street

In the late nineteenth century, the corner of the Upper Quarter that lay across Rampart Street from Storyville (see p.65) was known as the **Tango Belt**; a lively nightlife area of bars, cabarets, dance halls and jazz clubs that slowly shifted down to Bourbon Street after Storyville closed down. Today the old Tango Belt, centring on drab Iberville and Bienville streets, holds little of interest, but things improve considerably as you head downriver. Here the French Quarter becomes markedly more peaceful and residential, the tourists outnumbered by locals dog-walking, jogging, picking up provisions in corner groceries, or chatting on stoops. These quiet streets are fringed by some of the Quarter's finest **vernacular architecture**: narrow shotguns and Creole cottages, the hues of hand-tinted antique photos, standing flush with the sidewalk. Small courtyards are tended lovingly, with myrtle and magnolia blossoms tangling over cast-iron fences and fountains tinkling at the heart of hidden patios.

There are a number of popular gay bars, upscale restaurants, and bookstores above Bourbon, but, as you head toward Tremé (see p.63), these streets can be eerily isolated after dark; if you feel at all nervous, restrict your explorations to the daytime.

Musée Conti Wax Museum

Oddball and delightfully old-fashioned, the **Musée Conti Wax Museum**, one block north of Bourbon St at 917 Conti St (Mon, Fri & Sat 10am–4pm; $7; Ⓦwww.neworleanswaxmuseum.com), tells the story of New Orleans through a series of lurid tableaux, augmented by sound recordings (check out those French accents). Scenes include the Battle of New Orleans, with a wounded soldier rather gruesomely breathing (or not, depending if the mechanics are working), the arrival of the casket girls – portrayed here by a gaggle of department store manne-quins with groovy 1960s make-up – Napoleon proclaiming in his bathtub, a slave auction, wild-eyed voodoo dancers and a hard-faced, whip-wielding Madame LaLaurie (see p.50). The grand finale, apropos of nothing, comes in the Haunted Dungeon, where encounters with sundry ghouls are backed by recorded shrieking and wailing.

The Mississippi River

A resonant, romantic and extraordinary physical presence, the **Mississippi River** is New Orleans' lifeblood and its raison d'être. Some half a mile wide, it writhes through the city like an out-of-control snake, swelling against the constraining, man-made levees as it courses toward the Gulf of Mexico. Nineteenth-century visitors marvelled at this mighty highway into a still unexplored interior, writing long, lyrical accounts of its "vast and melancholy solitude", its power and its hazards; as the city's port grew, however, and river traffic increased, New Orleans gradually cut itself off from the water altogether, hemming the river in behind a string of warehouses and freight railroads.

More recently, as the importance of the port has diminished, a couple of downtown **parks**, plazas and riverside walks, accessible from the French Quarter and the CBD, have focused attention back onto the waterfront, capitalizing on its magnetic appeal. Most tourists combine a stroll by the river with a **shopping** trip at the French Market or Riverwalk Marketplace (see the "Shopping" chapter on p.184) or a visit to the **Aquarium of the Americas**. The superb **Southern Food and Beverage Museum**, and **Blaine Kern's Mardi Gras World**, are lesser-known attractions. The main draw, however, is the river itself, best seen from the **Moonwalk** or **Woldenberg Park**, or, even better, on a **cruise** aboard a restored steamboat or paddlewheeler. Some of these, which share river space with tugs and towboats, barges, naval tankers and darting water-taxis, take you as far as **Chalmette**, riverfront site of the 1815 Battle of New Orleans.

The **Riverfront streetcar**, which trundles between Esplanade Avenue and the Convention Center, can be useful if you're footsore, but river views are partial. You can get out onto the water on the **free ferry** from Canal Street, which

The Big Muddy: facts and figures

North America's principal waterway, the **Mississippi** – the name comes from the Algonquin words for "big" and "river" – is the third longest river in the world after the Nile and the Amazon. Starting in Minnesota just ninety miles south of the Canadian border, it writhes 2348 miles to the Gulf of Mexico, taking in more than one hundred tributaries and draining 41 percent of continental America, an area of more than a million square miles. **The Big Muddy** – so nicknamed because it carries two pounds of dirt for every thousand of water – is one of the world's busiest commercial rivers and one of the least conventional. Instead of widening toward its mouth, like most rivers, the Mississippi grows narrower and deeper. It is also, in the words of Mark Twain, who spent four years as a riverboat pilot, "the **crookedest** river in the world". As it extravagantly weaves and curls, it cuts through narrow necks of land to shape and reshape oxbow lakes, meander scars, cutoffs and marshy backwaters.

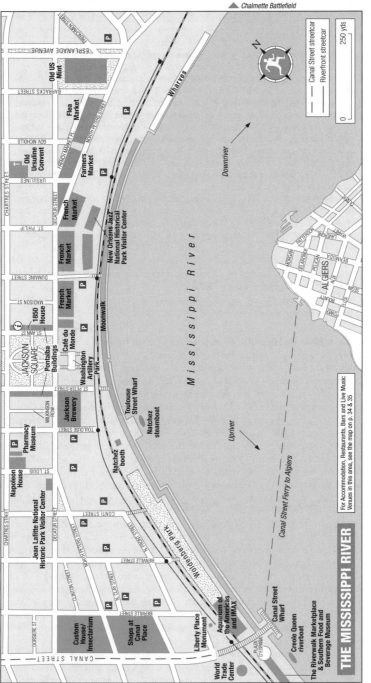

▲ Chalmette Battlefield

--- Canal Street streetcar
--- Riverfront streetcar

0   250 yds

Downriver

Mississippi River

Upriver

Canal Street Ferry to Algiers

ALGIERS

For Accommodation, Restaurants, Bars and Live Music
Venues in this area, see the map on p. 34 & 35

THE MISSISSIPPI RIVER

Old US Mint

ESPLANADE AVENUE

FRENCHMAN STREET

Flea Market

BARRACKS STREET

Old Ursuline Convent

GOV NICHOLLS

Farmers Market

CHARTRES STREET

URSULINES

French Market

DECATUR STREET

ST. PHILIP

New Orleans Jazz National Historical Park Visitor Center

French Market

DUMAINE STREET

MADISON ST

French Market

1850 House

ST ANN ST

JACKSON SQUARE

Pontalba Buildings

Café du Monde

Washington Artillery Park

Moonwalk

WILKINSON ROW

Jackson Brewery

ST PETER STREET

TOULOUSE STREET

Toulouse Street Wharf

Natchez steamboat

Pharmacy Museum

Natchez booth

Napoleon House

ST. LOUIS

Jean Lafitte National Historic Park Visitor Center

CONTI STREET

DECATUR STREET

NORTH PETERS STREET

CHARTRES STREET

TCHOUPITOULAS STREET

BIENVILLE STREET

N PETERS STREET

Woldenberg park

CLINTON STREET

IBERVILLE STREET

Custom House/ Insectarium

Shops at Canal Place

Liberty Place Monument

Aquarium of the Americas and IMAX

Canal Street Wharf

Creole Queen riverboat

The Riverwalk Marketplace & Southern Food and Beverage Museum

World Trade Center

CANAL STREET

PLACE D'ESPAGNE

▲ Blaine Kern's Mardi Gras World

River cruises

Quite apart from the sheer delight of churning along one of the world's greatest rivers on a big old sternwheeler, a short **cruise** on the Mississippi offers a fascinating glimpse into the workings of the nation's most important waterway.

Leaving from the Toulouse Street wharf behind the Jackson Brewery mall – its departure heralded by its hauntingly off-key calliope tunes, which float through the French Quarter for about forty minutes before the boat sets off – the **Natchez steamboat** heads seven miles or so downriver before turning back near the Chalmette battlefield. The captain gives a running historical commentary, audible only if you sit on deck; inside, you can dine on a buffet of fried chicken and red beans accompanied by a jaunty Dixieland band (daily 2.30pm, plus 11.30am at busy times; $24.50, $34.50 with lunch; evening cruise 7pm, $40, $64.50 with dinner; 2hr; ⊤586-8777, ⊚www.steamboatnatchez.com). Tickets are sold at booths behind Jackson Brewery and the aquarium.

Though less historic, the John James Audubon riverboat is a great option if you want to combine a cruise with a trip to the aquarium (see p.58), or Audubon Zoo (p.91), or both. Services were suspended after Katrina, but plans are afoot to get the cruises up and running again by the end of 2010; check the Natchez website.

struggles against the current to deliver you within minutes to the old shipbuilding community of **Algiers** on the west bank.

Some history

It took considerable persistence for the French-Canadian explorer Jean Baptiste le Moyne, **Sieur de Bienville**, to impose a city on the banks of a force of nature as powerful as the Mississippi River. His dream, however, of a mighty metropolis built on the back of lucrative river trade – a vision not shared by his critics, who could see only a soggy handful of cypress huts doomed by endless flooding – was eventually realized. By the nineteenth century, New Orleans' position on a portage between the river and Lake Pontchartrain, which opened into the Gulf of Mexico, made it an ideal **entrepôt** – the meeting point for the riverboats carrying cotton, sugar, tobacco and lumber down from the interior, ocean-going ships hauling the goods out to the rest of the world, and foreign vessels bringing manufactured and luxury commodities from overseas. In 1803, as the United States began its inexorable sweep westward, the Americans snapped the city up, under the terms of the **Louisiana Purchase**, which ensured them control of the entire river. Within a year, tonnage using New Orleans' port had increased by fifty percent, and for the next quarter century the number of flatboats and keelboats docking at the end of Tchoupitoulas Street averaged around a thousand per year. The flatboats, which came from the interior but were unable to negotiate the current and return upstream, were sold for lumber or transformed into floating brothels and gambling dens, while the boatmen – a lawless, brawling breed known derisively by the Creoles as "**Kaintocks**" (many came from Kentucky) – would kick up hell in the city before making their way back into the interior by land. **Pirates** plied the Mississippi, too, ready to hijack the cumbersome vessels. Most notorious among them were Jean and Pierre Lafitte and their band of **Baratarians** – named for their swampy hideout, around twenty miles downriver – who hatched countless plots in the coffeehouses and bars of New Orleans.

In 1812 the **steamboat** exploded – sometimes literally – onto the scene. Though these "floating palaces", with their puffing chimneys, fancy galleries and enormous paddlewheels, have become icons of the great days of river travel, the earliest packets, with their propensity to overheat and burst into flames, were seen as novelties only, and far too dangerous to carry passengers. By the 1840s, however, hundreds of them churned along the river, bringing goods, news, travellers and sharp-suited card sharks to the city, while their cousins, the flamboyant **showboats** – a common sight on the Mississippi well into the 1930s – staged vaudeville, circus, melodrama and Shakespeare for plantation owners, rough boatmen and straggling river communities.

Today, though New Orleans' antebellum golden era as the world's biggest export **port** – when scores of steamboats, ocean-going sailing ships, keelboats and barges lined the waterfront for miles on end – is a distant memory, in terms of tonnage New Orleans is still one of the busiest ports in the world. The river, meanwhile, maintains its awesome power behind the levee, as unpredictable and intractable as ever.

Washington Artillery Park and the Moonwalk

Directly across Decatur Street from Jackson Square, **Washington Artillery Park** is a rather grandiose name for a small, elevated strip of concrete, reached by steps, that gives superb photo opportunities of the square and St Louis Cathedral, and, in the other direction, of the Mississippi. Street performers use the space below on Decatur as a stage, while spectators lounge on the steps.

Descending the steps on the river side, walking through the break in the concrete flood walls, over the Riverfront streetcar tracks, and up another flight of steps, brings you to the **Moonwalk**, a riverfront promenade named for "Moon" Landrieu, mayor of the city from 1970 to 1978. It's a great spot, especially at sunset, when its iron benches fill with tourists gazing at the panorama upriver to the Mississippi River Bridge and, downriver, to the wharves that begin at Governor Nicholls Street. Gulls dip and dive in front of you, in the vain hope of plucking catfish out of the whirling eddies, while ships battle against the current at **Algiers Point**, the sharpest bend in the entire river, churned by a savage centrifugal force. Safe enough during the day – though you may have to contend with

▲ The Moonwalk

panhandlers, extrovert street punks and **hustlers** – the Moonwalk is best avoided late at night.

Woldenberg Park and the Aquarium of the Americas

Woldenberg Park curves upriver from the end of Toulouse Street in the French Quarter to the **Aquarium of the Americas**. Its riverside location makes it a great spot to sprawl on the grass with a picnic, watching the traffic on the Mississippi and the stream of humanity – tourists, bus boys, cops on cycles, buskers hurrying to their spot – flowing past. It's a key venue for live music during the city's numerous festivals, and for good reason; listening to live local music and filling up on New Orleans food with the Big Muddy as a backdrop has to be one of the definitive life-affirming experiences. Beyond the aquarium, you have to cut through the ugly concrete **Canal Street wharf**, terminal for the free ferry to **Algiers**, to reach the **Plaza d'España** and the touristy **Riverwalk Marketplace** shopping mall.

Aquarium of the Americas

The **Aquarium of the Americas**, one of a handful of city attractions owned by the Audubon Nature Institute (Tues–Sun 10am–5pm; $18, kids $11, IMAX $9/6; various combination tickets are available with other Audubon Nature Institute attractions; Ⓦwww.auduboninstitute.org) lies at the upriver edge of Woldenberg park near the Canal Street wharf. Entry is through a clear **tunnel** where tropical fish, rippling rays, ugly sawfish and hawksbill turtles whirl above and around you, and throngs of excitable infants press their noses against the Plexiglas. It's a vast place, with different environments recreated in lively detail – the steamy **Amazonian rainforest**, for example, demonstrates how monstrous fish, grown fat on the river's bounty, develop sensitive whiskers and an acute sense of hearing in order to make their way through the muddy water. Rainbow macaws flap above you as you cross a tree-top pathway, while thumbnail-sized poisoned-dart frogs and bird-eating spiders lurk menacingly in glass enclosures. The **Mississippi delta**, meanwhile, complete with its own mossy cypress trees, features Spots, one of New Orleans' white alligators (see p.91), ancient paddlefish, and the unnerving giant flathead catfish, who feed on geese, ducks and even dogs.

There are so many other things to see – including a **penguin** enclosure and a pair of hyperactive **sea otters** – that it can be a challenge to get around it all. Do, however, make time for the **sharks**, which range from weird-looking Australian wobbegongs to leathery nurse sharks – which you are encouraged to pet – and the infinitesimal **jellyfish** that sparkle in the dark blue water like tiny Christmas-tree lights. And on no account miss the **seahorse** exhibit, where you'll find the leafy sea dragon, nonchalantly disguised as a tangle of foliage, and the strange weedy sea dragon, hovering in the kelp like some arthritic Dr Seuss creature. The five-storey **IMAX** theatre shows the usual overblown epics of mountaineering, space exploration and other derring-do.

For details of the John James Audubon **riverboat cruise** between the aquarium and Audubon Zoo uptown, see p.56.

Plaza d'España and the Riverwalk Marketplace

Nudged in between the Aquarium and the Riverwalk Marketplace, the sunken **Plaza d'España** is a large circular space fringed with tiled representations of

The federal flood

"You know, they straightened out the Mississippi in places, to make room for houses and livable acreage. Occasionally the river floods these places. 'Floods' is the word they use, but in fact it is not flooding; it is remembering. Remembering where it used to be…"

Toni Morrison, "The Site of Memory"
in *Out There: Marginalization and Contemporary Cultures* (ed Russell Ferguson)

Although Katrina tends to be described as having been a natural disaster, the devastating flooding of New Orleans in 2005 was, in fact largely a man-made catastrophe: to most people in the city the failure of the levees will always be known as **"the federal flood"**.

At its highest point New Orleans reaches just 4.5m (15ft) above sea level, so the Mississippi's propensity to **flood** has always been a serious threat. Although the city was settled on a natural levee, this was little safeguard against flooding, and couldn't prevent the swollen Mississippi from sporadically wiping out sugar crops and entire cotton plantations. As New Orleans developed, it became crucial to find effective ways to tame this destructive force. As early as 1792 Governor Carondelet decreed that landowners should build and maintain artificial **levees**, imposing steep fines for noncompliance. The plan backfired, however, as landowners would send men out at night, under the guise of checking their own levees for **crevasses** (tiny cracks that could be caused by something as small as a crawfish), but in reality to force holes into the levees of their neighbours.

After the disastrous Great Mississippi Flood of 1927 wiped out entire communities throughout the Mississippi valley the 1928 **Flood Control Act** authorized the US Army Corps of Engineers to build protective measures all along the river that would be maintained by, and be the ultimate responsibility of, local levee boards. Many of the flood control projects built in New Orleans ever since have been problematic: the **Bonnet Carré Spillway**, for example, drains floodwaters into Lake Pontchartrain, which conservationists claim pours polluted water into the lake, putting wildlife at risk.

Meanwhile, numerous channels cut at the instigation of, among others, the **oil companies** – providing convenient short cuts from the Gulf to the city via the wetlands at the mouth of the river – have also had disastrous effects. These lead to dramatic erosion of the barrier islands that once provided natural hurricane protection, rendering the Mississippi valley increasingly **vulnerable** to storm surges, and threatening the very infrastructure of the city. With the natural flow of silt to southern Louisiana impeded and rerouted, New Orleans is slowly sinking.

One such navigation channel, the 76-mile **Mississippi River Gulf Outlet** (Mr-Go), built by the Corps of Engineers in the 1960s, funnelled cataclysmic amounts of water into the city after Katrina, laying waste to the Lower Ninth Ward and the neighbouring St. Bernard Parish. In November 2009, in a private suit brought by four individuals, a federal judge declared the Corps responsible for the collapse of Mr-Go, and **guilty of negligence**, ruling that "The Corps' lassitude and failure to fulfil its duties resulted in a catastrophic loss of human life and property in unprecedented proportions…Furthermore, the Corps not only knew, but admitted by 1988, that the Mr-Go threatened human life…and yet it did not act in time to prevent the catastrophic disaster that ensued." Fearing an onslaught of class action lawsuits, the Corps immediately appealed on a technicality, and the finding may still be overturned. For most people, however, the case has been amply proven: the worst engineering disaster in American history could have been avoided.

Spanish coats of arms and centering on a fountain. A pleasant enough place to hang out in the heat, it is most lively on Lundi Gras, when a free party, following the Zulu bash in Woldenberg Park (see p.173), celebrates the mayor handing over the city to Rex, King of Carnival.

From here you can enter the half-mile-long **Riverwalk Marketplace**, which tends to be scuttling with weekenders and conference delegates scooping up souvenirs as they rush between the convention center and the French Quarter. This isn't bad, as malls go, with at least some local character, but even more than the shopping (for more on which see p.184), it's worth strolling along its outdoor **promenade**, which is raised above river-level and dotted with illuminating historical plaques. It was here, in 1996, that a Chinese freighter, losing the battle against the current at Algiers Point, ploughed into the side of the mall in the middle of the afternoon, smashing much of the place up.

Southern Food and Beverage Museum

Hidden away on the Julia Street side of the Riverwalk Marketplace, the **Southern Food and Beverage Museum** (Mon–Sat 10am–7pm, Sun noon–6pm; $10; Ⓦ www.southernfood.org) is too easily overlooked. For anyone with the slightest interest in food, or in history, it is a must-see; enthusiastic, lively and with a fierce commitment to preserving Southern, and particularly Louisianan, food traditions and culture. While it deals with the cuisine and food cultures of other Southern states – Elvis features, along with exhibits on Tex-Mex food and a room on bananas – above all this is a love letter to Old New Orleans, its detailed installations telling the story of the city through its **cuisine**, and in particular its influences from Africa, Europe and the Caribbean. Panels on foodstuffs from pralines to chicory, king cakes to po-boys, are wordy but gripping, peppered with quotes from classic Louisiana literature and evoking the heady world of Creoles and free women of colour, Croatian oyster farmers and Sicilian grocers who helped define and form this unique city. The evolving collection includes pretty cups used to serve steaming *café brûlot* in grand Creole homes, a sno-ball machine used to fuel the city's passion for syrupy shaved ice, and a huge old 1840s wooden bar salvaged from *Bruning's*, a beloved lakeside seafood restaurant washed away by Katrina.

A room devoted to the **cocktail** – "a great American invention" – is full of treasures, from seventeenth-century syllabub cups to nineteenth-century cocktail manuals, Belle Epoque absinthe accessories, Art Deco cocktail shakers, and a whole host of cumbersome old bartending implements. Complaints cards handed out by Temperance campaigners outside movie theatres are pre-printed with huffy comments like "I didn't like the movie because it was too wet!" Prohibition memorabilia, meanwhile, includes the songsheet "Everybody wants a key to my cellar". Special emphasis is given to local drinks, like the Sazarac and the Ramos Gin Fizz; certainly the retro photos and etchings of various reprobates and lounge lizards have definite echoes of a New Orleans night out on the town.

The museum may well find new premises; keep track of it on the website.

Blaine Kern's Mardi Gras World

The cavernous "dens" of **Blaine Kern's Mardi Gras World** (daily 9.30am–4.30pm; $17.50; Ⓦ www.mardigrasworld.com), 1380 Port of New Orleans Place, out beyond the convention center past the Mississippi River bridge, are best reached on a free shuttle bus from the Canal Street ferry terminal (every 15min). This is a working facility, where year-round (except during the frenzied fortnight or so before Mardi Gras itself) you can see artists preparing, constructing and painting the overblown, brightly coloured papier-mache floats used in the official carnival parades. Kern's team, who have been building floats since 1947, are the leaders in their field, building props for parades and theme parks all over the world. They work for dozens of the krewes, including super krewe **Bacchus**, whose enormous King Kong family, Bacchawhoppa whale and Bacchagator hibernate here for most of the year, along with Orpheus's 120-foot-long, smoke-puffing **Leviathan**, emblazoned with multi-coloured fibre-optic lights. You can also see spooky floats made for Kern's own **Krewe of Boo**, a group that parades on Halloween to raise money for first responders still suffering after Katrina. It's a surreal experience wandering these paint-splattered warehouses, past piles of dusty, grimacing has-beens from parades gone by – limbless cartoon characters lolling over giant caved-in crawfish, beaming superstars snuggling up with long-dead presidents. Many figures are recycled for future parades, so little is ever thrown away. In keeping with the carnival spirit, there are plenty of opportunities to dress up, fool about and take photos – you're encouraged to try on colossal Marilyn and Nixon papier-mache heads, velvet cloaks and towering plumed headdresses – and each visitor gets free coffee and a slice of King cake. For more on Mardi Gras, see pp.163–174.

Chalmette Battlefield

About six miles downriver from the city, off Hwy-46 in St Bernard parish, the **Chalmette Battlefield National Historical Park** (daily 9am–4.30pm; free; Ⓦ www.nps.gov/jela/chalmette-battlefield.htm) was the site of the **Battle of New Orleans**, the final skirmish of the War of 1812. In 1814, having captured Washington DC, the British turned their sights to the Gulf, inviting the notorious pirates, the Lafitte brothers, to join them in the campaign against General Andrew Jackson. The double-crossing Lafittes, however, aligned themselves with Jackson and, though neither of them actually fought, furnished him with arms and troops, in exchange for which they were pardoned of all piracy charges.

On December 23, 1814, British General Edward Pakenham and his nine thousand Redcoats arrived five miles downriver of the city, to be met by Jackson's five-thousand-strong volunteer force of Creoles, Anglo-American adventurers, free men of colour, Baratarian pirates and Native Americans. Though at first the British troops succeeded in pushing back the ragbag American army, on **January 8, 1815**, after a battle of minutes, Jackson's men routed their opponents. The death toll came to seven hundred Redcoats, including Pakenham, and just a dozen or so Americans. Ironically, the battle, from which Jackson went on to become a national hero – and eventually US president – was unnecessary. Soon after it was fought, the news reached the city that the Treaty of Ghent had already ended the war in December 1814.

The Battle of New Orleans is commemorated by a 110-foot **obelisk** and an **interpretative exhibit**– a source of delight to war buffs but probably too much of a good thing for casual visitors. After the thirty-minute video that details the events leading up to the War of 1812 you can wander freely around the site (a loop of a mile and a half; a handy battlefield leaflet details six points of particular interest).

The Algiers ferry

A **ferry ride** (every 30min; free) from the bottom of Canal Street brings you within five minutes or so – depending on the current – to the west bank and the old shipbuilding community of **Algiers**. Seen from the riverbank, the ferry can be seen to swirl alarmingly with the river's flow – the Mississippi is at its deepest (nearly 200ft) here, and the current fierce, churning furiously around the extreme bend in the river. Even if you don't disembark, the views of both banks – especially at sunset – and the chance to see the river traffic up close make it well worth a ride in itself.

Settled a couple of years after New Orleans was established on the east bank, Algiers, a swathe of plantations originally belonging to Bienville, was entirely separate from the early city. The origins of its **name** are obscure, though one theory holds that, as a major eighteenth-century disembarkation point for the slave boats, it may have been named for the African slave port. In 1819 the first **shipyard** opened on the point, and settlement increased rapidly as a rash of dry docks, boat-builders and related industries spread along the riverfront. The coming of the **railways** and the development of the **shipbuilding industry** during the Civil War led to further growth, and in 1870 Algiers was incorporated into New Orleans. Here, in the same way as across the river, the saloons – haunts of gamblers, dockers, seamen and prostitutes – spawned some of the earliest **jazz** music, often created by freed slaves who had played in brass bands on the local plantations. Practically the whole town had to be rebuilt after a devastating **fire** in 1895; most of the buildings you see today date from just after that time. Algiers declined after the 1920s, and was touched little by the oil boom and subsequent modernizations that were inflicted on the east bank. Though you're safe enough walking around its quiet streets and admiring its vernacular **architecture** (Ⓦ www .algierspoint.org has a downloadable walking tour map) during the day, it's best not to wander too far off the beaten track, especially if you're alone.

Tremé

J ust footsteps from the heavily touristed French Quarter, the residential neighbourhood of **Tremé**, an area of Creole cottages and shotgun houses bounded by Canal, Rampart, Broad and St Bernard streets, is the oldest African-American community in the United States. Many of New Orleans' most enduring cultural and artistic forms – **jazz** music, jazz funerals, **Second Line parades** – were born here at the end of the nineteenth century, and Tremé is still home to a star-studded roster of musicians who play loose sets to crowds of friends and family in local bars. Despite its history, its music and its gorgeous vernacular architecture, however, Tremé is a poor neighbourhood, and has traditionally been depicted as a no-go zone for visitors. **North Rampart Street**, the run-down strip that separates it from the Quarter, has long been described – by locals and guide-books alike – as a barrier not to be crossed. Beyond here lie the projects, the reasoning goes, and unwitting tourists who expect the Quarter street party to continue as they head across the road are prime targets for muggings, or worse.

Attitudes were slowly beginning to change in the years just before Katrina, and towards Rampart Street in particular, whose crop of bars and music venues were establishing it as a de facto extension of the French Quarter. Then came the **floods**, and while the area was no more physically hurt than many others downtown, the attendant economic crisis and rising crime rates hit hard. Many of the bars and clubs on Rampart closed, and tourists once more stayed away in droves.

This is a huge shame. As an embodiment of the spirit of the city, the financially poor but culturally rich neighbourhood of Tremé deserves the attention and support of any visitor. Though there is some way to go before it feels entirely **safe** – it's certainly not recommended to wander around at night, when you should use cabs to get anywhere beyond Rampart Street – the re-emergence of a couple of popular bars and restaurants, along with the jazz **club** *Donna's* (see p.156) have helped put **Rampart Street** back onto the map, while the gradual recovery of **Louis Armstrong Park**, particularly as a place to hear music, has also breathed life into the neighbourhood. Meanwhile, the street culture remains as vibrant as ever, with the joyous, noisy Second Line **parades** growing, if anything, in importance since Katrina. Even if there are no parades scheduled during your stay, make sure to head out to the **Backstreet Cultural Museum**, a labour of love devoted to keeping street culture alive, and to **St Augustine's Church**, which is of huge historical significance. **St Louis Cemeteries** No.1 and No.2, two of the city's most important and beautiful above-ground Cities of the Dead, are also here, and best visited on a guided tour (see p.106).

Some history

Tremé is named for Claude Tremé, a free black hatmaker who in the nineteenth century owned a plantation on what is now St Claude Avenue. In the 1800s this

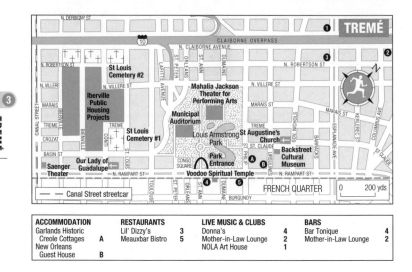

ACCOMMODATION		RESTAURANTS		LIVE MUSIC & CLUBS		BARS	
Garlands Historic		Lil' Dizzy's	3	Donna's	4	Bar Tonique	4
Creole Cottages	A	Meauxbar Bistro	5	Mother-in-Law Lounge	2	Mother-in-Law Lounge	2
New Orleans				NOLA Art House	1		
Guest House	B						

was a prosperous area, its shops, businesses, and homes owned and frequented by New Orleans' significant – and unique – free black population. It is commonly accepted that **jazz** evolved in Tremé, born from the Sunday slave gatherings in **Congo Square** (now part of Louis Armstrong Park) and developed in the "sporting houses" of **Storyville**, the area's long-defunct red-light district. Many of the free craftsmen, artists and labourers who built New Orleans in the second half of the nineteenth century were born here, along with hundreds of its most famous jazzmen. After Reconstruction, however, when the free people of colour found themselves stripped of the rights they'd had before the Civil War, the district took a downturn. In the 1890s, the blacks of Tremé began to form benevolent – or mutual aid – societies, paying dues to cover medical and funeral expenses. Later known as **Social Aid and Pleasure Clubs**, these societies also staged street parades and **jazz funerals**, which provided lifelines and forged essential cultural bonds for this beleaguered community.

Tremé's financial decline continued as the twentieth century progressed. In the 1960s, drug problems and violent crime blighted the area; matters weren't helped a decade later by the construction of the I-10 overpass, which hacked the community in half at Claiborne Avenue – which had been the neighbourhood's main street – and razed entire city blocks. By the 1980s, local **drug wars** had become so savage that Tremé's famed jazz funerals had degenerated into often violent "crack funerals"; the community was in crisis. Things shifted again with the rebirth of the brass bands and street parades – which inspired not only a growth in neighbourhood cultural pride but also increasing interest from the outside world – and in the early 2000s, when skyrocketing property prices in the Quarter tempted many residents to decamp to the pretty, and much cheaper, Creole cottages of Tremé. This **gentrification**, mostly apparent in the few blocks above Rampart, was met with mixed feelings by original residents – and was then halted in its tracks by the economic crisis that followed Katrina. Today, while Tremé is doing better year on year and has gained considerable visibility from David (*The Wire*) Simon's HBO series *Tremé*, many of its residents have yet to return, and numerous houses remain in bad shape.

Louis Armstrong Park and Congo Square

The entrance to **Louis Armstrong Park**, a huge twinkling arch visible the length of St Ann Street, may be a New Orleans icon, but it promises somewhat more than the park actually delivers. Unprepossessing, windblown, and not always safe – don't dream of venturing here after dark – the park nonetheless holds huge cultural significance, and is well worth a visit during its occasional community events or **music festivals**.

Many of these are held in **Congo Square**, the small paved area to the left of the entrance arch. In colonial times this was the Place des Nègres, where every Sunday slaves taken from all over West Africa would meet in their thousands to trade, perform religious rituals, make music and dance the **bamboula**, named after the large drums that beat the rhythm. At 9pm sharp a policeman would fire a cannon to signal the end of the proceedings – the penalty for breaking the curfew was twenty lashes. In the American era, the gatherings quickly became tourist attractions, thronging with vendors and sideshows, from which fascinated white visitors would return with shocked tales of weird **voodoo rituals** and depravity. The slave gatherings were banned between 1834 and 1845, while in 1851, when the transformation of the Place d'Armes into Jackson Square left the soldiers without a parade ground, this open area was chosen as a replacement.

Storyville

Much to the dismay of many tourists, there is nothing left of New Orleans' notorious red-light district, **Storyville**, long since torn down to make room for the Iberville housing projects. In 1897, in an attempt to control the **prostitution** that had been rampant in the city since its earliest days, an ordinance was passed confining the brothels to a fixed fifteen-block area enclosed by Basin, Iberville, North Robertson and St Louis streets. Rather than legalizing prostitution within these boundaries, the law simply decreed it to be illegal outside them; nonetheless, the trade continued to exist throughout the city and Storyville – nicknamed for the alderman who passed the ordinance, and more commonly known at the time as "the district" – simply became its most famous locale.

The district soon developed into a tourist attraction, with newspapers reporting the movements of its various **stars**, among them "Mayor" Tom Anderson, state legislator and oil company president, who owned many of the most notorious saloons. Anderson also produced the famed **blue book**, which advertised the "palaces" of landladies (they never called themselves madams) such as brawling Josie Arlington, who prided herself on her exotic continental girls, Emma Johnson, who staged lewd circuses in her "House of All Nations", and, Queen of Storyville, the diamond-bedecked Lulu White – Mae West's inspiration in her 1934 movie *Belle of the Nineties*. Though **jazz** was not, as is often claimed, invented in Storyville, it did evolve here, in its restaurants, cabarets and brothels, and many of the "professors" who played rumbustious piano to entertain the clients went on to become well-known musicians.

In 1917, the Secretary of the Navy decreed that red-light areas were bad for wartime "morale" – entering the World War with an army riddled with venereal disease was not deemed to be a good idea – and Storyville was **closed** down. Its denizens, however, are immortalized in the extraordinary, humane portraits taken by **E.J. Bellocq**, the hydrocephalic photographer adopted by the prostitutes as their official recorder. You may catch some of these haunting images, which show the women comfortable in their own milieu, staring directly at the camera, at the New Orleans Museum of Art (see p.96) or the Ogden Museum of Southern Art (see p.80).

After the Civil War, however, Congo Square resumed its central role in the **political** life of black New Orleanians. In 1867, local blacks staged a mass sit-in protesting against segregation on the mule-drawn streetcars, demanding that as emancipated citizens they be accorded the same civil rights as whites. Almost immediately the streetcars were integrated, and stayed so until 1902, after the Supreme Court Plessy vs Ferguson ruling had effectively retracted the civil rights won by blacks during Reconstruction (see p.222). In 1994, a group of Mardi Gras Indians and Native Americans blessed Congo Square as sacred ground, and three years later it was placed on the National Register of Historic Places.

Our Lady of Guadalupe

Our Lady of Guadalupe, 411 N Rampart St, the city's oldest surviving church, was built following a yellow fever epidemic in 1826 as a catholic mortuary chapel for the neighbouring St Louis No. 1 cemetery (see p.108). In those days both lay outside the city limits, protecting the population from what were believed to be poisonous miasmas that emanated from the mountains of corpses and from the back-to-back funeral processions. In 1870 it was designated as the church for the city's burgeoning Italian community, who had outgrown their church on Esplanade Avenue. A host of colourful shrines inside the church includes one to **St Jude**, patron saint of lost causes, piled high with hopefully placed novenas. Set into a niche in the front wall, to the right as you enter, stands the statue of the mysterious **St Expedite**, resembling a centurion and named, so the legend goes, because the unknown statue was delivered here in a crate simply stamped "expedite". The fact that a similar story had been flying around Paris in the late 1780s renders this version a little less convincing, as does the fact that a saint called Expeditus has been worshipped in southern Europe and the Caribbean since the eighteenth century. Whatever his provenance, he is revered by both the city's Catholics and its voodoo-ists – who often portray him as Baron Samedi, the spirit of death – particularly those needing a quick solution to a problem, or, oddly, help with lawsuits.

Backstreet Cultural Museum

Walking around the fascinating **Backstreet Cultural Museum** (Tues–Sat 10am–5pm; $10; Ⓦ www.backstreetmuseum.org), one block above Rampart Street at 1116 St Claude Ave at Gov Nicholls, you feel as though you've been invited into someone's home and allowed to rummage through their personal possessions. Your curator – and often your guide – is Sylvester Francis, an enthusiastic local who has spent the last thirty years documenting, preserving and celebrating local black street culture. Not only has he filmed and photographed scores of **jazz funerals and Second Line parades**, but he also set up this little museum, displaying the kind of indigenous but often unrecognized works of art that might otherwise be left to rot in a cellar. Above all, a visit here reveals the deep connections New Orleans has with Africa, Central America and the Caribbean; Tremé's folk, oral and street traditions, while unique in the US, vividly resemble those found in Trinidad, Haiti or West Africa.

As befits its location in an old funeral home, much of the collection revolves around **urban mourning customs**, often to very moving effect. Among the church programmes, news clippings and scrapbooks is a case of T-shirts, screen-printed with blurred photos of recently deceased loved ones – many of them boys killed by "lead poisoning", as locals call gun wounds – and inscribed with dates of the victim's "Sunrise" and "Sunset". All too many people in Tremé wear these customized shirts; seeing them contextualized as part of a long history of

▲ Backstreet Cultural Museum

mourning and celebration makes them all the more powerful. New Orleanians, and particularly those from Tremé, pay tribute to each and every soul who has passed; thus the museum gives as much space to a local jazz funeral held for a neighbourhood beer vendor as to the citywide parade held to mark the passing of nationally known R&B star and Tremé resident Ernie K-Doe.

As in the Caribbean, New Orleans' street culture is a flamboyant one, deeming decoration and creativity to be spiritual acts. Nowhere is this better defined than by the Mardi Gras Indians (see p.166), tribes of black men who take to the streets during carnival dressed in their magnificent hand-sewn **Mardi Gras Indian suits**, emblazoned with feathers, beads and sequins. Francis has an impressive selection on display here (suits are only designed to be worn once), along with photos honouring the proud chiefs who have passed on – "They lived like warriors; died like braves". Another display celebrates the local **Social Aid and Pleasure clubs**, whose members hold dressing to the nines to be an expression of the fiercest pride. Francis, who used to parade with the Gentlemen of Leisure, and whose daughter, who may be your guide, masks with the Fi-Yi-Yi Mardi Gras Indians, has a fine collection of natty **marching regalia**, from frilly satin Second Line umbrellas to hot-coloured suits, sharp hats and crocodile-skin shoes that cost $1000 a pair. You can also see the scruffy costumes and huge papier-mache skulls worn by the Skeletons, or **bone gangs**, whose dawn appearance marks the official beginning of black street carnival. The avowed message of these mysterious characters – that life is short – is scrawled onto butcher's aprons in the form of cheery slogans like "Come With Me to Hell" or "You Next". Light relief is given by the frilly bloomers and bonnets of the **Baby Dolls**, an irreverent Mardi Gras street group started by local women in the early 1900s.

The museum acts as a **social hub** during the city's major festivals, and a starting point for many parades. In particular, if you can rouse yourself at 5am on Mardi Gras morning, join the gathering that assembles here to witness the Skeletons drumming, rattling their tambourines and "calling out" to the community; a sacred way to start a day of masking and misrule.

Second Line parades

On Sunday afternoons throughout the year, but particularly in spring and autumn, clubs with names like the Jolly Bunch, the Black Men of Labor, the Moneywasters and the Sidewalk Steppers strut through New Orleans' black neighbourhoods in elaborate matching shoes, sharp hats and sashes, twirling huge feathered fans and frilly umbrellas to the syncopated beat blasted out by noisy brass bands. Known as **Second Lines** – for the unofficial string of dancers and followers they gather behind them as they go – these parades are as tightly woven into the fabric of the city as is Mardi Gras or the Mississippi, and a must for any visitor.

Some history

Enjoyed today as feel-good street parties, the parades in fact have a profound history, their very existence asserting black empowerment and community pride – not to mention the sacred power of music and dance. Following traditions upheld by their West African forefathers, in 1783 a group of former slaves in New Orleans formed the **Perseverance Benevolent and Mutual Aid Association**, whose members paid dues to cover medical and other expenses. By the end of the nineteenth century, when Reconstruction had stripped many black New Orleanians of rights they had previously held, benevolent societies were rife, members paying into policies not only to cover legal expenses and loans towards buying property or education, but also, crucially, to ensure proper burials in society tombs. While there were similar white organizations, following the model of European fraternal societies, the associations were particularly significant to the black community, and their roles soon expanded beyond the merely financial to become custodians of cultural and social traditions. By the turn of the twentieth century, the societies, now more commonly known as **Social Aid and Pleasure Clubs,** were displaying themselves to potential members via street parades, their members dancing and high-stepping behind noisy brass bands. The societies died out during the Depression and World War II, and by the 1980s, as insurance companies proliferated and New Orleans' traditional street culture declined, the number dwindled to a handful. A decade or so later, however, with the resurgence of the brass bands (see p.237), clubs began to parade once more.

St Augustine's Church

Directly across the road from the Backstreet Cultural Museum, the imposing Catholic **St Augustine's**, 1210 Gov Nicholls St, is the oldest mixed-race church in the USA, active since 1842. Founded and funded by whites and freemen of colour, it was designed by J.N.B. de Pouilly – who eight years later went on to remodel St Louis Cathedral in the French Quarter. Uniquely in the States, rows of pews were set aside exclusively for the use of slaves, making it the most integrated church in the nation. It was here, in the early 1890s, that the plot was hatched for Homer Plessy, a local Creole, to defy the state law that banned blacks from riding in the same railroad car or streetcar as whites – his action led to the Plessy vs Ferguson case, which established Jim Crow segregation laws throughout the South.

Today, the church welcomes visitors, and is fullest on the occasional Sunday **jazz masses** when a guest singer or musician joins the choir and the pews are packed

On the parade route

While Second Line parades have a close kinship with jazz funerals (see p.110), they are rowdier, more informal events, celebrating not only community but also the sheer pleasure of being alive. After Katrina, the gradual emergence of Second Lines back onto the streets was a lifeline, providing an essential sense of continuity and affording a shattered population the hope that their city, and their lives, might be saved. Weaving their way along a predetermined backstreet route, stopping at local bars along the way, the official club members – the Main Line – gather hundreds of spectators and dancers – the "Second Line", singing, shouting and twirling their handkerchiefs in the air – as they go. **Brass bands**, sometimes in formal peaked caps and suits, sometimes hanging loose in baggy T-shirts and jeans, blast out traditional and not-so-traditional street tunes, often battling with other bands en route and offering noisy background for the hollered calls and responses of the crowd. The best dancers, or **buckjumpers** – from the tiniest children to redoubtable octogenarians, from club members in their fancy suits to passers-by in shabby workclothes – stride, swoop and plunge in a formalized interpretation of old African bamboula, some of it highly sexual, but when it comes to joining in, pretty much anything goes. Meanwhile, vendors set up along the route, selling beer, water and home-made food.

Though primarily locals' events, Second Line parades are even more explicitly open to all than the city's jazz funerals. That's not to say they are without **tension** – as so often in New Orleans, violence, even death, can lurk in the shadows even at the most joyous moments. Shootings have been known, and in one famed case a bar owner shot a man dead for selling beer outside his joint. Nonetheless, such incidents are rare, and joining a Second Line will most likely be an extraordinary, life-affirming experience, one that epitomizes so much of what makes the city, and Tremé, unique.

Schedules and routes, which are finalized just a few days beforehand and often prone to change, are available at the Backstreet Cultural Museum (see p.66). You can also find good Second Line news, reviews and schedules on the blog pages of the city's free weekly, *Gambit* (ⓦ www.bestofneworleans.com).

with tourists. Its spruce, light interior is lined with tall white columns and illuminated by stained-glass porthole windows portraying French saints. It's also imbued with the influence of its radical, humanistic former priest **Father Jerome LeDoux**, who preached in traditional African robes from behind a cypress stump altar: bright, jazzy paintings portray Mardi Gras Indians and local musicians, while flags flutter from the ceiling printed with affirmations – Unity, Creativity, Self-Determination, Purpose – in English and Swahili.

St Augustine's aim, "to break the shackles of sin and oppression", is powerfully illustrated in the garden, where the moving **Tomb of the Unknown Slave**, a huge toppled metal cross entwined with balls-and-chains and shackles, honours "the nameless, faceless, turfless Africans who met an untimely death in Faubourg Tremé" and African and Native American slaves buried in unmarked graves throughout the United States.

Standoff at St Augustine's

After Katrina, **St Augustine's**, already of such spiritual and cultural signifcance to Tremé, became an intensely emotional symbol of the African-American community's struggle to rebuild and heal. Though the building had sustained heavy storm damage, the parish – led by its beloved priest, **Father LeDoux** (see p.69) – rallied. St Augustine's became a community hub for returning evacuees, and established schemes to aid victims in whichever way they needed. With a membership thirty percent higher than pre-Katrina, St Augustine's was thriving when, in the spring of 2006, New Orleans' Archbishop Alfred Hughes – head of a Church that was cash-strapped and stripped of resources following the storm – announced that St Augustine's, along with many other churches in the city, was to be closed. Father LeDoux was removed immediately – his final mass, on March 19, was a tearful occasion – and the announcement led to a storm of protest that extended far beyond neighbourhood and city boundaries to become national news.

Soon after LeDoux's departure, hurricane assistance volunteers began an **occupation** of the church's rectory that lasted three weeks. The mass on Sunday March 26th, held by the new Father Michael Jacques, was a tense affair. Jacques, joined by Archdiocese spokesman Father William Maestri and ten armed guards – to defend against the peaceful, placard-carrying protestors outside and the young occupiers within – announced that the church was to close that day. The fact that guns were brought into a mass inflamed the situation further, with reverends Jesse Jackson and Al Sharpton attending a church vigil in support. In April Hughes conceded: St Augustine's was to be given an eighteen-month stay of execution, during which various financial and administrative targets were to be met. In 2009, the church was finally taken off probation. The controversial Archbishop Hughes, meanwhile, retired the same year, to be replaced by New Orleans native Gregory Aymond, who has kept a low profile. Father LeDoux, though still regarded as a hero in Tremé, remains pastor in Fort Worth, Texas.

The CBD and Warehouse District

N either as visually stunning nor as immediately appealing as the neighbouring French Quarter, New Orleans' Central Business District, or **CBD**, is of more interest to visitors for its hotels and restaurants than for its sights. Historically, however, its significance can't be overstressed: this was where American New Orleans started, created by vigorous Anglo newcomers who, after the Louisiana Purchase in 1803, built a new suburb of exchanges, insurance companies, banks and shops – along with grand theatres and hotels – as they set about making themselves rich. Rivalling their equivalents in the Creole city, the developments marked the onset of New Orleans' **Americanization**, an era of phenomenal change and economic growth that lasted until the Civil War.

Upriver from the Quarter, across Canal Street, the CBD's sweep of offices, old bank buildings and fancy hotels stretches west as far as the Pontchartrain Expressway, bounded riverside by the Mississippi and, lakeside, by I-10 (Claiborne Avenue). Apart from the gargantuan **Superdome**, which lies at the lakeside edge of the CBD, most of what there is to see is in the **Warehouse District**, a flyblown area of low-rent studios and pricey loft apartments, loosely bounded by Poydras Street, the Expressway, Convention Center Boulevard and St Charles Avenue. A number of the neglected warehouses and old factory buildings have been given over to galleries, restaurants and bars, with a spirited arts community thriving on and around **Julia Street**. But while these and the slick **National World War II Museum** and superb **Ogden Museum of Southern Art** are raising the cultural profile of the district, there's still some way left to go. Despite assurances from the tourist literature that the area's many run-down, abandoned-looking buildings are, in fact, hives of creativity, the Warehouse District isn't necessarily a great place to walk around at night.

Some history

In the eighteenth century, much of the area now covered by the CBD was a vast sugar plantation belonging to **Bertrand Gravier**. Following the devastating fire of 1788, which destroyed most of the French Quarter, Gravier sold off parcels of his land to allow settlement along the river. The emergent suburb, **Faubourg Ste Marie**, named after his wife, remained sparsely populated until the Louisiana Purchase in 1803. Within fifteen years or so of annexation, however, the faubourg – its name now Americanized to St Mary – expanded rapidly, populated by the brokers, bankers and planters who flooded into New Orleans eager to exploit its

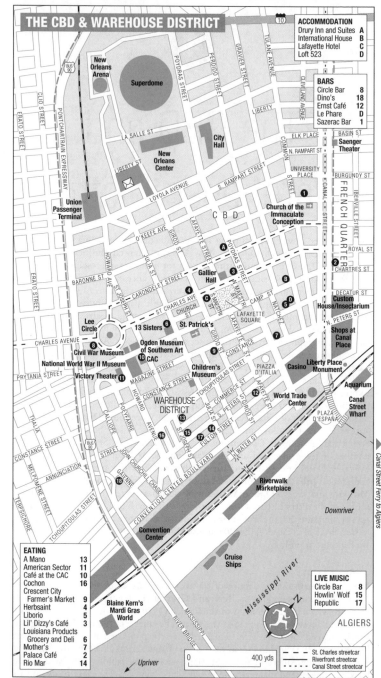

THE CBD & WAREHOUSE DISTRICT

ACCOMMODATION

Drury Inn and Suites	A
International House	B
Lafayette Hotel	C
Loft 523	D

BARS

Circle Bar	8
Dino's	18
Ernst Café	12
Le Phare	D
Sazerac Bar	1

New Orleans Arena

Superdome

New Orleans Center

City Hall

Union Passenger Terminal

Church of the Immaculate Conception

C B D

Gallier Hall

Custom House/Insectarium

Shops at Canal Place

Lee Circle

13 Sisters

St. Patrick's

Liberty Place Monument

Civil War Museum

Ogden Museum of Southern Art

CAC

National World War II Museum

Victory Theater

Children's Museum

Casino

World Trade Center

Aquarium

WAREHOUSE DISTRICT

PIAZZA D'ITALIA

Canal Street Wharf

PLAZA D'ESPAÑA

Riverwalk Marketplace

Canal Street Ferry to Algiers

Downriver

Convention Center

Cruise Ships

Blaine Kern's Mardi Gras World

Mississippi River

ALGIERS

MISSISSIPPI RIVER BRIDGE

Upriver

EATING

A Mano	13
American Sector	11
Café at the CAC	10
Cochon	16
Crescent City Farmer's Market	9
Herbsaint	4
Liborio	5
Lil' Dizzy's Café	3
Louisiana Products Grocery and Deli	6
Mother's	7
Palace Café	2
Rio Mar	14

LIVE MUSIC

Circle Bar	8
Howlin' Wolf	15
Republic	17

0   400 yds

- - - St. Charles streetcar
——— Riverfront streetcar
· · · Canal Street streetcar

booming port. The city's centre of commerce swiftly shifted away from the French Quarter to the "**American sector**", as St Mary was referred to, and eventually in 1836 New Orleans was carved into **municipalities**, each with its own council – a state of affairs which lasted until 1852. **Canal Street** was the dividing line between the first (Creole) and second (American) municipalities, and gradually took over from Royal Street in the French Quarter as the city's chief commercial thoroughfare. The Americans also built fine Federal-style townhouses for themselves, on and around **Julia Street**, while huge warehouses backed the bustling wharves.

After Reconstruction, as the French Quarter fell into decline, the CBD struggled on, keeping its head above water on the back of continuing cotton wealth; the warehouses, meanwhile, were turned over to wholesalers and meat packers. During the 1970s **oil boom**, many of the old banks and exchanges were torn down to make way for corporate towers (though building anything too high has always been a problem on this soggy soil), car parks, business hotels and the landmark hulk of the Superdome.

During the 1980s, when the boom went **bust** as suddenly as it had hit, the CBD experienced a mass exodus and eventually turned to tourism for its salvation. Since then, many of the older buildings, capitalizing on their proximity to the French Quarter, have been converted into boutique hotels and ritzy restaurants. The Warehouse District, meanwhile, revitalized to some extent by the 1984 **World's Fair**, held in restored buildings along the wharves, offers a string of highly regarded **art galleries**.

Canal Street

The widest main street (170ft) in America, and on the parade route for all the super krewes at Mardi Gras, the once glorious **Canal Street**, which runs from the Mississippi to Lake Pontchartrain, is looking rather down at heel. It is still the backbone of the city, however, literally dividing downtown (downriver) from uptown (upriver), its jaunty streetcar trundling all the way from the river to Mid-City.

There never was a canal here, though one was planned in the early 1800s, and you'll see a phantom waterway marked on many early maps. The street started as a rough ditch cut along the ramparts of the city, separating it from the plantations – and later the American suburb – beyond. It was eventually filled to become the town commons, and as the Faubourg St Mary grew, settlers built homes along its muddy expanse. When New Orleans was divided into municipalities, this was the "neutral ground" in the middle – the term still used by locals to describe the median at the centre of any city road – and many traders set up here in order to get business from both sides of the city. By the 1850s, all the homes had been replaced by department stores and opulent theatres.

Though the grand old department stores that gave Canal Street so much of its character have all but disappeared, the gorgeous **storefronts**, decorated in Beaux Arts, Italianate and Art Deco styles, for the most part remain, safe from the demolition that richer cities would have inflicted upon them. Today the lovely old buildings are filled with swanky chain hotels, tacky T-shirt and souvenir stores, fast-food outlets and none-too-reputable electronics shops.

The casino

Splayed out at the foot of Canal Street, *Harrah's* **casino**, all turrets and baubles, stands as a gaudy testament to a political saga of double-dealing and ineptitude in the great Louisiana tradition. In the early 1990s, political opposition to the very notion of legalizing gambling in New Orleans, on the grounds that to do so would siphon income away from the city's genuinely unique attractions, ensured that even when it did finally open, a decade later, the casino was more white elephant than cash cow. Forbidden to offer the themed attractions and flash restaurants that you'd expect in, say, Las Vegas, Harrah's, an unprepossessing warehouse stuffed with slot machines, remains pretty much devoid of interest.

The Insectarium

Mark Twain may have had a point when he dismissed the foreboding Classical exterior of the **Custom House**, 423 Canal St, as "inferior to a gasometer," but this

The Battle of Liberty Place

The riverside end of Canal Street, opposite the Custom House, was the site of one of the most significant battles in the city's bitter Reconstruction era (see p.222). On September 13, 1874, the Metropolitan police force, which included many freed slaves, seized a boat-load of arms destined for the **White League** – a militia formed by ex-Confederates committed to bringing down the radical Republican government and stamping out what they called the "Africanization" of their city. Claiming that the action of the police was an infringement of their constitutional right to bear arms, the League placed an advertisement in the *Times-Picayune*, calling for a mass demonstration in protest.

On September 14, some five thousand whites met at the Henry Clay statue, which stood at the heart of the city on Canal Street where it crossed St Charles and Royal. After a morning of rabble-rousing, during which the call was made to depose the hated Republican Governor Kellogg, the White Leaguers armed themselves and marched down Canal Street to the river, where they met a defensive line made up of the Metropolitan police and the black militia. A twenty-minute conflict ensued, which resulted in the police being chased back to Jackson Square in the French Quarter, where Kellogg was overthrown. Though just five days later President Grant sent in troops to reinstate him, the **Battle of Liberty Place**, which left eleven policemen and sixteen rioters dead, was seen by the White League as a victory for freedom, a blow against the Reconstruction government and – despite lame public assurances that their motives weren't racist – an assertion of white supremacy. The League was formally disbanded two years later, when, Reconstruction over, Louisiana returned to home rule.

The ramifications of the battle did not end there, however. In 1891, the **Liberty Monument**, inscribed with a list of the White League members who had died fighting, was erected at the foot of Canal Street. Well into the 1930s, Confederate supporters gathered at the granite obelisk every September 14 – their insistence that to do so was a celebration of political liberty was undermined somewhat by the plaque added to the monument in 1932, the wording on which blatantly rejoiced at the demise of Reconstruction and the victory of "white supremacy".

In 1981, "Dutch" Morial, New Orleans' first black mayor, ordered that the monument should be surrounded by tall bushes, effectively hiding it from view. Under increasing pressure from civil rights groups, who demanded that it should be torn down, and white reactionaries, who insisted it was part of the city's history, the city council vacillated for years, until eventually, in 1989, the monument was removed and put into storage. Spearheaded by David Duke, a former Grand Wizard of the Ku Klux Klan and candidate for Louisiana governor in 1991, a lawsuit was filed to return the monument to the street, and in 1993, amid violent demonstrations, the Liberty Monument was rededicated in an inconspicuous spot next to a parking lot behind the aquarium. Though its supremacist plaque was replaced by a list of the Metropolitan police killed in the battle, the new dedication: "In honour of those Americans on both sides of the conflict…A conflict of the past that should teach us lessons for the future…" is infuriatingly ambivalent, and the monument remains an ugly, graffitied testament to a century of vexed race relations.

dour granite colossus was key to New Orleans' grand antebellum building programme, a hymn to the city's optimism and commercial aspirations. Work started in 1848 on what was to be the largest federal building in the nation – rooting such a monster in the city's shifting, soggy soil proved difficult, however, and what with the break during the Civil War, the Custom House was not completed until 1881. In summer 2008, a similar optimism – and nearly as many years' delays – was in the air with the opening here of the **Insectarium**, one of a handful of city attractions owned by the Audubon Nature Institute (Tues–Sun 10am–5pm; $15, kids $10; various combination tickets are available with other Audubon Nature Institute attractions; ⓦwww.auduboninstitute.org). Like the other Audubon attractions, it's of most appeal to kids, though there's plenty of gleeful shrieking from adults, too, especially in the dark tunnel where you're invited to put your hand in various holes to feel the "bugs" inside. More genuinely scary are the true stories of the insects that have threatened New Orleans since its earliest days: not only the **mosquito**, who got away for centuries with ravaging the city with yellow fever until the discovery in 1900 that it was not "miasmas" from the swamps or graveyards that carried the plague, but these humming bloodsuckers. Roachophobes will be distressed to discover that these pesky New Orleans regulars can live for weeks without a head; thankfully, the city's **termites**, whose burrowing caused more damage than flood or fire until major pest control improvements at the end of the 1990s, are becoming less of a problem. The insectarium's swamp exhibit offers little solace: along with a tank of baleful baby gators, including two of Louisiana's rare white breed (see p.91), you'll be introduced to the **predaceous diving beetle**, which resembles an infinitesimal turtle but is far more vicious. Big hitters are found in the **Hall of Fame**, including elaborate, velvety moths and giant specimens like the 1.5ft-long stick insect, the two-inch-long horsefly, and the Queen Alexandra's Birdwing butterfly, bigger than two large human hands. The butterflies supply much of the eye candy, especially as they flutter around you in the humid, Asian-style **butterfly house**. This being New Orleans there's an emphasis on **food**, with regular cooking demonstrations and crispy Cajun crickets and salty fly larvae among the delights on offer in the gift shop – or, as it likes to call itself, the Flea Market.

The Church of the Immaculate Conception

Turning off Canal at Baronne Street – look for the wonderful old Walgreen's sign – brings you to the oddly Moorish **Church of the Immaculate Conception**, or Jesuit Church, worth a peek for its flamboyant arches, bright stained-glass, cast-iron spiral columns and pews. Designed by local architect James Freret, the gilded bronze altar, with its trio of onion domes, won first prize at the Paris Exposition of 1867. Like so many of New Orleans' buildings, the original church, built in 1857, threatened to collapse under its own weight into the swampy earth; what you see today – a perfect replica – dates from the 1930s. As you move upriver from the church and head down Common Street toward Carondelet, you come to the heart of the old CBD.

Lafayette Square

Laid out in 1788, **Lafayette Square** was the political hub of the American sector, an Anglo version of the Creole Place d'Armes (today's Jackson Square). Today, surrounded by dreary court buildings and offices, it's the venue for regular outdoor concerts featuring big-name local and regional bands. It centres on a bronze **statue** of early nineteenth-century statesman **Henry Clay**. When the statue was dedicated in 1860, it stood at the heart of the city, on Canal Street where Royal met St Charles, and provided a focal point for countless public meetings – including the rally that led to the race riot known as the Battle of Liberty Place (see p.74). In 1901 it was moved to this less conspicuous spot to make room for increasing traffic along Canal.

On the lakeside of the square, another bronze statue portrays **John McDonogh**, an outspoken abolitionist and leading light in the American Colonization Society, which advocated the return of slaves to Africa. Regarded as a miser during his lifetime, upon his death in 1850 he left his considerable riches to be divided between New Orleans and his native Baltimore for the establishment of racially mixed public schools. Many of New Orleans' public schools are the result of that legacy; the statue, designed in 1898 at a cost of $7000, was funded by nickel donations from the city's schoolchildren.

The magnificent **Gallier Hall,** across from Lafayette Square at 545 St Charles Ave, is the grandest example of Greek Revival architecture in New Orleans. Fronted by an ornate ninety-foot facade with ten fluted white Ionic columns and a pediment featuring Justice, Liberty and Commerce, it was designed by James Gallier Sr as the City Hall for the second municipality (the first municipality had its own, the Cabildo, on the Place d'Armes). By the time it was dedicated in 1853, however, New Orleans had reunited; thus the building served as seat of government for the whole city right up to the 1950s, when the new City Hall was built on Poydras. These days, Gallier Hall hosts civic events and receptions. Traditionally, too, it's the site of one of the premier **Mardi Gras** parade-viewing platforms, packed with assorted bigwigs, including the mayor. The enormous floats stop for quite a while here, and experienced bead-beggars know to stake out a spot across the street.

The Warehouse District

During the antebellum era, the **Warehouse District** was a bustling area of vast factories and warehouses storing sugar, cotton, grain and tobacco ready to be loaded onto ocean-going ships, and coffee, luxuries and manufactured goods from overseas waiting to be transported upriver by steamboat. After Reconstruction, however, as the port went into decline, the district deteriorated into a dangerous no-go zone, only reviving a century or so later after it was chosen as the site of the 1984 **World's Fair**. The fair was the first in history to lose money, but it did bring visibility to the area's previously neglected lofts and factory buildings, and the die was cast for the Warehouse District. Loft-living was big business in the 1980s, and there was no shortage of eager developers hungry to make a profit.

Tourist literature pushes the Warehouse District as a thriving **arts community**, buzzing with workshops, cutting-edge galleries and designer stores. However, though it features a couple of the city's major **museums** and the best of its **private galleries**, the many empty lots and derelict buildings do little to encourage you to wander around for very long. That said, there's enough to whet the appetite of anyone with an interest in **architecture**. Although many structures were demolished in the 1960s and 70s, a profusion of the original buildings – churches, factories and tall brick townhouses, as well as warehouses – remains, offering a counterpoint to the Creole flavour of the Quarter. Here, Federal, Neoclassical and Greek Revival styles dominate, reflecting the very American nature of the Faubourg St Mary.

Piazza d'Italia

On the outskirts of the Warehouse District, at 377 Poydras St, the **Piazza d'Italia** sets a suitably arty tone. An unlikely jumble of mock-Classical columns, arches, and relief facades, fashioned in marble, steel, and neon, it was designed in 1978 by

Charles Moore as a tribute to the city's Italian community. Having won a number of awards for its cutting-edge Postmodern design, the piazza fell into disrepair in the 1980s, becoming a flyblown wasteland best avoided. Today, spruced up by the swanky *Loew's* hotel next door, it's a colourful space once more, with a huge, staggered fountain that's great fun for kids on hot afternoons. It still feels somewhat forlorn, however: a knowing, grown-up playground that hasn't quite found its place.

Julia Street

④

When people talk about the **Arts District** (ⓦwww.neworleansartsdistrict.com) they're mainly referring to **Julia Street**, and in particular the stretch from Commerce Street up to St Charles Avenue, which has a growing reputation for showcasing the best in regional and national contemporary art. While strolling between the tony private **galleries** along here can while away a pleasant few hours, note that many keep irregular hours, and most of them close for summer; consult the listings papers *Lagniappe* or *Gambit* (see p.25) before setting off. Probably the best time to visit is on the first Saturday of every month from October to May, when the string of art openings pulls a mixed crowd of uptowners, art students and conventioneers, all nibbling cheese, sipping Chablis and checking out the art

---

The Julia Street galleries

The following is a list of some of the most consistently intriguing galleries on and around Julia Street. For a **full rundown** of current exhibitions, log on to ⓦwww .neworleansartsdistrict.com, pick up a copy of the free Arts District magazine *Art New Orleans*, or check the city's listings papers.

Arthur Roger Gallery Nos. 432 and 434 (Mon–Sat 10am–5pm; ☏522-1999, ⓦwww .arthurrogergallery.com). This prestgious and long-established gallery continues to innovate. It's a large, swish space for an eclectic and fascinating range of cutting-edge art, sculpture and video.

Canary Gallery No. 329 (Wed–Fri 2–5pm; ☏251-7745, ⓦwww.thecanarygallery .blogspot.com). Splendid multimedia gallery focusing on regional video art and installations, performance, mixed media and photography.

George Schmidt No. 626 (Tues–Sat 12.30–4.30pm; ☏592-0206, ⓦwww.george schmidt.com). Native New Orleanian, painter, banjo player and singer, Schmidt is an unapologetically nostalgic artist. His work – bold, vivid images of moments in history, and in particular New Orleans history – is haunting and affecting, invariable with a quirky angle.

Jonathan Ferrara No. 400a (Mon–Sat 11am–5pm; ☏522-5988, ⓦwww.jonathanfer raragallery.com). There's always something interesting going on in this large, airy space, where the abstract and figurative works from new and established artists range from watercolours to sculpture and multimedia.

LeMieux Galleries No. 332 (Mon–Sat 10am–6pm; ☏522-5988, ⓦwww.lemieuxgal leries.com). Contemporary art, folk art, photography and crafts from Louisiana and the Gulf Coast. Retrospectives have included the "Caribbean-Cubist" images of New Orleans by Paul Niñas, who painted the mural in the old-fashioned *Sazerac Bar* (see p.150). If you see only one Arts District gallery, make it this.

New Orleans School of Glassworks and Printmaking 727 Magazine St at Julia (artisans work Mon–Wed 9am–noon & 1–5pm; ☏529-7279, ⓦwww.neworleansglass works.org). Stunning, unusual handblown glass displayed in a working studio. You'll see glassblowers in action and may be able to try your hand at it yourself; contact them in advance about one-off, two-hour-long classes.

and each other. The biggest shindig of all, the place for the local art world to see and be seen, is **Art for Art's Sake** (see p.181), the official opening of the arts season, held on the first Saturday in October. In the evening the street is closed off, creating a block-party ambience, with nervous artists milling around, live music stages, and food – from some of the city's best restaurants – and drink stalls. **Jammin' on Julia**, in April or May, and **White Linen Night**, in August, are similar, though smaller-scale events. Incidentally, unless you're a serious collector, with a lot of money to shell out, gallery-hopping on Julia is strictly a spectator sport: the only place you'll be able to pick up anything half-way affordable is at the **Louisiana Crafts Guild** shop, reviewed in our shopping chapter on p.194.

In addition to the galleries, Julia is a good place to check out the **architecture** that characterized the American sector. At no. 545 you'll see three of the district's earliest warehouses – simple, shuttered structures built in 1833; compare these with the larger, utilitarian building at no. 329, New Orleans' first reinforced concrete construction. In the 600 block between St Charles Avenue and Camp Street stands a parade of spruce, renovated row houses known as the **Thirteen Sisters**. When they were built in 1833, these red-brick residences were the most desirable in the American sector, modelled in the Federal style favoured in the northeastern states; just sixty years later they had declined into slums. Today they're alive again, filled with galleries and antique stores, architects' offices, and a wonderfully old-time corner grocery/deli (see p.143).

Louisiana Children's Museum

The **Louisiana Children's Museum** (Sept–May Tues–Sat 9.30am–4.30pm, Sun noon–4.30pm; June–Aug closes 5pm; $7.50 adults and kids; ⓦ www.lcm.org) occupies a sturdy 1861 warehouse with cheery blue shutters at 420 Julia St. While on any given day you can bet some of the exhibits don't work, and others are a tad earnest, this place has its seriously underfunded heart in the right place, and though it could hardly be called high-tech there are enough things to wind up, push, pull, and plunge to keep younger ones diverted for an hour or so. Watching kids design their own buildings using pencil, paper and slide-rule in the section on local architecture, "New Orleans – Proud to Call It Home" – has an undeniably poignant edge in the post-Katrina city. Generally resisting the opportunity to practice calling 911, take a 911 call, or, even more ambitiously, to "put on some scrubs and do eye surgery", kids instead flock to the impressively stocked Winn Dixie supermarket, where they can shop, work the cash registers, and stack shelves, or the mock-café, where they can "dine", serve, or sweep to their hearts' delight.

Civil War Museum

Anyone who needs reminding about the historical horrors of the Deep South should take a look at the **Civil War Museum** (until very recently, and still unofficially, called the **Confederate Museum**), 929 Camp St at Lee Circle (Wed–Sat 10am–4pm; $7; ⓦ confederatemuseum.com). A gloomy Romanesque Revival hulk, purpose-designed by Thomas Sully in 1891 as a place for Confederate veterans to display their mementos, this so-called "Battle Abbey of the South" is a relic from a bygone age. Jefferson Davis, who died in New Orleans' Garden District in 1889 (see p.86), lay in state here briefly, and there remains a funereal air about the place, with its bittersweet remembrances of long-lost generals and their forgotten families. A caption states that its aim remains to tell "the story of insult and oppression…pillage and ruin…want and suffering and humiliation and insult and punishment"; it would be no stretch to believe that most of the written material here has not been updated since 1891.

Though he was in New Orleans for just nine months, **Major Benjamin Butler**, who commanded the military rule of the city after it fell to Union troops in 1862, is one of its most demonized figures. Dubbed **"Beast" Butler** by diehard Rebels, for what they saw as his cruelty and injustice – in June 1862 he hanged a man who had torn down a Union flag before the city was occupied – he has also been called "Spoons", a nickname that grew out of rumours that he pilfered his hosts' silver, including their cutlery. The truth, however, is that during occupation families who refused to swear allegiance to the Union may have had property – including silverware – confiscated. It is highly unlikely that "Spoons" pocketed the cutlery himself.

So unpopular was the Beast with Confederate supporters that local beauties – who, it is said, had his likeness painted in their chamber pots – would retch loudly as Union soldiers walked by. After a month or so of this, in a fit of pique at the behaviour of what he called "these she-adders", Butler announced the **General Order 28**, claiming "When any female shall by word, gesture, or movement, insult or show contempt for any officer of the United States, she shall be regarded and held liable to be treated as a woman of the town plying her vocation." The order, denounced by Jefferson Davis (who proclaimed that the general deserved to be hanged) and the British parliament (who saw it as terribly ungentlemanly), was recalled, as was Butler himself in December 1862.

Inside the church-like hall, wooden cases are filled with flags, swords, mess-kits, uniforms and helmets. There are wordy accounts of battles and of generals, but very little background detail – when the museum was built the "lost cause" would have been fresh in visitors' minds – and certainly no attempt at hindsight or analysis. That said, the place can have a strange pull. Along with affecting, fragile sepia photos – of the wealthy, muddy antebellum city, and sad-eyed youths awkward in uniform – oddities include a crown of thorns hand-woven by Pope Pius IX and sent to Davis, imprisoned after the war, as an encouraging gift, and genuine bullets bitten out of shape by soldiers undergoing amputations with no pain relief. There's also an account of the **Confederate Native Guards**, free blacks who signed up but weren't allowed to fight by the other Confederate states because of the colour of their skin.

The curators obviously feel that the exhibit on notorious Union **General "Beast" Butler** (see above) needs no introduction, and concentrate instead on miffed accounts of his corruption and cruelty, along with alarmingly personal attacks on his appearance, describing him as having, among other things, "baggy eyelids, a bald head and a protruding gut". The throwaway line, "justice requires that it be stated that he did feed the poor, clean up the streets and prevent disease", strikes an odd note given the rest of the invective, as does the startling assertion that after the war he befriended the widow of William Mumford – the man he hanged for tearing down the Union flag – and secured her "a government position."

Reconstruction, too, is covered in bitterest terms, charging that the US government deliberately kept the Southern states from recovery. Accounts of supremacist groups, such as the **White League** (see p.222), are puffed up with patriotic outrage, couched in terms of individuals seeking political liberty in order to protect themselves from the "police state". That the new Metropolitan police force was composed of many Union sympathizers and freed slaves is portrayed here as an affirmation of White League beliefs rather than a challenge to them. While the spiteful contemporaneous cartoons – one, showing an African-American politician and two white men holding their noses, has the caption "Scent to the Legislature" – are shocking, they do at least tell their own story, putting the lie once and for all to any claim that the Confederate cause was not based on tenets of white supremacy.

Ogden Museum of Southern Art

Just next door to the Civil War museum, the sleek, four-storey **Ogden Museum of Southern Art**, 925 Camp St (Wed–Sun 10am–5pm, Thurs also 6–8pm with live music; $10; Ⓦ www.ogdenmuseum.org) represents the South in all its complexity, strangeness and beauty, with a collection that runs the gamut from rare eighteenth-century watercolours through self-taught art to photography and modernist sculpture. While most of the artists are little known outside the South, it's a fascinating place, evoking a strong sense of this distinctive region so preoccupied with notions of the land, of family and religion, poverty and the past, ghosts and spirits, abandonment, migration and loss. Many of the works have an other-worldly, off-kilter quality; as the museum asserts, Southern art follows a different pace from the rest of the nation.

With a host of temporary exhibitions, and rotating shows from the permanent collection, it's pot luck as to what will be on show at any one time: safe bets, however, include the **photography** selection, with E.J. Bellocq's direct and humane portraits of Storyville prostitutes (see box, p.65), rendered both mysterious and mischievous in their striped stockings and masks; Clarence John Laughlin's haunting 1930s evocations of a devastated, ghost-ridden South; some fine hyper-realist portraits from Eudora Welty, commissioned to photograph the Deep South for the WPA in the 1930s, and stark Katrina pictures that still have the power to shock. Elsewhere, highlights include self-taught, visionary and **folk art**, with a good showing from Clementine Hunter, the African-American artist whose colourful paintings and quilts recall her plantation childhood in northern Louisiana, and the 1960s **portraits of Preservation Hall jazzmen** by painter Noel Rockmore, their dark, sparing daubs endowing the old men with

▲ Ogden Museum of Southern Art

a gloomy gravitas. The earliest work is Lulu King Saxon's intriguing oil painting *Uptown Street*, in which today's busy Magazine Street resembles a French Impressionist pastoral idyll; other landscape paintings veer beyond the simply Romantic into the Metaphysical, portraying a netherworld of misty marshes, dark bayous and dreamy swamps.

Before leaving make sure to visit the **gift shop**, a great place for Southern folk art, crafts, and books.

National World War II Museum

The colossal, always crowded **National World War II Museum**, 945 Magazine St (daily 9am–5pm; $16, $20 with admission to the Victory Theater; Ⓦ www .nationalww2museum.org), first opened its doors as the National D-Day Museum on June 6, 2000, the 56th anniversary of the Allied invasion of Normandy, France. Although it has since expanded to become the nation's official World War II museum, its core collection still concentrates on the various shoreline assaults that led to the downfall of both Nazi Germany and Japan, all of which it categorizes as D-Days. New Orleans may seem an unlikely choice for such a high-profile venture; however, shaped by the vision of local historian Stephen E. Ambrose, it was originally chosen because the amphibious craft that made the Normandy landings possible – the **LCVP**, or Landing Craft Vehicle, Personnel – was manufactured here. During the 1930s, Andrew Jackson Higgins developed a flat-bottomed vessel for use in the Louisiana bayous; by 1945 his factories were turning out hundreds of boats per month for the war effort.

Visitors spend most of their time in the upstairs **galleries** of the main building. Split evenly between the campaign in Europe and the endless island-hopping of the Pacific War, these trace the entire history of US involvement in World War II. While the sheer quantity of the hardware and uniforms, the blasts of statistics and the glaring computer visuals may exhaust all but diehard military buffs, the human impact of the war can still be explored via the old film footage, background material, and, especially, oral testimony from all sides of the conflict. The denouement is unquestionably chilling, with the outline plans for "Olympic", the never-implemented invasion of Japan. Actual footage of kamikaze attacks shows the potential ferocity of Japanese resistance; you're left in little doubt where your sympathies should lie regarding Truman's decision to drop the atomic bomb.

As the museum swells, the sheer gung-ho militarism is starting to swamp its few nods towards nuance. Its latest addition, the much-trumpeted **Victory Theater**, across the road from the main entrance, sets a dismal introductory tone with the "Beyond All Boundaries" 4-D movie (shows hourly 10am–4pm; $9, $20 with museum admission). Narrated by Tom Hanks, this 45 minutes of propaganda disguised as history reduces the devastating global conflict to a series of infantile super-effects (seats rumble as tanks plough through a battlefield, fake snow flutters onto the audience as an actor reads out letters sent home on Christmas Day). It hardly makes the museum's plans to cover several blocks with structures such as the "US Freedom Pavilion" sound promising.

The Contemporary Arts Center

Housed in a restored nineteenth-century warehouse and ice-cream factory, the **Contemporary Arts Center** (**CAC**), 900 Camp St, is the city's premier modern art gallery (Thurs–Sun 11am–4pm; ground-floor galleries free; changing exhibitions $5; Ⓦ www.cacno.org). A kind of hub for the Arts District, it's a large, peaceful space, and there's often something interesting going on, from the temporary shows on the ground floor to major exhibitions upstairs, with a lively programme of cutting-edge performances, movies, lectures and workshops to boot. It also hosts a number of arty fundraisers, climaxing in October's **Art for Art's Sake** bash (see p.181), when you can wander the galleries with a beer and a gumbo, dance to live bands, or watch a fashion show. The tranquil **café** (see p.141) is a good place to take a break in an area otherwise short on pit-stop opportunities.

The Superdome

The lakeside edge of the CBD, a tangle of busy grey highways, is dominated by the colossal home of the New Orleans Saints NFL team, the **Superdome**. At 52 acres, 27 storeys high and with a diameter of 207m, this is one of the largest buildings on the planet, completed in 1975 at a cost of nearly $200 million. While the Superdome can boast many superlatives – hosting the world's largest-ever indoor rock concert, for example (in 1981, when 87,500 fans watched The Rolling Stones) – its place in the world's consciousness has since been etched by rather more distressing events. The building was designed to function as a hurricane shelter – much needed in this storm-battered city, which, despite its obvious vulnerability has shockingly few designated shelters – and in 1998 it sheltered 14,000 people for two days as Hurricane Georges approached before veering sharply east at the last minute. It was during **Katrina**, however, that its putative capacity to be a "refuge of last resort" was shaken forever as it struggled to house some 30,000 evacuees in unthinkable conditions for six days. Though lurid tales of gang rapes, murders, and suicides were later discovered to have been urban myths based largely on racism, the Superdome became a byword the world over for the shocking neglect, chaos and sheer human rights atrocities that New Orleans was facing in the wake of the floods. Standing sentinel over the battered CBD for thirteen months after the storm, its damaged roof scarred and distressedly flapping, the stadium finally re-opened in September 2006 with a nationally televised, star-studded rock concert and a triumphant victory by the Saints over the Atlanta Falcons. Emotional in the extreme, the high-profile event provided a huge boost of confidence, and marked a turning point in the city's sense of its own recovery.

Things reached an even higher emotional peak in January 2010 when the Saints (previously nicknamed the Aints, due to their dismal record) defeated the Minnesota Vikings at home to win their first-ever place in the **Superbowl**. Coach Sean Payton's tearful words to the home crowd after the game – "four years ago, there were holes in this roof" – spoke to a city sick of being seen as the loser, and ready to show the world they were back. Even the Saints' eventual astonishing Superbowl victory over the Indianapolis Colts – which gained the highest TV ratings ever in the USA – could not quite match this moment; never had a football game, a team, or a stadium, signified quite so much.

Today, while it remains a mighty monument to the flooding, its instantly recognizable silhouette on the skyline a salutary reminder of that horrific time, as an arena the Superdome is back to its old self. In addition to providing a home for the Saints (Aug–Dec), it hosts the wildly popular **Sugar Bowl**, a college football game (early Jan), and the **Bayou Classic** (Thanksgiving weekend), along with the major African-American music festival **Essence** in July (see p.180); in 2013 it will also be the site of Super Bowl XLVII.

The adjacent **New Orleans Arena**, clinging to the Superdome like a kid brother, opened in 1999 as the home of the (now defunct) New Orleans Brass ice hockey team. Today it hosts the NBA Hornets and doubles as a downtown venue for big, tight-trousered rock bands. For details on booking for **events** at the Superdome and the New Orleans Arena, see p.197.

5

The Garden District and Uptown

The ravishing **Garden District**, a grand old residential neighbourhood around two miles upriver from the French Quarter, was given life in the 1840s by the energetic breed of Anglo-Americans who, having outgrown the Faubourg St Mary (today's CBD, see p.71), announced their ever-accumulating wealth by building sumptuous mansions in huge, lush gardens. Shaded by jungles of subtropical foliage, the glorious houses – some of them spick-and-span showpieces, others in shabby ruin – evoke a nostalgic vision of the Deep South in a profusion of galleries, columns and balconies. It's a deeply romantic spectacle, if somewhat Gothic – perfect for author **Anne Rice**, who was born nearby and bought and restored a number of local properties, as well as featuring several of them in her fiction, before moving away after the death of her husband.

The St Charles streetcar

There can be few more romantic ways of passing time in New Orleans than planting yourself on a mahogany bench on the **St Charles streetcar**, catching the breeze from the open window, and watching as one of America's loveliest avenues unfolds in front of you.

The streetcar, now a National Historic Monument, began in 1835 as the **New Orleans and Carrollton Railroad**, a steam-powered train that took a whole day to cover the six and a half miles from Canal Street, via Lafayette and a string of small faubourgs, to the resort town of Carrollton. After the Civil War, the inefficient steam engines were replaced by mules – a cleaner, quieter form of transport – until overhead electricity was introduced in 1893.

The streetcar network spread quickly, with cars travelling three abreast along tracks crisscrossing Canal Street and the French Quarter. Though Tennessee Williams was said to be inspired by the clanging of the trolley bell beneath his French Quarter apartment to pen his 1947 play *A Streetcar Named Desire*, the service was already dwindling by then, faced with competition from motorbuses, and by 1964 only the St Charles line remained.

In the 1980s, a new streetcar line, geared primarily toward tourists, was developed along a two-mile stretch of the **riverfront**, and in 2004 the old Canal Street line, which heads up via Mid-City and Carrollton Avenue to City Park, was reinstated. Neither, however, has quite the romantic, historic cachet of the sage green St Charles cars. For more on the practicalities of streetcar travel, see p.23.

The Garden District began in 1834 as the city of **Lafayette**, which remained separate from New Orleans until 1852. Development sped up with the arrival in 1835 of the **New Orleans and Carrollton Railroad** – forerunner of today's streetcar – which ran along St Charles Avenue, the broad street bordering the suburb on its lakeside edge. Lafayette's construction frenzy was brought to a halt by the Civil War, when occupying Union troops made themselves comfortable in the capacious homes. The turn of the next century, however, saw another spate of mansion-building, this time along **St Charles Avenue** and the crucial streetcar line, extending further and further upriver with each passing year. The august residences of the Garden District, meanwhile, remained in the hands of the monied elite, as they continue to do today.

The Garden District heralds the onset of **uptown** New Orleans, the big chunk of the city that extends roughly between Jackson and Carrollton avenues. While uptown is a mixed area, the stately, live-oak-lined St Charles Avenue is its showpiece boulevard, studded with fabulous mansions. The **St Charles Avenue streetcar**, which follows the same route as the early railroad, is still the preferred way to get to and around the area, affording front-row views of "the avenue", as St Charles is known locally. Clanging its way from Canal Street, it courses through the low-rent **Lower Garden District** before arriving at the Garden District proper, beyond which it continues past increasingly opulent houses. It eventually reaches peaceful **Audubon Park** and its **zoo**; beyond the park, the track turns inland to the studenty **Riverbend** area, where a cluster of great bars and restaurants lie on or around **Carrollton Avenue**.

Running parallel to St Charles, and forming the riverside boundary of the Garden District, funky **Magazine Street**, its shotgun houses filled with distinctive stores, galleries, restaurants and bars, is the other main channel between Canal Street and uptown.

The Lower Garden District

The **Lower Garden District** is a loose term for the area between the Warehouse District and the Garden District proper. Sprawling down through a cluster of streets romantically named after the Greek muses, via gentrifying **Coliseum Square** to the river, it's a hip, racially mixed neighbourhood, the once decorative, now decaying, nineteenth-century buildings housing a motley population of artists and poor families. While it's no great shakes for sightseeing, it does have a number of budget **hotels**, and lower **Magazine Street** – more countercultural here than along its uptown stretch – is superb for shopping, with various alternative galleries, thrift stores and places to eat. Below Jackson Avenue the street is peppered with desolate, run-down blocks, however, so keep your wits about you if you decide to walk it.

The Garden District

Pride of uptown New Orleans, the **Garden District** drapes itself seductively across an area just thirteen blocks wide and five deep, bounded by Magazine Street and St Charles, Jackson and Louisiana avenues. Here some of the swankiest homes in the city – during Carnival season, many fly the flag announcing that a resident has been honoured as King or Queen of Rex (see p.165) – stand in the shadow of hauntingly derelict piles.

The mansions of Lafayette were built in a variety of **architectural styles**, each according to the whim of its owner. The earliest homes stood one to a block,

Running parallel to St Charles Avenue, but providing a quite different experience, **Magazine Street** is the main commercial thoroughfare between Canal Street and uptown. You won't find opulent mansions and grand iron gates here, though, but instead clapboard shotguns, porches and stoops, with everything on a human scale. Offering a six-mile stretch – extending from the Lower Garden District up to Clay Avenue, a couple of blocks short of Audubon Park – of thrift and antique stores, designer clothes shops, coffee bars, restaurants and art galleries, this is one of the very best places to shop in the city, and is especially lively at the weekends. It's also eminently walkable – although aiming to see the entire street in one go will leave you pretty footsore, and its lower reaches can feel a little edgy when there are few shoppers around. Sadly the streetcars do not pass this way, and although it is fine to walk the five blocks down from St Charles Avenue to Magazine Street via the Garden District, the distance between the two main roads increases as the streetcar heads uptown, where in any case you may well feel unsafe. The #11 bus runs the length of the road from Canal Street to Audubon Park, but services are sporadic.

5

THE GARDEN DISTRICT AND UPTOWN | The Garden District

situated on the corners and fronted by brick flagstones that came over as ballast on ships returning from Europe. As fortunes were made, tastes became more and more flamboyant, each nouveau-riche planter and merchant trying to outdo his neighbour. Today you'll see ordered, columned Greek Revival structures; romantic, Italianate villas; Moorish follies; Second Empire piles and fanciful Queen Anne mansions, plus a number of buildings that defy categorization, with motifs mixed up together to form transitional, or hybrid, styles.

Other than a handful of fellow tourists, you'll come across little human activity on these rarefied streets, where the uncanny hush is interrupted only by birdsong and the buzzing of distant lawnmowers – worlds away from the crash and clatter of the Quarter. Though most come here to gaze upon the houses, the neighbourhood also lives up to its name with its fabulous **greenery**. Unlike the Creoles of the French Quarter, who were constrained by lack of space, the planters and traders who built in Lafayette revelled in its expansiveness, setting their mansions back from the street and surrounding them with lush gardens. Today, everywhere you turn, foliage threatens to overtake the place: huge, mossy live oaks form a canopy over the streets, while broad oleander trees and banana plants fight for space with vividly flowering azaleas, camellias and crepe myrtles. (It's not just for aesthetic reasons that so many gallery ceilings in the Garden District are painted sky-blue – the colour deters dozy insects, who thrive in the copious foliage, from nesting there.) The air is scented by jasmine, sweet olive and waxy magnolia blossoms – originally planted, it is said, to mask the odours from the tanneries and slaughterhouses of the **Irish Channel**, the working-class district that spread out beneath Lafayette toward the river and that still exists as a rough-and-ready neighbourhood today.

The Garden District can be explored on an official **walking tour** (see p.24) or by using one of the self-guided tours available from the Welcome Center (see p.28). We've pointed out the main landmarks in this chapter; the Garden District's cemetery, **Lafayette No. 1**, is covered on p.108, in the chapter devoted to New Orleans' Cities of the Dead. Note that the mansions are only open to the public during New Orleans' Spring Fiesta (see p.179).

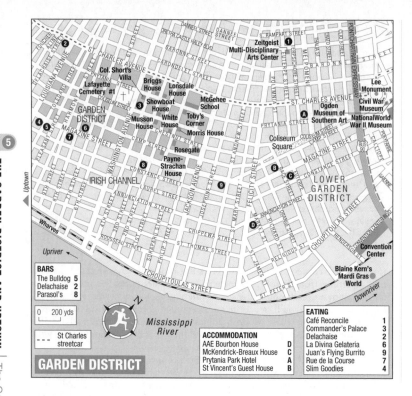

BARS
The Bulldog	5
Delachaise	2
Parasol's	8

0   200 yds

--- St Charles streetcar

Mississippi River

ACCOMMODATION
AAE Bourbon House	D
McKendrick-Breaux House	C
Prytania Park Hotel	A
St Vincent's Guest House	B

EATING
Café Reconcile	1
Commander's Palace	3
Delachaise	2
La Divina Gelateria	6
Juan's Flying Burrito	9
Rue de la Course	7
Slim Goodies	4

Rosegate

A gorgeous Italianate-Greek Revival hybrid on First Street between Chestnut and Camp, **Rosegate** was home to local novelist Anne Rice between 1991 and 2004. This was also the fictional home of her Mayfair witches, and appears in her final vampire novel, *Blood Canticle*, written before she left her beloved New Orleans following the death of her husband. Built in 1856, it was the first house on the block, and today its elaborate floriate iron fence encloses other, newer houses. Notice the Egyptian "keyhole" front door, flaring out at the base, and the sky-blue gallery ceilings so common in the Garden District.

Payne-Strachan House

The relatively unostentatious, columned **Payne-Strachan House**, 1134 First St at Camp, is a prime specimen of antebellum Greek Revival styling. Built in 1849 for the pro-Union planter Jacob Payne, the house is most notable for being where Jefferson Davis, president of the Confederacy, died in 1889, while visiting Payne's son-in-law. A granite slab outside commemorates the event.

Morris House and the White House

The **Morris House**, the lovely rose-pink villa on the corner of First Street and Coliseum, is a quintessential example of the dreamy Italianate style that swept through the Garden District in the 1860s. Its romantic aspect, enhanced by a delicate filigree of cast-iron galleries, is perfectly set off by the orderly, straight-down-the-line Greek Revival **White House**, opposite at 1312 First St.

Toby's Corner and the McGehee School

The oldest surviving house in the Garden District, the Greek Revival mansion known as **Toby's Corner**, 2340 Prytania St at First, was built in 1838 in unadorned plantation style, with a raised floor to prevent waterlogging. Thomas Toby himself, a Philadelphia native, had made a fortune by inventing a revolutionary cotton hauler, then promptly lost most of it backing the doomed Texan revolution of 1835.

Covering the entire block opposite Toby's Corner, fronted by mighty Corinthian columns, the private **McGehee School** is housed in what was formerly the residence of Union sympathizer Bradish Johnson. Built during Reconstruction, the showy Second Empire trophy was the envy of every sugar planter in town, boasting not only an exquisite domed marble staircase, but also a newfangled elevator, a sure sign of wealth and distinction.

Musson House and Showboat House

On Coliseum Street and Third, the Italianate **Musson House**, a fanciful pink clapboard structure fronted with fabulous cast-iron balconies, was built in 1850 for Michel Musson, the Creole uncle of the French Impressionist painter **Edgar Degas**. After the Civil War, having lost much of his wealth, Musson abandoned the Anglo-dominated Garden District in favour of Esplanade Avenue, the Creole equivalent of St Charles Avenue downriver. He went on to join the supremacist White League, and was a voluble presence at the rally that led to the Battle of Liberty Place (see p.74). Musson can be seen testing a cotton sample in the foreground of Degas' painting *A Cotton Office in New Orleans* (see p.93).

Opposite the Musson House, the gallery-swathed **Showboat House**, or Robinson Mansion, at 1415 Third St, is one of the Garden District's most palatial properties. An Italianate-Greek Revival structure built in 1860 by eminent architects Henry Howard and James Gallier Jr, it is best known, prosaically, for its early form of indoor plumbing, whereby the roof acted as a vessel to collect rainwater that was then channelled down into the house.

Briggs House

The Garden District's only neo-Gothic mansion, the stern-looking **Briggs House**, 2605 Prytania St at Third, was designed by James Gallier Sr in 1847. Though there are a couple of significant neo-Gothic buildings – also the work of Gallier – in the CBD, as a rule Southerners weren't keen on the narrow windows and arches that characterized the style. This building, whose pared-down aspect does look a little out of place in the overblown Garden District, was built for an English insurance broker.

Colonel Short's Villa

Yet another Henry Howard structure, the Italianate **Colonel Short's Villa**, 1448 Fourth St at Prytania, was built for $25,000 in 1859 – a relatively paltry sum, even then. Just a few years later, it was commandeered by Yankee forces, who enjoyed its facilities for the duration of the Civil War. While the building itself, with its columns and galleries, is undeniably striking, it's the cast-iron **cornstalk fence** that grabs your attention. A rural tangle of corn cobs and morning glories, it was picked, during the city's cast-iron craze, from the same catalogue as its twin in the French Quarter (see p.49). You'll spot crumbly patches, where the fence is rusting away: cast iron, despite its decorative qualities, tends to be less durable than the simpler, hand-wrought iron favoured in the early nineteenth century.

The turquoise Queen Anne building a block south of Colonel Short's Villa at 1403 Washington Ave is *Commander's Palace*, one of the city's most famous Creole restaurants (see p.134).

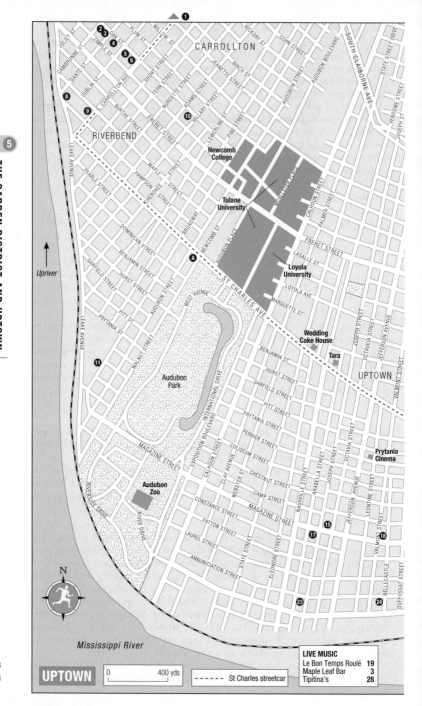

CARROLLTON

RIVERBEND

Newcomb College

Tulane University

Loyola University

Uptown

Wedding Cake House

Tara

UPTOWN

Prytania Cinema

Audubon Park

Audubon Zoo

Mississippi River

N

Upriver

UPTOWN

0   400 yds

- - - - St Charles streetcar

LIVE MUSIC
Le Bon Temps Roulé   19
Maple Leaf Bar   3
Tipitina's   28

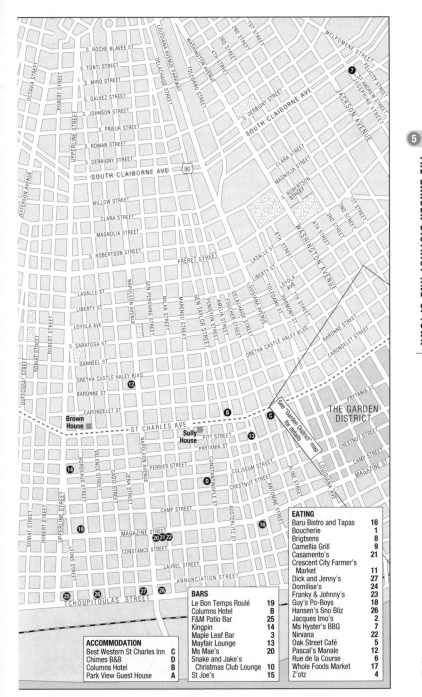

EATING

Baru Bistro and Tapas	16
Boucherie	1
Brigtsens	8
Camellia Grill	9
Casamento's	21
Crescent City Farmer's Market	11
Dick and Jenny's	27
Domilise's	24
Franky & Johnny's	23
Guy's Po-Boys	18
Hansen's Sno Bliz	26
Jacques Imo's	2
Ms Hyster's BBQ	7
Nirvana	22
Oak Street Café	5
Pascal's Manale	12
Rue de la Course	6
Whole Foods Market	17
Z'otz	4

BARS

Le Bon Temps Roulé	19
Columns Hotel	B
F&M Patio Bar	25
Kingpin	14
Maple Leaf Bar	3
Mayfair Lounge	13
Ms Mae's	20
Snake and Jake's Christmas Club Lounge	10
St Joe's	15

ACCOMMODATION

Best Western St Charles Inn	C
Chimes B&B	D
Columns Hotel	B
Park View Guest House	A

St Charles Avenue

A stately, live oak-lined swathe sweeping its way from Canal Street upriver to Audubon Park, **St Charles Avenue** is uptown's pride and joy. Most of its ostentatious homes were built in the late nineteenth and early twentieth centuries – after 1893, when the streetcar line was electrified, merchants flourishing in the post-Civil War South found that to live on "the avenue" was an ideal way to display their new wealth.

The **streetcar** (see p.22) is still by far the best way to see the avenue, which gets more magnificent the further uptown you go. **Lower St Charles** is a scrappy ragbag of empty lots and architectural nonentities; beyond the Garden District, however, the private mansions cut as impressive a dash as they did a century ago, the cut-glass windows in their mighty doors sparkling like priceless crystal. To see the best of them, continue on the streetcar and head uptown towards Audubon Park.

The *Columns Hotel*, 3811 St Charles (on the lakeside of the avenue), is a fabulous place to stop for a drink, either in the faded bar or on the avenue-side veranda, fronted by its stout Doric columns (see p.151).

The mansions

Beyond the Garden District, St Charles Avenue's showy **mansions** display a variety of styles, from Italianate through Romanesque to Queen Anne. Many of them – including his own little Queen Anne gingerbread home at 4010 St Charles (riverside) – are the work of eminent architect **Thomas Sully**, who is also responsible for some of the most important buildings in the CBD.

You can hardly miss the **Brown House**, a limestone Romanesque monster at no. 4717 (lakeside); it's the largest mansion on the avenue. Further along, at no. 5705, look out for the gleaming white 1941 replica of **Tara**, Scarlett's beloved home in *Gone with the Wind* (lakeside). Close on its heels at no. 5809, the aptly nicknamed **Wedding Cake House** (lakeside) is an ostentatious Greek Revival building, frosted with a layer of balconies, balustrades, cornices and columns.

▲ St Charles streetcar

Beyond, the handsome **university campuses** of Loyola and Tulane (lakeside) stand side by side facing Audubon Park.

Audubon Park

Built on plantation lands once belonging to Etienne de Boré – who in 1795 perfected the sugar granulation process, and went on to become the city's first mayor – Upper City Park was laid out in 1871. After hosting the 1884 Cotton Exposition, which, though it proved to be a financial flop, marked the onset of a nascent tourist industry in New Orleans, the park was redeveloped and renamed for celebrated Haitian naturalist John James Audubon, who stayed in the city in 1821 while compiling his seminal *Birds of America*. Today the 350-acre **Audubon Park** is an appealing, much-used space, dotted with lagoons and picnic areas, shaded by Spanish moss-swathed trees and looped by an extensive cycling and jogging path.

Audubon Zoo

The best thing about the **Audubon Zoo**, a ten-minute walk or a free shuttle ride (every 20–30min) from the park's St Charles entrance (Tues–Fri 10am–4pm, Sat & Sun 10am–5pm; $13, kids $8; various combination tickets are available with other Audubon Nature Institute attractions; Ⓦ www.auduboninstitute.org), is its beautifully recreated **Louisiana swamp**, complete with Cajun houseboats, wallowing alligators and knobbly cypress knees poking out of the emerald green water. Animals here include raccoons, otters, bears, cougars and the broadhead skink, Louisiana's largest lizard. If the snakes and reptiles leave you cold, you can take refuge with the fluffy bobcat kittens in the cosy swamp nursery.

Star of the swamp, is, of course, the **alligator**, and you'll find anything and everything gator-related here, from monstrous prehistoric skulls to the tank of tiny hatchlings perched precariously on small logs. The main attractions are the mysterious blue-eyed **white alligators**, two of eighteen leucistic hatchlings discovered by a Cajun fisherman in a nearby swamp in 1987. No one knows what causes their milky colouring, and as yet only two more batches of hatchlings have been found, again in southern Louisiana.

Throughout the swamp, a trail of panels puts the exhibits into historical and cultural context, while videos illustrate subjects ranging from Cajun dancing to cooking. At the barn-like **café**, you can eat gumbo and crawfish pie seated in a rocking chair on the veranda; look carefully and you'll see enormous snapping turtles just beneath the water's surface.

Some of the zoo's other recreated habitats, despite their lush vegetation and pleasant boardwalks, are showing their age. Many of the enclosures are simply too small, their inhabitants hemmed in and dispirited. Best bets are the **African savannah** – where, along with the hippos, leopards, and giraffes, Monkey Hill (which at 8m is proudly labeled as the highest natural point in the city), provides an informal staggered splash pool for overheated kids in summer – and **Jaguar Jungle**, where jaguars, sloths, anteaters and monkeys prowl, doze, snuffle and swing among mock Mayan ruins. Look out too for the komodo dragons, and, in the **Asian domain** the rare white tigers, who like the alligator are leucistic, with blue eyes. Kids will make a beeline for the cheery carousel of endangered species ($2), the safari simulator ($5) and the animatronic dinosaurs ($4); there is also a toy train that weaves through the zoo for anyone that's getting footsore ($5).

Each November, Audubon Zoo hosts the splendid **Swampfest**, featuring the best in Cajun and zydeco music, food and crafts. See p.182 for details.

Mid-City and City Park

Predominantly residential **Mid-City**, the large stretch of land that fans up from Tremé towards Lake Pontchartrain, is of most interest to visitors for **City Park** and the superb **New Orleans Museum of Art**. Snaking down the eastern side of the park and a mile or so beyond, **Bayou St John**, once an important waterway, today flows placidly through a desirable residential area; nearby, the **Fair Grounds** racetrack hosts New Orleans' annual **Jazz Fest** (see p.175), when it bursts at the seams with tens of thousands of music fans from around the world.

You may well also venture into Mid-City for its **restaurants** (see pp.137–139). There's an especially good cluster along **Esplanade Ridge** – the "high" ground (about 1.2m above sea level) that hugs either side of Esplanade Avenue. Beyond the ridge, however, it's not a good idea to wander around the poverty-scarred outskirts of Tremé; bus #91, running from the corner of North Rampart Street along Esplanade all the way to City Park, is safe enough during the day, but you should call a **taxi** (see p.22) after dark. You can also take the Canal Street **streetcar** to the Esplanade Avenue entrance of the park, convenient not only for the art museum but also for the nearby **Pitot House**, the area's only other formal attraction (take the cars marked "Museum" rather than "Cemeteries" to avoid having to change at Carrollton Avenue).

Esplanade Avenue

In the antebellum era, wealthy Creoles turned their sights toward broad, live oak-lined **Esplanade Avenue**, which sweeps up from the Mississippi River to City Park. Escaping the congested French Quarter, they lined the grand boulevard with large, fashionable homes, fronting them with voluminous, filigree cast-iron galleries. Today, many of the houses, though still hauntingly lovely, are decidedly run-down, and stretches of the road, particularly those on the fringes of Tremé, lie blighted and desolate. Restoration, monitored by a vocal preservation group, is gradually improving matters, and a handful of the homes have been converted into luxurious **B&Bs**.

St Louis No. 3 Cemetery, on Esplanade Avenue near Bayou St John, is covered in the chapter devoted to New Orleans' Cities of the Dead; see p.111.

Bayou St John

Were it not for **Bayou St John**, New Orleans might never have existed. Local Indians had long used the site of today's city as a portage: the alligator-filled bayou, an inlet of Lake Pontchartrain, provided a handy shortcut between the Mississippi and the Gulf of Mexico via the lake, bypassing the river's perilous lower reaches. As the city grew, the countryside around the bayou was carved into plantations

The Degas House

Built in 1854, the Italianate **Degas House**, 2306 Esplanade Ave at Tonti Street, was rented in the 1870s by the Mussons – Creole relatives of the French Impressionist painter Edgar Degas – who had been forced to sell their Garden District mansion following a downturn in their fortunes after the Civil War (see p.87). Degas lodged here for a while in 1872, painting about fifteen portraits of family members. He returned to Paris the next year, frustrated by the degenerative eye problem that prevented him from painting outdoors, but he did produce at least one important work during his stay: *A Cotton Office in New Orleans*, a complex commercial scene that works just as well as a family portrait, showing Michel Musson, Degas' uncle, at work in his cotton exchange, along with sundry nephews and sons-in-law. The artist also made three portraits of his blind cousin Estelle, who was married to his brother René until he ran off with a neighbour; one of the largest, and most affecting, of these is displayed at the New Orleans Museum of Art (see p.97). Today the house – which is, in fact, just half of the original building (the other half is now next door, standing a few feet away on the left) – is a pricey B&B (see p.120).

worked by African slaves, and in the early 1800s it evolved into a popular gathering place for local **voodooists** (see p.52). Though it remained a key waterway until the 1920s, today Bayou St John flows through the heart of a well-heeled residential neighbourhood – it's a favourite spot for fishing and dog-walking – with not an alligator to be seen. It is also the starting point, on the Sunday closest to St Joseph's Day (March 19th), for the downtown Mardi Gras Indian parade known as **Super Sunday**, a rare opportunity to see the amazing suits debuted at the preceding Mardi Gras (see p.178).

Pitot House

One of the prettiest houses in New Orleans, the **Pitot House**, 1440 Moss St (Wed–Sat 10am–3pm; $7), stands near the upper end of Esplanade on the banks

▲ Pitot House

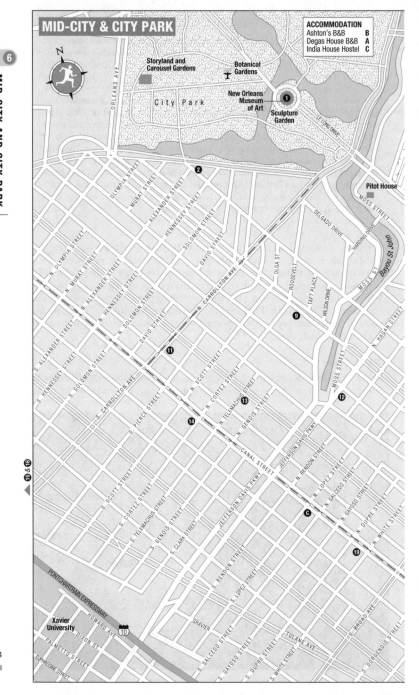

MID-CITY & CITY PARK

N

Storyland and
Carousel Gardens

Botanical
Gardens

City Park

New Orleans
Museum
of Art

Sculpture
Garden

Pitot House

ORLEANS AVE

LE LONG DRIVE

MOSS STREET

DELGADO DRIVE

HARDING DRIVE

MOSS ST

Bayou St John

OLYMPIA STREET
MURAT STREET
ALEXANDER STREET
HENNESSEY STREET
SOLOMON STREET
DAVID STREET

N. OLYMPIA STREET
N. MURAT STREET
N. ALEXANDER STREET
N. HENNESSEY STREET
N. SOLOMON STREET
DAVID STREET
N. CARROLLTON AVE

S. ALEXANDER STREET
S. HENNESSEY STREET
S. SOLOMON STREET
S. CARROLLTON AVE
S. PIERCE STREET

OLGA ST
ROOSEVELT
TAFT PLACE
WILSON DRIVE

MOSS STREET
N. HAGAN STREET

N. SCOTT STREET
N. CORTEZ STREET
N. TELEMACHUS STREET
N. GENOIS STREET

SCOTT STREET
S. CORTEZ STREET
S. TELEMACHUS STREET
S. GENOIS STREET
S. CLARK STREET

CANAL STREET

JEFFERSON DAVIS PKWY

JEFFERSON DAVIS PKWY

N. RENDON STREET
N. LOPEZ STREET
N. SALCEDO STREET
GAYOSO STREET
N. DUPRE STREET
N. WHITE STREET

S. RENDON STREET
S. LOPEZ STREET
S. SALCEDO STREET
S. GAYOSO STREET
S. DUPRE STREET
S. WHITE STREET

S. BROAD AVE
S. DORGENOIS STREET

PONTCHARTRAIN EXPRESSWAY

Xavier
University

HOWARD AVE

DIXON ST

PALMETTO STREET

EUPHROSINE STREET

GRAVIER

TULANE AVE

15 & 16

2

9

11

13

14

12

C

19

10

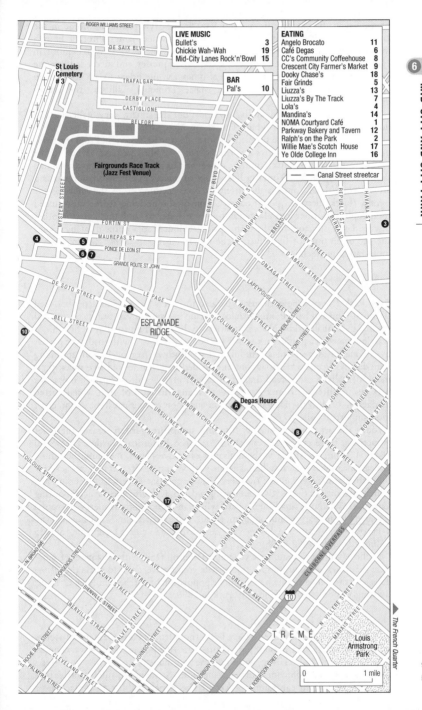

LIVE MUSIC
Bullet's 3
Chickie Wah-Wah 19
Mid-City Lanes Rock'n'Bowl 15

BAR
Pal's 10

EATING
Angelo Brocato 11
Café Degas 6
CC's Community Coffeehouse 8
Crescent City Farmer's Market 9
Dooky Chase's 18
Fair Grinds 5
Liuzza's 13
Liuzza's By The Track 7
Lola's 4
Mandina's 14
NOMA Courtyard Café 1
Parkway Bakery and Tavern 12
Ralph's on the Park 2
Willie Mae's Scotch House 17
Ye Olde College Inn 16

— — Canal Street streetcar

ROGER WILLIAMS STREET
DE SAIX BLVD
St Louis Cemetery # 3
TRAFALGAR
DERBY PLACE
CASTIGLIONE
BELFORT

Fairgrounds Race Track
(Jazz Fest Venue)

MYSTERY STREET
FORTIN ST
MAUREPAS ST
PONCE DE LEON ST
GRANDE ROUTE ST JOHN
DE SOTO STREET
LE PAGE
BELL STREET
ESPLANADE RIDGE
ESPLANADE AVE
BARRACKS STREET
GOVERNOR NICHOLLS STREET
URSULINES AVE
ST PHILIP STREET
DUMAINE STREET
ST ANN STREET
ST PETER STREET
TOULOUSE STREET
LAFITTE AVE
ST LOUIS STREET
CONTI STREET
BIENVILLE STREET
BERVILLE STREET
PALMYRA STREET
CLEVELAND STREET

GENTILLY BLVD
ROSIERE ST
GAYOSO ST
DUPRE ST
PAUL MORPHY ST
BROAD
AUBRY STREET
ONZAGA STREET
D'ABADIE STREET
LAPEYPOUSE STREET
LA HARPE STREET
COLUMBUS STREET
N. ROCHEBLAVE STREET
N. TONTI STREET
N. MIRO STREET
N. GALVEZ STREET
N. JOHNSON STREET
N. PRIEUR STREET
N. ROMAN STREET
KERLEREC STREET
BAYOU ROAD
ST BERNARD
REPUBLIC ST.
HAVANA ST.

Degas House

CLAIBORNE OVERPASS
ORLEANS AVE
N. VILLERE STREET
MARAIS STREET
N. VERDUN STREET
N. ROBERTSON STREET

TREMÉ
Louis Armstrong Park

► The French Quarter

0   1 mile

of the bayou. It's the only remaining West Indies-style plantation home in the city, built in 1799 and named for its fourth owner, James Pitot, a French merchant who came to the United States fleeing the 1792 slave rebellions in Haiti. Pitot developed one of the city's first cotton presses, and succeeded Etienne de Boré as mayor in 1804. The house also has a vague Edgar Degas connection (see p.93), as Pitot bought it from Marie Tronquet Rillieux, the artist's great-grandmother.

With its stucco-covered walls, ground-floor basement, airy galleries and double-pitched roof, it's a typical Caribbean-New Orleans structure (see p.40), and has been decorated in a simple, elegant style true to its period. From the front galleries you get lovely views out over the flower-filled parterre garden to the bayou, while crops of cotton, indigo, ginger and bananas form a patchwork across the small back garden. **Tours**, a lively mix of anecdote, historical snippets and architectural detail, draw your attention to everything from the *briquete entre poteaux* (bricks between posts) construction of the building to the customized food cupboards, their legs planted in bowls of water to confound ants and other insects. Look out, too, for the lush, apricot-coloured sofa in the drawing room: the site of an orgy of bloodlust in the movie *Interview with the Vampire*, here it looks rather genteel.

City Park

City Park (Ⓦ www.neworleanscitypark.com) covers some 1500 acres between Bayou St John and Lake Pontchartrain. Starting its days as a vast swathe of forested swampland, inhabited by Native Americans who traded on the Bayou St John, it was designated as a public park in 1854. Today, crisscrossed with roads, the park is by no means as peaceful as Audubon Park uptown (see p.91), but appealing nonetheless. Streaked with lagoons and shaded by centuries-old **live oaks**, their monumentally broad spread draped in ragged grey beards of Spanish moss, the park also features the Beaux Arts **New Orleans Museum of Art**, which started its days in 1911 as the Delgado Museum and soon established itself as the city's most important gallery.

Today the art museum and its stunning **sculpture garden** remain the chief attractions; there is also an appealing Art Deco **Botanical Garden** (Tues–Sun 10am–4.30pm; $6), filled with thousands of native plants, including blooming azaleas, magnolias and camellias. Anyone with young children in tow can head for the **Storyland** playground (Tues–Fri 10am–3pm, Sat & Sun 10am–6pm; $3), which, designed in the 1950s, is endearingly dated. Kids also like the neighbouring **Carousel Garden**, a small theme park where an indoor antique merry-go-round is joined by a miniature railroad, bumper cars, rollercoaster, the "slime bucket" and a Ferris wheel (days and hours vary seasonally; $3, plus $1 per ride, or $15 unlimited rides; Ⓣ 482-4888).

To the left of the museum, the venerable **Dueling Oak**, with a diameter of more than 4.5m, was a favourite spot for volatile young adversaries to settle the *affaires d'honneur* that felled so much of the male population of antebellum New Orleans; duelling was only outlawed in City Park in 1890.

New Orleans Museum of Art

Near the Esplanade entrance to City Park, the splendid **New Orleans Museum of Art** (NOMA; Wed noon–8pm, Thurs–Sun 10am–5pm; $16; Ⓦ www.noma .org) holds an impressive, wide-ranging permanent collection and hosts temporary shows and major touring exhibitions. Some works suffer a little from poor or nonexistent captioning – **Art of the Americas**, for example, whose astonishingly broad collection, including Maya stelae, delicate Costa Rican jade and gold, unsettling Olmec pathological figures, Navajo kachinas, fabulous Plains Indians beadwork, and Inuit granite anthropomorphic figures, is sporadically labelled. Not so the **Asian galleries**, however, where everything from tiny eighth-century Jain bronzes and Zen ink paintings to ferocious Tang Dynasty temple guardians and bombastic suits of Edo armour is put into context. There are some particularly intriguing objects from India, among them raffia baskets from the northeastern hill state of Nagaland decorated with real monkey skulls, and gruesome sixteenth-century wooden temple guardians from Kerala. Similarly, the **African galleries** – a dizzying array of tribal and religious art, with wonderfully immediate wooden masks and human figurines, beaded and feathered ceremonial costumes, and finely crafted fetishes – plots an admirably clear course through its jaw-dropping treasures. Highlights include a nineteenth-century memorial staff from Benin, topped with an entire scene played out in iron. The **Oceanic galleries** – which include, among other things, wizened shrunken heads and splendid spirit masks from Papua New Guinea, feathered currency rolls from the Solomon Islands, and fierce eighteenth-century Hawaiian temple figures – are also something to behold.

Of the **paintings**, French artists – naturally – are particularly well represented. Watch out for the lush and symbolic portrait of a regal *Marie Antoinette* (1788) by the young court painter **Élizabeth Louise Vigée-Lebrun**, and **Edgar Degas**' 1872 painting of his blind New Orleans cousin and sister-in-law, *Estelle Musson* (see p.93) – a melancholy, almost Impressionistic image of an unseeing woman reaching out through a shadowy interior to gently arrange a blazing red gladiolus. Degas himself was losing his eyesight when he made the work, which only adds to the poignancy. Another masterpiece born of impending blindness, **Claude Monet**'s *Snow at Giverny* (1893), painted when the artist's eyesight was at its worst, shrouds his beloved French home in a pearly, lavender-white blur.

▲ New Orleans Museum of Art

The museum has a strong collection of American works, highlights of which include **William Woodward**'s warm, Impressionistic paintings of the late nineteenth-century French Quarter. A keen preservationist, Woodward was eager to bring this historic, and neglected, neighbourhood to life, setting up his easel on the streets and using oil crayons to render the softness of the crumbling stucco and moist subtropical air. The Quarter doesn't look so different today, though it's a bit of a stretch to match Woodward's Bourbon Street of muddy, unpaved sidewalks and squat Creole cottages with today's version. Also on display is the masterful *Mother and Child in the Conservatory* (1906) from America's greatest Impressionist, **Mary Cassatt**, a typically intimate portrayal of the intense maternal bond. You'll also find one or two works each from names such as Magritte, Chagall, Picasso, Pollock, and Warhol, among other big-hitters.

An intriguing side-room is filled with the exquisite pieces of end-of-Empire decadence produced by Russian jeweller **Peter Carl Fabergé** and his contemporaries. Fabergé, commissioned in the mid-1880s by Tsar Nicholas II to make a precious decorated egg for his daughter, went on to design sixty ever more elaborate creations for the autocratic Russian court. The museum rotates its collection at regular intervals, and that first piece – an extravagant take on traditional Russian stacking dolls, with a silver egg containing a hinged jewelled chicken, sporting a gold crown, which, in turn, hides an emerald ring – may or may not be on show. You will see, however, other fantastical fairytale objects, including an 18-carat-gold tree holding 26 precious eggs, and humble dandelions and lilies magically transformed with platinum pods, gold stems, translucent nephrite leaves and seeds made from infinitesimal diamonds.

The NOMA **café**, whose picture windows overlook City Park's trees and lagoons, serves good coffee and lunches during museum hours.

NOMA Sculpture Garden

Behind the museum lies the impressive **NOMA Sculpture Garden** (same hours; free). Set in five landscaped acres of winding paths and lagoons, shaded by fat magnolias, richly scented jasmine, and ragged Spanish moss, many of the sculptures appear to have grown from the ground. One tree, strewn with giant necklaces, wittily evokes New Orleans' bead-bedecked branches left in the wake of Mardi Gras parades, while Louise Bourgeois' spindly giant spider seems as organic and gnarled as the venerable live oaks that surround it. Among works by such luminaries as Barbara Hepworth, Magritte, Isamu Noguchi, Alexander Calder and Henry Moore, Alison Saar's chilling *Travelin' Light* leaves a lasting impression – an African-American figure, cast in brass and hanging by his feet from a gallows, it tolls like a bell when you pull a chain at the back, its mournful call resounding through the park.

7

Faubourg Marigny, Bywater and the Ninth Ward

ust downriver from the French Quarter, across Esplanade Avenue, Faubourg Marigny is a happening, mixed and low-rent area of Creole cottages and shotguns populated by artists, musicians, and sundry bohemians. Its main drag and nightlife strip, **Frenchmen Street**, is a hugely popular place to hang out, revellers spilling out onto the streets, especially at the weekend and during festivals, to create a block party. For now the street keeps its edge, boasting some of New Orleans' best spots to hear live music, but recently its hipper – and hippier – credentials have been passed onto its neighbour, residential **Bywater**, another low-key, appealing artists' district. Bywater is officially part of the **Ninth Ward**, which, as one of the areas most drastically affected by the levee breaks and consequent flooding, has become a byword for the very worst of Katrina's horrors. The **Lower Ninth Ward**, in particular – downriver from the Industrial Canal – was particularly badly hit. A visit here, while a disquieting experience, can also be an inspiring one. Once a bustling neighbourhood, now battling against enormous odds to get back on its feet, the Lower Ninth has become a hauntingly surreal place, with new buildings, many of them financed by high-profile nonprofits, standing like sentinels of hope among a devastated landscape. There are ghosts in the Ninth Ward, certainly, and there is despair – but there is also no small amount of determination, hope, and even halting signs of joy.

Faubourg Marigny

The **Faubourg Marigny** – known more often as the Faubourg, or simply the Marigny – is named for the Creole Bernard de Marigny, a millionaire roué, expert duellist and gambler who in 1808, aged 18 and in drastic debt, divided his vast plantation into lots and sold them off. Many were bought by the planters, among them numerous free people of colour, who flooded the city in 1809 after the slave rebellions in Saint-Domingue (today's Haiti). By the 1820s, much of Esplanade and the Faubourg was populated by the free women of colour who,

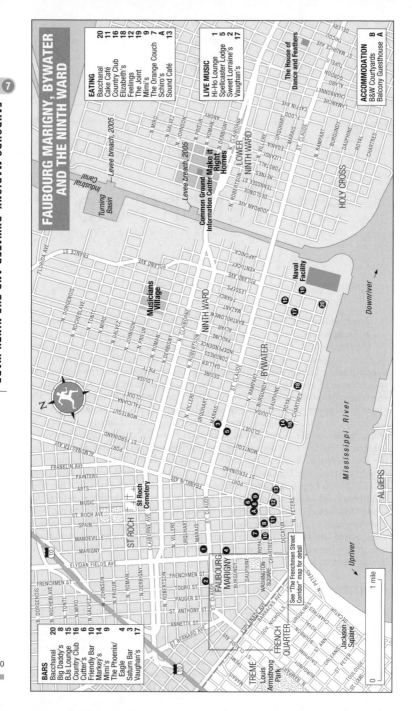

FAUBOURG MARIGNY, BYWATER AND THE NINTH WARD

BARS

Bacchanal	20
Big Daddy's	8
BJs Lounge	15
Country Club	16
Cutter's	6
Friendly Bar	10
Markey's	14
Mimi's	9
The Phoenix/	4
Eagle	3
Saturn Bar	17
Vaughan's	

EATING

Bacchanal	20
Cake Café	11
Country Club	16
Elizabeth's	18
Feelings	12
The Joint	19
Mimi's	9
The Orange Couch	7
Schiro's	A
Sound Café	13

LIVE MUSIC

Hi-Ho Lounge	1
Spellcaster Lodge	5
Sweet Lorraine's	2
Vaughan's	17

ACCOMMODATION

B&W Courtyards	B
Balcony Guesthouse	A

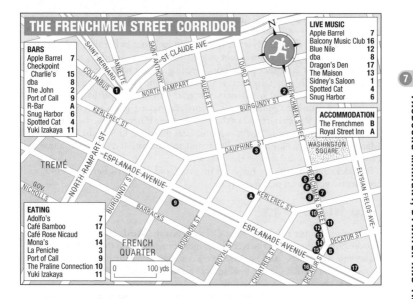

THE FRENCHMEN STREET CORRIDOR

BARS
Apple Barrel	7
Checkpoint Charlie's	15
dba	8
The John	2
Port of Call	9
R-Bar	A
Snug Harbor	6
Spotted Cat	4
Yuki Izakaya	11

LIVE MUSIC
Apple Barrel	7
Balcony Music Club	16
Blue Nile	12
dba	8
Dragon's Den	17
The Maison	13
Sidney's Saloon	1
Spotted Cat	4
Snug Harbor	6

ACCOMMODATION
The Frenchmen	B
Royal Street Inn	A

EATING
Adolfo's	7
Café Bamboo	17
Café Rose Nicaud	5
Mona's	14
La Peniche	3
Port of Call	9
The Praline Connection	10
Yuki Izakaya	11

under the semi-institutionalized system of plaçage (see p.221) lived with their French-speaking children in houses bought for them by their white "husbands".

The upriver boundary of the neighbourhood, forming its border with the French Quarter, **Esplanade Avenue** is a ravishing, if somewhat down-at-heel boulevard, lined with huge, twisted live oaks and decaying Italianate mansions. At the end of the nineteenth century, this was the grandest residential street in the declining Creole city; these days its faded glamour is part of its charm.

Beyond here lies **Frenchmen Street**, with its lively bars, clubs and good, inexpensive restaurants. Despite the bustle on this hipsters' drag, however, it's best not to wander too far beyond it after dark. The Faubourg, though largely safe, remains a marginal area; even **Elysian Fields Avenue** – where Stanley and Stella lived in Tennessee Williams' *A Streetcar Named Desire* – can feel dodgy, despite its heavenly name, with much of it neglected and depressingly bleak. Many residents get around by **bike**, and if you are going to be spending a lot of time in the neighbourhood it might be worth renting one yourself (see p.23). Frenchmen Street's **restaurants** are reviewed on p.130 and p.142, its **bars** on p.148, and its **live music** venues on p.157 and p.160.

Bywater

Spreading downriver from the Faubourg, **Bywater** began, like its neighbour, as a Creole suburb of the French Quarter and developed into a mixed, residential blue-collar neighbourhood. By the late 1990s, the cash-strapped bohos priced out of the French Quarter were drifting to the district's gorgeous Creole cottages and shotguns. Nowadays Bywater merges easily with the Faubourg while feeling just a tad more countercultural. Rather than the high-profile jazz clubs and bars of Frenchmen Street, here you will find yoga studios and artists' workshops sharing lots with radical grass-roots organizations and underground, offbeat little clubs. A few small galleries specialize in quirky art – the **Rusty Pelican Gallery**, for example, at 4031 St Claude Ave at Bartholomew (Wed–Fri noon–5pm, Sat & Sun noon–6pm; ☎218-5727, Ⓦrustypelicanart.com), whose offbeat and poignant sculptures are forged from the flotsam and jetsam of the Katrina-ravaged Ninth Ward. In general, though, Bywater is a place to hang out rather than sightsee. It is an easy place to enjoy as a visitor, not too self-conscious, and with a genuine, gentle bohemianism that is neither posey nor alienating. Along with the Ninth Ward, of which it is officially a part, Bywater is also the breeding ground for a super-cool but very inclusive **music and performance scene**; watch out in particular for gigs by organist/inventor Mr Quintron and his maraca-shaking puppeteer consort, Miss Pussycat. They, and characters like the New Orleans Bingo! Show, the Ninth Ward Rollergirls, the Society of St Anne Mardi Gras marching krewe, the Pussyfooters Marching Band, and Noisician Coalition sum up the creativity, skewed humour and eccentric chutzpah that defines the local scene.

Bywater's **restaurants** are reviewed on p.131 and p.142, its **bars** on p.149, and **live music venues** on p.157 and p.160.

The Ninth Ward

When most people think of New Orleans' **Ninth Ward**, and in particular the **Lower Ninth**, they recall the terrible images beamed around the world in the days following August 29, 2005: desperate residents pleading for help from bashed-in roofs, trapped for days in the searing heat above the deadly, stagnant floodwaters that swept through like a tsunami when the levees broke.

Shockingly, driving or biking through the Ninth Ward today, in a landscape that in places resembles a shantytown, the desolation remains all too apparent. That said, signs of life are beginning to appear. Some houses remain derelict: dark, dreadful holes that, it has to be suspected, may never again be filled. Others, gutted and expectant, await repairs, while a few are spruce and inhabited, their owners taking pride in their neat yards and porches. There's even a small museum, the

Out of the storm: post-Katrina art

From the Mardi Gras Indians meticulously sewing their fabulous suits to electropop eccentrics Quintron and Miss Pussycat, the Ninth Ward has always had a strong seam of creativity and artistic energy. Since Katrina, it has also given birth to some extraordinary site-specific art, its devastated terrain inspiring artists from the city and beyond. Much of the city-wide contemporary art biennale **Prospect1** (see p.177) was preoccupied with the neighbourhood's post-flood experience: installations set up on its ravaged streets included a huge beached ark made from materials salvaged after the storm, and **"Ms Sarah's House"**, created by artist Wangechi Mutu after she heard about Sarah Wester, the wife of Fats Domino's drummer, who was unable to rebuild her home after being defrauded, as happened to so many Ninth Ward residents, by a fly-by-night contractor. The "House", a skeleton frame suggesting a half-formed vision of a home, became a fundraising project to build a real house for Ms Wester; the finished house eventually became in itself the work of art. Meanwhile, in 2007 New Orleanians from throughout the city congregated at a makeshift outdoor stage at North Prieur and Reynes streets – the wasteland now being filled by Brad Pitt's modernist Make It Right homes (see opposite) – to watch local actor Wendell Pierce (Bunk in *The Wire*) in Beckett's **Waiting for Godot**, a play that could almost have been written for the place and the occasion, and that has historically been performed in troubled locations from San Quentin prison to Sarajevo. Since then, murals, sculptures and performance pieces have been created throughout the Ninth, some of them temporary, othes permanent, and all of them defiant signals that this historic, once vibrant district will not die.

▲ A Make It Right house

House of Dance and Feathers, celebrating the culture and traditions of the neighbourhood and determinedly acting as a beacon of hope for returning residents. Meanwhile signs for electricians, grass-cutters and construction businesses line the sides of the road like weeds; as you proceed further downriver into the Lower Ninth, however, where real weeds have been left to run rampant and grow head-high, it can be hard to remember you are in a city at all.

The Lower Ninth Ward

Crossing the Industrial Canal, whose levees broke so horrifyingly during Katrina, takes you into the **Lower Ninth Ward**, familiar from the acres of TV footage that revealed just how drastically the city was abandoned after the storm. This is one of the low-lying areas where the floods did their worst, and it was clear that, after the toxic soup had eventually drained away, the Lower Ninth – once a bustling blue-collar neighbourhood, populated by home-owners and families who had lived here all their lives, just as their parents and grandparents had done – could never be the same. Even those residents who had the money or wherewithal to come back – or could face coming back – found it almost impossible to heal the psychic devasta-tion of returning to a street where their home, or those of their neighbours, had been uprooted, smashed, drenched in toxic water and flung to the opposite side of the road.

Once you have crossed the canal, there is an almost palpable hush. Almost immediately you will see the **Make It Right** houses built by Brad Pitt's charity (see p.104): tall, modernist structures, they're incongruous but reassuring among the Lower Ninth's scrubby patchwork of empty lots, run-down trailers, and bare foundations. Beyond this stretch, things get quieter. Shadows on empty lots mark the spaces where houses once stood; in front, small hand-printed signs defiantly state "Roots run deep here". Many of these shadows, ghostly negatives, are fronted by three concrete steps – stoops, social spaces where neighbours once sat, talked and drank beer, that now lead to nowhere. Everything is eerily quiet, interrupted only by birdsong, the distant rumble of the expressway and, in certain pockets, the echoing clatter of construction workers. On a Sunday morning you may hear the hymns of a determined, if depleted, church congregation, gathered on garden chairs on a bare concrete foundation, raising their voices in hope above the silence.

7 Rebuilding the Ninth Ward

Rebuilding the Ninth Ward is a huge challenge. Many of the original population have been displaced forever, while others, attempting to return, still struggle with insurance claims, complex property-title issues, byzantine snafus regarding federal grants, difficulty in securing bank loans, and unreliable, if not corrupt, contractors. Despite early promises, the federal and city governments have done little to invest in a sustained rebuilding programme for this historic neighbourhood.

In the absence of any central plan, a gaggle of groups with good intentions and big ideas – private individuals, radical grassroots organizations, church groups, architects – have got busy, re-imagining, rebuilding, and remaking the environment. Probably the highest profile figure is Brad Pitt, who in 2006 established his **Make It Right** project, contacting a number of leading architects and sustainable development experts to design, in conjunction with community groups and displaced residents, safe, green housing in the Lower Ninth. Homes are built from sturdy, hurricane-resistant materials and produce as much energy as they consume; they also incorporate pragmatic elements such as easy internal access to the rooftop. Though they look startling – modernist arks raised on stilts, looming above a lonesome wasteland – to some extent they follow the same principles as the old neighbourhood, built on narrow lots not too far from their neighbours, and many of them with broad, sociable porches and traditional sloped roofs. Houses cost around $150,000 each, and are available to anyone who owned a home in the neighbourhood before the floods; Make It Right help out with interest-free open-ended loans and grants.

Founded in 2007, another nonprofit, **Build Now**, helps homeowners with everything from demolishing their old properties to sorting out the paperwork for rebuilding to actually erecting new homes. Rather than designing radical new structures, however, Build Now believes that old neighbourhoods should be rebuilt as they were in order to revive. The new Build Now homes closely resemble New Orleans' nineteenth-century shotguns, and are built on the same architectural logic, with natural ventilation, for example, provided by their transoms, tall ceilings, and porches.

Another key building project, organized by the construction charity **Habitat for Humanity** with the input of New Orleanians Branford Marsalis and Harry Connick Jr, is the **Musicians' Village** on Alvar and Prieur streets in the Upper Ninth Ward. These neat, small, raised cottages, each painted a different colour, with tidy front gardens and backyards, are available solely to musicians, providing not only housing for people who are traditionally among the city's least wealthy, but also a show of faith in New Orleans' precious musical heritage and a guarantee that it will be safeguarded for the future.

The Ninth Ward is evolving. It may never be, or even look like, what it once was, but, with the blast of a trumpet through an open window, the Sunday morning call of a preacher to his open-air congregation, and the hollers of children playing in its empty streets, there are signs it will thrive again.

If you are interested in **donating** time or money to help rebuild the Ninth Ward, check the following:

ⓦ www.buildnownola.com
ⓦ www.commongroundrelief.org
ⓦ www.habitat-nola.org
ⓦ www.lowernine.org
ⓦ www.makeitrightnola.org
ⓦ www.nolamusiciansvillage.org

The further towards the lake you go, however, the further behind you the city seems. Head as far as *Andry* and *Galvez* streets and you could almost be in the Mississippi Delta: grass grows to six feet high and above; shrubs thrust their way through old concrete foundations. Though the ghosts of civilization lie all around, nature has irrefutably taken over: egrets balance on rusty wire fences, while turtles creep dozily along the scarred and potholed roads.

The House of Dance and Feathers

In 2000, Rodney Lewis's wife, sick of the clutter in her home, gathered up her husband's Mardi Gras Indian memorabilia, scrapbooks and Second Line paraphernalia and threw them into the backyard. Incorrigible hoarder Lewis hurriedly bundled all his treasures into his garden shed, and thus was born the **House of Dance and Feathers**, a personal, eclectic collection that documents and preserves local black culture (call to arrange a visit; ☎957-2678). Lewis's home, and the shed/museum behind it, were ruined after the levees broke, but rebuilt by volunteer and nonprofit efforts. Today the museum, still in the backyard, looks more official than it once did: a small, modern building whose roof intentionally brings to mind the flood by sweeping up like a wave. Lewis' aim, much like Sylvester Francis' in Tremé's Backstreet Cultural Museum (see p.66), is to create a world of images, objects, and memories that celebrate his community and his ancestors, and like the Backstreet Cultural Museum, it is at once a personal, political and very powerful space. It also acts as a cornerstone for the Lower Ninth's rebuilding efforts, offering hope and inspiration for residents determined to reconstruct not only their homes and their lives but also their culture. Much space is devoted to the Mardi Gras Indians (see p.166) and Social Aid and Pleasure Clubs (see p.68) – rainbow-coloured Indian "suits" and headdresses, with their vast plumes of feathers and intricately stitched panels, hang from the rafters, while smart, handstitched shoes sported by parading Club members are displayed in glass cases. Wider in scope is the assemblage of photos, mementoes and personal objects which cover everything from domestic life in the Lower Ninth to artworks from the wider African diaspora. Bringing the whole place to life is Lewis himself – with his lively stories and insightful histories, embodying the pride, the fortitude and the sheer guts of the Lower Ninth.

The Cemeteries

Though picking your way through a crumbling, overgrown graveyard may sound more like a nightmare than a dream vacation, New Orleans' above-ground **cemeteries**, scattered throughout the city, are fascinating places. They're known as "Cities of the Dead", and amid their tangled pathways, lopsided marble-fronted tombs and decaying monuments to long-forgotten families, the city's history and folklore, and its strange love affair with death, seem to come alive.

New Orleans' **first settlers** buried their dead underground. This set-up wasn't ideal, however; so much of the city is at, or below, sea level that every time the city flooded waves of mouldy coffins would float to the surface of the sodden earth. Meanwhile, as the colony grew, so did the **death rate**, reaching a peak in 1783 when a yellow fever epidemic wiped out fifty percent of the population. With dismal sanitation, infections brought by sailors arriving from the Caribbean and fever-carrying mosquitoes proliferating in stagnant swamps and cisterns, the hot, filthy city was a breeding ground for disease.

Believing that germs were carried in miasmas emitted by decaying bodies, New Orleanians began to build their cemeteries outside the city limits, where, in traditional European style, bodies were stored in **above-ground** brick and stucco vaults, or in smaller vaults packed into the walls. Not only did this protect the coffins from flooding, but also it meant families could reuse tombs – a felony in other US states, but still legal in New Orleans.

By the **antebellum** period, New Orleans had the highest mortality rate in the country: in the summer of 1853 alone some 11,000 people – one tenth of the population – died from **yellow fever**. Meanwhile, a booming economy and a fad for French funerary design, as perfected in Père Lachaise cemetery in Paris, led to a demand for increasingly ornate resting places. The finest architects were commissioned to build tombs in various decorative styles, from Baroque and neo-Gothic to Italianate and Neoclassical. Many were set in little gardens surrounded by cast-iron railings, with benches where families could greet friends on All Saints' Day (see opposite). Wide avenues, designed to accommodate grand funeral processions, divided the cemeteries into blocks.

Family tombs stood two or more storeys high. The first coffin, placed on the top level, would remain there until the death of another family member, when it would be shifted down to the next level, and so on, until all levels were filled. After a year and a day, with the heat and humidity having sped up decomposition, the first body could be removed from its coffin, and the desiccated remains and ashes poked down into the damp pit at the base of the tomb. Eventually, the remains of numerous family members would be mixed together in this *caveau*, as the long lists of names on the tombs attest.

Bodies could also be stored in rented **wall vaults**, which followed the same "year and a day" principle but held only one coffin at a time. Jewish families built tombs in **copings** – elevated, walled frames containing soil, allowing the body to be buried in the earth, as the religion demands, and above ground, as geography dictates. The largest, most ornate tombs, with dozens of vaults, belong to New Orleans' many nineteenth-century mutual aid and **benevolent societies**; it was the African-American fraternal societies that popularized the city's famed **jazz funerals**, ritualized parades that bestow the highest honour upon the deceased (see p.110).

Because the marble enclosure tablets needed to be kept clear for the long lists of names, epitaphs are rare – as if to compensate, there's an overload of **symbolism** throughout the cemeteries, with a profusion of broken columns (signifying a life cut short), winged hourglasses (the passage of time), roses with broken stems, or arrows pointing downwards (death), rosebuds (the death of a child, also represented by lambs), and waterlilies (death while pregnant or in childbirth).

Visiting and safety

Though part of the thrill of venturing into the Cities of the Dead is fuelled by the vampires-and-witches tales of once-local horror author Anne Rice, many of which refer to specific cemetery locations, a real **danger** comes from a different source – the threat of being mugged, or worse. Though statistically the likelihood that you'll be attacked is slim, it nonetheless exists, and you should thus *always* visit the cemeteries on a guided tour. Many city tours include a quick jaunt around at least one of them, but if you're interested in more than an overview, contact **Save Our Cemeteries**, whose profits are donated to much-needed restoration work, or **Historic New Orleans Walking Tours** (for both, see p.24).

All Saints' and All Souls'

In New Orleans, **All Saints' Day** (November 1), the Catholic day of holy obligation when respect is paid to saints and martyrs, is traditionally when families would come to whitewash and repaint their tombs, trim the grass and shrubbery, and add fresh flowers – especially the long-lasting and vibrant yellow chrysanthemums and red coxcombs – to their plots. Well into the twentieth century this was a lively social occasion, when old friends, settling down on the iron benches with picnics, would exchange news and gossip. Orphans and nuns sold pralines and fruit outside the gates, while stallholders hawked raisin-filled "funeral pies" and hard Italian almond cookies called **ossi de muerte**, or bones of the dead – you'll still find both in the city's bakeries at the end of October.

Nowadays, though older New Orleanians still pay tribute to their ancestors, the All Saints' tradition is evolving. People still tend their family tombs at the end of October – you will see more candles flickering, more fresh flowers, and more rosary beads strung around the statuary around this time of year – but not necessarily on the day itself, and while devout Catholics are sure to attend afternoon mass, said by priests who drive along the ceremonial alleys sprinkling holy water on the tombs, few make a day of it. Of the cemeteries detailed in this chapter, **St Roch** is the liveliest on All Saints', the day when former residents return to reconnect with their childhoods and their old community. Outside the cemeteries All Saints' – along with **All Souls' Day** (November 2), the day of remembrance for those souls who have not been sainted – does not go unmarked, either. Voodoo rituals, parties and arts events are held throughout town, while in Tremé, a Second Line devoted to deceased neighbourhood figures winds through the streets before ending up at the Backstreet Cultural Museum (see p.66).

The most touristed cemeteries are **Lafayette No. 1**, in the Garden District opposite *Commander's Palace* restaurant (see p.134), and **St Louis No. 1**, on the border of Tremé and the French Quarter near the Iberville housing project. **St Louis No. 2**, a few blocks away, surrounded by the Iberville projects, and **St Louis No. 3**, out in Mid-City near City Park, are less visited. **St Roch**, in the Bywater, has an intriguing chapel but isn't on the cemetery tours' itineraries; take a cab and visit in a group.

Lafayette No. 1

Lafayette Cemetery (Mon–Fri 7.30am–2.30pm, Sat 7.30am–noon; free), in the heart of the Garden District at 1400 Washington Ave, was built in 1833 for the wealthy, Anglo-American population of Lafayette City (see p.84). The place was filled to capacity by 1852; in that year alone two thousand yellow fever victims were buried here.

Today, Lafayette No. 1 is a moody place, its wide intersecting avenues swathed with overgrown foliage. Many of the tombs are sinking into the gunge below, and as the soft red brick cracks and the marble tablets buckle, some of them are slowly opening, revealing the *caveau* within. It's no surprise that all this decaying grandeur should capture the imagination of author **Anne Rice**, who for many years lived nearby and used the place in a number of her novels – in 1995, she even staged a mock jazz funeral here to launch publication of *Memnoch the Devil*; the "corpse" was herself, dressed in an antique wedding dress, in an open coffin carried by pallbearers.

St Louis No. 1

St Louis No. 1 (Mon–Sat 9am–3pm, Sun 9am–noon; free), 400 Basin St between Conti and St Louis streets, is the oldest cemetery in the Mississippi valley. It was built in 1789, outside the city limits in an attempt to protect the population from the fatal fumes they believed emanated from corpses, and its tombs vary from early Spanish structures made of brick and plaster to later mausoleums designed by eminent architects including Benjamin Latrobe and Jacques de Pouilly. Its position on the lakeside fringe of the French Quarter makes the cemetery a regular stop on the tour-bus circuit. There is invariably a huddle of people by the simple tomb of "voodoo queen" **Marie Laveau** (see p.52), graffitied with countless brick-dust crosses. They're usually being told some tall tale about how, if you knock on the slab three times and mark a cross on her tomb, her spirit will grant you any favour. The family who own it have asked that this bogus, destructive tradition should stop, not least because people are taking chunks of brick from other tombs to make the crosses. Voodoo practitioners – responsible for the candles, plastic flowers, beads and rum bottles surrounding the plot – deplore the practice, too, regarding it as a desecration that chases Laveau's spirit away. Nearby, the enormous circular white marble structure topped by a cross and angel is the 1857 **Italian Benevolent Society** mausoleum, which has space for thousands of remains. This is where Peter Fonda and Dennis Hopper writhed and sobbed in their LSD-induced hell in the movie *Easy Rider*; local gossip has it that the tomb's headless statue of Charity was decapitated by a crazed Hopper during filming.

The Barbarin family tomb, belonging to one of the city's great jazz dynasties, was designated in 2004 as a **Musicians' Tomb**, providing space for those poor black New Orleanians who would otherwise be relegated to a pauper's grave. The first non-family member to be laid to rest here was Lloyd Washington, vocalist in the Ink Spots, in 2004.

▲ St Louis No.1

St Louis's other famous dead include the city's first African-American mayor, **Ernest "Dutch" Morial**, and **Homer Plessy**, whose refusal in 1892 to move from the whites-only section of a train led to the historic Plessy vs Ferguson case. His defeat gave rise to the Supreme Court's "separate but equal" ruling, which effectively stripped blacks of the civil rights they had won during Reconstruction and established segregation in the South for another sixty years.

St Louis No. 2

St Louis No. 2 (Mon–Sat 9am–3pm, Sun 9am–noon; free), 200 N Claiborne Ave between Iberville and St Louis streets, is one of the most desolate of the Cities of the Dead, hemmed in between Tremé's Iberville housing project and the interstate. Built in 1823, it's a prime example of local cemetery design, with a dead-straight

The jazz funeral

Rooted in the city's long tradition of military brass band parades, African processions and vibrant street culture, the **jazz funeral** is unique to New Orleans. "Funerals with music" actually pre-date jazz, having emerged in the 1840s when decorous marching bands, black and white, would parade through the streets playing brass instruments from sheet music. Jazz funerals as we recognize them today evolved at the end of the nineteenth century, when Reconstruction's erosion of the rights of black citizens prompted a corresponding boom in black benevolent and mutual aid societies (see p.107). For a small fee, society members could guarantee themselves a fine, celebratory funeral – one way to maintain pride and a sense of community in the face of Jim Crow degradations. Meanwhile, jazz was emerging, and while the parades kept the old hymns and dirges, they began to see a more improvisational, looser playing style. By the start of World War II, these musical funerals had become almost entirely black.

Jazz funerals were led by brass bands who, after playing dirges and hymns on the route to the cemetery would offer a slow drum roll as the body was taken away to be interred, a moment known as "turning the body loose". Parades were directed by a strutting **Grand Marshall** – whose formal dress included a stuffed white dove on one shoulder, to represent the soaring spirit of the deceased – and other standard bearers, kitted out in sashes and gloves. The band, officials and close family were followed by a "**Second Line**", mourners, neighbours and stragglers alike, who joined the funeral as it paraded through the streets. Once the body was in the ground, the band, moving away from the cemetery, would burst into a joyful tune – sometimes irreverent, like "I'll Be Glad When You're Dead, You Rascal You" – to mark the start of the celebration ritual. Marshalls and officials would dance their elegant, ritualized steps, while Second Liners caroused and waved handkerchiefs above their heads to represent the end of wiping away tears.

Post-war, New Orleans' parade tradition dwindled. Not only did the benevolent societies decrease in importance (though their social function remained; see p.69), but also by the 1970s many older band players had died and few young musicians were taking their place. The brass band renaissance was largely due to banjoist-composer **Danny Barker**, who returned to New Orleans in the mid-60s after thirty years in New York, and through a local church taught youngsters not only to play the music but also to honour the spirit of the old marching bands. As the music revived, so did the street culture, and parading came back in force. During the late 1980s,

centre aisle, and many grandiose Greek Revival mausoleums, designed by de Pouilly. A second **Marie Laveau**, believed to be the famed voodoo queen's daughter, has a tomb here – daubed with red-chalk crosses, like the original in St Louis No. 1 – as do Baratarian smuggler **Dominique You** and his friend **Mayor Nicholas Girod**, who plotted together to return Napoleon from exile (see p.43).

More recently, St Louis No. 2 has become the resting place for some of Tremé's most important cultural guardians. Mardi Gras Indian chief **Tootie Montana**, whose 52 years of masking Indian (see p.166), passionate championing of the black Indian tradition, and enormous, dazzling 3-D "suits", earned him the title of "Chief of Chiefs", was buried here after suffering a fatal heart attack while addressing the city council about police harassment of Indians. His jazz funeral, in July 2005, saw a rainbow of feathers, sequins and rhinestones take to the streets of Tremé as dozens of Indian gangs, dressed in their finery, came together to chant, play percussion and dance their respects to this proud warrior. Also here is eccentric local R&B star **Ernie K-Doe**, the self-named "Emperor of the Universe", who was interred in 2001 after the largest jazz funeral and Second Line New Orleans has ever seen, attracting 5000 celebrants. Two years later this however, a new kind of jazz funeral emerged. Faced with the rise of crack cocaine, savage drug wars and a staggering number of gang-related deaths, families in the projects began to call upon hip young bands like the **ReBirth** and the Soul Rebels to play at the funerals of their peers. The bands sometimes joined the funeral party for just a few blocks, leading the way to the victim's home, a corner where they used to hang out, or even the spot where they were killed. Unlike in earlier funerals, the bands played furious, fast-paced music, sometimes foregoing the dirges altogether, and the Second Line predominated, with noisy mourners drinking heavily and spraying beer over the coffin (not an insult, but an honour derived from African funerary rituals in which drinks are poured into the ground for the dead to enjoy in the afterlife). The potential for violence seemed such that when Barker died in 1994 his family announced there would be no jazz funeral – though they were eventually persuaded to change their minds by the many musicians who wanted to pay homage to their teacher and mentor.

Today, the jazz funeral is alive and well, although in transition. As the outside world becomes increasingly intrigued by New Orleans' street culture – in part due to the visibility brought by Katrina – in the city itself debate rages among commentators, musicians and historians: to many, the legacy of the so-called "crack funerals", and the gradual disappearance of the dirges represent the loss of a crucial spiritual element. Others recognize a deep spiritual continuity even as the tradition evolves, welcoming the infusion of hip-hop and rap stylings into a ritual that can trace its ancestry back to African slaves. Meanwhile, while white New Orleans whoops it up at tacky mock-funerals – to mark divorces and liquidations, to promote book launches and conferences – genuine jazz funerals are still held on the streets of **Tremé** for musicians, local Mardi Gras Indians and even Second Liners. While it's inappropriate for tourists to gatecrash the more local events, everyone is welcome to the larger, higher-profile funerals – held for well-known musicians, for example. There is no better way to pay your respects: dancing in the streets as a celebration of both life and death offers not only an intimate approach to understanding this exceptionally spiritual city, but also an unforgettable, profoundly personal, experience.

For more about **Second Line parades**, which are closely related to jazz funerals, see p.68.

quintessential New Orleans character was joined by his friend, dynamic R&B guitarist **Earl King**, and then, in 2009, by his one-of-a-kind wife and champion **Miss Antoinette**, who died at their Tremé *Mother-in-Law Lounge* (see p.150) on Mardi Gras day that year.

St Louis No. 3

Built in 1856 on the site of a leper colony, **St Louis No. 3** (daily 10am–3pm; free), in Mid-City at 3421 Esplanade Ave, is a peaceful and well-kept burial ground; all the **priests** of the diocese are buried here, and fragile angels balance on top of the tombs. It also holds the family tomb of **James Gallier Jr**, designed by the architect himself, and that of photographer **E.J. Bellocq**, whose remarkable images of the Storyville prostitutes (see p.65) have become icons of a lost era. One stretch, dubbed for obvious reasons "Chefs' Corner", holds the tombs of fine old **restaurant dynasties** the Tujagues, Prudhommes and Galatoires. Mardi Gras Indian **Donald Harrison Sr**, Chief of the Guardians of the Flame tribe and father of the well-known jazz saxophonist Donald Harrison Jr, was also entombed here in 1999. Harrison was one of the best loved and respected of the old chiefs, whose

8

▲ St Louis No.3

tireless work to earn recognition for the Indians took him from lecture tours in the public schools of New Orleans to the reservation of the Seneca tribe.

St Roch

Dedicated in honour of the patron saint of plagues after the local congregation was saved from the 1867 yellow fever epidemic, **St Roch cemetery**, 1725 St Roch Ave (Mon–Sat 9am–3pm, Sun 9am–noon; free) sits out in the arty though crumbling (and not always safe) district of the same name near Bywater. Also known as the Campo Santo, the cemetery is particularly notable for its little Gothic Revival chapel, finished in 1876. This shiveringly damp space is an intriguing spectacle, its small side room paved with bricks printed with "Merci" or "Thanks", and lined with ex-votos thanking the saint – or appealing to him – for his intervention in curing ailments. Given in the same spirit as the silver milagros found in Hispanic churches, here the offerings include plaster replicas of body parts, including eyeballs, teeth and hearts, along with calipers, shoes, spectacles and the like, many of them strewn with rosaries. The odd plastic offering – ears, dentures, doll parts – adds to the eeriness.

Listings

Listings

Accommodation

N ew Orleans has some lovely **places to stay**, from rambling old guesthouses seeping faded grandeur to hip boutique hotels in restored historic
buildings. **Standard room rates**, never low (you'll be pushed to find
anything half decent advertised for less than $75 a night), increase
considerably for Mardi Gras, Jazz Fest and major football games. At other times,
and especially during summer weekdays, when things slow down, it's worth
checking hotel websites for, or calling and asking about, **special promotions**. It's
a fiercely competitive market post-Katrina, and you will probably find, or be able
to negotiate, prices far lower than quoted rates. (Always call to confirm with the
hotel direct the rate you'll be actually paying.)

This is not a city where you want to be stranded without a room, and though it's
possible to take a chance on last-minute cancellations and deals, you should ideally
make **reservations** in advance. This is especially true during the big festivals and
special events and at weekends throughout the year. (Note also that some places,
especially in the Quarter, require **minimum stays** during special events.)
However, if you do turn up on spec, head immediately for the **Welcome Center**
on Jackson Square (see p.28), which has racks of **discount leaflets** offering savings
on same-day bookings (generally weekdays only).

Most people choose to pay a bit more to stay in the **French Quarter**, in the heart
of things. Many accommodations here are in **guesthouses**, the majority of them
in old Creole cottages or townhouses, furnished with antiques. These are some of
the most beautiful and atmospheric lodgings in the city, ranging from shabbily
decadent places with iffy plumbing and the odd insect to romantic honeymooners'
hideaways. In any one place, rooms can vary considerably in size, comfort, and
amenities, so be specific if you have certain preferences – and ask for a room away
from the street if you want peace and quiet. The odd few can be dark and a little
musty inside – in the Creole tradition, they're shaded from the heat, sun and rain
by lush patios and cranky wooden shutters – but many also have courtyards,
balconies, verandas and pools. Bear in mind that the city is still in recovery, and
that housekeeping can, occasionally, be eccentric. None of the guesthouses we've
listed below should be dirty, but you may have to ask if you want your linens
changed daily during a two-night stay, for example. Very few hotels offer free
on-site **parking** (those that offer any kind of parking are mentioned below), and
Quarter car parks are outrageously expensive. Many visitors choose to leave their
car in one of the lots down by the river for the duration.

If you prefer to stay outside the Quarter – if you're on a very tight budget, say,
or want to base yourself somewhere less intense – there are a number of possibilities
throughout town. The **Garden District** offers a handful of budget options near the
streetcar line, while the funky **Faubourg Marigny** specializes in friendly, affordable bed and breakfasts – many of them gay-owned – and **Uptown** has a couple of

gorgeous old places in historic buildings. The **CBD** is the domain of the city's upmarket boutique and chain hotels, catering mostly to conventioneers. These are much of a muchness – and unless you hook a special deal, you can usually find better value elsewhere – but we've reviewed the best of them in this chapter.

If you want to get **out of the city** altogether, many of the grand old plantation homes strung along the River Road offer B&B accommodation; they're reviewed in the "Out of the city" chapter (see p.203).

Rates shown here represent the standard prices quoted by the hotels, and refer to the least expensive double rooms available for weekdays between October and May outside of festival times. Especially in the bigger, more expensive hotels, however, where rates are subject to all sorts of web-only deals and promotions, they should be taken as a guideline only; prices change on a daily basis and are often dependent on occupancy. Always do your research online. Where places offer a choice of en-suite rooms and rooms with shared bath, we quote rates for both. Costs shown do not include the **room tax**, which varies between 11 and 13 percent depending on the size of the hotel.

The French Quarter

All the following places are marked on the map on pp.34–35.

Biscuit Palace 730 Dumaine St at Bourbon ☏525-9949, ⓦ www.biscuitpalace.com. Well-run, friendly and charming guesthouse in a good central location, named for the vintage biscuit ad painted on its outside wall. It's housed in an 1820 mansion, complete with a pretty flagstoned courtyard, fish pond and tropical plants. The eight rooms, with balconies and antique baths, are spacious and creatively decorated, and there's a two-room attic apartment that sleeps six. From $105; from $115 with front balcony.

Bon Maison Guesthouse 835 Bourbon St at St Ann ☏561-8498, ⓦ www.bonmaison.com. Hidden from the road and laid out around a brick courtyard, this Creole townhouse has been converted into a laid-back, no-fuss, non-smoking guesthouse. The atmosphere is peaceful, considering its location, partly because there are just five suites, all with baths and tiny kitchenettes, and some with balconies. It's particularly popular with gay guests, but everyone is welcome – though children are not allowed. $95–145 for two guests, $165 for three, $175 for four.

Bourgoyne Guest House 839 Bourbon St at Dumaine ☏524-3621, ⓦ www.bourgoynehouse .com. Good-value guesthouse in an 1830s Creole mansion, furnished with homely antiques. There are two kinds of accommodation: five worn but cosy studios (with small kitchenettes) around the subtropical

courtyard, and two fancier suites. The plum is the rather lovely Green Suite, accessed by a sweeping staircase, and boasting two bedrooms, a kitchen, parlour, and Bourbon Street balcony (which can, of course, make it noisy, depending on when you're here). Studios $92; Green Suite $130.

Chateau Hotel 1001 Chartres St at St Philip ☏524-9636, ⓦ www.chateauhotel.com. All the rooms are comfortable in this simple, clean hotel in the quieter part of the Quarter, but some are far better than others, so if you feel yours is too small or a tad dark, ask to see what else is available. The attractive, plant-filled brick courtyard is a boon, with a pretty (if small) pool. Rates include continental breakfast (which you can have in your room or the courtyard) and a free daily paper. Valet parking $16 per day. From $110.

Cornstalk Hotel 915 Royal St at Dumaine ☏523-1515 or 1-800/759-6112, ⓦ www .cornstalkhotel.com. Casually elegant, somewhat faded place in a turreted Queen Anne house, surrounded by a landmark cast-iron fence decorated with fat cornstalks. The twelve appealing, high-ceilinged rooms are each individually furnished with antiques and have lots of period detail. They vary considerably in size, but all have showers, and some have baths. Free wi-fi. From $140.

Dauphine Orleans 415 Dauphine St at Conti ☏586-1800 or 1-800/521-7111, ⓦ www .dauphineorleans.com. A historic complex of buildings with more than one hundred nonsmoking, good-looking, quite upmarket rooms. The best are set in brick cottages around tranquil, palm-filled patios and have their own jacuzzis. There's a pretty outdoor saltwater pool, a gym, snug bar (once the site of a brothel) and library. Rates include welcome cocktails, a hearty breakfast, and afternoon tea. Free wi-fi. On-site valet parking $28 per day. From $130.

Hotel Monteleone 214 Royal St at Iberville ☎523-3341 or 1-800/535-9595, ⓦwww .hotelmonteleone.com. This handsome French Quarter landmark is the oldest hotel in the city, owned by the same family since 1886, and hosting a fine array of writers and luminaries since then. At sixteen storeys, it's also the tallest building in the Quarter, something of a gentle giant towering over genteel Royal Street. It has been restored and modernized somewhat over the years – and now has more than 600 rooms – but manages to keep its distinctive character with a handsome baroque facade, stunning old marble lobby, comfy rooms, and the atmospheric revolving *Carousel* bar (see p.146). There's a small gym and a heated rooftop pool, and pets are welcome. From $180.

Olivier House 828 Toulouse St at Bourbon ☎525-8456 or 1-866/525-9748, ⓦwww .olivierhouse.com. Though a bit dark in places, this atmospheric, quintessentially New Orleans guesthouse offers good value and real character. It's a family-run place, spread across three handsome Creole townhouses with a warren of corridors,

▲ *Olivier House*

balconies and stairwells. The 42 rooms (all with bath and kitchenettes) vary considerably in size and quality, but most of them are appealingly old-fashioned, with funky antique furniture, chandeliers, plush sofas, tall, shuttered windows, and some have small patios. It's worth negotiating about rates; if money's no object, go for the two-storey Garden Suite, which has its own internal tropical garden and fountain. There's a courtyard, and a tiny pool. Free valet parking in a small lot nearby. From $100.

Omni Royal Orleans 621 St Louis St at Royal ☎529-5333, ⓦwww.omnihotels.com. Large, landmark French Quarter hotel, built on the site of one of the key hotels of the Creole city (see p.47). Very upmarket without being snooty, it has an old-fashioned New Orleans elegance that never intimidates, with very comfortable rooms and wonderfully low-key service. The rooftop pool is lovely. From $170.

Place d'Armes 625 St Ann St at Chartres ☎1-800/366-2743, ⓦwww.placedarmes.com. There's nothing special at this friendly (and very kid-friendly) hotel, but you can get good online rates and the location, behind Jackson Square, is superb. The eighty or so slightly faded standard hotel rooms, in a complex of restored nineteenth-century buildings set around a courtyard and a pool, vary hugely in quality – some have no windows – so discuss your needs in advance. They also serve a satisfying complimentary continental breakfast, which you can eat in the breakfast room, courtyard or your room. From $99.

Prince Conti 830 Conti St at Dauphine ☎1-800/366-2743, ⓦwww.princecontihotel .com. This quiet French Quarter hotel, owned by the same people as the Place d'Armes, offers very affordable promotional rates at non-busy times. Rooms can be tiny or huge, but many of them have charm, with brick walls and high ceilings. The free continental breakfast is nothing to shout about, though. Free wi-fi. From $89.

Hotel Provincial 1024 Chartres St at Ursulines ☎581-4995 or 1-800/535-7922, ⓦwww .hotelprovincial.com. Set in a quiet part of the Quarter, this sprawling – yet somehow intimate and relaxed – place has nearly one hundred rooms, many of which open onto one of five peaceful, gaslit courtyards. Some are filled with antiques, others are more ordinary, but the whole place has a welcoming feel. There are two nice outdoor pools (but avoid rooms nearby if you mind the noise), and a fancy restaurant, *Stella!* (see p.130) on site. Booking in advance through the website gets you good deals, and if you turn up without a reservation you may find leaflets offering low weekday rates in the Welcome Center (see p.28). Free wi-fi and complimentary continental breakfast. On-site valet parking $22 per night. From $99.

Le Richelieu 1234 Chartres St at Barracks ⊤529-2492 or 1-800/535-9653, ⊛www .lerichelieuhotel.com. Handsome hotel in a restored factory and neighbouring townhouse. Though the old-world ambience of the lovely lobby is not continued in the rather ordinary rooms, they are nonetheless comfortable and clean, and staff are extremely friendly. There's a small (unheated) outdoor pool overlooked by a café serving light meals and coffee, and, uniquely, free on-site self parking. They also offer a baby-sitting service. Free wi-fi. From $99.

St Peter House Hotel 1005 St Peter St at Burgundy ⊤1-800/535-7815, ⊛www .stpeterhouse.com. Thirty or so darkish, budget rooms – some set around a courtyard, others with access to the wrap-around balcony – popular with a mixed gay and straight clientele. Though it's certainly basic – and can be noisy if you're staying at the front – it's efficiently run, and has a certain macabre cachet if you're into that kind of thing: Johnny Thunders of the New York Dolls died here in suspicious circumstances in 1991. From $79.

Soniat House 1133 Chartres St at Gov Nicholls ⊤522-0570, ⊛www.soniathouse.com. There's something magical about the *Soniat House*, where a warren of stunning, antique-filled rooms are scattered throughout the carriage houses and main buildings of two peaceful Creole townhouses. Rates are high, but you are paying for a particular kind of luxury here: not fussy, nor pretentious, nor showy, but simply laid out for you to share. The service is kindly and refreshingly laidback; unless asked they may well not even tell you about the free wi-fi, honour bar system, or hot biscuits and fresh coffee breakfast that you can eat in your room ($12.50 per person). The owners' quirky but impeccable taste and the buildings' venerable history aren't crammed down your throats, either: you'll feel as relaxed and comfy as the

sleepy hotel cat, whether lazing in rooms filled with nineteenth-century French books and bold Creole art, eating warm biscuits on your flower-filled balcony, or enjoying a drink in the sweetly candlelit flagstoned carriageway. From $200.

Ursuline Guest House 708 Ursulines St at Royal ⊤525-8509 or 1-800/654-2351, ⊛ursulineguesthouse.com. Not a place for people who like to be alone; the laid-back *Ursuline* is friendly, sociable and occasionally noisy, with impromptu get-togethers in the courtyard. Some of the sixteen individually furnished and decorated rooms, all of which have baths (and one of which has bunk beds), open onto a broad gallery or the courtyard (which has a clothing-optional jacuzzi). Rates include continental breakfast and a nightly wine and cheese party. From $100; $59 for bunk-bed room.

Hotel Villa Convento 616 Ursulines St at Chartres ⊤522-1793, ⊛www.villaconvento .com. You can take the buggy-drivers' insistence that this is the original House of the Rising Sun with a pinch of salt. It is, however, a friendly, family-run place with the feel of an old European boarding house and a loyal band of repeat visitors. The public spaces are rather shabby, as are some of the furnishings, but the 25 no-frills rooms are clean and comfortable; some have very small balconies, while others open onto a patio, and there are a few budget options. From $89.

W Hotel French Quarter 310 Chartres St at Bienville ⊤581-1200, ⊛www.whotels.com. Smaller and slightly less pretentious than its CBD counterpart (at 333 Poydras St), this boutique branch of the *W* chain offers the usual concept, with modern rooms, a trendy bar – the "Living Room" – in-room CD- and DVD-players, and even a dash of local flavour in the New Orleans courtyard. Despite the shop-bought style, however, this is really a business hotel, geared toward expense-account travellers. There's a nice pool and a superb nouvelle Italian restaurant, *Bacco*, on site (see p.124). From $130.

Tremé

The following places are marked on the map on p.64.

Garlands Historic Cottages 1129 St Philip St at N Rampart ⊤523-1372, ⊛www .garlandsguesthouse.com. Lovely luxury B&B

footsteps from the Quarter. With one- to four-bedroom cottages and one- and two-bedroom suites, accommodation ranges from cosy to palatial; the whole place is extremely tasteful and romantic. The delicious full breakfast, which you can eat in the garden (which also has a little hot tub), is a plus. Free onsite parking. From $115.

New Orleans Guest House 1118 Ursulines St at N Rampart ☎566-1177, ⊛www.neworleans .com/nogh/. The flamingo pink decor, carried through from the exterior into the courtyard, may not be to everyone's taste, but this gay-friendly guesthouse offers cheery B&B (breakfast is a croissant and coffee) in slightly faded rooms at good rates. Free onsite parking. From $89.

CBD and Warehouse District

The following places are marked on the map on p.72.

Drury Inn and Suites 820 Poydras St at Caron-delet ☎529-7800, ⊛www.druryhotels.com. Though it offers zero New Orleans character, if you're after a good-value, reliable chain hotel, this is your best CBD bet. Rooms are small and adequate, service is efficient, and they offer lots of nice freebies: a hot breakfast; early evening drinks and snacks; an hour's worth of long-distance phone calls per day; and free wi-fi. There's also a small heated rooftop pool. Parking $17 per night, which is reasonable for the area. From $99.

International House 221 Camp St at Gravier ☎553-9550 or 1-800/633-5770, ⊛www.ihhotel .com. Contemporary boutique hotel in a beautifully restored Beaux Arts bank building. Beyond the swish design and stultifyingly cool vibe – the whole place seems to be trying just a bit *too* hard – it does at least attempt to engage with its location, changing its decor to fit in with the season or the latest local festival. The smallish, very beige guest rooms are comfortable, lined with photos of jazz musicians, but those facing the street can be noisy. *Loa*, the candlelit lobby bar, fills with beautiful people as the night proceeds. Good rates available online. From $119.

Lafayette Hotel 600 St Charles Ave at Girod ☎524-4441, ⊛www.thelafayettehotel.com. Gently faded, with more than a hint of shabby French chic, the *Lafayette*, which has been in operation since 1916, has a tad

more character than many CBD hotels, and is quiet. It's worth looking out for good online deals here, but otherwise you may well find better value elsewhere; the best rooms have been newly renovated – ask when you book. From $119.

Loft 523 523 Gravier St at Magazine ☎200-6523, ⊛www.loft523.com. If you can swallow the pretension – "an urban canvas that sets the design muse free" – and are after a huge, modern, room, *Loft 523*, in an 1880 warehouse building, might fit the bill. Designed to within an inch of their lives, the lofts are comfortable and minimal; but be sure to ask for one as far away from the noisy downstairs club/bar, *Phare* (see p.150) as possible. From $129.

The Lower Garden District and Garden District

The following places are marked on the map on p.86.

AAE Bourbon House 1660 Annunciation St at Market ☎1-304/268-8981, ⊛bourbon.aaeworld hotels.com. This very friendly budget place in the Lower Garden District is the newest of the city's hostels, open since 2008. With mixed and single-sex dorms and inexpensive private rooms sleeping one to eight, it has its plusses and minusses – while there is no soap in the common bathrooms, for example, they are, at least, clean. Common rooms can be scruffy, but they offer a decent pancake breakfast and free daytime pick-up and drop-off to the train/bus stations. At busy times, like Mardi Gras, they add airbeds in the dorms ($42) and offer limited tent space ($35). There is a small surcharge for paying by credit card. Free wi-fi. Dorm beds $16; doubles from $35.

McKendrick-Breaux House 1474 Magazine St at Race ☎586-1700 or 1-888/570-1700, ⊛www .mckendrick-breaux.com. Quiet B&B with just nine rooms in a restored nineteenth-century home. The large, antique-filled rooms are prettily decorated; all have baths (clawfoot tubs abound) and some feature galleries overlooking the patio (which has a jacuzzi). Rates include a good continental breakfast. Free off-street parking. From $125.

Prytania Park Hotel 1525 Prytania St at Terpsi-chore ☎524-0427 or 1-800/862-1984, ⊛www .prytaniaparkhotel.com. One of the Lower Garden District's better deals, the *Prytania*

Park is popular with business travellers (though the wi-fi is patchy), and attracts quite a bit of repeat business. It's an unusual place with a selection of historic and modern rooms spread across four buildings, including lofts that sleep four or five. All rooms have fridges and microwaves; rates include a simple continental breakfast, which you can eat in the small courtyard, and free parking. Rates vary widely, but you can find some excellent prices via their site; in addition, the Welcome Center (see p.28) on Jackson Square usually has brochures detailing weekday discounts. From $79.

St Vincent's Guest House **1507 Magazine St at Race** T 302-9606, W www.stvguesthouse.com. Budget Lower Garden District lodging with more than seventy simple rooms with private bath, in a huge 1861 orphanage. The atmosphere is cheery, if a little institutional, and some rooms are far better than others. Rates include breakfast, served in the pretty, very friendly restaurant. There's a pool, too, but don't expect luxury: you get what you pay for. Dorms from $20; doubles from $45.

Uptown

The following places are marked on the map on pp.88–89.

Best Western St Charles Inn **3636 St Charles Ave at Foucher** T 899-8888, W www .bestwesternlouisiana.com. This small (forty-room) *Best Western* offers reliable, if unexciting, accommodation in a prime location just beyond the Garden District, right by the streetcar stop. Staff are friendly and efficient, and rates include a decent continental breakfast and free covered parking. From $110.

Chimes B&B **1146 Constantinople St at Coliseum** T 899-2621, W www .chimesneworleans.com. You're in a pretty part of town at this peaceful, arty, casually stylish B&B mid-way between Magazine Street and the St Charles streetcar. Each of the five rooms – all with their own private entrance from the gorgeous courtyard – is comfortable, light and airy, beautifully furnished without being fussy, and full of intriguing period detail. The charming hosts rustle up a nice European-style breakfast, too. Free off-street parking. From $110.

Columns Hotel **3811 St Charles Ave at General Taylor** T 899-9308 or 1-800/445-9308, W www.thecolumns.com. Deliciously atmospheric, quirky hotel in a stately 1883 Italianate mansion right on the streetcar line. Standing in for a Storyville bordello in the 1977 movie *Pretty Baby*, the whole place seeps louche glamour, especially the faded Victorian bar (see p.151) and the veranda, with its stately namesake columns; both are essentials on any drinking itinerary. The nineteen rooms vary widely – some are decorated on themes, some come with four-poster beds, some are bordering on shabby, others have balconies and fabulous views of St Charles Avenue – but all have hardwood floors and antique furnishings. There are no TVs, and most rooms have showers only, with no tub. A complimentary full breakfast is served in their little tearoom, but it's not fantastic. Rates increase enormously at Mardi Gras, due to its excellent parade-viewing location on the Avenue. From $120.

Park View Guest House **7004 St Charles Ave at Walnut** T 861-7564, W www.parkviewguest house.com. Built for the 1884 Cotton Exposition, this 21-room B&B on the edge of Audubon Park has an appealing, lived-in feel, with lofty ceilings, mismatched furniture, hardwood floors and a roomy veranda. Rooms are comfortable, if a little uninspired; many have balconies and views of the park. Rates include a good cooked breakfast. Free wi-fi. From $125.

Esplanade Ridge and Mid-City

The following places are marked on the map on pp.94–95.

Ashton's B&B **2023 Esplanade Ave at N Johnson** T 942-7048, W www .ashtonsbb.com. Luxurious yet homey B&B in a Greek Revival mansion with eight gorgeous rooms. Each has its own character, immaculately decorated with antiques and personal touches; those in the main building are larger and more expensive than the cosier rooms in the patio wing. Some have clawfoot tubs, others whirlpools. The gourmet breakfasts will set you up for the day. Free wi-fi. From $130.

Degas House B&B **2306 Esplanade Ave at N Tonti** T 821-5009, W www.degashouse.com. Art-fans will love this guesthouse, which was the family home of Edgar Degas's maternal relatives, and where the artist lived and painted for a few months in 1872–73 (see p.93). The small details are lovely – chocolates, fruit and cheese, and fresh flowers in your room to greet you – but the main appeal is its sense of history. Cheapest are the "garret" rooms, set in the eaves, which have no windows, but sleep three people. Be sure to take a free tour of the whole property, which is now split into two, to see where and what the artist painted while he lived here. From $150.

India House Hostel 124 S Lopez St at Canal ☎821-1904, ⓦwww.indiahousehostel.com. The Mid-City location of this funky, somewhat run-down backpackers' hostel, a little away from the heart of things – except during Jazz Fest and Voodoo Fest – doesn't seem to bother its young, enthusiastic crowd, and the Canal Street streetcar is close by. Owned and run by keen travellers, it's probably the most sociable, and booziest, of the hostels, with TV, DVD, and Playstation, the occasional jam session, crawfish boils, and regular rowdy pool parties. Accommodation is in mixed and single-sex dorms, with a few basic rooms with ensuite or shared baths. The area isn't great at night. Free wi-fi. Dorms $17–20; rooms from $45 (shared) or $55 (en-suite).

Faubourg Marigny and Bywater

Most of the hotels reviewed here are shown on the map on p.100; those on or near Frenchmen Street are shown on the map on p.101.

B&W Courtyards 2425 Chartres St at Mandeville ☎945-9418, ⓦwww.bandwcourtyards.com. Welcoming, homey and stylish B&B with six rooms – all different, and with lovely artistic flourishes – surrounding the small, tranquil courtyards with a gently burbling fountain and hot tub. The continental breakfast is light but tasty, and provides an opportunity

to hang out with the friendly, informative owners. No children. Free wi-fi. From $130.

Balcony Guesthouse 2483 Royal St at St Roch ☎945-4425, ⓦwww.balconyguesthouse.com. Live like a local in a great spot right in the heart of the Faubourg Marigny – four blocks from Frenchmen Street – above a popular neighbourhood grocery/café, *Schiro's* (see p.132). The four rooms, though basic and not exactly spacious, are quite stylish, with hardwood floors and sleigh beds; two have doors out onto the communal wraparound balcony, which can also be accessed from the shared parlour. Rates include a full breakfast during the week and a continental breakfast on Sun. Free wi-fi. From $99.

The Frenchmen 417 Frenchmen St at Decatur ☎1-800/831-1781, ⓦwww.frenchmenhotel .com. Basic Faubourg Marigny guesthouse right on Frenchmen (avoid streetside rooms if you are bothered by noise at night), with a variety of rooms, from tiny to spacious, spread across two 1860 townhouses. There's a patio, a small pool, and a hot tub, but it's not fancy, and can be noisy. Rates include continental breakfast. Free wi-fi. From $90.

Royal Street Inn 1431 Royal St at Kerlerec ☎948-7499, ⓦwww.royalstreetinn.com. This good-value, funky Faubourg Marigny lodging sits right above the *R-Bar* (see p.149), footsteps from Frenchmen Street, and is run by the same people. Quirky New Orleans style meets big-city boutique hip in the five suites (some with balconies) with their stripped wooden floors, bare brick walls and leather sofas; all have bath, DVD players, iPod docks and free wi-fi. It's favoured by a young crowd who hang out in the bar, and can be noisy at weekends, but the comfort, location, and the price, can't be bettered. Rates include one free drink per person at the bar. From $75.

Eating

New Orleans is a gourmand's dream. Many visitors come here for the restaurants alone, while locals will spend hours arguing about where to find the fattest po-boy, the briniest raw oysters or the tastiest gumbo. Post-Katrina, the halting reappearance of some of the city's most beloved eating places, many of them simple, family-owned joints or generations-old holes in the wall, made headline news here and, occasionally, around the nation. Never had it been clearer that in New Orleans restaurants are far more than places to eat: from the haughtiest *grandes dames* of Creole cuisine right down to rough-and-ready po-boy shacks, they are fiercely cherished as the guardians of community, culture and heritage. While many restaurants will never return, others have come back with a vengeance, and, fired with a passion for their city, have, if anything raised their game. Today once more the comings, goings and latest creations of local celebrity chefs are daily gossip, and food festivals litter the calendar.

When deciding **where to eat** it can be difficult to choose between the city's fabulous special-occasion restaurants and its many neighbourhood joints. Indeed, some of the best food in the city is served in scruffy little dives that you'd barely give a second glance elsewhere. That said, the atmosphere alone at New Orleans' swankiest, **old-guard restaurants** – including *Brennan's, Commander's Palace* and *Galatoire's* – all of which serve haute-Creole cuisine in elegant, jacket-and-tie surroundings, makes it worth splashing out for a special occasion. Many of them are owned by members of the extended Brennan family, a dynasty that has ruled the city's dining roost since the 1950s. Though this is a city that values well-loved tradition far above modernity for its own sake, occasionally a few vibrant, **cutting-edge restaurants** have established themselves, with ambitious young chefs throwing even more influences – Fusion, Asian, and, in particular, Latin American – into the pot. Now that TV darling Emeril Lagasse – who stormed the restaurant scene in the 1990s after cutting his teeth at *Commander's* – has taken his place in the ranks of grand old men of New Orleans cooking, chefs such as Susan Spicer (*Bayona*), Donald Link (*Cochon, Herbsaint*), Scott Boswell (*Stella!*), and John Besh (*August, Lüke, The American Sector*) have risen up to take his crown. A significant post-Katrina trend, interestingly, is the increasing number of restaurants serving beautifully executed **Southern-style homecooking** – pulled pork, shrimp and grits, chicken and dumplings: perfect comfort food for a city that is still very much in need of it.

New Orleans also has a number of good places to eat **Black Creole** cuisine. These, while they may resemble soul food restaurants – and dish up amazingly good fried chicken, collard greens, and the like – also offer a distinctively different

For more on the specifics of **Creole cuisine**, see the Big Easy cuisine colour section. And for a full **glossary** of New Orleans' unique **food terms**, see p.246.

Don't miss...

For a true New Orleans experience, don't miss:

Cannoli at **Angelo Brocato**	see p.141
Grit fries at **Boucherie**	see p.135
Sweetbreads and duck gumbo at **Bayona**	see p.124
Raw oysters on the half-shell at **Casamento's**	see p.136
Boudin balls at **Cochon**	see p.133
Jambalaya at **Coop's**	see p.125
Chargrilled oysters at **Felix's**	see p.126
Lunch and a *café brûlot* at **Galatoire's**	see p.126
"Da Bomb" po-boy at **Guy's**	see p.137
Cream of nectar with condensed milk sno-ball at **Hansen's Sno Bliz**	see p.141
Alligator sausage cheesecake at **Jacques Imo's**	see p.137
Barbecue shrimp po-boy at **Liuzza's By The Track**	see p.138
Early drinks and antipasto at **Napoleon House**	see p.129
Ya-ka-mein at a **Second Line**	see p.248
Fried chicken at **Willie Mae's Scotch House**	see p.139

(10)

EATING | Restaurants

range of African-influenced dishes, including gumbos and fried seafood, that can only be found here. Meanwhile, although New Orleans does have a couple of good **Cajun** restaurants, little of what most places call Cajun cooking has much in common with the one-pot country food, cooked in a very dark roux, that is dished up along the bayous. After all, despite the nonstop accordion music that jangles from the tackiest tourist shops, New Orleans is not actually in Cajun country, which lies well to the west and southwest. Famed local chefs Paul Prudhomme (*K-Paul's Louisiana Kitchen*) and Donald Link (*Cochon, Herbsaint*) may hail from Cajun country, but their restaurants offer a more sophisticated, Creolized take on its cuisine.

Vegetarians need to be careful at Creole restaurants; even dishes that sound innocent – red beans and rice, collard greens – will probably yield fat chunks of smoked sausage or ham hocks, or will at the very least have been stewed with some juicy lump of flesh. The best bets are **ethnic** places – African, Middle Eastern and Indian – of which the city has a few. New Orleans' significant **Vietnamese** community, largely based in the east of the city, also has an increasingly high profile on the restaurant scene; Vietnamese bakeries, in particular, are prized for their po-boy bread.

Gratifyingly, **prices** are not that high compared to other US cities – even at a fancy restaurant you could get away with $50 per head for a three-course feast with wine. Lunch, in particular, can be a bargain, especially at the more upmarket places. And if you're on a really tight budget, don't despair: one of the great pleasures of New Orleans' dining scene is the scores of excellent neighbourhood joints serving colossal portions at low prices.

New Orleans' best **coffeehouses**, most of which serve light lunches and snacks, are reviewed on pp.139–142. For **picnic food**, turn to the reviews of delis and food stores on p.143.

Restaurants

No neighbourhood can rival the **French Quarter** for sheer volume and variety of eating options, its narrow old streets jam-packed with everything from downhome dives to old-guard dining rooms serving glorious haute cuisine. If you can drag yourself away from the Quarter, your best bet for a special occasion is one of the smarter restaurants in the **CBD**, **Garden District** or **uptown**. At the other end of the scale you'll find a clutch of funky neighbourhood joints in the **Faubourg**, **Bywater**, and **Lower Garden District**, and a crop of good inexpensive restaurants in the studenty **Riverbend** area uptown. You should head out to **Mid-City** for at least one meal: much of this blue-collar neighbourhood was practically wiped out by the floods, and the fact that so many old family-owned restaurants have re-opened is testimony not only to the city's passion for good home-cooked food, but also to its fierce sense of community. These are the places that make New Orleans special, as much as any of the grand old Creole dining rooms, and breaking bread at any one of them is to pay respects.

The French Quarter

The places reviewed here are shown on the map on pp.34–35. For coffeehouses, delis, and food stores, see p.139.

Acme Oyster House 724 Iberville St at Bourbon ☎522-5973, ⓦwww.acmeoyster.com. Sun–Thurs 11am–10pm, Fri & Sat 11am–11pm. With its checked tablecloths, tangle of neon signs, marble-topped oyster bar and fast, smart-talking staff, this noisy, touristy place has been the French Quarter hangout for raw oysters and ice-cold beer for generations. A dozen briny bivalves on the half-shell costs $10.99, or you can get a fried platter (with fries and a side dish) for around $15.99. In season, don't miss the fresh, buttery mudbugs, boiled in a delicious, pepper-hot stock. Or try the gut-busting medley of gumbo, jambalaya, and red beans and rice with sausage ($11.99) – not the finest in the city, but unbelievably filling.

Bacco 310 Chartres St at Bienville, in the W hotel ☎522-2426, ⓦwww.bacco.com. Sun–Thurs 11.30am–2pm & 6–9pm, Fri & Sat 11.30am–2pm & 6–10pm. Elegant, unstuffy nouvelle Italian – all Venetian chandeliers, Gothic-style iron arches, and ivory-coloured booths scrawled with Italian love proclamations – owned by Ralph Brennan of the city's top restaurant clan. It's upscale, but not always expensive, especially at lunch, when there's a two-course pasta deal for $15, and a three-course prix-fixe for around $25 (with which you can also get astonishingly tangy 10¢ martinis). Dinner can set you back, however (entrées $19–34), and the tasty homemade pasta can be pricey. Good appetizers include vermouth-steamed mussels ($11.50), and the black truffle fettuccine ($13.50) while for an entrée you could try the wood-oven-roasted Gulf

shrimp ($21.50). Reservations recommended for dinner.

Bayona 430 Dauphine St at Conti ☎525-4455, ⓦwww.bayona.com. Mon & Tues 6–11pm, Wed–Sat 11.30am–2pm & 6–11pm. Splendid, romantic restaurant in a seventeenth-century Creole cottage. The lovely patio, complete with fountain, feels more relaxed than the more formal dining rooms, though the service throughout is charming. Superchef Susan Spicer creates unfussy "global cuisine", using organic ingredients and giving local staples an Asian, Southwestern or European twist. It's all great, but the best dishes are the simplest: the garlic soup, meltingly good sweetbreads, and lamb dishes are out of this world. The wine list is excellent, too, with more than 250 selections from around the world. Best of all is lunch, when you can get three courses for less than $30, or even a dazzling grilled cashew butter, duck, and pepper jelly sandwich with crisp apple slaw for a staggeringly low $11 (you could easily spend as much as this on a far less classy po-boy at the cheap-and-cheerful *Johnny's*; see p.128). Reservations recommended for dinner.

Bennachin 1212 Royal St at Barracks ☎504/522-1230. Sun–Thurs 11am–9pm, Fri & Sat 11am–10pm. Historically, New Orleans owes a lot to West Africa, including much of its traditional cuisine. In this informal, family-run, neighbourhood restaurant, the hefty portions of inexpensive, delicious food from Cameroon and Gambia bring Creole food right back to its roots. The long menu abounds in inexpensive treats – the black-eyed-bean fritters, peanut-infused stews, grilled fish in ginger sauce, and sautéed spinach with coconut rice and plantains are all good bets, while the iced ginger-honey tea is a treat on a steamy New Orleans evening. Avoid the shrimp, however, which tends to be uninteresting. Lunch specials (before 3pm, for around $8) are a very good deal. They're often busy, with the tiny open kitchen cooking up food to take out as well as eat in, so be prepared to sit back and wait awhile. This should be no problem, especially if you get the prime seating on the sofa by the window. BYOB. No credit cards.

Brennan's 417 Royal St at Conti ☎ 525-9711, Ⓦ www.brennansneworleans.com. Mon–Fri 9am–1pm & 6–9pm, Sat & Sun 9am–2pm & 6–9pm. Historic, formal Creole restaurant, the first in the city's Brennan empire, with a dozen dining rooms and a tropical courtyard. It's famed for its long, luxurious breakfasts (served until 2.30pm) – choose from more than twenty poached-egg dishes, hair-of-the-dog cocktails, grillades and grits, and the like. Though locals balk at spending $50 on eggs, tourists can't get enough of the place. Dinner proves better value, with four-course prix-fixe meals for $48. The lengthy menu includes turtle and oyster soups, shrimp *sardou* (with an artichoke, creamed spinach, and hollandaise sauce), the definitive Bananas Foster (see p.246), and wonderful *café brûlot*, while the wine list runs to 65 pages. Dress up and reserve.

Café Angeli 1141 Decatur St at Gov Nicholls ☎ 504/566-0077. Open daily till late. A hit with French Quarter night owls, this big, open, dimly lit room is virtually an extension of the Lower Decatur scene outside. Picture windows allow diners to see and be seen, while cult movies flicker across the wall above the bar. The inexpensive Mediterranean salads, sandwiches, fresh pizzas, and pasta won't blow you away, but there are some good veggie options and this can be a convenient stop-off on a wild night out.

Clover Grill 900 Bourbon St at Dumaine ☎ 598-1010, Ⓦ www.clovergrill.com. Daily 24hr. Camp all-night diner – "We love to fry and it shows" – with retro counter seating and a few booths, usually crowded with a gay Bourbon Street clientele filling up on fries, burgers (from $5.50), omelettes ($5 with hashbrowns or grits and toast), pork chops and eggs ($8) and shakes. It's always lively and can get rowdy: come for a post bar-crawl breakfast of waffles, pancakes or Froot Loops, then sit back and enjoy the scene.

Coop's 1109 Decatur St at Ursulines ☎ 525-9053, Ⓦ www.coopsplace.net. Sun–Thurs 11am–2am, Fri & Sat 11am–3am (bar open later). *Coop's* is a merry fixture on the heavy-drinking, late-night, Lower Decatur bar scene, a dark-wood dive with locals folded over the round bar, a handful of rickety tables and leatherette booths, and a pretty grey cat keeping everything in order. It's a good place to drink, but the amazing surprise is the truly delicious food. This is gourmet stuff, at ridiculous prices – the jambalaya, with rabbit and tasso, costs just $10, as do three pieces of crispy fried chicken, with the jambalaya as a side dish. The "Taste of Coop's", meanwhile, gets you a tasty seafood gumbo packed with fat oysters, shrimp Creole, jambalaya, red beans and rice, *and* spicy crispy fried chicken for an astonishing $13. You simply can't go wrong here.

Country Flame 620 Iberville St at Exchange Alley ☎ 522-1138. Daily 11am–8.30pm. To say this friendly little Mexican/Cuban place is grungey would be an understatement, but the burritos, enchiladas, fajitas, and chimichangas aren't bad for the price (all around $7), and the Cuban specialities – including *ropa vieja* (shredded beef or chicken in red sauce with rice and black beans; $7.75); or the *puerco frito* with yucca ($10) are substantial and authentic. Avoid the chips and salsa, though.

Court of Two Sisters 613 Royal St between St Peter and Toulouse ☎ 522-7261, Ⓦ www .courtoftwosisters.com. Brunch daily 9am–3pm. New Orleans' only daily jazz brunch, where a Dixieland trio plays 45-minute sets in a big, wisteria-draped brick courtyard, and visitors gorge themselves on the all-you-can-eat buffet of local specialities including spicy oysters, turtle soup, sweet potato with andouille, Bananas Foster, and bread pudding, along with mounds of boiled seafood. It's a tourist trap, and certainly not gourmet, but tasty and very reasonably priced at $28 for all you can eat. Reserve.

Eat NO 900 Dumaine at Dauphine ☎ 522-7222, Ⓦ www.eatnola.com. Tues–Fri 11am–2pm & 5.30–10pm, Sat 9am–2pm & 5.30–10pm, Sun 9am–2pm. Modern Southern (shrimp and grits, fried green tomatoes, and the like) and contemporary American food served in a relaxed, airy corner space with huge picture windows, cool blue walls and fresh flowers on each table. Though you can find dining rooms like this in most major cities, the sunny simplicity makes a change from the Quarter's overriding Creole aesthetic, and has a soothing effect. Locals flock here for Sunday brunch; although the menu looks pricey ($8 for a granola starter, $11 for a spinach and artichoke omelette), the portions are huge – the granola, packed with fruit and nuts, is a meal in itself – and lovingly prepared. For lunch and dinner you can get similarly simple home-style dishes such as pot-roasted chicken, a side and a salad, for $16. BYOB.

Felix's Oyster House 739 Iberville St at Bourbon ☏522-4440, ⊛www.felixs.com. Mon–Thurs & Sun 10am–10pm, Fri & Sat 10am–midnight. Just across the road from the *Acme*, but less crowded and more relaxed, *Felix's* is something of a secret. Their raw oysters on the half-shell are as fresh and delicious as their rival's – and slightly cheaper – and they also offer a broader range of seafood dishes (fabulous chargrilled oysters, oysters Rockefeller, seafood gumbo, crawfish cakes) along with some very tasty local favourites (don't miss the succulent blackened alligator with sweet potato fries) in friendly, unfussy surroundings. Good po-boys, too.

Fiorella's 45 French Market Place/1136 Decatur St at Gov Nicholls ☏528-9566. Mon & Thurs–Sun noon–9pm. You can ignore the po-boys, the red beans and rice, and the fried seafood platters. There are just two things to go for – if your cholesterol levels can take it – at this rough-and-ready French Market diner: the fried pickles appetizer (crispy thin, salty, and deliciously herby), followed by the Southern fried chicken ($8.95–12.75 with beans, fries or mash).

Galatoire's 209 Bourbon St at Iberville ☏525-2021, ⊛www.galatoires.com. Closed Mon. If you want to eat at one of the *grandes dames* of Creole cuisine, make it this, Tennessee Williams' favourite

▲ *Café brûlot* at *Galatoire's*

restaurant, open on this spot since 1905. With its dark wood panelling, black-and-white tiled floor, ceiling fans, and antique mirror-lined walls, it's quintessential old New Orleans – elegant, relaxed, and not at all stuffy. Prices (from $10 for an appetizer, around $25 for a main, and sides extra at $7) mount, but you are paying for the experience here as much as the rich, indulgent French-influenced food. It's best at lunchtime, on Friday or Sunday especially, when you can join the city's old guard (gents in seersucker, Southern belles in pearls) whiling away long, convivial hours gorging on dishes like turtle soup, oysters Rockefeller, shrimp *rémoulade*, and crabmeat *sardou* (huge chunks of lumpmeat with an artichoke, creamed spinach and hollandaise sauce). Mingling between tables is common, with the crusty old waiters keeping everyone in order. Finish with a fragrant *café brûlot*, prepared tableside. Reservations are taken only for the less atmospheric, upstairs room, so arrive

The Farmers Market

As well as selling fresh produce (see p.42), the French Quarter **Farmers Market**, an extension of the French Market, is also a good place to head for reasonably priced Creole homecooking, dished up at counter seating among the food stalls. Whether you fancy an alligator and crawfish sausage on a stick or a substantial softshell crab dinner, head along here to see what's on offer.

early and be prepared to wait; lines often snake out into the incongruously rough-and-ready setting of Bourbon Street, which is all part of the fun. Jackets required after 5pm and all day Sunday.

Galvez 912 N Peters St at Decatur ☎585-1400, Ⓦwww.galvezrestaurant.com. Tues–Sun 5–10pm, Sun brunch 11am. Given that New Orleans lies so low, a restaurant needs to be up at least one flight of stairs and directly next to the water to have any chance of river views – which is one of Galvez's great advantages. Huge picture windows let you watch the river traffic drift by as you eat, and on a warm evening the outdoor terrace is one of the most romantic spots in the city. Food is regional Spanish, with a good selection of tapas (empanadas, clams in white wine, shrimp ceviche) from $7, and an à la carte menu featuring caldo gallego (Galician green broth; $8) and sopa de ajo (garlic soup; $8) alongside the more familiar gazpacho ($5) and paella (from $18). The white sangria is refreshing, and they have some nice albariño wines from Galicia, too.

Green Goddess 307 Exchange Alley at Bienville ☎301-3347, Ⓦwww.green goddessnola.com. Mon–Wed 11am–4pm, Thurs–Sun 11am–4pm & 5pm–midnight. Don't be misled by the name – this is no whole earth veggie café, but instead a gorgeous, relaxed restaurant devoted to the richest sensory pleasures imaginable. It's tiny, with a few outdoor tables, some counter seating beside the open kitchen, and just four tables inside, but diners are more than willing to wait. From the Deco-influenced decor to the mismatched crockery, everything exudes a laid-back stylishness, but it's the food, a kind of contemporary Creole-Mediterranean-Southern fusion, using amazingly fresh ingredients, that steals the show. Menus change seasonally, but brunch ($7–14) might include light cactus chilaquiles with poached egg and salsa verde, or the richer blue corn crepes with the rare huitlacoche corn fungus, lobster mushrooms and brandy ragout. For lunch, don't miss the stupendous garlicky barbecue shrimp with grits ($14); dinner could be foie gras with black rice and blood orange pepper jelly ($13) or smoked duck and chestnut pasta ($17). Excellent sides include a mean manchego grits ($5) and sweet potato biscuits with orange honey butter ($3), while

to finish, the ciabatta French toast with chocolate and sweet cheese is irresistible. It's also a lovely place to come for a drink (see p.147) and an artisan cheese plate. No reservations.

Gumbo Shop 630 St Peter St at Chartres ☎525-1486, Ⓦwww.gumboshop.com. Sun–Thurs 11am–10.30pm, Fri & Sat 11am–11pm. Though it's not gourmet food, this touristy Creole restaurant is a relaxed, convivial spot for a quick lunch or to fill up before a night out, housed in an eighteenth-century building lined with murals of old New Orleans. Naturally the gumbo – seafood, chicken and andouille, or z'herbes – is the highlight; dark, subtly flavoured, and excellent value ($5). Entrées are good, too – try the crawfish étouffé, or the succulent blackened grilled catfish smothered with shrimp Creole (both $15.99); for vegetarians, the white beans and rice are a tasty, satisfying option. The complete Creole dinners, three courses plus side dish for $24, are a bargain.

Irene's Cuisine 539 St Philip St at Chartres ☎529-8811. Mon–Sat 5.30–10pm. There are only limited reservations available at this intimate, lively old Creole-Italian place, long treasured by local diners, so lines – and waits – can be very long indeed. No one minds: settling down in the comfy piano bar with a good Italian wine is part of the experi-ence. The dining room itself, lined with bookshelves and paintings, is just as cosy, with elbow-to-elbow-packed diners tucking into garlicky roast chicken rosemarino ($17.90), seafood and fish, or rich pasta dishes. Prices are slightly on the high side, but you're paying partly for the ambience and the sense of in-the-know satisfaction.

Iris 321 N Peters St at Conti in the Bienville House hotel ☎299-3944, Ⓦwww .irisneworleans.com. Mon, Wed & Sat 6–11pm, Thurs & Fri 11.30am–2pm & 6–11pm. If you're craving white linen table-cloths, smart New American cuisine, and superb service, but don't want to break the bank, this chic, unstuffy little hotel restaurant will hit the spot at lunchtime, when it offers a superb two-course-plus-sorbet prix-fixe lunch for $20. The appetizers – mussels with coconut curry broth, fresh summer rolls, smoky baby octopus with arugula and citrus – are especially tasty, while mains revolve around light white fish or richer meat dishes.

Johnny's Po-Boys 511 St Louis St at Decatur
☎524-8129, ⊛johnnyspoboy.com. Mon–Fri
9am–3pm, Sat & Sun 8am–4pm. A French
Quarter institution for four generations, this
no-frills, checkered-tablecloth joint feels like
a cheap find, though actually prices aren't
all that low. Still, it's a nice, bustling place to
get a po-boy fix, and is heaving at lunchtime
with local workers and loyal repeat-visit
tourists. It's famed for its po-boys, of
course, made to order – the mind-boggling
choice of fillings (around fifty; $6–14)
includes pork chop, French fries, chicken
Parmesan, boudin, oysters, roast beef, and
alligator – but they also serve breakfasts
and plate lunches ($7.50–10). Prepare to
wait at lunchtime, or call for local deliveries.
No credit cards.

K-Paul's Louisiana Kitchen 416 Chartres St at
Conti ☎596-2530, ⊛www.kpauls.com. Mon–
Wed 5.30–10.30pm,Thurs–Sat 11am–2pm
& 5.30–10.30pm. Renowned, rustic-smart
restaurant serving the delicious "blackened"
cuisine, slathered in butter and spices, introduced to the nation by Cajun chef Paul
Prudhomme in the 1980s. If you like your
food heavy, rich, and full of complex
flavours you'll love it here. Highlights among
dinner entrées (around $30) include the
insanely good bronzed swordfish with "Hot
Fanny" sauce – roasted pecans, jalapeños,
veal glaze, and garlic butter. Gumbos are
good, too: try the chicken and andouille.
You may prefer to come for the "deli lunch"
(reservations not taken), when prices are far
lower (po-boys from $9; $11 for plate
lunches like sticky chicken or shrimp
grillades with bacon and parmesan grits),
and there's time afterwards to walk it all off.

Maximo's 1117 Decatur St at Ursulines
☎586-8883, ⊛www.maximosgrill.com. Mon–
Thurs 6–11pm, Fri & Sat 6pm–midnight,
Sun 3–10pm. Pricey northern Italian food in
a slick urban bistro, with counter seating,
booths, and moody black-and-white
photos. It's especially busy at weekends,
when people pile in to eat late. Entrées start
at $20: you can't go wrong with the pasta,
especially penne crawfish diablo in a zippy
cream sauce ($21.95), and any of the veal
dishes (from $23; osso bucco $35). There
are around fifty good Italian wines on the list
of hundreds, many of them served by the
glass.

Meauxbar Bistro 942 N Rampart at St Philip
☎569-9979, ⊛www.meauxbar.com. Tues–Sat

6–10pm. Though the French-accented food
– *moules marinières*, bouillabaisse, duck
confit – is good, it's not the primary reason
for heading to this neighbourhood bistro, a
soothingly pared-down space at the furthest
reaches of the Upper Quarter, decorated
with just a few big mirrors, simple prints,
and globe lights. Its slightly upscale, unfussy
vibe offers a comfortable place to hang out
and kick back, whether you fancy a burger
or pan-fried frogs' legs. Appetizers $7–14,
entrées $12–28.

Mona Lisa 1212 Royal St at Barracks
☎522-6746. Tues & Wed 5–10pm, Thurs–
Mon 11am–10pm. Candlelit at night, with
brick walls, cobblestone floors, and endless
kitschy renditions of the mysterious Mona,
this funky, cosy place is a favourite with
Quarterites. You can get pasta, sandwiches,
and salads – along with daily specials like
butternut squash soup ($3) or tapenade
($4.50). The pizzas, though, are the best
thing here; try the Mediterranean, with
spinach, feta, garlic, olives, and sun-dried
tomatoes. A 12in ($11–15) is more than
enough for two. Free delivery in the Quarter
and Faubourg.

Moon Wok 800 Dauphine St at St Ann
☎523-6910. Mon, Tues, Thurs & Sun
11am–8.45pm, Fri & Sat 11am–9.45pm. If
you're after something very-cheap-and-
quite-cheerful, this ramshackle Vietnamese-
Chinese diner (the only place for Chinese
food in the Quarter) is a good bet, with big
bowls of phô ($6) and various vermicelli
bowls with peanuts, shallots, and greens
(from $6.95). At lunch it's the haunt of
penny-pinching locals and a few stray
tourists, while evening diners are usually
filling up before a big night out. BYOB.

Mr B's Bistro 201 Royal St at Iberville
☎523-6727, ⊛www.mrbsbistro.com.
Mon–Sat 11.30am–2pm & 5.30–9pm, Sun
10.30am–2pm (jazz brunch) & 5.30–9pm.
Another Brennans' winner: a casually chic
brasserie-bistro with dark-wood booths, lots
of etched glass, a relaxed, chatty buzz and
spectacular food. It's difficult to choose from
the star-studded contemporary Creole
menu: the garlic chicken ($21) is the city's
finest, served drowned in a satiny reduction.
The same accolade could go to the delec-
table barbecue shrimp ($24.50) in sloppy,
rich, buttery sauce – they tie the bib around
your neck for good reason. Other signature
dishes include gumbo ya-ya with chicken

and andouille ($8) and Creole bread pudding with whisky sauce ($7). Prices can mount if you order wine, but lunch is good value. Walk-ins are welcome.

Napoleon House 500 Chartres St at St Louis ☎524-9752, ⓦwww.napoleon house.com. Mon 11am–5.30pm, Tues–Thurs 11am–10pm, Fri & Sat 11am–11pm. This ravishing, historic old place – all crumbling walls and shadowy corners – is one of the best bars in the nation (see p.147). Since 1914 it has been owned and run by the same Italian family, and though their fabulous full-service bistro has yet to re-open post-Katrina, the old-timer bow-tied waiters continue to serve their nice bar/café menu. Everyone comes for the muffulettas, which they heat up to melt the cheese and mellow the flavours, but it's worth trying their Mediterranean paninis (the Franco, say, packed with herby mushroom salad, spinach, and smoked mozzarella; $8.25), the tasty seafood gumbo ($7.95), salads (the Greek comes with baby spinach, roasted red peppers, and warm grilled flatbread; $4.50/$7.50), and antipasto plates ($7.50). Eat in the gaslit front room, at tables spilling out through the shuttered French doors into the street, or in the gorgeous subtropical courtyard; you won't want to leave.

Olivier's 204 Decatur St at Iberville ☎525-7734, ⓦwww.oliviers.com. Tues–Sat 11am–3pm & 5–10pm, Sun & Mon 5–10pm. Delicious Black Creole food, served in casually elegant surroundings in a charming old building. Family-owned, it's very welcoming, and the menu describes how each dish is cooked according to the recipe of a different family member. To start, they offer four gumbos – the Creole variety is fantastic, packed with sausage and shrimp – while entrées ($18 or $19) include poulet au fromage, baked with five cheeses, and Creole rabbit with oyster stuffing doused in a dark, herby sauce. They also do an expert, finely flavoured crawfish étouffé.

Port of Call 838 Esplanade Ave at Dauphine ☎523-0120, ⓦportofcallnola.com. Sun–Thurs 11am–midnight, Fri & Sat 11am–1am. Strung with tatty old rigging, lifebuoys and Hurricane lamps, this lively, casual neighbourhood bar (see p.148) is the place for freshly made, half-pound burgers. The menu is short and to the point, ranging from a plain burger ($9.50) to one with mushrooms

and melted cheese ($11.75), all served with a huge, buttery baked potato. Eat at the bar, in the cosy pub-like room or in the (very slightly) more formal dining area next door.

Redfish Grill 115 Bourbon St at Iberville ☎598-1200, ⓦwww.redfishgrill.com. Daily 11am–3pm & 5–10pm, oyster bar open all day. Casual, Ralph Brennan-owned fish restaurant. The brash ragwashed walls, naïf fish motifs and metallic palm trees are slightly twee, but the food isn't bad at all, especially for a well-priced lunch – try the shrimp and crabmeat Creole ($15 lunch/$22 dinner). Well-priced two-course lunch specials ($12) feature a gourmet po-boy and soup or salad, or you can get a dozen raw oysters on the half shell for $15. Dinner options include five fresh grilled fish, from fresh speckled trout ($21.50) to hickory-grilled snapper with shrimp ($23.50).

Sekisui Samurai Sushi 239 Decatur St at Bienville ☎525-9595, ⓦwww.sekisuiusa.com. Sun–Thurs 11.30am–10pm, Fri & Sat 11.30am–10.30pm. Though it may seem a bit perverse to nibble on raw fish in gluttonous New Orleans, sometimes a palate-cleansing tuna and asparagus nigiri roll is just the thing. This is the only sushi place in the Quarter (and one of just a few in the city), offering rolls and nigiri along with sushi and sashimi plates, udon noodle soups (from $10), teriyaki (from $15) and a plate of tasty fried softshell crabs served with ponzu sauce ($8). Lunch specials include sushi plates from $10.50, or sashimi at $14.50, along with some hot dishes from $7.

Stanley 547 St Ann St at Chartres, Jackson Square ☎587-0093, ⓦwww.stanleyrestaurant .com. Daily 7am–7pm. Chef Scott Boswell, the mastermind behind the stellar *Stella!* (see p.130) presents his delightfully casual alternative. Fresh, airy and spacious, with huge picture windows overlooking the square and little posies of fresh flowers on the marble-and-iron tables, it's a modern place with an unfussy retro feel, offering a simple, perfectly judged menu of all-day breakfasts and brunches, salads and sandwiches. Best bets are the various creative twists on Eggs Benedict ($9–19), including Eggs Stanley, with cornmeal-crusted oysters, and the delicious Breaux Bridge Benedict with boudin, smoked ham and cheese (both $12.50). Sandwiches ($9–15) include a nicely turned-out burger, soft-shell crab po-boys and a superior Reuben. Wash it down with an ice cream soda ($4), and if you have space, try the Stella Uptown sundae: carrot cake, rum-and-raisin ice cream, cream cheese sauce and whipped cream ($8.75).

Stella! 1032 Chartres St at Ursulines
☎587-0091, ⊛www.restaurantstella.com. Daily 5.30–10.30pm. One of the hottest tables in town, headed by local star Scott Boswell, and one of the very few where you will find such newfangled items as beetroot "air" and black truffle ice cream. The menu may be fancy (and a wee bit witty), but the service and the setting – two simply furnished, wooden-floored, brick-walled rooms – are welcoming and unpretentious. To start, the beet plate – beet carpaccio with beet sorbet, confit of baby beets, spun beet honey and the aforementioned froth of "air" ($17) is phenomenal, while for an entrée you can't go wrong with the miso- and sake-glazed Japanese sea bass with udon, green tea and soba noodles in a lobster, lump crab and shrimp broth ($38). Desserts include a killer grilled cheese sandwich (sweet cheese and chocolate ganache on brioche). If you're wanting to spend $150, without wine, on a gourmet experience for two, then *Stella!* will fit the bill.

Tujague's 823 Decatur St at Madison
☎525-8676, ⊛www.tujaguesrestaurant.com. Daily 5–10pm. Things are kept simple, and very traditional, at the beloved *Tujague's* ("Two-Jacks") – which at 150 years old is the second oldest restaurant in the city. Eating in the classic New Orleans dining room, both relaxed and elegant with its bentwood chairs and checkerboard tiled floor, has changed little since the 1850s, when butchers, dockers, and French Market traders enjoyed its famed seven-course Creole feasts. Today the (five-course) prix-fixe menu always starts with a classic shrimp rémoulade, soup, and a meltingly tender boiled brisket with Creole sauce, goes on to offer a choice of four classic entrées, and closes with bread pudding and coffee. Depending on your entrée, you'll pay about $35 – but it's not really done to ask the price in advance. If money's tight, simply order the tasty chicken "Bonne Femme"

(fried chicken with garlic and parsley) at the beautiful old bar (see p.148).

Tremé

The restaurant reviewed here is shown on the map on p.64.

Lil' Dizzy's 1500 Esplanade Ave at N Robertson
☎569-8997. Mon–Fri 7am–2.30pm, Sat 7am–2pm. Honest Creole soul food served in a cramped, convivial space owned and run by the Baquets, one of the city's great restaurant families. It's best (and most crowded) on Sunday, when there's a lively jazz brunch (BYOB) with a superb buffet – mac cheese, fried chicken, seafood gravy, creamy grits – and an omelette station where they'll rustle you up a delicious crawfish omelette. If you can't make that, the trout Baquet (doused in garlic butter and crabmeat) is an excellent bet, along with the delicate filé gumbo, home-made hot sausage, and any of the side dishes. They have a second branch in the CBD (see p.133) which is slightly less good.

Faubourg Marigny and Bywater

Most of the restaurants reviewed here are shown on the map on p.100; those on or near Frenchmen Street are shown on the map on p.101. For coffeehouses, see p.139.

Adolfo's 611 Frenchmen St at Chartres
☎948-3800. Daily 5.30–10.30pm. Gutsy Italian-Creole food prepared by an Argentine with New Orleans flair. The funky dining room, tucked above the tumbledown *Apple Barrel* bar (see p.148), and decorated with Christmas-tree lights, candles, and splashy art on the brick walls, is a romantic, cosy setting for enjoying robust, rich pasta, fish and seafood dishes ($15–25). Non-pasta meals start with a tasty spaghetti appetizer; to follow, choose from entrées such as pan-sautéed softshell crab stuffed with shrimp, or redfish with crawfish étouffé. Pasta dishes include cannelloni stuffed with crabmeat, sweetcorn, and ricotta. The kitchen is tiny, so service can be slow – BYOB (the wine they offer is rough) and hunker down for the evening. Cash only.

For a full **glossary** of New Orleans' unique **food terms**, see p.246.

Bacchanal 600 Poland St at Chartres

☎948-9111, ⓦ www.bacchanalwine.com.
Daily 11am–9pm. If you weren't sitting right under the shadow of the Mississippi levee you could imagine you'd washed up in an old European bodega in this gorgeously ramshackle little corner dive. Bacchanal may have the feel of a friendly, artfully distressed, thrift store-cum-living room – all bare brick walls, peeling stucco, wooden barrel seating and ancient, overstuffed bookcases – but it's actually a very good wine bar. There are some very classy wines here, many available by the glass (see p.149), while the simple food is fabulous, with huge deli sandwiches made from delicious European cheeses (the ambrosial grilled taleggio with portobello mushrooms is enough for two people at $11). Live bands play in the big subtropical courtyard, which is lit by lanterns; on Sunday nights from 6pm, guest chefs prepare fuller dinner menus.

Café Bamboo 435 Esplanade Ave at Frenchmen

☎940-5546, ⓦ www.cafebamboo.com.
Mon–Sat 11.30am–10pm (with a reduced window service till 2am). Downstairs at the Dragon's Den music club (see p.160), and with the same rough-and-ready, youthful ambience, this is one of the city's very few veggie restaurants, with a few vegan options and a lot of soya-based mock "chicken". Though the emphasis is on soul food and Southern, dishes run the gamut from Caribbean tofu wraps ($8) to a barbecue "chicken" with cornbread, mash and greens (at $13, the most expensive thing on the menu). None of it is fancy, but the vindaloo rice bowl ($10), a curry with tofu, zucchini, potatoes and pepper, hits the spot. Free delivery in the Quarter and Marigny.

Cake Café 2440 Chartres St at Spain

☎943-0010, ⓦnolacakes.com. Tues–Sun 7am–3pm. This casual corner joint is one of the Faubourg's hottest neighbourhood spots for a Sunday brunch or lunch, when the delicious smells wafting from the kitchen and the sociable hubbub make you feel right at home. Steve Himmelfarb started out selling his scrumptious homebaked cakes door-to-door, but has settled here and extended his menu to include brilliantly cooked local dishes. Whether you fancy a red velvet cupcake to go, an oyster and crab sandwich, a warm slice of artichoke and goat cheese quiche or a breakfast of fried tilapia, grits, and eggs, this is the place to come. No reservations.

Country Club 634 Louisa St at Chartres

☎945-0742, ⓦ www.thecountryclubneworleans .com. Restaurant daily 11am–10pm. Though this is predominantly a gay men's club (see p.149), it's open to all, offering delicious Southern/Louisianan cooking – from boudin balls or crawfish pies to glazed pork chops and Gulf fish with crabmeat – at very reasonable prices. You can dine on the veranda, in the stylish, airy dining room, or, if you pay for membership ($10 till 5pm; $7 after 5pm), poolside. The simple brunch menu (Sat & Sun 11am–3pm; $8–14) is popular. Don't let the naked bathers in the pool put you off; feel free to join them.

Elizabeth's 601 Gallier St at Chartres

☎944-9272, ⓦ www.elizabeths-restaurant .com. Tues–Fri 11am–2.30pm & 6–10pm, Sat 8am–2.30pm & 6–10pm, Sun 8am–2.30pm. Even Elizabeth's logo, a cheery pig, can't prepare you for the size of the portions at this popular Bywater spot, which started as a simple breakfast diner and has kept its grassroots, homey feel even while upscaling its menu. It still pulls in a loyal crowd of local artists and blue-collar workers, but nowadays people come from all over the city for the delicious Southern/Creole home cooking. Brunch and lunch are the most popular, featuring traditional calas rice fritters ($4.50) and a tempting praline bacon appetizer ($5), along with fried chicken livers with a chunky home-made pepper jelly. Interesting mains include a salmon and brie grilled sandwich with eggs and hash browns ($14.50) or Cajun bubble and squeak with grits ($13.50). It can get crowded, and reservations aren't taken, so order a Bloody Mary at the bar and be prepared to wait. Dinner is a bit fancier and more relaxed – try the seafood sampler, with crab and avocado salad, braised fish and seared scallops.

Feelings Café 2600 Chartres St at Franklin

☎945-2222, ⓦ www.feelingscafe.com. Thurs 6–9.30pm, Fri & Sat 6–10pm, Sun 11am–2pm & 6–9.30pm. Though it doesn't look like much from the outside, this is a lovely, romantic restaurant set in a complex of restored plantation buildings with a shady brick courtyard. The old-world New Orleans/Caribbean ambience is the perfect place to eat the classic French-Creole food – lots of shrimp, seafood, steak, and duck – though prices may be just a tad on the high side (entrées, including pork tenderloin, or Gulf fish with Dijon mustard, spinach, and shrimp go for $19–25).

The Joint 801 Poland Ave at Dauphine ☎949-3232, ⓦwww.alwayssmokin.com. Mon & Tues 11.30am–2pm, Wed–Sat 11.30am–9pm. This tiny yellow shed hides one of the best barbecue joints in the city, with its own smokehouse out back. Plonk yourself down on a wooden bench and join the crowds of noisy locals chowing down on juicy, crispy ribs (half rack $11.50), succulent slow-cooked pulled pork, Cajun chaurice (sausage) and meltingly tender beef brisket (each around $10), dousing it all in the amazing smoky sauce. If you can't choose, settle on the combo plate, which gets you three meats plus one side for $15. Don't miss the home-made sides, either; the baked beans, and the ambrosial mac n' cheese, are particularly good. Fabulous jukebox, too. Expect a wait at busy times.

Mimi's 2601 Royal St at Franklin ☎872-9868, ⓦwww.mimisinthemarigny.com. Bar daily 4pm–5am; food served Tues–Sun 6pm–late. The coolest Faubourg/Bywater hipsters have made this bar (see p.149) a home away from home not only for the drinks, the DJs, and the live music, but for the cheap and very tasty tapas, served upstairs. Everything costs around $6, from the goat cheese croquettes to the beef empanadas to the herby shrimp with jamon serrano.

Mona's 504 Frenchmen St at Decatur ☎949-4115. Mon–Thurs 11am–10pm, Fri & Sat 11am–11pm, Sun 11am–9pm. There's no fuss at all at this popular café, attached to a Middle Eastern grocery, though the food – kebabs, flatbread pizzas, meze, beef kibby, split red lentil soup – is well worth fussing over. It's all wonderfully fresh and zingy, with lots of excellent veggie choices. At $9.99 the delicious vegetable platter, with hummus, babaganoush, tabbouleh, and falafel, is a steal, but you can't go wrong whatever you choose. BYOB, or simply enjoy a refreshing mug of their hot mint tea. They have a couple of uptown branches, at 4126 Magazine (☎894-4115) and 1120 S. Carrollton (☎861-8175).

La Peniche 1940 Dauphine St at Touro ☎943-1460. Thurs–Mon 24hr. Very mixed, and decidedly non-hip, little neighbourhood restaurant, whose round-the-clock hours, home-made comfort food, and low prices

see off-duty bartenders eating alongside old timers, worse-for-wear tourists alongside local families. Diner staples share space with New Orleans standards, but the best choices are the breakfasts (waffles, eggs Benedict, gator sausage with gravy, savoury Creole bread pudding with sausage and cheese) or the burgers, all of which go down a treat after a long night of partying.

The Praline Connection 542 Frenchmen St at Chartres ☎943-3934, ⓦwww.praline connection.com. Mon–Sat 11am–10pm, Sun 11am–9pm. Though there are better soul food restaurants in town – and the shtick, with wait staff wearing black fedoras and black ties, feels a bit tired – if you want a quick fried chicken fix ($13) on Frenchmen, or need to fill up on mac cheese and mustard greens, this inexpensive place will fit the bill. The best things on the menu are the fried chicken livers ($7), which, though offered as an appetizer, with their crackly cornmeal crust and zingy green pepper jelly make a meal in themselves.

Schiro's 2483 Royal St at St Roch ☎944-6666, ⓦwww.schiroscafe.com. Mon–Sat 11am–9.30pm. A corner grocery store-cum-neighbourhood restaurant (with a guest house upstairs; see p.121) serving simple food. Choose from a few Indian dishes (all around $10, including a nice vegetarian aloo mutter paneer) and New Orleans favourites (hot lunch specials, including red beans and rice or fried catfish, go for $7–10) and po-boys.

Yuki Izakaya 525 Frenchmen St at Decatur ☎943-1122. Tues–Thurs 6.30pm–midnight, Fri & Sat 6.30am–2am, Sun 6–10pm. Superhip little Frenchmen bar (see p.149) serving tasty Japanese snacks – skewered shiitake mushrooms ($6), sautéed fishcakes with yam ($5), Korean kimchee ($4), and seared tuna with ponzu sauce ($10).

The CBD and Warehouse District

The restaurants reviewed here are shown on the map on p.72. For coffee houses, see p.141; for delis and a farmers' market, see p.143.

A Mano 870 Tchoupitoulas St at St Joseph ☎208-9280, ⓦamanonola.com. Wed–Fri 11.30am–2.30pm & 6–10pm, Mon, Tues & Sat 6–10pm. Chef Adolfo Garcia, of *Rio Mar* fame (see p.134) is behind this excellent Italian restaurant. Its name means "by hand", and it specializes in house-cured meats and handmade pastas ($8–12) from the Siena region. This is rustic food, with no hint of Creole: big hitters include the ricotta gnudi (dumplings) with mushroom and sage butter ($12) the braised tripe in Fiorentina sauce ($7), and, among the simple, robust entrées ($18–25), the rabbit with olives, garlic, and thyme ($18).

American Sector 945 Magazine St at Andrew Higgins Drive ☎528-1940, Ⓦwww .americansector.com. Daily 11am–11pm. Linked to the National World War II Museum's Victory Theater (see p.81) this restaurant – from the stable of local star John Besh – is currently one of the hottest in town. The relentless retro theming (servers in 40s garb, vintage lunchboxes for the kids, home-made pickles served in a jar) jars slightly with the minimal, modern space, and could probably be toned down a bit, as it threatens to detract from the superb food. Classic homecooking, blue plate specials, Southern favourites and diner/deli staples are all given a stylish upgrade, from the short rib sloppy joe ($11.50) to the satisfying meatloaf and mash ($13), pork cheeks with corn bread and black-eyed peas ($15.50), and the phenomenal blue crab and sausage stew ($16). Sides ($2.50–4) range from jalapeno cheese grits to Southern greens, while to drink you could go for a Bananas Foster malted shake or a Ramos Gin Fizz. If you're in a hurry or not very hungry, grab a snack dish like rabbit paté ($9) or fried chicken gizzards ($7).

Cochon 930 Tchoupitoulas St at Andrew Higgins Drive ☎588-2123, Ⓦwww .cochonrestaurant.com. Mon–Fri 11am–10pm, Sat 5.30–10pm. Cajun chef Donald Link prepares boudin and andouille from scratch at his on-site boucherie – and it's this kind of care and expertise that defines his superb restaurant. Very comfortable with itself, its simple, rustic-modern decor enlivened only by a few jars of pickles and old photos, it's an upscale but unintimidating place, full of blissed-out diners from businessmen to bearded hipsters. This is authentic, finely presented Cajun food – not hot, spicy, and stodgy, but flavoursome, complex, and with a heavy emphasis on pork. Everything, from the melt-in-the-mouth fried boudin balls to the tangy sweet potato and andouille flan, ham hock soup, and cochon with turnip and cracklin', is utterly delicious. There are

some fine seafood dishes, too, but the meat dishes have the edge. Entrées $14–22, appetizers from $8; a little less at lunchtime.

Herbsaint 701 St Charles Ave at Girod ☎524-4114, Ⓦwww.herbsaint.com. Mon–Fri 11.30am–10pm, Sat 5.30–10pm. Another of Donald Link's restaurants (see *Cochon*, above), this is an effortlessly elegant, relaxed bistro offering affordable French-influenced Southern food. It's especially appealing at lunchtime, when people come to enjoy themselves rather than to grab a hurried business lunch, and the streetcar rumbles past the huge windows. The food is deceptively simple, using fresh ingredients in classics like steak-frites or fried catfish. Dinner options include a splendid duck leg confit with black rice and citrus. Entrées $15–25 at lunch, slightly more at dinner.

Liborio 321 Magazine St at Gravier ☎581-9680, Ⓦwww.liboriocuban.com. Mon 11am–2.30pm, Tues–Sat 11am–2.30pm & 5.30–9pm. This family-run lunchtime favourite is also good for inexpensive dinners. Traditional Cuban dishes include home-made tamales ($7), *picadillo*, a garlicky beef hash with raisins ($11), and *ropa viejo* ("old clothes") – shredded beef in garlicky tomato sauce with brown rice, black beans, and plantains ($13) – while the *medianoche*, sweet bread stuffed with ham, cheese, pork, and pickles, is an interesting variation on the classic Cuban sandwich ($8). Don't miss the side dish of yucca with garlic ($4).

Lil' Dizzy's in the Whitney Hotel, 610 Poydras St at Camp ☎212-5656. Mon–Sat 7am–2pm & 5–9pm, Sun 10am–2pm & 5–9pm. The second branch of the Tremé soul-food restaurant (see p.130) is not quite as successful as the original, and seems a little lost in this vast, high-ceilinged, marble pillared room, which was once a grand bank. The all-you-can-eat Sunday brunch buffet ($20) can be hit-and-miss (head instead to the original restaurant for that), but breakfasts (till 11am) and lunch entrées – pot roast, fried chicken, trout Baquet (with garlic butter and crabmeat), gumbo – are good value. As so often with soul food restaurants, the side dishes steal the show.

Mother's 401 Poydras St at Tchoupitoulas ☎523-9656, Ⓦwww.mothersrestaurant.net. Mon–Sat 6.30am–10pm, Sun 7am–10pm. Though tourists go into a tizzy about *Mother's*, thrilled to be eating N'Awlins home cooking in a downhome restaurant that has changed little since the 1930s (brick walls, concrete floors, brusque counter service), locals complain that it's become too touristy. That said, the portions are huge, and the food will satisfy, especially if you go for breakfast and choose the right things – black ham (the sweet, crunchy skin of a baked ham) is a favourite, dished up with buttery biscuits and grits – or one of their overstuffed po-boys (try the signature Ferdi, with ham and beef debris, for $9.75). The blue plates – fried chicken, beans and rice with sausage, white bean soup and so on – are not for the faint-hearted. No credit cards.

Palace Café 605 Canal St at Chartres ☎523-1661, ⓦwww.palacecafe.com. Mon–Sat 11.30am–2.30pm & 5.30 till, Sun 10.30am–2.30pm & 5.30 till. Another hit from the Brennans stable: a lovely, casually elegant dining room in a grand old music-store building on the edge of the Quarter. Always buzzing, with the ambience of a nineteenth-century European café, it's big and airy, with marble tables, check-tiled floors, a spiral staircase sweeping up to a mezzanine and sunny walls lined with vintage French posters. The food, contemporary Creole, is first-rate, from the fragrant oyster pan roast ($8) to the potato pie mashed with cochon du lait debris, spinach, melted cheese, and gravy ($13). At lunch, which is considerably cheaper than dinner, they offer a "light" option (fish, usually); after that why not go on to ruin all the good work with a slab of white chocolate bread pudding ($6)? The Sunday jazz brunch is lovely, with the favourite à la carte choices joining fancy egg concoctions and indulgent *pain perdu*, and a trio of strolling musicians who play requests.

Rio Mar 800 S Peters St at Julia ☎525-3474, ⓦwww.riomarseafood.com. Mon–Fri 11.30am–2pm & 6–10pm, Sat 6–10pm. New Orleans seafood meets Latin cuisine in this terrific Warehouse District restaurant from local chef Adolfo Garcia. It's a comfortable, welcoming space, decorated in sunny yellows and glossy, warm woods: a cosy setting for the utterly delicious, reasonably priced food. Lunchtime is tapas time, with perfectly executed plates including chorizo in Rioja, tuna empanadas, some lip-smackingly garlicky shrimp dishes, baked oysters, and jamon serrano. At dinner, you can order many of the same

dishes, plus flavoursome Spanish staples like gazpacho, bacalao, seafood stews, hunks of juicy octopus dusted with paprika, and zingy South American ceviches, all of which can be washed down with robust wines from Argentina and Spain.

Lower Garden District, Central City and the Garden District

Unless otherwise stated, the restaurants below are shown on the map on p.86. For coffeehouses, see p.139.

Café Reconcile 1631 Oretha Castle Haley Blvd at Terpsichore ☎568-1157, ⓦwww .cafereconcile.com. Open for lunch, Mon–Fri. Something special: a grass-roots, non-profit venture, spearheaded by a Jesuit church, where local at-risk teens are trained for jobs in the hospitality industry. The bustling dining room, in the blighted but slowly recovering neighbourhood of Central City, north of the Lower Garden District, is warm, welcoming, and spotless. The prices are ridiculously low (nothing over $9), and the food – fried chicken, catfish, jambalaya, white beans and shrimp, along with daily specials like pot roast, shrimp Creole, and smothered pork chops – beyond delicious.

Commander's Palace 1403 Washington Ave at Coliseum ☎899-8221, ⓦwww.commanders palace.com. Mon–Fri 11.30am–2pm & 6.30–10pm, Sat 11.30am–1pm & 6.30–10pm, Sun 10.30am–1.30pm & 6.30–10pm. The world-famous *grande dame* of the Garden District is set in a turquoise-and-white 1880s mansion with a maze of rooms and a tropical, oak-shaded courtyard. The heart-thumpingly rich Creole food deserves the hype; it can get pricey (dinner entrées from $26), but the prix-fixe menus are very reasonable (two-course lunch from $16, three-course dinner from $36). Specialities include the traditional (turtle soup; an oyster and absinthe "dome" in a flaky pastry shell), the innovative (the fancy foie gras du monde – peach and foie gras *beignets* with foie gras café au lait, pecans, cane syrup and a chicory "mist"), and a killer bread pudding soufflé with whisky sauce. At the hugely popular Sunday jazz brunch (three courses from $28), you can enjoy the likes of foie gras pain perdu or white truffle scrambled eggs, but the sheer numbers of people here at this time can make it feel a little like mass catering. Jacket required for dinner and all day Sunday; no shorts, T-shirts, running shoes, or jeans at any time. Reservations essential.

Delachaise 3442 St Charles Ave at Louisiana ☎ 895-0858, ⓦ www.thedelachaise.com. Food served daily 6pm–midnight. Buzzy, welcoming winebar, just beyond the Garden District, that pulls as many in-the-know locals for its tasty Louisianan/European/ Mediterranean fusion food as for its drink. Options range from small tapas-style dishes and simple cheese plates to more substantial portions – the juicy smoked salmon Johnny cakes, made from roasted corn and served with salmon and vodka crème fraiche ($13) are a winner, as are the steak frites ($22; the frites deliciously fried in duck fat), the spicy frogs' legs ($10), and lots of creative varieties of crème brulée. No reservations; if you want to dine you'll have to wait for a table, which can take a while.

Juan's Flying Burrito 2018 Magazine St at St Andrew ☎ 569-0000, ⓦ www.juansflyingburrito .com. Mon–Thurs 11am–10pm, Fri & Sat 11am–11pm, Sun noon–10pm. Mainstay of the Lower Garden District boho scene, a funky, cheerful Tex-Mex joint with (loud) groovy music, local art on the walls and rock-bottom prices. Stars on the very long menu include the overstuffed burritos, loaded with sour cream, black beans, and guacamole. If you don't fancy the namesake flying version, with grilled steak, chicken and shrimp ($8.25), try jerk chicken ($7.50) or the grilled mixed vegetables ($6.95). The fajitas, quesadillas and tacos are also good – light choices include the Mardi Gras Indian tacos, crunchy with grilled squash, roasted corn and red cabbage ($7). Daily specials, which are slightly pricier, might include blackened redfish tacos or brisket enchiladas. Portions are huge; unusually for New Orleans, they offer very cheap kids' versions of some of the simpler dishes. There are also happy-hour deals on bottled beers and margaritas. No reservations. There's another branch in Mid-City at 4724 S Carrollton Ave at Canal Street (same hours; ☎ 486-9950).

Ms Hyster's Barbecue 2000 S Claiborne Ave at St Andrew ☎ 522-3028. See map, p.89. It's well worth driving out to the depths of Central City to find this friendly little joint: they serve amazingly good barbecue, with colossal portions of succulent ribs, fall-off-the-bone chicken, and warm, mellow

cornbread to mop up the sweet-tangy sauce. The Black Creole side dishes are unmissable, too, especially the smothered mustard greens, cooked with pork to a salty, delicious mush. You can eat well for around $5.

Slim Goodies 3322 Magazine St at Toledano ☎ 891-3447. Daily 6am–3pm. Hip neighbourhood diner serving offbeat all-day breakfasts to a young, tattooed, crowd. Prices range from around $5 for the Guatemalan (eggs, black beans, plantains) to $10 for the Jewish Coonass (potato latkes with spinach, eggs, crawfish étouffé and a biscuit). As well, the menu includes pancakes, salads, sandwiches and blue plate diner specials, all of them with global influences. Lots of veggie options, including tofu scramble and sweet potato pancakes. No credit cards.

Uptown

The restaurants below are shown on the map on p.89. For coffeehouses see p.139; for delis and for a farmers' market, see p.143.

Baru Bistro and Tapas 3700 Magazine St at Amelia ☎ 895-2225. Sun & Mon 5.30–10pm, Tues–Thurs 11.30am–2.30pm & 5.30–10pm, Fri & Sat 11.30am–2.30pm & 5.30–11pm. Casually romantic little place serving delicious, garlicky, Latin American and Caribbean tapas, with lots of Columbian specialities – try the *mazorca*, a dish of grilled corn topped with crumbly cheese, pink sauce and potato sticks (trust us!; $6) or the *picada cartagenera*, a mix of shrimp, chorizo and bell peppers sautéed in wine and spices ($12). Entrées are just as good; from the fish of the day with coconut rice to the *lechon Cubano*, a slow-roasted shoulder of pork ($18). BYOB; $8 corkage fee. No reservations.

Boucherie 8115 Jeannette at Carrollton ☎ 862-5514, ⓦ www.boucherie-nola .com. Tues–Sat 11am–3pm & 5.30–9.30pm. Chef Nathaniel Zimet started out serving startling tasty late night eats from a purple catering truck, *Que Crawl*, outside legendary nightclub *Tipitina's*. The truck is still going, but Zimet now also has a permanent space in this pretty, cosy uptown cottage. This is sophisticated, creative, Southern food with a few bistro specials – and it's all invariably delicious, from old *Que Crawl* favourites (home-made boudin balls, pulled pork, grit fries – fingers of fried grits with cheese and hot sauce) to steamed mussels with collard greens, green-tea-braised flounder with black-eyed peas, or artisan cheese plates. For dessert, the krispy kreme bread pudding is a favourite, but the chilli chocolate chess pie is great, too. Small plates go for around $5, larger plates about twice that.

Brigtsen's 723 Dante St at Leake ☎861-7610, ⓦwww.brigtsens.com. Tues–Sat 5.30–10pm. It's hard not to like this refined, old-fashioned, and unpretentious restaurant – a real local favourite – spread through a handful of cosy rooms in an old Riverbend house. The long, handwritten menu of hearty Creole-Cajun dishes changes daily; of the entrées ($25–32) the seafood is especially fine, whether served in a gumbo or fragrant bisque (try the shrimp and butternut variety), blackened, or smothered in creamy sauces. You can't go wrong with roast duck, either, served with cornbread dressing and dried cherry sauce. Reservations advised.

Camellia Grill 626 S Carrollton Ave at Hampson ☎866-9573. Sun–Thurs 8am–11pm, Fri & Sat 8am–1am. Housed in a crumbling, columned Riverbend building, this classic chrome-and-formica diner is a New Orleans institution for burgers, omelettes, fries and grilled sandwiches. A maître d' seats you on leatherette banquettes until a stool becomes free at the double-horseshoe counter; there, brisk wait staff, in jackets and bow ties, bark your orders to the cooks frying right behind them. You're here more for the ambience than the food – though the chilli cheese omelette, with potato and onion, packs a punch. Lines can be long, especially at weekend. No credit cards.

Casamento's 4330 Magazine St at Napoleon ☎895-9761, ⓦwww .casamentosrestaurant.com. Tues–Sat 11am–2pm, plus Thurs–Sat 5.30–9pm; closed June–Aug. Spotless, wonderfully old-fashioned oyster bar – all cream, aqua, and floral tiles – that's been going since 1919. Other than the ice-fresh oysters, shucked at the marble bar ($4.50 for six; try them with a grilled cheese sandwich on the side), good choices include the fried crab claws, the oyster stew ($5.50) or the trout "loaf," a buttery, overstuffed sandwich made with hunks of white bread ($6.45/$12.90).

▲ Oysters at *Casamento's*

Friendly and bustling, this is an unmissable New Orleans experience. No credit cards.

Dick and Jenny's 4501 Tchoupitoulas St at Jena ☎894-9880, ⓦdickandjennys.com. Mon–Thurs 5.30–10pm, Fri & Sat 5.30–10.30pm. This rather bleak stretch of Tchoupitoulas is a surprising setting for such a delightfully cosy restaurant, set in a funky little clapboard house. The atmosphere may be casual, but the food is classy: the menu of creative Creole comfort food (entrées $16–28) changes seasonally, but might include such dishes as sautéed Gulf shrimp with cheddar-andouille grits, pork tenderloin stuffed with cheese and pine nuts, or a roasted portobello mushroom and blue cheesecake. No reservations, and it's hugely popular; take a drink out onto the porch and relax while you wait.

Domilise's 5240 Annunciation St at Bellecastle ☎899-9126. Mon–Sat 10am–7pm. One of the city's definitive po-boy joints, a family-owned little time-warp of a place where grandma Dot and her clan can assemble your sandwich, on very fresh bread, in front of your eyes. Of the many fillings, fresh-fried oysters are always a winner, but many swear by the meatballs or the roast beef with gravy. Prices can go up to $15 for a large fried shrimp po-boy. No credit cards.

Franky & Johnny's 321 Arabella St at Tchoupitoulas ☎899-9146, ⓦ www.frankyandjohnnys
.com. This homely, noisy neighbourhood
Italian-American restaurant – with red
checked tablecloths, sassy waitresses, and
Italian crooners and New Orleans R&B on
the vintage jukebox – gets packed at
weekends with families and large parties.
Food is downhome Cajun-Creole – alligator
soup, gumbo, softshell crabs, spicy boiled
crawfish, stuffed artichoke, and the like, with
very little over $10. They also do seriously
good po-boys ($8–13) and muffulettas
($10–16).

Guy's Po-boys 5259 Magazine St at Bellecastle
☎891-5025. Mon–Sat 11am–4pm. Another
of the classic hole-in-the-wall po-boy joints
that Uptown specializes in, where huge
po-boys are prepared to order and lines
snake down the block. Everyone has their
favourite, and the friendly Guy is always
willing to make recommendations, but safe
bets include the sloppy roast beef with
Swiss, the pork chop, or "da bomb": spicy
catfish with fried shrimp and cheese,
created by local funk band Galactic. Wash it
down with a bottle of root beer. No credit
cards.

Jacques Imo's 8324 Oak St at Dante
☎861-0886. Mon–Thurs 5–10pm, Fri & Sat
5–10.30pm. The quirky, rowdy bar and
wildly colourful covered patio at this popular
Riverbend restaurant are a little at odds with
the cuisine, an inventive, gourmet Creole-
Caribbean take on soul food. Everything on
the long menu – garlicky fried oysters,
chicken livers, grilled amberjack with spicy
green tomato-avocado crab sauce,
ambrosial alligator sausage cheesecake,
smothered rabbit with cornbread dressing,
deep-fried roast beef po-boy to name but a
few – is good, though costs do mount
(entrées $14–25). Sides include macque
choux, sweet potatoes, or butterbeans with
rice – you'll leave feeling stuffed. It's *the*
place to eat before seeing the ReBirth Brass
Band at the *Maple Leaf* (see p.161), but
they don't accept reservations for parties
smaller than five, so arrive early or settle
down at the bar for a long wait.

Nirvana 4308 Magazine St at General Pershing
☎894-9797, ⓦ www.insidenirvana.com. Tues–
Sun 11.30am–2.30pm & 5.30–10.30pm.
Authentic Indian food, spanning the range
from Goan dishes via biryani and tandoori to
creative fusions. Vegetarian choices are

recommended: go for the potato patties
topped with curried garbanzo beans, the
naurattan curry with vegetables and creamy
paneer, or a thali. Entrées range from
$10–16; the buffet (lunch daily; dinner Thurs
& Sun), which includes hot naan bread,
tangy chutneys, tandoori and saag chicken,
and three vegetarian entrées (including the
garbanzo beans) is great value at $9.95.

Oak Street Café 8140 Oak St at Dublin
☎866-8710, ⓦ www.oakstreetcafe.com. Mon &
Wed–Sat 6.30am–2pm, Sun 7.30am–2pm.
Cheery, old-fashioned and cosy neighbourhood diner, dishing up a huge variety of
inexpensive hot breakfast/brunches from
fluffy omelettes to tacos, biscuits and gravy
to breakfast po-boys. A few inexpensive blue
plate specials (from $6) feature southern
Louisiana favourites (Cajun boudin and the
like). Occasional live jazz piano. Free wi-fi.

Pascal's Manale 1838 Napoleon Ave at Baronne
☎895-4877. Wed–Fri 11.30am–2pm &
5–10pm, Mon, Tues & Sat 5–10pm. Dishing
up Italian-Creole classics since 1913, this
wonderfully old-fashioned restaurant is the
kind of place that New Orleans holds very
dear. The signature dish is barbecue shrimp,
and you have to order it ($24 for ten
enormous shrimp) – the bubbling, buttery,
garlicky, peppery sauce sets the bar for
every restaurant in town. Other dishes –
heavy pastas, steaks, breaded and fried
seafood – are less interesting (entrées from
$15), but you could spend a happy hour or
two slurping fresh raw oysters and cold
cocktails at the old-fashioned oyster bar.

Mid-City and Esplanade Ridge

The restaurants below are shown on
the map on pp.94–95. For coffeehouses
see p.141, and for a farmers' market, see
p.143.

Café Degas 3127 Esplanade Ave at Ponce de
Leon ☎945-5635, ⓦ www.cafedegas.com.
Wed–Sat 11am–3pm & 6–10pm, Sun
10.30am–3pm & 6–9.30pm. Cosy little
French-style bistro with a very pretty
covered deck amongst the trees. The
seasonally changing menu uses the freshest
ingredients in well-executed classics like
escargots, mussels and warm goat-cheese
salad. Good mains might include
pan-seared monkfish ($17) and roasted
lamb chops ($18), with local favourites, like
shrimp and grits, done equally well.

137

Dooky Chase's 2301 Orleans Ave at Miro
☏821-0600. Tues–Fri 11am–2pm; takeout
sometimes available till 7pm. Classy Black
Creole food dished up in a refined dining
room that like so many in the district, had to
struggle to return after the storm. Since its
triumphant return, and since Barack Obama
declared himself a fan, doughty matriarch
Leah Chase has become something of a
cult heroine, much like her fellow Mid-City
restaurateur Willie Mae (see p.139). Though
things are not quite back to normal yet –
opening hours are limited, and some menu
items aren't available – the food, and the
experience, is still wonderful. Of the entrées
($10–20), the crispy fried chicken, oyster-
stuffed chicken breast, and gumbo – made
with chicken, ham, veal, crab, shrimp, and
spicy and smoked sausage – are all great.
As for the sides, the sweet potatoes are
meltingly good. For the best value, go for
the buffet ($15.95).

Liuzza's 3636 Bienville St at N Telemachus
☏482-9120, ⓦwww.liuzzas.com. Tues–Thurs
11am–9pm, Fri & Sat 11am–10pm. This
homey Creole Italian restaurant has been
pulling a gritty, friendly, neighbourhood
crowd since the 1940s. While they do a
superior red beans and rice, and a seafood-
packed gumbo, it's best to order classic New
Orleans Italian – meatballs, pasta and red
gravy; stuffed bell peppers; and enormous
artichokes stuffed with breadcrumbs, garlic,
lemon, anchovies and olives – and wash it
down with a frosted beer. It's all very reasonably priced, with entrées from $7 to $20.

**Liuzza's By The Track 1518 N Lopez at Ponce
de Leon** ☏218-7888. Mon–Sat 11am–7pm.
Not related to the other *Liuzza's*, but adored
with a similar passion, this is an old corner
tavern serving top-notch Bloody Marys, a
brilliant gumbo, and fantastic po-boys. Try
them stuffed with garlic oysters or the
phenomenal, peppery, buttery BBQ shrimp,
which is so sloppy that you'll need a knife
and fork. If you're not in a po-boy mood
there are plenty of other items on the menu,
including an astonishingly garlicky roast
beef, that will hit the spot.

Lola's 3312 Esplanade Ave at Mystery
☏488-6946. Sun–Thurs 5.30–9.30pm, Fri &
Sat 5.30–10pm. Noisy, colourful little
restaurant that's a firm local favourite for

mouthwatering, cheap, and authentic
Spanish food. To start, choose from lentil or
garlic soup, gazpacho, or lip-licking grilled
shrimp, perhaps following with grilled rack
of lamb. Star turns, however, are the paellas
($12–22), cooked to order in the open
kitchen, served in a cast-iron skillet and
packed with seafood, meat, or vegetables,
or all three. Fresh bread comes warm, with
garlic-packed butter. No reservations, so
arrive early or wait, and no credit cards.
BYOB, or choose from their short wine list
(including sangria).

Mandina's 3800 Canal at S Cortez ☏482-9179,
ⓦwww.mandinasrestaurant.com. Mon–Thurs
11am–9.30pm, Fri & Sat 11am–10pm, Sun
noon–9pm. Mid-City's neighbourhood
restaurants struggled to return after Katrina,
which hit this area very hard – and many of
them never did. Today the reassuring
old-fashioned *Mandina's* – a family-owned
Italian-Creole place open since the 1930s,
which cleaned itself up and came back with
a vengeance after the flood – is a symbol of
recovery for its loyal locals, many of whom
have been coming here all their lives. The
food is quintessential New Orleans-Italian,
home-cooked, and served in vast portions
by no-nonsense bow-tied waiters. Highlights
include *bruccialone*, veal stuffed with
spinach and egg ($15), or the simple
spaghetti with Italian sausage and red gravy
($12.50). Traditional Creole dishes are done
well here, too, including a chunky turtle
soup, a silky oyster and artichoke soup, and
a very fine gumbo with a dash of sherry (all
$5.25), and a delicious trout amandine
($18); you can also get a killer Sazerac at
the lively bar. No credit cards.

**Parkway Bakery and Tavern 538 Hagan St at
Toulouse** ☏482-3047, ⓦwww.parkway
bakeryandtavernnola.com. Wed–Sun
11am–10pm. Fans come from all over the
city to get po-boys from this pretty, lovingly
restored old restaurant overlooking the
Bayou. It's not just the food: *Parkway* is
decorated with the kind of neighbourhood
memorabilia that this nostalgic city loves,
and they serve local brands including Barqs
root beer and Hubig's pies. The award-
winning po-boys are simple, inexpensive,
huge, and tasty – try the roast beef,
dripping with gravy.

For a full **glossary** of New Orleans' unique **food terms**, see p.246.

Ralph's on the Park 900 City Park Ave at
Dumaine ☎485-1000, ⓦwww.ralphsonthepark
.com. Mon–Thurs & Sat 5.30–9pm, Fri
11.30am–2pm & 5.30–9pm, Sun
11am–2pm & 5.30–9pm. Classy, friendly
Ralph Brennan-owned restaurant in a
gorgeous, historic, and light-filled dining
room right opposite the park and its
wrought-iron gate. The food is modern
Louisianan and very delicious – try the cauli-
flower soup with a mini blue crab cake ($7),
the saffron-braised lamb cheeks with beets
and garbanzo beans ($25.50), or the spiced
cream-cheese-encrusted grouper ($19). The
views of City Park's stately old Live Oaks,
draped with Spanish moss, are great – and
even better from the veranda, where you
can sit when the weather is good.

Willie Mae's Scotch House 2401 St Ann
St at N Tonti ☎822-9503. Mon–Sat
11am–3pm. Pre-2005 this was a simple
fried chicken shack in a poor neighbourhood, where the octogenarian Miss Willie
Mae Seaton, who lived on site, kept an
appreciative bunch of locals fed with
home-made soul food. Then came Katrina,
which submerged Willie Mae's restaurant
and her home under water. Almost immediately, a bunch of passionate volunteers –
locals, visitors, restaurateurs, students – set
to rebuilding it, their progress followed by
news stations, food magazines and blogs
around the nation. The re-opening of *Willie
Mae's* in 2007 came to represent the city's
spiritual rebirth, and the (by now nonoge-
naerian) Willie Mae the tenacity and

courage of every Katrina victim. Run today
by Willie Mae's granddaughter, it's a
pilgrimage site for anyone who cares about
this city. The peppery, hot, crunchy fried
chicken ($10) and warm, sweet cornbread
at *Willie Mae's* will truly feed your soul,
while reminding you never to forget. No
credit cards.

Ye Olde College Inn 3000 S Carrollton Ave at Fig
☎866-3683. Tues–Sat 4–11pm. After this
neighbourhood restaurant, which had been
serving since the 1930s, was devastated by
Katrina, it was bought by local boy John
Blancher, owner of the fabulous *Rock 'n'
Bowl* music venue (see p.162), and moved
next door. Soon after, Blancher moved his
bowling alley to the same block, which
makes *Ye Olde College Inn* a convenient
and very jolly place to fill up before a night
dancing to zydeco or swamp pop. It's a
restaurant that has adapted to survive, but
Blancher has done a great job of keeping its
character. The wood-panelled dining room,
lined with photos of New Orleans
landmarks, memorabilia, and newscuttings
about local figures, evokes all the atmosphere of the original 1930s dining room,
while the mural of old Canal Street, big old
wooden bar, and rugs on the bare floor give
it a funky, comfy, feel. Food is Southern
Creole, with nice fried green tomatoes with
shrimp remoulade ($8), foot-long gourmet
po-boys, including one with oysters, havarti
and bacon ($13), and tasty grilled redfish
topped with crawfish or lump crabmeat
($18–22).

Coffee, snacks and light meals

European-influenced New Orleans has always been the American city for **coffee**.
Fresh, strong and aromatic, it's been a big part of life here since long before Seattle
laid claim to the notion, and today locals drink twice the national average.

The city's fondness for smoky **chicory** coffee – which for many visitors takes
some getting used to – dates back to the early European colonists, who had
learned to stretch out their precious coffee supplies back home by adding the
ground root of the endive plant. This money-saving ruse became particularly
popular in New Orleans during the impoverished days of the Civil War – when
the entire city developed a taste for the stuff – and has endured ever since.
Chicory coffee should be mellow, never bitter, and is best served as a **café au lait**.
It's one of the city's great traditions to drink a cup accompanied by the sugary
puffed donuts known as **beignets** in the French Quarter's historic *Café du Monde*
(see p.140).

Most of the coffeehouses listed below serve inexpensive **snacks**, sandwiches and
pastries, too, and many will rustle up **breakfasts** and light **lunches**.

The following places are marked on the map on pp.34–35.

La Boucherie 335 Chartres St at Conti
☎581-6868. Daily 7.30am–4pm. The coffee is pricier and the scene less interesting than at other French Quarter coffeehouses, but the patisserie (usually delivered around 10am) is delicious, and it's a convenient spot in this part of the Quarter for free wi-fi.

Café Beignet 334 Royal St at Conti ☎524-5530, ⓦwww.cafebeignet.com. Daily 8am–3pm. Casual little coffeehouse, the starting point for many of the city's walking tours. The front is open to the street, which gives it an airy feel (watch out for sparrows pecking around your feet) and there is some seating in a small patio right next to the police station. Enjoying café au lait and *beignets* here isn't quite the same as making the pilgrimage to the *Café du Monde* (see below), but it's a good pitstop in this part of the Quarter. They serve some hot food, including breakfasts, but you can get better elsewhere.

Café du Monde 800 Decatur St at St Ann ☎525-4544, ⓦwww.cafedumonde.com. Daily 24hr; closed Christmas Day. Resistance is futile: despite the hype, the crowds and the sugar-sticky tabletops, this old French Market coffeehouse – serving from this spot since 1862 – is an undeniably atmospheric place to drink steaming café au lait, imbued with chicory, and snack on piping hot, sugary *beignets* for a couple of dollars; apart from orange juice and hot chocolate, they serve little else. Prime seating is on the large outdoor patio shaded by its landmark striped awning – come early, when it's quiet, or join the night owls in the wee hours, when you can gaze at the starry sky.

Café Envie 1241 Decatur St at Barracks ☎524-3689. Daily 7am to midnight. With its bare brick walls, huge old wooden bar and French windows flung open to the street *Envie*'s good looks are a big draw for passing tourists – who are sometimes then taken aback to encounter a quintessential Lower Decatur scene of oddballs and lost souls, gutter punks and hipsters hanging out inside. It all adds up a happy, quirky mix, however, everyone enjoying the coffee, gooey cakes and veggie paninis (from $7).

Hot breakfasts (till 1pm Mon–Fri, till 2pm Sat & Sun) range from grits and gravy for $5 to a big tomato-basil tortilla filled with egg, sausage, cheese, peppers, onions and salsa for $7.

CC's Community Coffeehouse 941 Royal St at St Philip ☎581-6996. Daily 7am–9pm. Quarterites linger for hours in this friendly branch of the local chain, either at the counter or in the plump leather armchairs, chatting, reading or people-watching through the open French windows. The brews are good and strong – try the Mochassippi, a creamy iced espresso with a choice of flavours. Also smoothies, quiches, pastries and muffins, and teas. The other French Quarter branch, at 505 Decatur St (daily 7am–6pm) is cramped and subdued in comparison. Free wi-fi.

Croissant d'Or 617 Ursulines St at Chartres ☎524-4663. Wed–Mon 6.30am–2pm. Quirky, old-fashioned little patisserie/café in a converted ice-cream parlour. Lines form down the street at breakfast time for the delicious French pastries, tarts and stuffed croissants, plus quiches, baguettes, salads, and steaming café au lait. There's a small, bare-bones courtyard, but inside, with its marble floor, tiled walls, stained-glass and iron chairs, is even more atmospheric. No credit cards.

▲ *Croissant d'Or*

EATING | Coffee, snacks and light meals

La Divina Gelateria 621 St Peters at Chartres ☎302-2692, ⓦwww.ladivinagelateria.com.
Mon, Tues & Thurs 11am–10pm, Fri–Sun 8.30am–11pm. The big draw at this little place by the cathedral is their delicious, unusual, gourmet ice cream – try the Earl Grey and biscuits, or strawberry with balsamic (from $2 for a cup) – but they also serve good espresso, paninis, and salads from $7.50. The main, larger, branch is on Magazine Street (see below).

Royal Blend 621 Royal St at St Peter ☎523-2716. Daily 8am–6pm.
The pretty, peaceful courtyard, dotted with fountains and statuary, is the main appeal of this coffeehouse – as well as its convenient, central location. In addition to drip coffees, espressos and herbal teas, they offer a limited menu of deli sandwiches. They also profess to offer internet service ($5.50/30min), but it's usually down.

The Warehouse District

The following place is marked on the map on p.72.

Café at the CAC 900 Camp St at St Joseph ☎523-0990. Mon–Fri 9am–4pm, Sat & Sun 11am–4pm. A welcome Warehouse District pitstop, linked to the contemporary art gallery (see p.81), and selling a few design books and gifts. A quiet spot to sip espresso, tea, or wine, with bagels and pastries to boot.

Garden District and Uptown

Unless otherwise stated, the following places are marked on the map on pp.88–89.

La Divina Gelateria 3005 Magazine St at Seventh ☎342-2634, ⓦwww.ladivinagelateria .com. See map, p.86. Sun–Thurs 11am–10pm, Fri & Sat 11am–11pm. Artisan gelato, espressos and panini (from $8.50); the ice cream (from $2) is really special. Flavours change daily, but honey sesame goat milk and the very refreshing pineapple mint sorbet are regulars. There's a smaller branch in the French Quarter (see above).

Hansen's Sno Bliz 4801 Tchoupitoulas St at Bordeaux ☎891-9788, ⓦwww.snobliz.com.
May–Aug only; usually daily 1–7pm. This unassuming cinderblock building hides a New Orleans institution, which only barely survived Katrina, and which is treasured even more so because of it. Owner Ashley Hansen's grandparents started their sno-ball business in the 1930s – he invented an ice-shaving machine and she created the special, secret-recipe syrups – and set up on this spot in the 1940s. Both died soon after the floods, after which Ashley took up the reins, still using her grandmother's recipes and her grandfather's patented machine. You'll have plenty of time to peruse the memorabilia lining the walls, as lines can get very long, and it can take some time to create these fluffy cups of shaved ice saturated with syrup, condensed milk and, if you wish, cream and ice cream. Everyone has their own favourite flavour: cream of nectar with condensed milk, or the less sweet satsuma, are excellent bets (from $2). No credit cards.

Rue de la Course 3121 Magazine St at Ninth ☎899-0242. Mon–Fri 6.30am–11pm, Sat & Sun 7am–11pm. With their café-au-lait decor, ceiling fans, pressed-tin or dark wood walls, and green reading lamps, New Orleans' *Rue* coffee shops exude an old-Europe ambience. This, and the Riverbend branch (1140 S Carrollton Ave at Oak St, ☎861-4343; same hours), which is in a huge, grand old former bank, are usually teeming with students poring over fat textbooks or playing Scrabble. The coffee, brewed with beans from around the world, is strong and inexpensive, and there are a few biscotti, cakes, and bagels. No credit cards. Free wi-fi.

Z'otz 8210 Oak St at Dublin ☎861-2224. Daily 6.30am–1am. A little piece of the Marigny transplanted uptown, this decrepit, bohemian coffeehouse offers an alternative – in all senses of the word – to the preppier *Rue* down the street, though the friendly crowd at both can mix and match. It began its days near Frenchmen Street, and it's as if they transported the customized armless mannequins, ripped velvet sofas, Tibetan mandala jigsaw puzzles and tatty used books all the way up here wholesale. There's a tiny patio at the back if you begin to crave the light. Good coffee, plus herbal teas, pastries and tasty roast vegetable sandwiches.

Mid-City

The following places are marked on the map on pp.94–95.

Angelo Brocato 214 N Carrollton Ave at ☎486-1465, ⓦwww.angelobrocatoicecream.com.
Tues–Thurs 10am–10pm, Fri & Sat 10am–10.30pm, Sun 10am–9pm. A New Orleans classic, this third-generation Sicilian ice cream joint had been dishing out freshly made gelato, cannoli, fig cookies and biscotti for a hundred years when Katrina devastated it. Its re-opening – complete with old signage, huge glass cases of treats, and the dear old espresso machine – was a much-needed sign that the city could and would come back, and it remains close to New Orleanians' hearts.

CC's Community Coffeehouse 2800 Esplanade Ave at De Soto ☎482-9865. Mon–Sat 6.30am–9pm, Sun 7am–9pm. Esplanade Ridge branch of this local coffeehouse chain, with peaceful outdoor seating under Esplanade's enormous live oaks, good coffee, and a few snacks to boot. Free wi-fi.

Fair Grinds 3133 Ponce de Leon at Mystery ☎913-9072, ⓦwww.fairgrinds .com. Daily 6.30am–10pm. Friendly local hangout colourfully decorated with painted timber walls and mismatched furniture, serving fairtrade and organic coffee, juice and very simple snacks (some vegan options from $3) to a laptop-toting crowd. There's a strong community vibe here, with Scrabble, yoga, life drawing and movie nights. No credit cards.

NOMA Courtyard Café NOMA, City Park ☎488-2631, ⓦwww.noma.org. Wed noon–8pm, Thurs–Sun 10am–5pm. In 2010, this peaceful refuelling spot, with big picture windows overlooking City Park's trees and lagoons, was temporarily being run by Ralph Brennan and offering his typically unfussy, sophisticated take on soups, salads, and sandwiches. Whether Brennan ups and moves on remains to be seen (check the museum website), but either way the café will continue to serve coffee, drinks, and light meals.

Faubourg Marigny and Bywater

Unless otherwise stated, the following places are marked on the map on p.100.

Café Rose Nicaud 632 Frenchmen St at Chartres ☎949-3300. See map, p.101.
Daily 7am–6pm. This comfortable, spacious neighbourhood coffee bar, decorated in warm reds and ochres, is a friendly, delightfully mixed place, and a firm favourite with the local academics, artists, and musicians who linger for ages around the marble-topped tables, in the capacious armchairs, or outside. The coffee is inexpensive and good, and there's a wide range of herb teas and smoothies, plus light meals served all day. It's all very veggie-friendly, with sandwiches ($5) and lots of eggy options for breakfast (till noon) and creative salads (try the spinach and strawberry for $7) later on. Free wi-fi.

The Orange Couch 2339 Royal St at Marigny ☎267-7327, ⓦwww.theorangecouchcoffee .com. Daily 7am–10pm. Cool designer minimalism is not a natural New Orleans trait, and certainly not one you'd associate with the battered old Marigny, but this peaceful place has carved a niche for itself by providing a stylish, airy, alternative to the chaotic junk store aesthetic of the area's other hip coffeehouses. Perhaps these white walls, big windows, and retro fittings – yes, there's an orange leatherette couch – could be anywhere, but the non-posey, inclusive vibe is very New Orleans and, crucially, the coffee is delicious. They also offer ice cream, cookies, Japanese mochi sweets, and quiches.

Sound Café 2700 Chartres St at Port ☎947-4477. Mon–Fri 7am–8pm, Sat & Sun 8am–6pm. There's a laidback vibe at this friendly Bywater corner joint, which acts as a kind of local hub, hosting occasional communty events, live bands and kids' workshops in a cavernous, unadorned space (just a small piano, a few armchairs and simple tables with retro plastic chairs). The coffee is great, as are the simple all-day breakfasts (around $5), which include waffles or granola. There are also salads (including a vegan option with hummus, sprouts and red onion; $6.25), and wine by the glass ($5). Free wi-fi, and a sweet bookstore next door (see p.188).

Delis, food stores and markets

For wine and **alcoholic drinks,** see Vieux Carré Wine and Spirits (p.148).

Central Grocery 923 Decatur St at Dumaine, French Quarter ☎523-1620. **See map, pp.34–35.** Tues–Sat 9am–5pm. Famed for its muffulettas (half for $6.95, whole for $12.95), this fragrant old Italian deli, open since 1906, offers a range of picnic staples, with giant cheeses and salamis hanging from the ceiling and big tubs of olives marinating in herby oils. Most people take out – it's just a short hop across to the river – but there is some counter seating. No credit cards.

Crescent City Farmers Markets ⓦwww .crescentcityfarmersmarket.org. New Orleans has three farmers' markets: on Tuesday uptown at 200 Broadway at the river (9am–1pm; see map, pp.88–89); on Thursday in Mid-City at 3700 Orleans Ave by the bayou (3–7pm; see map, pp.94–95); and on Saturday in the Warehouse District at 700 Magazine St at Girod (8am–noon; see map, p.72). Stalls sell fresh seasonal fruit and vegetables, breads, cheese, cut meats, and organic wines; there are also good coffee, pastry and lunch stands, live music, and celebrity chef demonstrations.

Louisiana Products Grocery and Deli 618 Julia St at Camp, Warehouse District ☎529-1666. **See map, p.72.** Mon–Fri 7am–4pm. Delightfully nostalgic old-time general store, slightly incongruous among the surrounding contemporary art galleries, serving simple lunch specials and po-boys at low prices.

Rouses 701 Royal St at St Peter, French Quarter ☎523-1353, ⓦwww.shoprouses.com.

See map, pp.34–35. Daily 7am–1am. Locally owned *Rouses* is the largest supermarket in the Quarter, and always bustling: you'll rub shoulders with horn players and living statues, tourists, and bus boys all "making groceries," as shopping for food is known in these parts. There's a deli counter, readymade sandwiches and heat-up food available, wine and beer, and a selection of fresh fruit and salad vegetables.

Verti Mart 1201 Royal St at Gov Nicholls, French Quarter ☎525-4767, ⓦwww .vertimarte.com. **See map, pp.34–35.** Daily 24hr. Decrepit corner grocery with an astonishingly good hot-food take-out counter: pick up mountains of baked chicken, fried oysters, blackened catfish, stuffed eggplant, dirty rice, mac cheese and gumbo for ridiculously low prices – you can fill two people easily for around $10. Nice po-boys, too. Perfect after a night out on the town. Free delivery in the Quarter and Faubourg.

Whole Foods Market 5600 Magazine St at Joseph, Uptown ☎899-9119, ⓦwww.whole foodsmarket.com. **See map, pp.88–89.** Mon–Sat 8am–9pm, Sun 8am–8pm. If you've overdone it on gutbusting Creole feasts, you may want to freshen your palate at this vast, lively outpost of the international chain. A wide range of take-out food includes boiled seafood, sushi, artisan breads, fresh sandwiches (try the blackened catfish po-boy), wheat-free chocolate fudge cake, and, to top it all a coffee stand serving café au lait.

⑩

EATING

Delis, food stores and markets

Drinking

As befits its image as a hard-drinking, hard-partying town, New Orleans has dozens of truly great **bars**. Locals love to drink, and tourists, it seems, even more so, and there are more than enough places to cater for all of them. The drinking scene, like the city itself, is remarkably unpretentious and inclusive: whether sipping Sazeracs in the golden glow of a historic cocktail bar or necking an Abita in a tumbledown dive, you'll more than likely find yourself in a high-spirited crowd of bohemian barflies. Gratifyingly, too, in this city of neighbourhoods, many establishments are within walking distance of each other, making bar-hopping all the easier. It can be difficult to separate the drinking scene from the **live-music scene** – most bars feature music at least one night of the week, and many places now known best as live-music venues started their days as humble taverns. Many establishments listed in this chapter feature occasional live music, but are not best known for it – see the "Live Music" chapter, p.153, for more on music venues that double as great places to drink.

Despite the popular misconception, there's more to drinking in New Orleans than the French Quarter, and there's far more to drinking in the French Quarter than **Bourbon Street**. A boozy enclave of beer stalls, karaoke clubs, strip joints and daiquiri bars – and even the odd jazz venue – Bourbon is usually heaving by nightfall, along with many of its denizens, leaving plenty of room in a host of great bars elsewhere in the Quarter. That said, it's a pretty unusual first-time visitor who doesn't spend at least an hour or so on Bourbon Street, stumbling through the hollering crowds with a "Big-Ass Beer" or a lurid cocktail to go – perhaps in a pink plastic goblet moulded into the form of a nubile woman, or a neon-green alien-shaped beaker – before dipping out again to find more atmospheric haunts nearby. The bedlam of dance music and shrieking revellers at the gay clubs *Oz Napoleon's Itch* and *Parade* (all reviewed on p.199), on the 800 block, where Bourbon meets St Ann, heralds the predominantly **gay** stretch of Bourbon Street. Beyond here, the further you head toward Esplanade Avenue, the quieter and more residential the street becomes. Once you've crossed Esplanade you're in the **Faubourg Marigny**. **Frenchmen Street**, the city's favourite nightlife stretch, features a string of bars and music venues that attract a stylish, arty and youthful crowd. Further into the Faubourg, and in the neighbouring **Bywater**, the scene becomes more local, with some wonderfully quirky one-offs.

With a few exceptions, bars in the **CBD** and **Warehouse District** tend to be after-work drinking holes or the kind of hotel bars you can find in any major city – not bad for a quick beer, but little competition for more characterful places elsewhere. The **Lower Garden District**, the **Garden District** and **Uptown** yield some classic New Orleans drinking holes – from classy to grungy – many of which are accessible from the streetcar line along St Charles Avenue.

While many tourists come to New Orleans intending to drink the place dry of **cocktails**, the city also offers some interesting **beers**. Abita is the local brew, with varieties including the caramelly Amber, raspberry-flavoured Purple Haze, and the chocolatey dark Turbodog, along with seasonal brews including a Christmas Ale.

Though **24-hour drinking licences** are common, don't expect every bar to be open all night – even on Bourbon Street many places close whenever they empty, which can be surprisingly early during slow periods. Uniquely in the United States, it's legal to drink alcohol on the streets – for some visitors it's practically *de rigueur* – though not from a glass or bottle. Simply ask for a plastic "**to go**" cup in

Cocktails

It is said that the **cocktail** was invented in New Orleans – although, as with so many historical anecdotes about this romantic place, that's pushing the truth a bit. From its earliest days New Orleans had been a drinking city: a rambunctuous port, with a stream of merchants, immigrants, and seamen passing through and a vibrant "café society" (for which read bar scene) to serve them. Many influences combined to create the city's taste for mixed drinks: among them the French fondness for absinthe and cognac and the Caribbean penchant for cane sugar and rum. The story goes that in the 1830s, operating from 437 Royal St, Haitian pharmacist Antoine Peychaud served medicinal tonics of brandy and bitters in little china egg-cups called **coquetiers**, which Anglo-Americans translated as "cocktails", and which took the city by storm. In fact, mixed drinks had been served in New Orleans and elsewhere long before then; as early as 1806 the term "cocktail" was defined in print as "a mixture of spirits, water, sugar and bitters, vulgarly called a bittered sling". Peychaud's mixed drinks, however, were a cut above, his ingredients of superior quality – and Peychaud's bitters, still sold today, are essential at any cocktail bar worth its salt. Since then, several potent concoctions have been dreamed up in New Orleans, many of them the signature drinks of the city's classier establishments.

Hurricane The number-one choice for gonna-drink-till-we're-sick out-of-towners; a headache-inducing, lurid red concoction – made with sugar, fruit juice and rums – which many bars refuse to serve. Popular since the 1940s, it's traditionally drunk, in reckless quantities, by the tourists at *Pat O'Brien's* (see p.147), but in fact *Lafitte's* (see p.147) shakes up a better one. Anyone with a death-wish can buy additive-laced Hurricane mixes in plastic packs from the tourist stores.

Pimm's Cup The speciality of the *Napoleon House* (see p.147), a gin-based drink served simply in a long cool glass with a slice of cucumber.

Ramos Gin Fizz A frothy swirl of gin, lemon juice, milk, eggwhite, powdered sugar and orange-flower water, invented by barman Harry Ramos around 1900. It was later perfected at the *Sazerac Bar* (see p.150) in the swanky *Roosevelt Hotel* – still the best place to order one.

Sazerac The city's official drink, today's Sazerac – a mellow, caramel-coloured mix of rye whisky, bitters, lemon, and ice, stirred together in a glass rinsed out with Herbsaint (an absinthe-like liqueur) – has a long history. In the 1830s, a coffeehouse on Exchange Alley in the French Quarter became the city's sole importer of a cognac called Sazerac-du-Forge et fils. Changing its name to the *Sazerac Coffee House*, the bar became a hit, mixing Sazeracs – which at that time combined cognac, Peychaud's bitters, and lemon – for a cocktail-crazy population. In the 1870s, a devastating phylloxera epidemic, which wiped out most of the vineyards in France, had two major consequences for the Sazerac: cognac, now less available, came to be replaced by whisky, and absinthe, which was being imported in huge quantities to replace the unavailable wine, was added. In the 1940s, the drink became closely associated with the *Roosevelt* hotel and its Art Deco *Sazerac Bar* (see p.150), but can also be enjoyed at many of the city's grand old cocktail bars.

any bar and carry it with you. You'll be expected to finish your drink before entering another bar, however. The **legal drinking age** is 21; you should carry photo ID, though few bartenders bother asking for it.

True drinks connoisseurs will want to check out the annual **Tales of the Cocktail** conference/festival/pilgrimage, held in the French Quarter; see p.178 for details.

For **gay** and **lesbian** bars, most of which welcome straights, see p.199.

The French Quarter

Café Lafitte in Exile, the *Golden Lantern*, *Good Friends*, *Rawhide 2010* and *Rubyfruit Jungle* are reviewed in our **Gay** chapter, which starts on p.198. They, and the following places, are marked on the map on pp.34–35.

Bar Tonique 820 Rampart St at St Ann ☎324-6045. Daily 5.30pm till. On the run-down border between the Quarter and Tremé, this is an unexpected, sexy little place, from the same people as Uptown's better-known *Delachaise* (see p.151). Creative cocktails are *de rigueur* here, made with their home-made infused tonic water and lots of local ingredients, but it's the ambience that makes it quite so appealing. Relaxed and friendly, comfortable and cosy with its creamy banquettes and flickering candles, *Bar Tonique* has more than a whiff of inclusive, shabby chic hip. It's unsigned, which only adds to the feeling that you're in on a secret.

Carousel Bar Hotel Monteleone, 214 Royal St at Iberville ☎523-3341. Daily 11am–2am. Inside the *Monteleone* (see p.117), an elegant literary hotspot, this quirky, historic bar is as much loved by local bon viveurs as by a high-spirited conventioneer and tourist crowd. Kitted out like a fairground carousel, with the stools set on a revolving floor, the 1940s-vintage bar takes fifteen minutes to do one full rotation. Drinks are a little pricey, but you get free snacks, and it's an essential stop on a French Quarter bar crawl. If you're feeling dizzy you can settle into stationary booths illuminated by a *trompe l'oeil* starlit sky (complete with intermittent shooting stars), but that's missing the point somewhat. Their speciality drink is the Vieux Carré cocktail (Benedictine, bitters, rye, cognac and vermouth), invented here in 1938 and served up to various literary bigwigs ever since. Pianist John Autin plays Wed–Sun from 9pm.

Chart Room 300 Chartres St at Bienville ☎522-1708. Very friendly, shabby corner bar with cheap drinks, Frank Sinatra and Patsy Cline on the jukebox, and a happy crowd of off-duty service industry workers, local residents, and loyal repeat-visit tourists who linger all day. Its facade opens on to the street, which makes it a great place to watch the world go by.

Coop's 1109 Decatur St at Ursulines ☎525-9053, ⓦwww.coopsplace.net. Daily 11am–3am. One of the best of the raucous Lower Decatur dive bars, with a pool table, jukebox, and a noisy crowd of regulars. It's a fun, much-loved place to drink, especially late at night, but it's the amazingly good food that sets it apart (see p.125).

The Dungeon 738 Toulouse St at Bourbon ☎523-5530, ⓦwww.originaldungeon.com. Tues–Sun from 10.30pm. Hidden away down a dingy side-alley, this down-and-dirty Stygian hideout is said to appeal to visiting rock stars, who enjoy anonymity in the web of nooks and crannies lit only by the dimmest red lightbulbs: skulls, cages, and cobwebs abound. With a dancefloor and three bars, it features specials (watch out for the lurid green "secret recipe" Dragon's Blood cocktail), and occasional Goth and fetish nights. $3 cover on weekends.

Fahy's 540 Burgundy St at Toulouse ☎586-9806. This laidback, often quiet, place is the friendliest of the French Quarter's handful of Irish bars, with an established local clientele, a friendly dog, a couple of pool tables, and only a few clued-up tourists to be seen.

French 75 Arnaud's restaurant, 815 Bienville St ☎523-5433, ⓦwww .arnauds.com/bar.html. Daily from 5.30pm. Hidden away in *Arnaud's*, one of the *grandes dames* of the city's old French-Creole restaurants, this bar is something of an in-the-know joint in the Quarter. The epitome of old New Orleans elegance with its dark mahogany walls, bevelled glass doors, glowing etched-glass lamps – and a hat rack for the gentlemen – it's classy but unintimidating, just the place to dress up, settle back, and sip on classic drinks. Watch the bow-tied waiters rustle up one of the brandy and champagne cocktails for which the bar is named, or try an expertly made Ramos Gin Fizz.

Green Goddess 307 Exchange Alley T301-3347, W www.greengoddessnola .com. Mon–Wed 11am–4pm, Thurs–Sun 11am–4pm & 5pm–midnight. This gorgeous, intimate restaurant (see p.127) is also a lovely place for a drink and an artisan cheese plate (around $14). Their range of creative cocktails includes the Green Fuse (absinthe, sugar and lime; $9), the French Guillotine (gin, Floc, Armagnac and hibiscus syrup; $12), and the Harem's Secret (rose petal syrup, pomegranate juice and gin; $8). The classy wine list features lots of European varieties by the glass for around $8 – including a nice Basque white – and beers from as far away as Scotland.

Lafitte's Blacksmith Shop 941 Bourbon St at St Philip T593-9761. Dim, candlelit bar frequented by local bohos and high-spirited tourists. One of the oldest buildings in the Quarter, bought by notorious pirate Jean Lafitte in 1809 (see p.52), it's practically unchanged since the 1700s. Despite some exterior sprucing, it's a tumbledown shack with beamed ceilings, peeling stucco walls, and a blackened brick fireplace where Lafitte's treasure is said to be stashed. Because of its historical appeal, it can get very crowded with a bolshy Bourbon Street crowd on busy weekends, and is far nicer at quieter times. There's a patio for those who want to get out of range of the piano player, who pounds out cocktail-lounge standards to a gaggle of drunken reprobates.

Molly's at the Market 1107 Decatur St at Ursulines T525-5169, W mollysatthe market.net. Once famed for being a genuine local Irish bar, haunt of politicos and media stars, Molly's is now a French Quarter institution and community hub, pulling in a rowdy crowd of locals, tourists, off-duty service industry workers and grungy street punks. It's a very New Orleans kind of place – remaining open through Katrina, the flooding, and subsequent evacuation, and organizing street parades for Mardi Gras, St Patrick's Day and Halloween –old memorab-lilia covering the walls from ceiling to floor.

There's good Guinness on tap, splendid Bloody Marys, and filling Tex-Mex/Southern food from the kitchen around the back.

Napoleon House 500 Chartres St at St Louis T524-9752, W www.napoleon house.com. Mon 11am–5.30pm, Tues–Thurs 11am–10pm, Fri & Sat 11am–11pm. Exuding a classic, relaxed New Orleans elegance, the family-owned Napoleon House is quite simply one of the best bars in the United States. The venerable, time-stained building was once the home of Mayor Girod, who schemed with Jean Lafitte to rescue Napoleon from exile (see p.43). The shadowy, softly lit interior is romantic in the extreme, its crumbling walls lined with age-blackened oil paintings and the old, well-stocked mahogany bar dominated by a marble bust of the frowning emperor. The customers, an interesting mix of tourists and regulars, dally for hours, either indoors, where chatter mingles with classical music on the CD player, or in the delightful tropical courtyard, fringed with lush plants; on a warm night the Napoleon House courtyard is one of the best places on earth to be. Good café food (see p.129) too, including their trademark heated muffuletta.

Pat O'Brien's 718 St Peter St at Bourbon T525-4823, W www.patobriens.com. Opened during Prohibition (but in this location since 1942), this is probably the most famous bar in New Orleans and, for many, an obligatory stop on the Bourbon Street circuit. While it's easy to turn your nose up at the hype, the crowds, and the prices, you'd have to be very churlish indeed not to have some fun here. A genuine slice of old Bourbon Street, with no little atmosphere, it's a vast, noisy complex, spilling over with drunken tourists, most of whom are guzzling the requisite Hurricane cocktail (see p.145), served, if you so wish, in 29oz hurricane-lamp glasses ($3 deposit). As well as the main bar, there's a huge patio, complete with kitsch multi-coloured water-and-flame fountains, and a raucous "dueling" piano bar, where bawdy players compete to play loudest. Less well-known, the small side-room attracts a friendly local crowd on Sunday afternoons.

Pirate's Alley Café 622 Pirate's Alley at Jackson Square T524-9332, W www.piratesalleycafe. The pirate theming occasionally goes completely nuts at this little corner bar hidden away in the alley behind the cathedral. Not only is it a regular on the ghost tour circuit, when you may find yourself invaded by a crowd of Goths, giggly tourists, and moustachioed gentlemen wearing top hats, but also it hosts pirate conventions, pirate costume contests, and pirate weddings. At other times, it's a quiet spot for a quick drink, a postage-stamp-sized old space with French shutters open to the street and some outdoor seating next to the cathedral garden. In addition to rum drinks – what else? – they serve absinthe, which adds to the campy vibe.

Port of Call 838 Esplanade Ave at Dauphine ☎523-0120, ⊛portofcallnola.com. This unpretentious neighbourhood joint, notorious hereabouts for its juicy fresh burgers (see p.129), is a cheery place to drink, crammed with a noisy mix of Quarterites, Faubourg denizens, and in-the-know tourists putting the world to rights around the large wooden bar or at small tables. A vaguely retro Caribbean theme – they serve a few exotic Tiki cocktails (try the Monsoon) – and a scattering of grubby nautical accoutrements are the only concession to style: this place is the archetype of a guileless American bar. Don't miss the eclectic jukebox, packed with New Orleans classics.

Pravda 1113 Decatur St at Ursulines ☎581-1112. Though the postmodern Tsarist boudoir-cum-Social Realist styling is a little chaotic, this relaxed bar, with dim red lighting, comfy velvet banquettes, and rugs covering the bare floor makes a nice alternative to the down-and-dirty Decatur bars along this stretch, especially if you want a quiet drink or even a quick espresso. The pretty courtyard out back is particularly appealing on a warm night. As you'd expect, they offer more than fifty vodkas, but their speciality is actually bona fide absinthe, prepared the traditional French way with the burning sugarlump. Free wi-fi.

Tujague's 823 Decatur St at Madison ☎525-8676. Wonderfully atmospheric old guard New Orleans dining room (see p.130) with a beautiful stand-up bar. It's particularly good fun on Sunday, when regulars gather to catch up and gossip. If you can't afford dinner at the restaurant, do as the locals do and order a boiled brisket po-boy or a scrumptious chicken Bonne Femme (fried with heaps of garlic and parsley) to eat in the bar.

Vieux Carré Wine and Spirits 422 Chartres St at St Louis ☎568-9463. Mon–Sat 10am–9pm. Liquor store selling a huge range of wines, bottled beers and spirits – a few of them somewhat obscure – from around the world. Though it's basically a corner store, with its TV and couple of tables it's something of a meeting place for local *bons vivants* and off-duty service industry staff.

Faubourg Marigny

Big Daddy's, Cutter's, Friendly Bar, and *The Phoenix* are reviewed in our **Gay** chapter, which starts on p.198. Unless otherwise stated, the following places are on the map on p.101.

Note that all the bars along Frenchmen Street host **live music** at least some of the week; turn to p.157 and p.159 for reviews of venues that, though best known for their live music, are also great bars.

Apple Barrel 609 Frenchmen St at Chartres ☎949-9399. Tiny place beneath *Adolfo's* restaurant (see p.130). Its cosy, pub-like atmosphere holds its own on this supercool bohemian stretch with a core group of regulars and drop-ins from the Frenchmen Street bar-hop circuit. Cheap drinks and occasional live music – mainly blues, folk and acoustic.

Checkpoint Charlie's 501 Esplanade Ave at Decatur ☎947-0979. Daily 24hr. Boozy, dingy laundromat/bar, which hosts unknown grunge and hardcore rock bands and serves sandwiches and burgers until late. The young, grumpy-looking crowd makes more use of the pool tables, slot and pinball machines than the lending library or coin-operated washing machines.

dba 618 Frenchmen St at Chartres ☎942-3731, ⊛www.drinkgoodstuff.com. Housed in an old theatre, with picture windows and high ceilings, this dimly lit bar sashayed into town in 2000 flashing its big-city credentials (the original *dba* is in New York) and a choice of beers that still leaves most local bars reeling. It's a little slick – not very New Orleans – but cosy with its cypress walls, and the drinks are good, if pricey, with more than twenty draught premium beers, classy cocktails and a range of spirits. Superb live local music, too (see p.157).

The John 2040 Burgundy St at Frenchmen ☎942-7159. Daily 24hr. A down-and-dirty late-night neighbourhood bar complete with a couple of abandoned toilets as decoration. There's no music here; the crowd, from exhausted off-duty bartenders to lost souls on a bender, are here to do nothing more than imbibe vast quantities. Drinks are suitably inexpensive, especially the cocktails. There's also a big-screen TV and a pool table in the back.

Mimi's 2601 Royal St at Franklin ☎872-9868, Ⓦwww.mimisinthemarigny.com. See map, p.100. Daily 4pm–5am. Its location beyond the Frenchmen strip and on the Bywater border means that *Mimi's* stays pretty local, with a lively, cool crowd of creative types from the Faubourg and arty Bywater bohos. They serve good tapas ($5–6) from 6pm to the wee hours along with wines from Spain, Portugal, and Latin America. Head upstairs for good live local music or funk/rare-groove DJ sets from hugely popular local girl Soul Sister.

R-Bar 1431 Royal St at Kerlerec ☎948-7499, Ⓦwww.royalstreetinn.com. The quirky, thrift-store decor at this shabby-hip bar – Buddhist prayer flags, peeling bordello mirrors on the red walls, 1970s armchairs and a pool table played by some of the coolest sharks in town – keeps it popular with a convivial twentysomething set that includes visitors staying at the guesthouse upstairs (see p.121). On Monday night you can pay $10 for a haircut and a hand-steadying shot.

Yuki Izakaya 525 Frenchmen St at Decatur ☎943-1122. Tues–Thurs 6.30pm–midnight, Fri & Sat 6.30am–2am, Sun 6–10pm. One of the coolest spots on the Frenchmen circuit, a tiny, dark nook of a bar with scarlet walls, a shelf of lucky golden cats, and a very interesting drinks menu including sake, hot sake ($4/$7), Japanese beers, and the lethal, vodka-like shochu (from $8). Good Japanese snack food, too (see p.132). Occasional DJs.

Bywater

The following places are on the map on p.100.

🏃 **Bacchanal** 600 Poland St at Chartres ☎948-9111, Ⓦwww.bacchanalwine.com. Daily 11am–9pm. Romantic and ramshackle, the Bywater's bohemian take

on an old Spanish *bodega* is a lovely place for a glass of fine wine and a plate of simple but delicious cheese or deli food (see p.131). Choose from some eighty wines, mostly from France or Italy, all of which reflect the friendly owner's tastes; bottles from $10–25. Regular events include free wine tastings on Saturdays, guest chef nights, and live music in the funky patio out back (bring mosquito repellent).

BJ's Lounge 4301 Burgundy St at Lesseps ☎945-9256. Hidden away in the deepest Bywater, this mellow joint is rarely found by tourists, but welcomes anyone and everyone. Get buzzed in to join the waifs, strays, and contented locals drinking inexpensive beer, chatting, playing pool, and enjoying classy roots music on the jukebox. Occasional live music and neighbourhood cookouts.

Country Club 634 Louisa St at Royal ☎945-0742, Ⓦwww.thecountryclubnew orleans.com. Daily 10am–1am. Only in New Orleans…a mostly gay (though straights, especially camp, extrovert straights, are also very welcome) members' club in a pretty mansion with a subtropical courtyard and lovely swimming pool. For the price of a daily membership ($10 till 5pm; $7 after 5pm), you can drink in the cute cabana bar, sip cocktails in a hot tub while watching big-screen sports or cult movies, or even dine on tasty Southern food (see p.131) by the clothing-optional pool. Martini happy hour Mon 6–11pm.

Markey's 640 Louisa St at Royal ☎943-0785. Attitude-free neighbourhood bar where a huge variety of locals – from tattooed hipsters to grizzled old-timers – come to hang out, play shuffleboard, and watch the big screen TVs. Drinks are inexpensive, and the standard bar food (po-boys, burgers, even a few good salads) not at all bad.

Saturn Bar 3067 St Claude Ave at Clouet ☎949-7532. Mon–Fri 4pm till, Sat & Sun noon till. This junk-filled neighbourhood dive has to be seen to be believed. Its decrepitude, even by funky New Orleans standards, is off the scale, with easy-going regulars – artists, young rockers, intellectuals, barkeeps and buskers – joined by wandering cats, dogs, and all manner of lost souls. Occasional live indie bands and DJ nights – Saturday's mod dance party gets unbelievably crowded.

Tremé

Mother-in-Law Lounge 1500 N Claiborne Ave at Columbus ☎947-1078, ⓦwww .k-doe.com. See map, p.64. After the untimely death in 2001 of eccentric local R&B legend Ernie K-Doe (he of the 1961 hit *Mother-in-Law*), his equally extraordinary wife Miss Antoinette kept their Tremé lounge (basically their living room, fixed up with a bar, some chairs, and a small stage) open as a shrine to the self-styled "Emperor of the World," complete with "Ernie in Heaven" mannequin holding court in an ever-changing array of natty suits and new manicures. When Miss Antoinette, who having fostered more than twenty children, revived the Baby Doll Mardi Gras marching group (see p.38), taken various Bywater musicians under her wing, and re-established her bar practically from scratch after Katrina, died of a heart attack on Mardi Gras day 2009, the city was left broken-hearted. Today, her daughter Betty is valiantly attempting to keep things going, mannequin and all – and, with the support of its fiercely loyal extended family of fans, the *Mother-in-Law Lounge* has, for now at least, remained open. Whether you hit an old school New Orleans R&B show or simply end up spending the afternoon

▲ *Mother-in-Law Lounge*

chatting to the neighbours and plugging quarters into the jukebox (featuring Ernie and New Orleans classics, naturally), you'll feel at once like you're in a movie and in a kindly aunty's front room. Hop in a cab and join the combination of supercool hipsters and unimpressed locals that make this place unique, and so very important. Occasional cover if there's a show.

The CBD and Warehouse District

For a review of the *Circle Bar*, see p.161. The following places are on the map on p.72.

Dino's 1128 Tchoupitoulas St ☎558-0900. In a neighbourhood with not too many good bars to choose from, this no-fuss, quiet place, sweetly lit with candles, can be a welcome stop-off; it's a popular after-work haunt. If you want an expertly made cocktail or nice cold beer in a stress-free atmosphere, give it a shot.

Ernst Café 600 S Peters St at Lafayette ☎525-8544. Mon & Tues 3pm till, Wed–Sun 11am till. Friendly blue-collar tavern that looks much as it did when it opened in 1902, with pressed-tin walls and a fine old wooden bar. Quiet during the day, it fills in the evening with an older, mellower set of regulars than you'll find in the other CBD after-work haunts. You can soak up the beer with blue-plate specials, gumbo and po-boys, served in the bar or in a small dining room.

Le Phare in Loft 523, 523 Gravier St at Magazine ☎636-1890, ⓦlepharenola.com. This cooler-than-thou minimal space, linked to the boutique loft hotel (see p.119) is more of a nightclub than a bar – especially at the weekend, when DJs spin very loud music. It's predominantly a singles scene, with the buzzy, dressed-up, young crowd sipping expensive cocktails and checking each other out. Occasional salsa nights.

Sazerac Bar Roosevelt Hotel, 123 Baronne St at Canal ☎529-4733. Swanky, historic Art Deco bar in the grand old hotel that once hosted the likes of Huey Long ("the Kingfish"). With its original walnut fittings and colourful "Caribbean-Cubist" street scene murals by Paul Niñas, it attracts a well-dressed uptown and business clientele. Serving champagne, fine wines and tip-top cocktails, it's the best place in town to dress up and sip their signature cocktails – the

Sazerac, naturally, and the Ramos Gin Fizz (see p.145).

Lower Garden District and Garden District

The following places are on the map on p.86.

The Bulldog 3236 Magazine St at Pleasant
℡891-1516. The main appeal at this tavern is the wide range of beers – some fifty on tap and more than 100 in bottles – from around the world. It's lively with a thirty-something after-work crowd and a convivial local scene at night. Video trivia games are hugely popular, and in warm weather the patio – complete with beer-tap-style fountain – buzzes until the wee hours. Happy hour Mon–Fri 2–7pm, plus weekday specials.

Delachaise 3442 St Charles Ave at Louisiana
℡895-0858, ⓦ www.thedelachaise.com. Daily 5pm till. Garnering rave reviews for its gourmet food (see p.135), this appealing wine bar – in an old room with a traditional tin ceiling, sitting stranded on a small island of its own just beyond the Garden District – is a lovely place to drink, especially if you like wines, including sparkling and rosé, by the glass. Also boutique beers from around the world and all the usual cocktails.

Parasol's 2533 Constance St at Third
℡897-5413, ⓦ www.parasols.com. Anyone in town on or around St Patrick's Day should make a beeline for this Irish Channel bar – their street parade is a blast, awash with green beer, green beads and green-haired revellers. The rest of the year, it's a welcoming neighbourhood spot, with good roast beef po-boys, fries, boudin sandwiches and sport on the TV. Take a cab there and back.

Uptown

The following places are on the map on pp.88–89. See also *Le Bon Temps Roulé*, reviewed on p.161.

Columns Bar 3811 St Charles Ave at General Taylor ℡899-9308. This gorgeous, atmospheric hotel (see p.120) on the edge of the Garden District, has a louche old bar, richly decorated in dark wood, stained glass and faded velvet. You can drink in a number of rooms, all of which exude faded Southern grandeur with their

▲ Columns Bar

chandeliers, baroque mirrors and vases of plump pink roses. On warm evenings, make for the namesake columned veranda, which overlooks the St Charles streetcar line. Occasional live Latin, jazz and piano.

F&M Patio Bar 4841 Tchoupitoulas St at Lyons
℡895-6784, ⓦ www.fandmpatiobar.com. A favourite on the post-*Tipitina's* (see p.161) circuit since the 1960s, this friendly (heavily studenty) hangout gets going late, with everything any drunken, high-spirited night owl might want – pool tables, a patio, frenzied dancing to the great jukebox, and cholesterol-packed cheese-fries served until late. Traditionally it's *de rigueur* to guzzle Bloody Marys and dance on the pool table, but no one will mind if you don't.

Kingpin 1307 Lyons St at Prytania
℡891-2373. Daily from 3pm. Though it's nominally themed with all things retro, rockabilly and Trash Vegas, with lots of heartfelt tribute paid to the King, this tiny neighbourhood bar is a very friendly place for a beer (they have nearly 20 varieties) and a relaxed chat. Try their speciality Dirty Pompadour cocktail.

Mayfair Lounge 1505 Amelia St at Prytania
℡895-9163. Daily from noon; closes 8pm on Sat. Timewarpy old place with lots of authentic 40s and 50s detail, and few concessions to hipness. Strung with Mardi Gras memorabilia and sundry pre-loved

trash, it's a friendly place to drink, with a pool table at the back. Buzz them to be let in. No credit cards.

Ms Mae's 4336 Magazine St at Napoleon
T 895-9401. Open 24hr. Another post-*Tipitina's* haunt that attracts a mixed crowd of serious-drinking locals and students for its extremely inexpensive alcohol (well drinks are just $1). The atmosphere is less frenetic than at *F&M*, and the pool table sees more cue balls than pratfalls (there's also foosball and air hockey), but it's still very lively, especially at weekends.

Snake and Jake's Christmas Club Lounge 7612 Oak St at Hillary
T 861-2802, W www.snakeandjakes.com. Daily from 7pm. Dim, debauched and derelict, strewn with ancient Christmas tree lights, this tumbledown shack is the quintessential New Orleans dive bar. Nothing much happens before 2am, when it fills up with a spicy crowd of musicians, journalists, students and twisted locals. The jukebox is superb, with a playlist of New Orleans music, classic soul and R&B. Happy hour 7–10pm.

St Joe's 5535 Magazine St at Joseph
T 899-3744. The decor at this toney bar is exotic – Oriental lanterns, High-Church Catholic memorabilia, folk art crosses – but the atmosphere is down-to-earth, with a mixed crowd of regulars enjoying the nice lamplit patio, the pool table, and their signature blueberry mojitos.

Mid-City

Pal's Lounge 949 N Rendon St at St Philip T 488-7257. See map, pp.94–95. Mon–Thurs & Sun 3pm–4am, Fri & Sat 3pm–5am. Local boy Rio Hackford, son of Taylor, has a magic touch with bars, as fans of his now-defunct French Quarter haunts will testify. Gussying up (slightly) a rough old blue-collar tavern and bringing in a mixed local crowd, he has created a true community drinking hole in this borderline but gentrifying neighbourhood. They serve good food specials for a dollar, including tacos, sloppy joes or pasta, and there's enough humour and style (from the $1 Pabst blue ribbon beers to old-school arcade games – not to mention the vintage Playboy porn clearly visible behind the saloon doors of the gents) to keep everyone happy.

Live music

New Orleans is quite simply one of the best places in the world to hear **live music**. From lonesome street musicians, through the shambling, joyous brass bands, to international names like Dr John, the Neville Brothers, or Juvenile, music remains the heartbeat of the Crescent City, the thread that stitches the whole place together. At any time of year – especially during the festivals – the sheer quantity, variety and quality of what's on offer is staggering.

While the French Quarter has its share of atmospheric clubs and bars, there are plenty of good venues elsewhere. To decide **where to go**, check the free weekly *Gambit* (Ⓦ www.bestofneworleans.com) and the music monthly *Offbeat* (Ⓦ www .offbeat.com) – both of which can be picked up at restaurants and bars all around town – and collect fliers in French Quarter **record stores** such as Louisiana Music Factory, 210 Decatur St (see p.195). Keep an ear tuned, too, to the fabulous local **radio station WWOZ** (90.7 FM), which features regular gig information and ticket competitions. You could also take potluck: most clubs have an eclectic booking policy, but as a general rule you can be pretty sure of seeing sophisticated **modern jazz** at *Snug Harbor*, **trad jazz** at *Donna's, Palm Court* and *Preservation Hall*, **blues**, **brass bands** and **R&B** at the *Maple Leaf*, quirky **indie bands** and **Bounce** acts at *One-Eyed Jack's*, and a **mixed bag of roots music** at *Rock'n'Bowl* and *Tipitina's*.

If you want to be even more spontaneous, you could simply wander around until you hear something you like. That said, visitors making a beeline for **Bourbon Street**, hoping to find it crammed with cool jazz clubs, will be disappointed by the string of 3-for-1 cocktail stands, drab strip joints and drunken karaoke bars. Still, even this tawdriest of streets has a couple of good places to hear jazz and blues, and at any time of day you may well stumble upon superb musicians – Guitar Slim Jr, Loose Marbles, Rockin' Dopsie Jr – playing happy-hour sets in even the dingiest alcohol-soaked dives. A better bet, however, is **Frenchmen Street** in the Faubourg Marigny, packed back-to-back with characterful bars and music venues; at weekends the crowds create one big block party. As for timings: with **24-hour drinking licences** common (see p.145), the music often doesn't get going until around midnight, even if the show is listed as starting at 10pm. However, many venues put on two sets a night, often by different performers, so with a little creative club-hopping you could easily see three outstanding bands in one evening. During Mardi Gras and Jazz Fest many places get started early and stay open for all-night jams.

In addition to the listings papers, the comprehensive New Orleans music portal Ⓦ **www.satchmo.com** is well worth a look for its wealth of gig listings, music news, music-related TV listings, message boards, CD release news, and links to local music-related websites.

Coming home: New Orleans music after Katrina

While the devastation wrought by the **post-Katrina flooding** hit many musicians – who are among the less wealthy of the population – particularly hard, leaving them homeless and scattered, those who were able to do so returned as soon and as often as possible, commuting hundreds of miles to play regular gigs or to appear at festivals. Through the intervention of nonprofit organizations including the **Tipitina's Foundation**, linked to the city's famed club, and the **New Orleans Musician's Relief Fund**, and the construction of a **"Musicians' Village"** in the devastated Ninth Ward (see p.104), some musicians have been able to return for good; energies are now being expended on music education for children in the hope of safeguarding traditions for future generations. Meanwhile, New Orleans continues to heal its wounds the best way it knows how: mourning, remembering, celebrating, and surviving, by making and dancing to music.

If you are interested in helping to preserve the city's musical culture and heritage, check out the following charitable organizations:

Ⓦ**www.musicrising.org** Replaces instruments lost by professional musicians, churches and schools during hurricanes Katrina and Rita.

Ⓦ**www.neworleansmusiciansclinic.org** Provides access to healthcare and welfare services for local, generally uninsured, musicians.

Ⓦ**www.nolamusiciansvillage.com** Rebuilding homes – and a musical culture – in the Ninth Ward.

Ⓦ**www.nomrf.org** The New Orleans Musicians Relief Fund provides all manner of economic support and physical items, from musical instruments to school band uniforms, furniture and toys for the children of displaced musicians.

Ⓦ**www.SweetHomeNewOrleans.org** Umbrella organization working to provide musicians, Mardi Gras Indians and Social Aid and Pleasure Club members with anything from loans to medical assistance.

Ⓦ**tipitinasfoundation.org** Supporting all aspects of music education, the *Tip's* foundation provides business skills training, supplies instruments for school bands, runs workshops, and offers internships.

Another distinctive feature of New Orleans' nightlife is that many shows can be seen – and heard – from the street. Perhaps it's something to do with the climate – faced with a room of hot, dancing, drinking people on a warm evening there's little to do but fling doors and windows open wide. If you hear something you like, but don't want to pay the **cover charge** – low or nonexistent in bars, but as much as $20 in some clubs – it's perfectly acceptable to stand outside with a "to go" cup (see p.145), drifting on when the fancy takes you.

Oddly, for a city so defined by its music, it can be difficult to predict how big a **crowd** will turn up to a gig. New Orleans is a small place, with a lot of clubs and a diminished population, and occasionally, especially during slow times, you may find yourself in the extraordinary position of sitting with just two or three others, listening to a local legend who sold the place out the night before.

For a **history** of New Orleans' music, with a **discography** of essential CDs, see p.234.

Jazz

Jazz, especially trad jazz, is **dance music** in New Orleans – inclusive, joyous, and sexy. It remains a living, evolving art form, and you're spoiled for choice for places to hear it, whether in Second Line parades (see p.68), at the city's many festivals, in dive bars or sophisticated lounges. You may or may not get to see world-famous names such as pianist **Allen Toussaint** or trumpeters **Terence Blanchard** and **Nicholas Payton** (except during a festival, perhaps), but you will without doubt discover an astonishing range of exciting local talents that play well within the city's unique music traditions while being open to new influences. Bigger clubs showcase the sophisticated stylings of horn-players **Irvin Mayfield** and **Troy Andrews** (also known as Trombone Shorty), the sheer virtuosity of Ellis, Delfeayo and Jason **Marsalis** of the multitalented local dynasty, and the super-smooth clarinet of **Dr Michael White**. Meanwhile, there is an equally enjoyable **indie trad** scene, incubated on the streets of the French Quarter and in the bars of Frenchmen Street. Whether you catch Linnzi Zaorski's sophisticated swing-with-an-edge or the New Orleans Cottonmouth Kings' fast-paced Depression-era jams, the gypsy-Balkan-klezmer frenzy of the Panorama Jazz Band or the Loose Marbles' ragtime hobo-hip – you'll join a happy, high-spirited mix of gutter punks and slick hipsters, delighted tourists and lindy-hopping locals. Even **Preservation Hall**, the holy grail for trad fans, doesn't rest on its laurels, keeping things fresh with guest musicians – in particular the über-hip master of all trades **Clint Maedgen** – and ever-evolving line-ups for its famed house band.

At the heart of it all, though, are the **brass bands**. Although brass bands have been integral to New Orleans' street music and parade culture since the nineteenth century, their resurgence in the 1980s and 1990s led to an explosion of energy on the local jazz scene. Ragtag groups of musicians, many of them from Tremé, the brass bands blast out a joyful, improvised and eminently danceable cacophony of horns, a kind of homegrown party music that goes down as much of a storm in the student bars as on the backstreet parades. Favourites include the **ReBirth** and the **Soul Rebels**, whose ear-splitting spin on anything from trad jazz and carnival music to hard funk, hip-hop, and reggae has won them a massive following. Still younger bands, like the the Stooges, TBC, and the all-female Pinettes, continue the tradition, honing their craft in street parades and in the clubs. The more traditional bands, meanwhile, like the **Tremé** and **Olympia**, whose line-up will typically include octogenarian old hands and up-and-coming youngsters, play music that is just as danceable and equally popular. One of the city's best-loved performers, trumpeter **Kermit Ruffins**, cut his teeth with the ReBirth. A fine jazz stylist and consummate performer, Kermit, and his band the Barbecue Swingers, guarantee a great New Orleans night out.

On any given week you'll find a handful of brass bands in the music listings, but it's even more fun to catch them at neighbourhood bars, parades and festivals in **Tremé**, when they really let rip. These are some of the hardest-working musicians in town: don't be surprised to find that the bunch of horn-blasting buskers attracting crowds in Jackson Square is made up of the phenomenal musicians you paid $10 to see at a club the night before. **Glen David Andrews**, cousin of the more famous Troy, is a case in point: a charismatic horn-player/singer who spends his days fronting loose brass bands in Jackson Square or driving crowds wild on a Second Line, and his nights gussied up in shirt and tie in *Irvin Mayfield's Playhouse* or getting everyone dancing at *dba* on Frenchmen.

Though the venues reviewed below are best known for, or exclusively devoted to, jazz, given that New Orleans music endlessly crosses boundaries and mixes things up so dramatically, be sure not to overlook the **"other" live music venues** in the section of this chapter that starts on p.158. Nearly everywhere in New Orleans will feature jazz, in some shape or form, some nights of the week.

Anyone with the slightest interest in New Orleans music should also visit the **New Orleans Jazz National Historical Park Visitor Center** (see p.42), which hosts regular short gigs and workshops and hands out free self-guided jazz walking tours.

The French Quarter

The following places are on the map on pp.34–35.

Donna's 800 N Rampart St at St Ann ☎596-6914, ⓦwww.donnasbarandgrill.com. Run by the formidable Donna and husband/chef Charlie, the ramshackle *Donna's* feels like a locals' place – you may have to elbow your way through a crowd of horn-players to get to the bathroom – but it attracts a big out-of-town crowd. With a roster of trad, indie trad, and modern jazz acts, with a few brass and Mardi Gras Indian funk bands, it's a must-visit. This is especially true during Jazz Fest and Mardi Gras, when you'll come across some of the finest jam sessions – incorporating spirituals, R&B, and blues – you're likely to hear. Tasty, simple food, too – ribs, chicken, red beans and rice – at low prices (and free on Mondays). Cover varies; around $10 plus one drink minimum.

▲ *Donna's*

Fritzel's 733 Bourbon St at Orleans ☎586-4800, ⓦwww.fritzelsjazz.net. Trad bands have been tearing the roof off this old bar, in the heart of karaoke-and-*Tropical-Isle* hell, since the 1960s, and it's still one of the best places in town to hear them. Every night is a blast, but look out in particular for Tim Laughlin, Tom McDermott, and Wendell Brunious, or

the youthful indie trad jazz favourites Loose Marbles; there will always be surprises in store, anyhow, with visiting vocalists invariably called up from the audience to guest on a few numbers. In keeping with its name, there are lots of German beers and schnapps on offer, which you can drink on *bierkeller*-style picnic benches. Shows 9pm. No cover, but drinks are expensive.

Irvin Mayfield's Playhouse Royal Sonesta Hotel, 300 Bourbon St at Bienville ☎586-0300, ⓦwww.sonesta.com. Dapper trumpeter Mayfield, a champion of the New Orleans music scene, dreams of bringing classy jazz back to Bourbon Street. This newish venue, all plush banquettes and red velvet curtains, certainly has a 1940s cachet, and the performers are undeniably superb – Mayfield himself, plus brass bands, pianists, burlesque troupes, Kermit Ruffins, Jason Marsalis, and more. Monday nights feature old-timer Bob French and his Original Tuxedo Jazz Band, when guest musicians/dancers/singers are invited up from the audience. Most nights will see some dancing and even some Second Lining (see p.68). Ultimately, however, location is an issue – it's basically a hotel bar, with punters literally passing through from lobby to elevator, paying no more attention to the band in the corner than they would a cheesy cover band, and bellowing over the music. Still, if you've got neither the time nor the inclination to go further afield, you're guaranteed to see the cream of the local jazz scene here. No cover. Shows at 8pm & midnight.

Palm Court Jazz Café 1204 Decatur St at Gov Nicholls ☎525-0200. Wed–Sun 7–11pm. Top-notch Dixieland jazz played to a tourist-dominated crowd in convivial, if rather staid, supper-club surroundings. It's a classically New Orleans dining room, lined with jazz photos – they also sell collector's items and records. Reservations are recommended for dinner, which is nothing special and rather pricey; you'd do better simply to sit at the bar. Shows 8pm; cover $5.

Preservation Hall 726 St Peter St at Bourbon ☎522-2841, ⓦwww.preservationhall.com. This shabby, ancient, and picturesque building – with no bar, a/c, or toilets, and just a few hard benches for seating – has long been lauded as the best place in New Orleans to hear trad jazz. Though the building is as old as it looks, the hall itself only opened in the 1960s, since when it has changed little. That's not to say it hasn't adapted with the times, particularly post-Katrina: while a core Preservation Hall Jazz Band remains, it changes its roster every once in a while, and regularly welcomes and works with guest musicians – Thursday night, for example, is brass band night. Performances are invariably wonderful, life-affirming and energetic, building steam as the night goes on. It's always bursting at the seams with tourists, and lines form well before doors open. You can stay for as many sets as you like, however, and people move out steadily, so you're bound to get a seat in the end. Nightly sets every 45min 8–11pm. $10 cover.

Faubourg Marigny and Bywater

Unless otherwise stated, the following places are on the map on p.101.

dba 618 Frenchmen St at Chartres ☎942-3731, ⓦwww.drinkgoodstuff.com. While the bar itself (see p.148) can attract a slightly brattier, frattier crowd than many of the others on Frenchmen, it does have a superb, in-the-know booking policy, and the cypress-wood-room is a warm, comfortable space to listen to great local music. The hottest jazz, R&B, brass bands, pianists and roots performers play nightly, with regular sets from Glen David Andrews and the New Orleans Cottonmouth Kings, among other Frenchmen Street favourites. Cover from zero (when there's a 50c surcharge on all drinks) to $5.

Snug Harbor 626 Frenchmen St at Royal ☎949-0696, ⓦwww.snugjazz.com. Sophisticated, prestigious jazz club in a small, two-storey space packed tight, cabaret-style, with small tables and chairs. Regulars include Astral Project, who play cool modern jazz, clarinet maestro Dr Michael White, scat singer Charmaine Neville (of *the* Nevilles), pianist Ellis Marsalis, and his drummer son, Jason. The cosy restaurant, which serves Creole standards, closes at 11pm (midnight at weekends), but the bar, from where you can hear the gigs – and watch them, on the tiny closed-circuit TV– stays open late. Shows 8pm & 10pm; cover varies, but can be as much as $25.

Spotted Cat 623 Frenchmen St at Royal ☎943-3887. With nightly roots music and hobo jazz, this friendly, quite drunken

little bar has become *the* place to see the New Orleans Cottonmouth Kings, whose high-octane, swinging twist on trad is impossible not to dance to. If you can't find space among the super-talented lindyhoppers and cute charleston kids, join the crowd outside enjoying the show through the huge picture windows and open door. Shows 6pm & 9.30pm. No cover.

Sweet Lorraine's 1931 St Claude Ave at Touro ☎945-9654, ⓦwww.sweetlorrainesjazzclub.com. See map, p.100. This classy supper club – on the blighted fringes of Tremé and the back end of the Faubourg – has established itself as a top spot for contemporary jazz, especially at the weekend. The room is small, but musicians love to play here, certain of an enthusiastic, attentive response, and the Creole food is great. There are also black poetry nights, blues, and a Sunday jazz brunch (11am–2.30pm). The crowd is dressy, overwhelmingly local, and includes a number of local movers and shakers. Cover varies.

Vaughan's 4229 Dauphine St at Lesseps, Bywater ☎947-5562. See map, p.100. Quintessential New Orleans neighbourhood bar – all paint-peeling clapboard and old neon – that fills to bursting on Thursday, when Kermit Ruffins plays jubilant jazz with his Barbecue Swingers band. It's very lively, with the band crammed against the hard-dancing audience – a mixed bunch of high-spirited college students, the players' friends and family, boozy locals, and fellow musicians. Between sets, help yourself to all-you-can-eat beans and rice from a massive pot. Take a cab and prepare for a magical New Orleans evening. Show 9pm; cover $10 (Thurs only).

Tremé

See also *Sweet Lorraine's*, above.

Sidney's Saloon (Kermit's Lounge) 1200 St. Bernard Ave at St Claude ☎947-2379. See map, p.101. This neighbourhood bar, owned by Kermit Ruffins, is a fiercely local community hub, and little known outside Tremé itself – to see who is on and when, check ⓦwww .wwoz.org. It's a safe bet that there will be some good music here around Jazz Fest time, however, when performances from Kermit and his friends are enjoyed by a happy mix of savvy tourists, local musicians, and New Orleanians from all over town. Take a cab.

Bullet's 2441 A P Tureaud Ave at Rocheblave
☎948-4003. See map, pp.94–95. Though less
well-known than his Thursday night gig at
Vaughan's (see p.157), Kermit Ruffins'
standing Tuesday night show at this worry-
ingly named but reassuringly welcoming bar
is just as much fun. It's a casual joint where
friends and family gather to catch up, laugh,
drink, and enjoy good barbecue. Show
7pm; no cover.

Other live music

There's far more to New Orleans than jazz alone. Though the "**New Orleans sound**", an exuberant, carnival-tinged hybrid of blues, parade music and R&B, had its heyday in the early 1960s, and many of its greatest stars have now passed, some are still going strong, and their shows, crowded with devoted locals, make for a quintessentially New Orleans night out. Check listings papers for appearances from Al "Carnival Time" Johnson, especially around Mardi Gras – and be prepared to sing along. After a two-year break post-Katrina, the Neville Brothers are back playing their legendary Jazz Fest closing set; Aaron's traditional rendition of *Amazing Grace* is a spiritual event for New Orleanians, and one not to be missed if you are in town. The brothers appear in various combinations year-round: most commonly Art, with his band the funky Meters. You may also see Irma Thomas, whose classics *Breakaway*, *It's Raining* and *Ruler of My Heart* never fail to send shivers down the spine. Super-talented songwriter-producer Allen Toussaint, who gave many of these R&B legends their big breaks, is still hard at work, too, showcasing new acts, recording and performing. If you are particularly blessed you may even get to see a rare appearance from Fats Domino.

Since the 1960s New Orleans has also been known for its homegrown **funk** – along with Art Neville's funky Meters, big local names include Galactic, Papa Grows Funk, Ivan (son of Aaron) Neville's Dumpstaphunk, Groovesect, and the ear-shattering brass of Big Sam's Funky Nation. If you want to see New Orleanians really let rip, however, try to catch a rare show from greying local heroes The Radiators, whose down-and-dirty blend of R&B, funk and rock has been bringing the house down for decades. **Blues** fans should look out for soulful blues-R&B fusion of Walter "Wolfman" Washington, who started his career backing Lee *Working on a Coalmine* Dorsey; Delta-blues guitarist John Mooney; Washboard Chaz, who sends the indie crowd wild with his *frottoir*-based acoustic swing; and the up-and-coming Honey Island Swamp Band, who have boozy country blues licked.

Hip-hop has its own special place in New Orleans music history, largely due to the phenomenal international success of local rap labels No Limit – whose star-studded roster in the 1990s included Mystikal, Master P, C-Murder, Mia X, and Soulja Slim – and Cash Money, who followed hot on their heels with B.G, Juvenile, and Lil Wayne, among others. **Bounce**, which emerged in the 90s using the call and response traditions of street parades and Mardi Gras Indians, is still huge in the city that created it: if you have a yen to back your thang up, look for gigs in the smaller or underground clubs by old-school Bounce maestro DJ Jubilee or the fabulous, uniquely New Orleanian "**sissy rappers**" Big Freedia, Sissy Nobby, and transsexual Katey Red, who attract huge crossover crowds.

Though many people associate New Orleans with the accordion jangle of **Cajun** music, it's not indigenous to the city. That said, locals do love to *fais-do-do* (the Cajun two-step), and there are a couple of fantastic places to dance to **zydeco**, its bluesier black relation. Watch out for gigs by accordion/harmonica/*djembe* player Bruce "Sunpie" Barnes, whose "Afro-Louisiana" music is a heady mix of zydeco, blues and R&B. Sentimental, melodic and easy to dance to, **swamp pop**, the region's distinctive mix of country, New Orleans R&B and Cajun music, had its heyday in the 1950s but still has a strong following among old-timers; you'll hear bands like Lil' Band of Gold at festivals and some of the more local clubs.

New Orleans **rock** is alive and kicking, in its own inimitably quirky style: theatrical, countercultural, and infused with the history and traditions of the city. Best of all, it rarely takes itself too seriously. Towering above the indie-rock scene are king and queen of the Ninth Ward, Quintron and Miss Pussycat, along with multitalented bandleader Clint Maedgen, who divides his time between his skewed, hugely enjoyable, vaudevillian cabaret **The New Orleans Bingo! Show**, various rock bands, and the venerable Preservation Hall Jazz band. Also worth checking out are the carnivalesque horns and accordions of avant-garde circus punks Why Are We Building Such A Big Ship?, and MyNameIsJohnMichael – formed after John Michael Rouchell took on a bet to write and record a song every week for a year – who infuse their twangy indie guitar rock with New Orleans soul and brass.

The city has also taken **klezmer** to its heart; in addition to outfits like the Panorama Brass Band, who bang out a frenzied blend of Yiddish folk, jazz and punk, look out for The Zydepunks, whose soulful, multilingual blend of zydeco with Klezmer, gypsy and Irish music is impossible not to dance to.

Finally, if you get the chance to catch a **Mardi Gras Indian performance** (see p.148) you should move hell and high water to be there. With its ancient chants, call-and-response hollering, spiritual intensity and improvised percussion beat, Indian music is at the heart of all New Orleans music, and to share in it is an experience that borders on sacred. The tribes proper only parade a few times a year, but offshoot bands like the Wild Magnolias, or the funk/Indian fusion 101 Runners play gigs all year-round, especially at festival times.

The French Quarter

The following places are on the map on pp.34–35.

Balcony Music Club 1331 Decatur St at Esplanade ☎599-7770. Daily 6pm–1.30am. Cosy, relaxed club with etched glass doors invariably thrown open to the street. Its eclectic booking policy – anything from Industrial DJ sets to salsa, brass bands to indie rock, swing to blues – features both local and visiting bands.

Chris Owens 500 Bourbon St at St Louis ☎523-6500, ⊛www.chrisowensclub.net. Chris Owens' one-woman hour-long variety show brings you Bourbon Street bawdiness at its old-fashioned best. Glitzy, spangly, and unashamedly camp, local institution Ms Owens has been a fixture here since 1967, high-kicking and grinding her way through Latin, Las Vegas, and pop standards, and shows no sign of stopping. Call for times.

House of Blues 225 Decatur St at Iberville ☎310-4999, ⊛www.hob.com. Large, slick venue, part of the national chain, with Southern folk art-themed decor. While the high prices and un-New Orleans attitude (bouncers, wrist tags) can be off-putting,

they book big names in a range of genres from blues, funk, reggae and zydeco to rap, hip-hop and rock. Artists have included Bob Dylan, Ray Charles, Willie Nelson, the B-52s and Lee "Scratch" Perry, as well as local stars like the Nevilles and Dr John. There's a gospel brunch on Sunday (10am; call to reserve) and regular DJ dance nights. Cover varies.

One-Eyed Jack's 615 Toulouse St at Chartres ☎569-8361, ⊛www .oneeyedjacks.net. Hip bar/club that successfully throws together an offbeat mix of music and styles for an in-the-know, artsy crowd. Loosely conceived as a decadent cabaret lounge in old Bourbon Street style, *Jack's* is slightly dark and a little daring, but it's a friendly place for all that, and never takes itself too seriously. While indie rock dominates, you'll find anything from burlesque to sissy rap, trad jazz, swing and punk. Cover varies.

Faubourg Marigny

If you're looking for roots R&B, local rock and blues, see also *dba* (see p.148). The following places are on the map on p.101.

Blue Nile 532 Frenchmen St at Decatur ☎948-2583, ⒲www.bluenilelive.com. This old bar/music venue has seen a few name changes over the years. With its dark corners, hippyish starlit ceiling, and large dancefloor, it remains a likeable stalwart on the Frenchmen strip. Nightly funk, reggae, rock, Latin, and brass, with regular gigs from Kermit Ruffins and the Soul Rebels downstairs, plus weekly improvised jazz jams in the smaller upstairs room on Tuesdays. From no cover up to $10.

▲ Blue Nile

Dragon's Den 435 Esplanade Ave at Frenchmen ☎949-1750, ⒲www.myspace .com/dragonsdennola. Balancing perilously above the *Café Bamboo* (see p.131) in a crumbling townhouse, this bohemian, opium-den-style bar/club is a favourite of local bright young things and grungy indie kids. While there is some seating on the alarmingly decrepit balcony, most people loll on the velvet floor cushions, crowd the low tables, or dance like demons next to the tiny stage; there's also a patio out back. Music is a mixed, sometimes obscure bag of acoustic, avant-garde, funk, indie punk, and the occasional brass band. Cover varies.

The Maison 508 Frenchmen St at Decatur ☎309-7137, ⒲508maisonmusique.com. Large, loose and easy Faubourg club. With two

stages, a big dance floor, and a wraparound balcony, it's a flexible space for a good variety of local jazz, brass, funk, and soul. Cover around $10.

Bywater

The following places are on the map on p.100.

Hi-Ho Lounge 2239 St Claude at Elysian Fields ☎945-4446. There's something quintessentially New Orleans about this club: perhaps it's the borderline location, on the fringes of Tremé, the Faubourg, and Bywater; perhaps the ambience, which is quirky but comfortable, with vintage booths and an old Deco bar, domino games and table football; or perhaps the unpretentious, enthusiastic mix-and-match booking policy. The mainstay is local indie rock, but it attracts a friendly crowd of in-the-know groovers for everything from bluegrass jams to burlesque cabaret, hardcore punk, Mardi Gras Indians, avant-garde performance art and old-school R&B. Cover varies.

Spellcaster Lodge 3052 St Claude Ave at Clouet ⒲www.quintronandmisspussycat.com/lodge .html. Painfully hip but outrageously enjoyable underground club/speakeasy run by Quintron and Miss Pussycat in the very turquoise, puppet-populated basement of their studio-home. The occasional gigs tend to be word-of-mouth, or detailed on flyers or Ninth Ward fanzines, though the biggest dos are also heralded on their website. You'll join an arty youthful crowd wigging out to circus acrobats and psychedelic electrorockers, sissy rappers and punkish marching bands, crazed puppetry from Miss Pussycat, and frenzied electronic beats from Mr Quintron and his trusty Drum Buddy.

Tremé

The following places are on the map on p.64.

Mother-in-Law Lounge 1500 N Claiborne Ave at Columbus ☎947-1078, ⒲www .k-doe.com. Since the deaths of local R&B legend Ernie in 2001, and his extraordinary wife Antoinette on Mardi Gras day 2009, this offbeat, warmhearted Tremé lounge (see p.150) has been kept open by Antoinette's daughter Betty, and is still enjoyed by the legions of fans who are making it their life's work to keep the K-Doe spirit alive. While gigs are rarer nowadays, the lounge still hosts occasional and unmissable music shows. Joining the K-Does' motley extended clan of die-hard fans, birth family and Ninth Ward cool cats, while a neighbourhood blues or R&B superstar belts his heart out three feet away from you – life doesn't get much better.

Nola Art House 1614 Esplanade Ave at Claiborne Ⓦwww.1614esplanade.com. The funky Art House, a decrepit Creole mansion, is home to a loose array of musicians, DJs and artists whose underground steampunk-art school-BYOB party nights have gained a feverish following – especially since the installation of an ever-evolving multilevel treehouse, complete with rope bridges and slides. It's a surreal experience, listening to noisy indie-rock bands while barefoot bohemians swig from bottles and scamper among the ropes. Look for flyers or check their Facebook page to find out what they've got up their sleeves next.

The CBD and Warehouse District

The following places are on the map on p.72.

Circle Bar 1032 St Charles Ave at Lee Circle Ⓣ588-2616. Run by the same people who brought you *Snake and Jake's* (see p.152), the offbeat and charmingly shambolic *Circle Bar*, incongruously set in a crumbling house standing alone in the shadow of the Expressway, crams live bands into its tiny space most nights. With an eclectic booking policy, it's renowned for resurrecting R&B legends from ignominy, though nowadays it's mostly hosts indie rock. Either way, it always pulls a gorgeous, hard-partying crowd of hippies, rockabillies and hipsters, all rubbing along nicely with the mumbling barflies propping up the bar. It gets very crowded, and half the party usually ends up mingling on the sidewalk. Cover varies.

Howlin' Wolf 907 S Peters St at St Joseph Ⓣ522-WOLF, Ⓦwww.thehowlinwolf.com. With its eye-catching mural of local musicians outside, and its huge mahogany bar salvaged from Al Capone's *Lexington Hotel* and the exteriors of a few shotgun cottages inside, the *Howlin' Wolf* has a passionate,

quirky sense of history. The big, warehouse-like space hosts alternative rock, brass bands, funk, and R&B, with a strong emphasis on local names, but also national acts. Cover varies.

Republic 828 S Peters St at Julia Ⓣ528-8282, Ⓦwww.republicnola.com. They sell this place as a sophisticated nightspot, where you can sip Sazeracs while enjoying anything from Bounce and Dirty South rap to old-school New Wave and brass-band funk. Gigs are great; the weekend club nights (indie, rock and electropop), however, which bring in a very young crowd and a very non-New Orleans door policy (no hats; no graphic T-shirts), are best avoided. Cover varies.

Uptown

The following places are on the map on pp.88–89.

Le Bon Temps Roulé 4801 Magazine St at Bordeaux Ⓣ895-8117. A spirited mix of locals and hard-drinking students fill this attractive, appealing neighbourhood bar – the name is a variation on the Cajun phrase "laissez les bon temps rouler", or "let the good times roll", and is generally shortened to "Lay-bon-tom". The Soul Rebels' standing Thursday night gig is always phenomenal, and free. Other evenings you'll get a mixed bag of blues, acoustic, funk, jazz, zydeco, R&B, or rock. They also offer food specials – free oysters, red beans and rice and the like – a wide selection of beers, a quiet front bar with two pool tables, a great jukebox and a patio. Low or no cover.

Maple Leaf 8316 Oak St at Dante Ⓣ866-9359, Ⓦmapleleafbar.com. Classic old New Orleans bar with pressed-tin walls, a large dance floor and a patio. Established for more than 30 years, it's been home base for some of the greats – including pianist James Booker – and is a much-loved institution. Locals fill the place, and the sidewalk outside, for a nightly menu of New Orleans piano, R&B, brass (the ReBirth Brass Band's legendary Tuesday night gigs are unmissable) and blues. There's chess and pool, too, and poetry readings on Sunday afternoons. Cover varies.

Tipitina's 501 Napoleon Ave at Tchoupitoulas Ⓣ895-8477, Ⓦwww.tipitinas.com. Legendary

▲ *Maple Leaf*

venue, named for a Professor Longhair song and sporting a banner with his likeness above the stage. Though it's no longer the must-see it once was, *Tip's* still has a consistently strong line-up of funk, R&B, brass, ska, soul and reggae, spanning the range from local favourites to national acts. And the Cajun *fais-do-do*, or dance (with free lessons; Sun 5–9pm) is great fun. Cover $7–20.

Mid-City

The following places are on the map on pp.94–95.

Chickie Wah Wah 2828 Canal St at S White ☎304-4714, ⓦwww.chickiewahwah.com. This relatively upscale music-lovers' club is a beacon of light in the flood-ravaged neighbourhood, with retro folk art-meets-neon decor and a superb jukebox of local music. You'll see an intelligently selected mixed bag here, from folk to blues via brass and jazz, with regular sets from John Boutté (Creole jazz/soul), Anders Osborne (folk-rock), and the wonderful jazz clarinettist Evan Christopher; unusually, many shows start early, at around 7pm or 8pm. There's a good beer selection, and an inexpensive menu of Creole/Southern staples. Free wi-fi. Cover varies; some shows free, others from $5.

Mid-City Lanes Rock'n'Bowl 3000 S Carrollton Ave at Earhart ☎861-1700, ⓦwww.rockandbowl.com. Joyful, rambunctious, and carefree, this eccentric ten-lane bowling alley-cum-live music venue is pure New Orleans, and fantastic fun. Thursday night is zydeco night, when greats such as Geno Delafose stir the local, all-ages, hard-dancing crowd into such a frenzy that you can barely hear the crashing of the pins. For the rest of the week they book good local R&B, blues, funk, swamp pop and swing. Cover varies.

Mardi Gras

Nothing sums up the unique nature of New Orleans as profoundly as **Mardi Gras**. Already one of the liveliest cities in North America, New Orleans lurches into an irresistible frenzy during carnival season, which starts on Twelfth Night and runs for the six weeks or so until Ash Wednesday. Though the name defines the entire season, Mardi Gras itself – an official holiday – French for "**Fat Tuesday**," is simply the last day of a whirl of parades, parties, bohemian street revels, and secret masked balls, all inextricably tied up with the city's byzantine social, racial, and political structures. It's hard to imagine another city in the developed world that could, for more than a month, devote all its energy and resources to the simple pursuit of pleasure – krewe news makes headlines, major streets are closed for days to make way for parades, and everyone, from bus boys to bigwigs, engage in lively debates about which krewes have come up with the best parades and which ones have been stingy with their throws. While it's by far the busiest tourist season, when the city is invaded by millions, Mardi Gras has always been, above all, a party that New Orleanians throw for themselves. Visitors are wooed, welcomed, and shown the time of their lives, but without them carnival would reel on regardless, dressing wildly, drinking, and dancing its bizarre way into Lent.

Much of official carnival revolves around the members-only **krewes**, who as well as organizing the public **parades** also hold elite society **balls**, glittering, arcane affairs that are strictly invitation-only. But visitors are more likely to be drawn into **unofficial carnival**: a whirlwind of satirical shindigs thrown by **alternative krewes**, impromptu parades and spur-of-the-moment carousing, and always, everywhere, the city's phenomenal **live music**. Of course, there's also the heavy drinking, stripping off and throwing up on **Bourbon Street**, where carnival gets down to its barest, basest essentials. However, despite what the national news media might have you believe, the fratpack shenanigans on Bourbon Street go nowhere near defining the true experience of Mardi Gras.

For more on Mardi Gras, see the **colour** section.

Some history

Mardi Gras was brought to New Orleans in the 1740s by **French colonists** who continued the European custom, established since medieval times, of marking the imminence of Lent with partying, masquerades, and feasting. Their **slaves**,

Mardi Gras is always the day before Ash Wednesday, exactly 47 days before Easter: in **2011** it falls on March 8, in **2012** on Feb 21 and in **2013** it's on Feb 12.

Top ten carnival tunes

Carnival in New Orleans reels along to its own exuberant **soundtrack**, much of it penned during the 1950s and 1960s, when Crescent City R&B was in its heyday. Anyone who has danced to Mardi Gras music knows it to be an expression of sheer life-affirming joy: a peculiarly New Orleans cocktail of R&B mixed with Mardi Gras Indian patois, Second Line beats, barroom boogie-woogie, blasts of brass and Caribbean and African rhythms. Every local recording artist includes a handful of Mardi Gras songs in his or her repertoire: the versions listed below – in chronological order – are agreed to be the definitive and the best, and you'll hear them repeatedly all over town throughout the entire season.

Carnival Time **Al "Carnival Time" Johnson**
1950s Mardi Gras anthem, all catchy lyrics, driving piano and ear-splitting horns.

Jock-a-Mo **Sugar Boy Crawford**
Infectious calypso-tinged hit (with its catchy Iko-Iko refrain), recorded in 1953, that flings together Mardi Gras Indian patois with hard-driving guitar from Snooks Eaglin.

Mardi Gras Mambo **The Hawkettes**
1950s R&B-meets-mambo hit, featuring a 17-year-old Art Neville on vocals and keyboards.

Go to the Mardi Gras **Professor Longhair**
The usual piano wizardry from the Prof, plus a young Mac Rebennack (who later reinvented himself as Dr John) on guitar.

Big Chief Part 2 **Professor Longhair**
Probably the finest carnival song ever; a fabulously danceable tribute to the Mardi Gras Indians, to New Orleans and to the crazy pleasure of being alive.

Indian Red **Wild Tchoupitoulas**
Venerable Mardi Gras Indian incantation recorded in 1972 by the Neville Brothers and the Wild Tchoupitoulas tribe.

New Suit **Wild Magnolias**
Hard funk homage to the Indians and their spectacular handmade outfits, driven by the foghorn vocals of Big Chief Bo Dollis.

Do Watcha Wanna **ReBirth Brass Band**
A gutsy Second Line and football game classic, penned by Kermit Ruffins and performed with their customary verve by the elder statesmen of the contemporary brass bands.

Gimme My Money Back **Tremé Brass Band**
Contemporary Second Line parade favourite from a band who span the range from tradition to funky street beats.

Do the Fat Tuesday **Kermit Ruffins**
High-spirited call to dance in tongue-in-cheek 1960s style.

meanwhile, were celebrating African and Caribbean festival traditions based on musical rituals, masking and the donning of elaborate costumes.

Mardi Gras takes shape

The Creole city celebrated in its informal way for more than a century, but what we recognize today as "**official**" carnival took its current form in 1857, when a mysterious torchlit procession, calling itself the "Mistick Krewe of Comus, Merrie Monarch of Mirth," took to the streets, initiated by a group of wealthy, white Anglo-American businessmen who had recently moved to the city from Alabama. **Comus** was an all-male, secret society, and its parade was strictly members-only. Based on the theme of

Milton's *Paradise Lost*, it featured beautifully designed floats and masked riders dressed as the demon actors of the epic – very different from the city's earlier, wilder processions, rowdy affairs with masked revellers flinging flour, mud, and bricks.

Almost immediately, the concept of the **krewe**, a secret carnival club whose mythological name afforded it a spurious gravitas, was taken up enthusiastically by the Anglo elite. More and more krewes were formed, each electing their own king and queen – usually an older businessman and a debutante – who, costumed and masked, and attended by a fairytale court, would reign over a themed parade and a ceremonial ball, centred on that great nineteenth-century obsession, the tableau vivant.

Though official carnival trailed off during the Civil War, it gathered strength during the city's volatile Reconstruction era. Dominated by the **white supremacists** whose resistance to the Reconstruction government often exploded into violence, the krewes also used their parades to attack the Republicans, northern politicians and the newly liberated blacks, often representing them as beasts, insects and grotesques. In 1872, newspapers published an arcane announcement heralding the imminent arrival of a "King of Carnival," ordaining that, "under penalty of Royal displeasure," the city be closed down for the day and handed over to him. On Mardi Gras morning, the masked **Rex** arrived by riverboat to preside over a brilliantly executed parade, which, though it boasted none of the dazzling floats created by Comus, featured hundreds of maskers and mounted horsemen. Composed of leading civic figures, Rex was formed partly to greet the Russian Grand Duke Alexis Romanoff, who was visiting the city for Mardi Gras that year. Despite his claim to be "king" of carnival, Rex himself, usually a philanthropist or public leader – and always born in New Orleans – bowed

to the venerable Comus; while Rex's motto is pro bono publico ("for the good of the public"), Comus' is sic volo, sic iubeo ("as I wish, I command"). Comus and Rex, along with newly formed krewes Proteus and the satirical, right-wing Knights of Momus, came to dominate organized carnival, their self-appointed monarchs sweeping through crowds of subjects on parades that wallowed in romantic, exotic, and exalted themes.

As the secret krewes grew, street masking and public balls – **"unofficial"** carnival – became the domain of the poor, the black, and the fallen women. A number of smaller, informal groups satirized the pomposity of the big krewes and more than once the Comus parade was blocked by jeering hordes. By the end of the century women were masking in gangs, dressed as men and carrying sticks to beat off attacks; newspapers complained that "few [of the street revellers] are of a class among whom one would care to mingle socially". The underworld held its own masques, or "French balls": raucous, drunken affairs that were curtailed in 1917 in part of a city clean-up campaign that included the closure of the notorious Storyville red-light district (see p.65).

Black carnival

Throughout much of the nineteenth century, the role of **black New Orleanians** in official carnival was limited to that of torch-carrier, float-hauler, or brass-band-member. Blacks had always celebrated carnival within their own communities, however; in 1823 one visitor reported "some 100 negroes…following the king of the wake", who wore a crown made from "oblong, gilt paper boxes…tapering upwards like a pyramid…from the end hang two huge tassels". In the 1880s, groups of black men began to organize themselves into **Mardi Gras Indian** tribes (see p.166), leading their own, often violent, processions through local neighbourhoods. In the same period came the **"Skull and Bone Gangs"** – men costumed as raggedy skeletons, wearing massive skulls and using bones as percussion – who would wander the back streets at dawn, knocking on doors, calling and drumming, frightening the children, and providing a salutory *memento mori*. Much like the Indians, the Skeletons were organized in hierarchical gangs, with chiefs, but were more secretive. Their avowed message – that life is short – was handpainted onto bloodstained butcher's aprons in the form of phrases like "Come With Me to Hell" or "You Next". As the years passed the groups

began to interact, with the Skeletons' calls heralding the imminent arrival of the Mardi Gras Indian gangs onto the streets. The Jazz Age saw the emergence of the **Baby Dolls**, loose gangs of black women who pranced through the streets in satin bloomers and bonnets, sucking pacifiers, and generally being bawdy.

There were also formal black carnival clubs. **Zulu**, the best-known black krewe, was established in 1909, when a band of labourers formed a benevolent society, called themselves The Tramps, and paraded with a king dressed in rags. In 1916, the society, now called the Zulu Social Aid and Pleasure Club,

The Mardi Gras Indians

New Orleans' **Mardi Gras Indians**, or **black Indians**, are not, in fact, Native Americans, but low-income black men who organize themselves into tribes, or "gangs." Today there are some twenty or so tribes, each with between ten and fifty members, who, on Mardi Gras morning ("that day" in Indian parlance) parade through their local neighbourhoods, debuting the extravagant beaded costumes and feathered headdresses that they've spent the last year sewing. Though there are reports of groups of New Orleans blacks "masking Indian" as early as 1872, the standard story starts in the 1880s, when Becate Battiste, of Native American and African blood, turned up in a bar in Tremé with a bunch of friends and introduced themselves as the **"Creole Wild West"**. Why they did so, and why the practice spread is unclear. Some say it developed out of a widespread craze for all things Native American after the Buffalo Bill Wild West show, complete with genuine Plains Indians, stopped in the city during its nationwide tour of 1884. Others argue that it harks back to the early days of the settlement, when indigenous tribes harboured and intermarried with African slaves, and that the tradition of masking Indian stretches back to the eighteenth century, albeit on a far smaller scale. Many see the tradition in the broader context of the African diaspora throughout the New World: in Trinidad, Haiti and Brazil, blacks celebrate carnival by donning huge feather headdresses, playing percussion and chanting.

The first New Orleans Indians dressed simply – copying the apparel of local tribes and Caribbean Amerindians – and fought neighbourhood gang wars on designated "battlefronts." Since the 1950s, however, largely due to the efforts of the late **Tootie Montana** – a descendant of Battiste and chief of the Yellow Pocahontas for fifty years, who died of a heart attack at a city council meeting in 2005 while protesting about police discrimination against Indians – they have competed instead with dances and chants and for the "prettiest" costume. These **"suits"** – which are worn in layers, so sections can be revealed one by one – can weigh as much as 45kg (100lb), their tunics, leggings, and moccasins heavy with beads and rhinestones (favoured by the Uptown gangs) and sequins (Downtown style). Each ensemble is topped with a towering plumed headdress known as a crown; those worn by the Big Chiefs, quivering with more than 350 feathers, are colossal. Traditionally, suits, painstakingly designed and hand-sewn by the Indians at a cost of thousands of dollars, aren't recycled from one Mardi Gras to the next, though they may be worn again at gigs and special events, and on **Super Sunday**, the only other time the Indians formally take to the streets (see p.178).

paraded in black-face and grass skirts on palmetto-shaded floats. Two years later the king parodied Rex's portentous arrival on the Mississippi by arriving in a tugboat along the New Basin Canal, waving a hambone as a sceptre, and as each year passed Zulu's lampoon of white carnival – and the reclamation of black stereotypes – intensified. By the 1940s Zulu had become one of the most important black organizations in America. In 1949, local boy **Louis Armstrong**, who had left the city as a young man, rode as Zulu king, an appearance that pushed Mardi Gras, and the city, into the public eye. Less publicized, however, was Armstrong's post-carnival avowal that he would never again return to his hometown, sickened as he was by its segregation and racism. Today Zulu is one of New Orleans' biggest krewes, and its Mardi Gras Day parade, a raucous and politically incorrect cavalcade of black-face savages in wild Afro wigs, is among the most popular of the season.

The twentieth century

After a hiatus during World War I, when masking was banned once again as potentially subversive and the organized krewes stopped parading, carnival was revived during the **Jazz Age**. By 1925, Rex, Comus, Momus, and Proteus were parading once more, while crowds of citizens took to dancing in the streets, accompanied by small jazz bands on motorized trucks. Many of the official parades also featured brass bands, followed by dancing Second Liners. Proteus, Comus, and Rex continued to parade throughout the **Depression**. Meanwhile, newer krewes, like Hermes, were being formed to attract tourists to carnival, and local writers like famed essayist Lyle Saxon were working hard to resurrect interest in the dwindling art of street masking.

In 1941 the **Krewe of Venus** was the first female krewe to parade, dodging the heckles and food hurled at them by the crowds. Mardi Gras grew in the 1950s, becoming a highly visible tourist attraction. The early 1960s saw the first openly **gay** carnival organizations, including the **Krewe of Yuga**, whose unofficial ball, a travesty that mocked straight carnival, was raided by the police, and **Petronius**, who established themselves as the first official gay krewe. In 1969, when the city was facing one of its most difficult economic periods, **Bacchus** emerged on the scene – a very different kind of krewe, less concerned with exclusivity than with cheerful excess. Bacchus's debut parade boasted the biggest floats, a widely trumpeted celebrity king (Danny Kaye), and, in place of the hush-hush ball, a public extravaganza open to anyone who could afford a ticket. Thus began the era of the colossal **super krewes**, with members drawn from the ranks of New Orleans' new wealth – Bacchus founders included float-designer Blaine Kern and Irish restaurateur Owen Brennan – who were barred from making inroads into the gentlemen's-club network of the old-guard krewes. Characterized by expensive, flashy floats, in their 1980s and 90s heyday, just one super krewe parade could last as long as four hours. Other super krewes include the colossal **Endymion**, who first paraded in 1974 (and whose motto, relating to the tradition of flinging beads into the crowds – see p.171 – is "throw till it hurts"), and the racially mixed **Orpheus**, established by Harry Connick Jr in 1993, which traditionally boasts the longest string of marching bands and a number of celebrity riders each year. In 1998, Orpheus debuted its 138ft-long Leviathan float, which, with its constellation of 54,000 flashing fibre-optic lights, set the bar high for the other super krewes.

In 1992, after months of widely publicized and bitter wrangling, the city government instigated a **nondiscrimination** policy for the parading krewes, requiring that, in order to be granted a parade license, they sign affidavits confirming that their organizations were open to all people, regardless of race or religion. While the super krewes agreed to the new conditions – as did Rex – Comus, along with Momus and Proteus, refused to comply, insisting that their membership be kept secret. From 1992 until 1999, none of them paraded, though they continued to stage their lavish balls, as exclusive and all-white as ever.

In 2000, **Proteus** finally backed down, and has since taken a prime Lundi Gras parade slot.

Twenty-first-century Mardi Gras

By the turn of the twenty-first century, the super krewes and official carnival were becoming a little tired. They were given a massive shot in the arm with the arrival in 2000 of the all-female krewe **Muses**, who pepped up the pomp of the old-line parades with the youthful street cred of unofficial

Mardi Gras 2006

Following **Katrina**, many national commentators believed that 2006's Mardi Gras would, or should, be cancelled. Few of the naysayers, however, understood either carnival's strong ties to history, community and family or just how crucial its heady blend of spirituality, decadence and fun are to the city's sense of identity. But New Orleanians knew what they were doing. After some six months of rebuilding – not only flood-ravaged neighbourhoods (which were not so much rebuilt as gutted), and not only thousands of devastated lives, but also the traumatized psyche of a decimated city – New Orleans needed normalcy. The city needed something positive, a sign for itself, and for the rest of the world, that it would be back. Above all, it needed to share its sorrow and lick its wounds. Like some massive jazz funeral, **Mardi Gras 2006** was a place as much to mourn as to celebrate.

Faced with a severe shortage of funds, a reduced police force, a diminished and partly transient population, a ravaged infrastructure and a struggling tourist industry, it was an extraordinary achievement that the city was able to throw a carnival as successful and sustained as it did. Naturally, there were changes. The parade season was shorter, as were the parades. Some were heralded by the blasting high-school brass bands, high-kicking and baton-twirling as if their lives depended on it, but these were far fewer than in previous years. There just weren't enough schools open. Long-established parade routes had to be redirected and shortened. Some streets were still too difficult to pass. Floats and costumes had been destroyed in the floods, and like those in any other profession, costumiers and float decorators were scattered throughout the country. The krewes that chose to parade approached the limitations with gusto, however, patching up and recycling old floats, even pairing up on parades where possible. **Zulu**, having lost a number of its members in the floods, postponed the crowning of a king or queen till 2007 and paraded with real-live Zulu warriors. **Rex** halted its parade and called for a moment of silence to honour the Katrina victims, New Orleanians stranded far from home, and relief workers, while church bells tolled throughout the city.

Much of the **satire** was, naturally, Katrina-related, poking fun at anything from Dubya and FEMA to the levee boards and local officials. **Costumes** were creative: street revellers swathed themselves in the bright blue tarpaulins that had patched up so many thousands of rooftops since the storm, dressed as the unusable refrigerators that had lined the streets like weeds for weeks after the floods, or simply donned plain rags blighted by a high brown tide-mark. Close to the edge, tinged with pain, this carnival offered not only catharsis but also huge courage. In the poor, black-dominated neighbourhoods that suffered inconceivable damage, Mardi Gras Indians paraded their decimated gangs through devastated, depopulated neighbourhoods, their battle cries and ancient songs echoing like hymns through the empty streets.

carnival, and whose beautiful nighttime parades have become must-sees.

The biggest shock to Mardi Gras, however, was of course **Katrina** (see box, opposite). The carnival of 2006, though shortened, diminished and appropriately muted, was above all cathartic – a crucial ingredient in the city's emotional and physical recovery. Many evacuees who had yet to be able to move home returned to meet friends and honour their city, creating a more emotionally charged event than usual. With the majority of functioning hotel rooms accommodating first-response staff and FEMA workers, and with a limited number of flights arriving at the airport, **tourist numbers** were, of course,

down. However, there was still a strong showing from people who knew and loved the city and wanted to support its renewal, as well as first-timers brought by curiosity, some believing that this might be their last chance to experience Mardi Gras in the so-called Big Easy. Since 2006, and partly due also to the global recession, the official Mardi Gras parades, though resplendent, have yet quite to return to their overblown 1990s excess. Unofficial carnival, meanwhile, reels on in its own transgressive way and visitor numbers have increased and evened out. As an emotional and economic lifeline for a still-recovering population, Mardi Gras remains absolutely essential.

Celebrating Mardi Gras

You need stamina to survive Mardi Gras, which gets increasingly frenzied as it progresses. For the most fun, you'll want to go with the flow: catch a couple of the big parades, rifle the thrift stores and costume outlets (see p.190 & p.191) for disguises, masks and weird gear (you'll feel left out, and have far less fun, if you don't throw together a **carnival outfit**), keep your eyes open for **flyers**, and listen to the **local radio** (WWOZ; see p.26) for news of the best gigs and parties. Official events and parade schedules are advertised in the press and in the widely available glossy handbook **Arthur Hardy's Mardi Gras Guide** ($4.99). For details of unofficial carnival events, check the **listings** at *Offbeat* (Ⓦ www.nola.com) and *Gambit* (Ⓦ www.bestofnola.com) and keep your eyes open in the hippest bars and stores.

For more on the best **Mardi Gras parades**, official and unofficial, see the **colour section**.

Unofficial carnival

While official carnival is hardly staid, and certainly not without satire (the krewes of Muses, Chaos, and d'Etat in particular are known for the biting wit of their parades), the spirit of old Mardi Gras, when maskers took to the streets to create their own parades and parties, is kept alive today in the city's many alternative or unofficial krewes.

In addition to the exquisite **Krewe of St Anne** (see p.173), who parade on Mardi Gras itself, and the black carnival of **Mardi Gras Indians** and **Skull and Bone Gangs** (see p.166), chief player in unofficial carnival is the

anarchic **Krewe du Vieux** (from Vieux Carré, another name for the French Quarter). Their irreverent ball, "the Krewe du Vieux Doo" – basically a wild party, open to all – is the first of the season, starting with a weird and wonderful night-time parade that weaves its way from the Faubourg through the French Quarter. Makeshift costumes and bizarre mule-hauled mini-floats satirize current local affairs and scandals, while the city's funkiest brass bands blast the roofs off and hip, artsy marching bands strut and twirl. As usual with New Orleans' walking parades, anyone is welcome to join in, and within minutes a raggle-taggle

Second Line will be dancing behind them. Uptown, the **Krewe of OAK** ("Outrageous And Kinky"), provides a similar, if smaller and somewhat more local, experience, finishing up at the marvellous *Maple Leaf* bar (see p.161) for live music and food well into the early hours. Other parades to look out for include the **Red Beans and Rice Second Line**, held in the Bywater on Lundi Gras, in which, echoing Mardi Gras Indian tradition, members debut new suits each year. Rather than sequins or beads, however, these suits, portraying local images – musicians, Mardi Gras Indians, French Quarter landmarks – are decorated with delicately assembled beans and rice kernels. Keep your antennae out, too, for the irreverent and arty **Box of Wine krewe**, **Noisician Coalition**, who make a lot of noise on any kind of homemade instrument possible, and the **Krewe do Craft**, who specialize in handmade and recycled throws.

Growing out of the city's love affair with circus, burlesque and dressing up are a number of rowdy, bawdy, glamorous **female dance troupes** – baton-twirling, candy-coloured-wig-wearing women of all shapes and sizes who worship all that is glittery and camp. Stars of the scene include the **Pussyfooters**, the **Cameltoe Ladysteppers**, and the subversive **Bearded Oysters**, a loose dance group for whom the only require-ment is that its members wear beards and pubic wigs.

And then there's the **Mystic Krewe of Barkus**, made up of dogs, more than a thousand of whom gather in Louis Armstrong Park in the morning before their proud trot through the French Quarter – all spiffed up on some spurious theme (Saturday Bite Fever, say, or perhaps Fistful of Collars), and presided over by their own king and queen. The dogs, along with owners and onlookers, then stop by the *Good Friends* gay bar (see p.199) to be toasted before scampering off to a happy party in Louis Armstrong Park.

Indian carnival

Once the **Skull and Bone** gangs (see p.166) have woken up Tremé with their ghoulish calls, ominous drums and rattling tambourines, Indian tribes set out from Big Chief's home early on **Mardi Gras morning**. They're led by the **spy boy**, who looks out for other gangs, and the **flag boy**, who alerts the chief when a rival gang comes into view. When gangs meet – usually swamped by now with Second Line crowds and camera-toting onlookers – they gather in circles and communicate with dances, hand gestures, percussion-rattling and improvised calls-and-responses which go on until Big Chief signals for it all to stop. Influenced by Native American, Haitian, and African chants, and peppered with mysterious pidgin and patois, the songs lament lost tribe members, recall past battles, and brag about fine suits. **Mardi Gras Indian music** has been a key influence on the New Orleans sound, and many famous carnival records, including the much-covered favourites *Iko Iko* and *Hey Pocky Way*, were originally Indian composi-tions. Other tracks to listen out for include *Indian Red* and *Meet De Boys on*

▲ Mardi Gras Indian

the Battlefront, whose combination of sacred incantation and blustering swagger create a powerful, spiritual intensity.

At Mardi Gras the tribes **parade** through local neighbourhoods where tourists, although not invited, are tolerated. However, the lack of any official starting times or starting points means that it's hit or miss as to whether you will witness them, or one of their standoffs – of course, this mysterious, mercurial quality makes the experience all the more special if you are lucky enough to be in the right place at the right time. For the best chance, aim to get out to the **Backstreet Cultural Museum** in Tremé (see p.66) by 5am or 6am. Here you'll witness the Skeletons' morning ritual, and maybe the early emergence of a few Indian gangs. You could also wait for the gangs to gather in the late afternoon at the Claiborne Underpass in Tremé, or head uptown to LaSalle and Washington, which is sacred ground for the Uptown Indians. Some tribes have taken their funky music and formed actual **bands**, and many of the more famous groups – the Wild Magnolias, for example – play gigs around town in the run-up to carnival. Don't miss these; the Indians' chest-thumping blend of funk, African beats, and New Orleans party music is some of the best dance music you're likely to hear.

Parades, throws and beads

More than fifty krewes organize major **parades** in the weeks leading up to the big day. Though they occur throughout the city, the biggest parades head downtown and attract hundreds of thousands of people. The crowds, and the size of the floats, make it impossible for the parades to pass through the French Quarter; they head instead along broader, safer roads such as Canal Street, Poydras Street and St Charles Avenue. Parades increase in number as the season goes on; the busiest days are the two weekends before Mardi Gras itself.

Huge, overblown events based around a theme (and using lots of spurious jokes and rotten puns), official parades follow **routes** of up to six or seven miles and can last for hours. Colourful, multi-tiered floats populated by masked, costumed krewe members hurling "throws" at the shrieking crowds are joined by the city's famed high-school marching bands – whose ear-splitting blast of drums and brass can be heard for miles – along with weirdly masked horsemen, stilt walkers, and sundry walking groups and dancing troupes who trail behind. Night parades may also be accompanied by black flambeaux carriers, whose nerve-wracking swirling and leaping as they carry their heavy torches, oil drums strapped to their backs, is rewarded by a scattering of quarters thrown by the crowds.

Good **viewing areas** include **Canal Street**, which sees the densest crowds, and **Lee Circle**, which provides a detailed "in-the-round" view as the parades loop around the Lee monument, but can get congested. Some people keep moving with parades, dipping in and out of side streets to catch up and overtake the rumbling floats, but this can be risky – you may end up at the back of a huge mass of bodies unable to see anything. There's more of a local scene on **St Charles Avenue**, especially between First and Jackson; the further away from downtown you get, the less touristy the crowd, with local families colonizing whole swathes of sidewalk with picnic boxes, folding chairs, and stepladders. Bear in mind when staking your place that parade **schedules** tend to be approximate – a broken down float, for example, can lead to delays or stoppages for as long as three hours.

For more on the best Mardi Gras parades, see the **colour section**.

Throws

Though street maskers had been tossing candy up to women on French Quarter balconies since the 1830s, the first parade **"throws"** appeared in 1871, lobbed at spectators by a member of the Twelfth Night Revelers dressed as Santa Claus. By the early twentieth century riders were slinging ribbons, confetti and glass beads as a matter of course, the crowds jostling and jumping in order to catch them – much to the umbrage of commentators who complained that it made "hoodlums of the boys and mendicants of the girls, both failing to enjoy the real beauty and grandeur of the floats in their wild desire to get something for nothing".

Nowadays this "wild desire" has reached fever pitch. For many visitors (and some locals) the whole point of carnival is to bedeck themselves in as many strings of shiny plastic Mardi Gras beads as possible, and the parades are all about the throws – not only the beads but also the toys and the doubloons, all etched with krewe insignia, flung by float riders into the crowds. And to truly enjoy a parade you should find yourself hollering "Throw me somethin' mistah" with the best of them, jostling your rivals to the ground in your frenzy to grab a Frisbee or a plastic beaker, and sporting your beads with pride. **Super krewes** (see p.167) are notorious for their generous throws, as are the all-female **Muses**, whose stylish gifts, from powder puffs to bracelets, rain down on the crowds like hail stones, and whose personally customized glittery ladies shoes are highly prized. Most desired of all are the **Zulu coconuts**, daubed with glitter and paint, and handed down rather than thrown, for obvious reasons. Each float-rider supplies their own throws; it is not unusual for a super krewe member to spend at least $1000 on beads.

The one break in all this scrabbling and tussling is when Bacchus' **King Kong** family – giant father, mother and baby gorilla in bonnet – rumble by. This time the crowds overturn tradition and throw beads at the floats rather than the other way round.

Incidentally, if you don't fancy scrabbling on the sidewalk for plastic trinkets it's possible to pay for a place on a **stand**, often linked to a hotel or restaurant, where $40 or so gets you a good view and an elevated vantage point for catching throws – but this isn't quite playing the game.

Beads

Throw frenzy rages long after the parades have rumbled past, triggering a drunken flirtation ritual whereby complete strangers, usually already heavily laden with **beads**, approach each other begging to swap some particular string (known by locals as a "pair of beads") in exchange for another. Over the years the stakes have become higher, giving rise to the famed **"Show your tits!"** phenomenon – female out-of towners, from co-eds to biker mammas, leaning over Bourbon Street balconies and responding to the challenge, chanted by goggling street mobs below, by pulling up their shirts in exchange for strings of beads and roars of boozy approval.

In recent years the guys have started to join in the fun, eagerly pulling down their pants at the slightest provocation. Especially popular among high-spirited gay boys, this, unlike the tits display, is officially illegal. However, although stripping off uptown, where carnival is more of a family affair, is certainly a no-no, in the French Quarter pretty much anything goes. New Orleanians leave these antics to the tourists: anyone desperate to see (or join) the show should head for **Bourbon Street** – a tacky strip at the best of times, and sheer drunken mayhem during Mardi Gras.

Lundi Gras

The day before Mardi Gras, **Lundi Gras** is one of the liveliest of the season. Things formally get going by mid-morning, when some of the city's best performers, most of whom will have been gigging till daybreak for the past two weeks, play at Zulu's free riverside music festival at **Woldenberg Park**. After a few hours relaxing on the grass, snacking on fried chicken and cold beer, listening to fine R&B, jazz, and blues, at 5pm it's time to leap up again to see Zulu's king and queen arrive by boat. When they've disembarked, you can head just around the corner to the Plaza d'España, where at 6pm, in a formal ceremony unchanged for more than a century, the mayor hands the city to Rex, King of Carnival. Everyone cheers, and the businessman in the golden robes, page-boy wig, and false beard shakes his sceptre graciously. A ceremonial meeting between **Zulu and Rex** ensues, which recognizes the popularity and political importance of the black krewe while bowing to the historical supremacy of Rex. The party continues with bands and fireworks, after which many people head off for the Proteus and Orpheus parades or to embark on yet another frenzied evening of live music. Most clubs are still hopping well into Mardi Gras morning.

Mardi Gras day

The fun starts early on **Mardi Gras** day – particularly if you head for Tremé at daybreak. If you can rouse yourself early enough to do this, it's worth every jolt of caffeine you'll need to get through the rest of the day, placing the ritual and theatre of carnival into a spiritual, sacred perspective. **Skull and Bone gangs** roam the streets waking the neighbourhood, while the resplendent **Mardi Gras Indians** gather to parade, preparing for their afternoon stand-offs. The Backstreet Cultural Museum (see p.66) and the *Mother-in-Law Lounge* (p.150) are good places to hang out for a while, as many Indians, Skeletons, Baby Dolls, and other black Tremé groups drop by. Meanwhile **Zulu**, scheduled to set off at 8.30am – but usually starting much later – heads from Uptown to Canal Street, its float-riders daubed in war paint and dressed in grass skirts. Following Zulu, the

refined **Rex** parade, dominated by the colossal Boeuf Gras – a fatted calf, symbolizing the last flesh before fasting – hits Canal Street in the afternoon. Ironically, however, by the time Rex turns up, most people have had their fill of the official parades. The wildest party is going on in the **French Quarter**, which is teeming with masked, costumed merrymakers, bead-strung tourists, strutting drag divas, tit-flashing teens, and banner-carrying out-of-state Evangelists preaching hellfire and brimstone. Most of the action is on the streets – indeed, many bars and restaurants close for the day – but some restaurants offer special packages whereby $50 or so gets you a day pass that includes food, drink, and, crucially, use of the restrooms.

Though it's best to do as most people do and drift through the maelstrom, there are a couple of high points to know about. The surreal **St Anne walking parade**, a stunning procession of the most extraordinary costumes

▲ Dressing up for Mardi Gras

gathers in the Bywater and hits the Quarter at around 11am, usually stopping for drinks at the *R-Bar* (see p.149) before parading through the Quarter and Jackson Square to the Mississippi River. Ragtag brass, klezmer and jazz bands provide accompaniment as they throw ashes into the river to remember friends lost during the year, with spontaneous outbursts of spirituals such as "I'll Fly Away". Anyone is welcome to prance through the streets with them, or to share their moving remembrance rituals; you'll fit in best if your costume is wild, beautiful, or creative. Meanwhile, on the corner of St Ann and Bourbon streets, the outrageous gay costume competition known as the **Bourbon Street Awards** gets going at noon. This is one to watch rather than join – unless, of course, you're a drag queen

who has just happened to wander by in a twenty-foot-high sequinned seahorse ensemble.

Late afternoon, hipsters head to the Faubourg, where **Frenchmen Street** is ablaze with bizarrely costumed carousers and drummers in a Bacchanalian scene as skewed as any medieval misrule. The fun continues throughout the Quarter and the Faubourg until **midnight**, when a siren wail heralds the forceful arrival of mounted police who sweep through Bourbon Street and declare through megaphones that carnival is officially over. Some bars do stay open later, but most people, masks askew, are drifting home by 1am. Like all good Catholic cities, New Orleans takes carnival very seriously. Midnight marks the arrival of the sanitation trucks and the onset of **Lent**, and repentance can begin.

Festivals

A s befits this party-loving, parade-crazy, multicultural city – a city that places huge emphasis on tradition and ritual – New Orleans' calendar is packed with **festivals**. The big one, of course, is the pre-Lenten bacchanalia of **Mardi Gras** (which is covered in its own chapter, and in the colour section) – closely followed by the enormous roots music festival **Jazz Fest** – but whenever you come your visit is bound to coincide with a celebration, be it a saint's day or a sinner's beanfeast. Whatever the festivity, music and food feature prominently, as do **street parades**, which occur at the drop of a hat throughout the year. Parades are particularly important in Tremé, where local Social Aid and Pleasure clubs organize lively processions featuring the city's best **brass bands**, followed by a dancing Second Line (see p.68).

If you're planning to come to New Orleans for Mardi Gras, Jazz Fest, French Quarter Festival, Essence, or Voodoo, be sure to reserve a hotel room well in advance; see p.115.

Jazz Fest

The internationally acclaimed **New Orleans Jazz and Heritage Festival** (**Jazz Fest**; Ⓦ www.noJazz Fest.com) is held during the last weekend (Fri–Sun) in April and the first weekend (Thurs–Sun) in May, at the Fair Grounds racetrack near City Park. Started in 1969 as a small-scale celebration of local roots music, it has mushroomed to become a colossal affair, rivalling Mardi Gras in size and importance. Detractors complain that it has suffered as a consequence, but gripes about overcrowding, corporate sponsorship, occasional poor acoustics and inappropriate headliners (the bombastic Bon Jovi and po-faced Kings of Leon in 2009 caused a particular stir) apart, it's still a fantastic show, attracting a mellower, slightly older audience than Mardi Gras. The "jazz" of the title is taken as a loose concept, with a dozen stages hosting R&B, gospel, funk, blues, African, Caribbean, Latin, Cajun, folk, bluegrass, reggae, country, Mardi Gras Indian and brass band music. Here, even more than at any other of New Orleans' festivals, the **food** is as big a deal as the music, with dozens of stalls, run by local restaurants, dishing up truly spectacular local cuisine. You'll find different dishes each year, but perennial favourites include the crawfish Monica, a creamy, spicy crawfish pasta dish; *cochon de lait* po-boys; and the plates of fried chicken livers with green pepper jelly from the *Praline Connection* stall.

At the Fair Grounds themselves, the **Thursday** of the second weekend, traditionally one of the quietest days of the festival, before the weekenders have hit town, is a favourite with locals. The **second Saturday**, on the other hand, has been known to draw more than 160,000 spectators, and was up at 90,000 in 2009. With some ninety bands playing each day, most Jazz Festers have to make tough decisions, foregoing a few of their favourites rather than dashing from stage to stage in a doomed attempt to catch them all. Don't overlook the interviews and workshops staged in the **Grandstand** – the tranquil, air-conditioned building is a great place to cool off and chill out, and it also benefits from proper, flushing toilets. **Schedules** are listed a couple of months in advance on the **website**, and during the festival itself in the *Times-Picayune* and *Gambit* (see p.25) The best pull-out programme comes free with the music paper *Offbeat* (ⓦwww.offbeat .com). If you really want to be in on all things Fest, however, you can join the **Threadheads**, the passionate, active group of fans that have grown out of the official Jazz Fest forum (see opposite).

Tickets, available from Ticketmaster (ⓣ1-800/745-3000 or ⓦwww.ticket master.com), cost $45 per day; you can also buy them for $60 on the day at the gate, though you may have to wait in a long line. There are also a limited number of discount **multi-day packages** available ($120 for the first weekend, $160 for the second) – these usually run out by mid-February – and various VIP combos that give you extra perks and privileges (see the Jazz Fest website for details). The official evening concerts, which book up fast, cost between $25 and $35, but there is plenty going on throughout town that will cost less.

Off-site: the fringes of the Fest

While some people spend all their Jazz Fest time at the Fair Grounds, others prefer to spread themselves about. There's plenty going on in town throughout the ten-day festival period, including free in-store performances by Jazz Fest acts at local **record stores** (see ⓦwww.louisianamusicfactory.com and ⓦwww.peachesrecords neworleans.com, for example) and free outdoor concerts at **Lafayette Square** in the CBD on Wednesdays from 5–7.30pm (though these run throughout April, May and June, and are not specifically linked with Jazz Fest, they are particularly lively at festival time).

Usually held on the Wednesday between the two weekends, **Chazfest** (ⓦwww .chazfestival.com) provides a refreshing antidote to the increasing corporatization of Jazz Fest, showcasing only local bands – many of whom haven't been invited to play the bigger festival – at a truck farm on St Claude Avenue in Bywater. It's a delightfully laidback and local affair. Tickets cost $30 on the gate, or less if bought in advance.

Meanwhile, many **clubs** feature superb line-ups, concert series and unofficial jam sessions into the early hours. **Preservation Hall** puts on special funk, brass and blues midnight shows; **Open Ears Music** (ⓦopenearsmusic.org) hosts special improvised jazz sessions, often featuring visiting musicians jamming with locals; and **Superfly Productions** (ⓦwww.superflypresents.com) presents interesting combinations of local roots music, R&B and rock in a range of venues.

The Jazz Fest period also sees some **big-name concerts**. In 2009, for example, the New Orleans Arena hosted a benefit gig featuring B.B. King, Chuck Berry, Little Richard, Wyclef Jean, Taj Mahal and Keb Mo among others. The Monday after the first weekend presents a difficult choice: you'll have to decide between **Piano Night**, a benefit for local radio station WWOZ (see p.26) that features a jaw-dropping roll-call of the city's famed piano professors tearing the roof off whichever club is hosting them, and Tipitina's **Instruments a Comin'**, an epic ten-hour-long brass-funk blowout that raises funds to buy musical instruments for New Orleans' public schools.

Mardi Gras

The best thing about Mardi Gras is that you get to participate, not only in the parties but also in the parades. The best of these wind through the backstreets – noisy, loose processions featuring stupendous brass bands and crowds of umbrella-twirling Second Liners. And though the official Mardi Gras parades are more formal and more overblown – featuring elaborate, motorized floats and eerie-looking masked riders hurling plastic coins and beads at the shrieking crowds – the invitation to join in is just as strong.

Begging for beads ▲
Zulu coconuts ▼

Super krewe parade ▼

The big parades

Though Mardi Gras parades roll all over the city, the biggest head downtown and attract crowds in the hundreds of thousands. **Krewes** – carnival organizations – compete to put on the best, wittiest, or most beautiful spectacles, and marvelling at a particularly inventive, elaborate, or just plain funny float (and bitching about the lame ones) is part of the fun. Most people, however, are here to do more than just watch. Everyone, from the wiry, hyper kids with jabbing elbows to the fierce old ladies hovering above the crowds on customized stepladders, is out to catch "**throws**", be they strings of beads, fluffy toys, beakers, trinkets or doubloons (tin coins marked with krewe insignia). Once the towering float-riders start throwing, the leaping and screaming begins. It's *de rigueur* to holler "Throw me somethin' mista! Throw me somethin'!", and it's futile to imagine you'll be able to resist. Competition is fierce, and the krewe members milk the hysteria for all it's worth, taunting the hoi polloi below.

Souvenirs vary in worth: the bright, cheap strings of beads that adorn balconies everywhere are the most common. The most treasured, however, are **Zulu's coconuts** – each one painstakingly customized by an individual krewe member, and handed down from the floats rather than thrown – and anything from **Muses**, especially their personally embellished high-heeled shoes, sparkling with glitter and beads. Old-guard krewes, including the stately and traditional Rex, tend to be more restrained, while super krewes are generous to the point of excessive. **Endymion** float-riders, in particular, are known for their throws, showering the streets with bagfuls of fat beads, perilous towers of plastic beakers, and a rainstorm of doubloons.

Unofficial parades

Unofficial parades feel more like a block party than the more formal parades, and, because they don't have the lumbering motorized floats, can weave their way through smaller, more local neighbourhoods.

For many New Orleanians, the parade held by the satirical **Krewe du Vieux** – a crazed nighttime procession that winds its way from the Faubourg Marigny through the French Quarter on a Saturday night three weeks or so before Mardi Gras – marks the start of unofficial carnival season. Its floats, many of which look as though they may have been thrown together the evening before, celebrate the profane and the politically incorrect, while its costumed members, a motley band of poets, dreamers, ne'er-do-wells and barflies, stride alongside. The quirky local hero lucky enough to be voted king or queen waves benignly from their mule-drawn carriage, while hip young brass bands lead a Second Line that swells with excited spectators.

Uptown, the **Krewe of OAK**'s parade (read: bar crawl) is a similar, though smaller-scale affair, starting from and climaxing at the *Maple Leaf* – one of the best bars in a city that boasts the finest in the world. OAK ("Outrageous And Kinky") costumes reveal as much flesh as possible. Unofficial parades are joined by not only the coolest, loudest local brass bands, but also the artsiest marching groups, from the risqué all-female **Bearded Oysters**, whose minxy bearded members flash merkins to the crowd; the unsettling anarcho-punks **Noisician Coalition**, who, dressed in scarlet and black, make as much racket as possible on anything that makes a noise; a band of Vegas-era Elvi, and a sassy gaggle of high-kicking glamour-girl troupes including the **Pussyfooters** and the **Muffalettas**.

▲ Krewe du Vieux

▼ Getting in the mood

Barkus ▲

Mr Big Stuff, Zulu ▼

Seven must-see parades

▶▶ **Barkus** Nutty parade in which dressed-up mutts trot through the streets with their proud owners while spectators holler with glee. See p.170.

▶▶ **Endymion** A nighttime parade for the most super of the super krewes, with enormous, elaborate floats, obscenely generous throws, and crowds craning for a view of celebrity kings and queens like Britney Spears or Al Green. See p.167.

▶▶ **Krewe Du Vieux** Boozy and rude, ribald and wild, this French Quarter parade sums up the satirical, all-inclusive misrule of street carnival. See p.169.

▶▶ **Krewe of St Anne** Mardi Gras morning sees these wildly creative costumed revellers walk from the Bywater to the Mississippi, before paying respects to the dead in a poignant ritual. See p.173.

▶▶ **Mardi Gras Indians** The Indians take to the backstreets of Tremé and Uptown on Mardi Gras morning, showing off their amazing "suits" and taunting rival gangs with songs and chants. See p.166.

▶▶ **Muses** Stylish, spectacular and irreverent, the all-female Muses krewe has made official carnival hip once more. Their parades meld gorgeous float artistry and generous throws with the kind of ragtag revellers – from scooter-riding Elvi to fire-eating gutter punks – more usually seen in the unofficial parades. Fabulous throws include customized shoes, eye masks and mini lava lamps. See p.172.

▶▶ **Zulu** Everyone loves Zulu, for its energy, its humour and its history. It's the only krewe in which members ride unmasked (albeit in black face), and in which recurring characters, like Mr Big Stuff and the Witch Doctor are met with cheers of recognition. See p.166.

The Threadheads

What started out in the mid-1990s as a standard fan forum (at ⓦ www.noJazzFest.com) has evolved into a global online network of festival-goers – known as the **"Threadheads"** – united by their passion for New Orleans. Following Katrina, the Threadheads immediately took on a crucial role in the restoration of the city. In addition to their annual party (or, as the Threadheads call it: "patry"), held in the days between the festival weekends to raise funds for musicians' charities and grassroots organizations, the Threadheads also donate money, and volunteer time, to various community and charity booths at the festival itself. In 2006 the Threadheads created **FestAid** (ⓦ www .festaid.com), offering volunteer opportunities on a score of post-Katrina projects – from restoring wrecked homes to sorting food donations – during the festival period. They also established the Fest4Kidz fund, raising money for children at a local musicians' clinic to be able to attend the festival. The most recent project is **Threadhead Records**, a revolutionary, non-profit record company that, through Threadheads' loans, has financed CDs from local artists, new and established, including Glen David Andrews, Shamarr Allen, John Boutté and Alex McMurray.

For more information on the various Threadhead **charitable projects**, visit ⓦ www .threadheads.org.

To **get to the Fair Grounds**, if there are two or more of you, **taxis** are convenient and cost around the same as the shuttle bus (see below): they'll charge around $15, or $5 per head (whichever is higher), to take you from a downtown hotel to one of two designated ranks near the Fair Grounds, and vice versa. There is also a Gray Line **shuttle bus** from downtown – with stops at the end of Toulouse Street by the river, on Canal Street, and Poydras Street ($16 roundtrip, or one-way *from* the Fair Grounds only $10; ⓦ www.grayline neworleans.com) – but it's a bit of a walk from the drop-off point to the actual festival site entrance. If you have time, you could also use **public transport** ($1.25 per journey; ⓦ www.norta.com), either by taking the Canal Street streetcar (marked City Park/Museum), which can be picked up along the riverfront line or on Canal Street, or bus 48/91 up Rampart and Esplanade, which passes right by the festival site.

If you're interested in **volunteering** to work for Jazz Fest, check the website for an application form (which must be submitted by March).

A festival calendar

The following list covers a wide spread of festivals, but is by no means exhaustive. For a **full rundown**, including details of sporting events such as New Year's **Sugar Bowl** game (see p.82), check ⓦ www.neworleansonline.com. **Neighbourhood events** are also announced on WWOZ radio station (ⓦ www.wwoz.org), and detailed in *Gambit* (ⓦ www.bestofneworleans.com) and the *Times-Picayune* (ⓦ www .nola.com). Festivals that are especially recommended have been denoted with ⚘.

Moveable feasts

The following events are held at different times on different years; check their websites for details.

Prospect/New Orleans Biennale This hugely exciting international exhibition, lasting three months, is the largest contemporary art show in the US, with conceptual artists from around the world presenting cutting-edge work. Exhibition spaces include not only all the city's major galleries but also a number of neighbourhood locales, from abandoned houses in St Roch to tiny Tremé chapels.

During Prospect.1, in 2008, much of the work was Katrina-related, revolving around devastation and loss – with, for example, a giant ark made from plywood and flyers moored next to a flood-wrecked house in the Ninth Ward, and FEMA trailers set up as "emergency response studios" where visitors could make art. The aim of Prospect.2 – November 2011 to February 2012 – will be to pull focus away from the storm and concentrate on the site-specific possibilities of the city's distinctive neighbourhoods. See Ⓦwww.prospectneworleans.org.

Tales of the Cocktail Devoted to the fine art of drinking fine drinks, this annual conference also acts as a gathering point for all cocktail-lovers, with bar crawls, tasting sessions, awards ceremonies and galas in addition to industry seminars on marketing, mixology and such like. See Ⓦwww.talesofthe cocktail.com and Ⓑtalesblog.com.

January & February

Mardi Gras (see pp.163–174 and the colour section) – January 6 to the day before Ash Wednesday.

March

St Patrick's Day New Orleanians celebrate the Irish saint's day (**March 17**) with gusto, with much swigging of green beer and Guinness. The fun starts on the Friday before with a typically funky French Quarter parade that sets off from *Molly's at the Market* bar (see p.147). Featuring some of the city's coolest and most irreverent marching groups and bands, this is always a riot. The next day, a more traditional, gentlemen-only parade hosted by the Irish Channel St Patrick's Day Club (Ⓦwww .irishchannelno.org) heads through the Irish Channel – the blue-collar neighbourhood between the Garden District and the river – with tuxedo-clad float-riders throwing cabbages and sundry vegetables to a green-bead-swathed bunch of roisterers. On March 17 itself there is also a popular daytime block party in the Irish Channel, organized by *Parasol's* Irish bar, 2533 Constance (see p.151; Ⓦwww.parasols .com). In the evening the Downtown Irish Club walking parade heads from the Bywater to the French Quarter, stopping at all the best bars on the way to Bourbon Street. And of course, the Irish bars in the

Quarter, including *Pat O'Brien's* (see p.147) are even livelier than usual, hosting their own parties, open to all.

St Joseph's Day The Sicilian saint's day, which falls on **March 19**, roughly halfway through Lent, is a big deal in this most Catholic of North American cities. Massive altars of food, groaning with bread, fig-cakes, cookies, and stuffed artichokes are erected in churches all around town (including St Louis Cathedral's garden) and the French Market; check the *Times-Picayune* for listings. Meanwhile, devout worshippers also continue the tradition of taking out newspaper ads inviting the public to come and admire their family shrine and to share food, though these tend to be more common in the suburbs nowadays. On the Saturday before the 19th, the Italian-American Marching Club parade through the French Quarter, female float-riders ("maids") flinging flowers and lucky fava beans.

St Joseph's Day is also significant for the **Mardi Gras Indians** (see p.166); in addition to their more formal parades on Super Sunday (see below), it's also common for Indian gangs to take to the streets of their neigh-bourhoods on the evening of March 19. These are local affairs, so keep your ears to the ground if you want to witness such a gathering.

Super Sunday The **Sunday closest to St Joseph's Day** is marked by two Mardi Gras Indian parades (see p.166). Rather than engaging in mock tribal battles, as they do on Mardi Gras morning, Super Sunday gives the gangs an opportunity to come together to celebrate their culture, displaying the costumes debuted on Mardi Gras day, chanting, and playing percussion. The parades, following set routes and times, make it easier to see the Indians than during Mardi Gras or on St Joseph's Day, when they can be more elusive. These are well-attended family-friendly affairs, and the many kids parading and masking represent the continuation of old traditions. The Indians are joined by Social Aid and Pleasure Clubs, brass bands, Second Lines, and guest musicians. Both parades start at around 11am or noon. Downtown, the Tambourine and Fan club – a social aid club devoted to educating children in the city's black cultural traditions – organizes a parade from Bayou St. John to Hunter's Field (St Bernard and Claiborne avenues), while uptown, the Mardi Gras Indian Council sets off from A.L. Davis Park at Washington and LaSalle streets. Check *Gambit*, the *Times-Picayune* or Ⓦ www.backstreet museum.org for details.

🏃 **Tennessee Williams Literary Festival** This superb five-day festival, in **late March**, attracts a host of internationally known actors and writers to the French Quarter – recent attendees have included Richard Ford, Margaret Atwood, David Simon and Edward Albee. Though ground zero is the Petit Théâtre du Vieux Carré (see p.45), many of the readings and discussions – on subjects as varied as presidential speeches, Elvis, and the Civil War in fact and fiction – are held in local bars, restaurants and hotels. Related events include master classes, panel discussions, walking tours, performances of Williams' plays, foodie events, movie screenings, poetry slams, and numerous music performances. The finale, the free Stanley and Stella (from *A Streetcar Named Desire*) shouting contest, in which overwrought Stanleys compete in Jackson Square to holler "Stellaaaa!" as loudly as they can, has become a cult. Recently, Stellas have begun to shout for Stanley, too, so it all gets wonderfully noisy. Prices aren't low – $25–60 for panels and master classes – but the organizers are always looking for volunteer ushers, stewards and ticket-takers. For schedules and full details, check Ⓦ www.tennesseewilliams.net.

March/April

Spring Fiesta Perfect for nosy parkers and decorative-arts fans alike – five days, spread across **the two weekends after Easter**, during which the public is invited to ogle the interiors of many of the poshest private homes in the French Quarter, Garden District, and Uptown. It's all rather genteel, with the presentation of a debby fiesta queen and her "court" at Jackson Square. Walking tours cost $15, house tours $25, or less if booked in advance. For details, see Ⓦ www.springfiesta.com.

Louisiana Roadfood Festival Held on **three days (Fri–Sun) at the end of March or in early April**, this foodie fest, in association with Ⓦ www.roadfood.com, provides yet another excuse to gorge on local food – along with a few regional specialities from other states – and listen to experts talk about regional

cuisine. During the day restaurants set up stalls along Royal Street showcasing dishes like cochon de lait, gator on a stick and crawfish pies. Evenings offer gala roadfood dinners, awards events, and a crab boil in the bayou ($75–95). Check Ⓦ www.new orleansroadfoodfestival.com for full details.

April

🏃 **French Quarter Festival** Excellent, highly recommended free music festival in **early April** that has come to rival Jazz Fest (see p.175) not only for the quality and variety of its local roots music – brass, R&B, Latin, trad jazz – on offer, but also the numbers it attracts (around 510,000 people in 2010). For three days (Fri–Sun) the Quarter is even more vibrant than usual, with seventeen stages and scores of food stalls along Royal and Bourbon streets, in Jackson Square and Woldenberg Park, plus free gigs, parades, workshops, tours and fireworks. See Ⓦ www.fqfi.org.

▲ Lazing by the river at French Quarter Festival

End April/early May

🏃 **Jazz Fest** See p.175.

May

Mid-City Bayou Boogaloo Mid-City's lower key and family-oriented version of the French

Quarter Festival, this free three-day (Fri–Sun) music festival, at the **end of May**, features a crowd-pleasing range of local performers – jazz, brass, hip-hop, Cajun, zydeco, blues, funk, Latin, reggae, Mardi Gras Indians and indie rock – playing on three stages. Plus crafts, food stalls, and an art market. See Ⓦwww.thebayouboogaloo.com.

June

Vieux-To-Do For two days (Sat & Sun) in **mid-June** the lower French Quarter celebrates three festivals in one: the French Market hosts the **Creole Tomato Festival**, marking the season when the local tomato is at its sweetest, and the **Louisiana Cajun-Zydeco Festival**, while the nearby Old US Mint is ground zero for the **Louisiana Seafood Festival**. It's a touristy affair, but fun, with music stages featuring the biggest names in Cajun and zydeco, cooking demonstrations, arts and crafts and kids' entertainment. There are also, of course, plenty of opportunities to guzzle tomatoes and seafood, from Bloody Marys, Creole tomato basil crepes and Creole tomato ice cream to shrimp and grits or chargrilled oysters. See Ⓦwww.louisianaseafood.com/festival, www.jazzandheritage.org/cajunzydeco/ and www.frenchmarket.org.

July

🏃 **Essence Music Festival Fourth of July weekend.** What started in 1995 as a one-off "party with a purpose" organized by the eponymous African-American magazine, this three-day event has become a huge deal – in 2009 it brought in more than 425,000 visitors for the best in black music, writing, seminars and theatre. Previous musical acts have included Beyoncé, Earth Wind and Fire, and Mary J Blige, along with a raft of brilliant local stars, all performing in the Superdome. From $159 for a three-night package. Ⓦwww.essencemusicfestival.com.

Running of the Bulls Early July. A nutty mix of hard-core runners, homesick Spaniards, Hispanophiles, show-offs, parade-rats and motley absurdists take to the streets of the French Quarter to pay homage to Pamplona's fiesta de San Fermin. The "bulls" here, however, are wiffle-bat-wielding, hotpants-wearing members of the local roller derby

team the Big Easy Rollergirls, who may or not be joined by the rollerskating krewe of the Rolling Elvi. Don white T-shirt and red neckerchief and join the fun. See Ⓦwww.nolabulls.com.

August

🏊 **Satchmo SummerFest** Extremely enjoyable free three-day festival celebrating Louis Armstrong's birthday. Talks and exhibits, staged at the US Mint and the Presbytère in the Quarter, focus on Satchmo's far-reaching cultural influence, while jazz and brass bands play on three stages set up on the grounds. Plus parades, Second Lines, special gigs, dance contests, and a jazz mass at Tremé's St Augustine's church. Festivities close with the Satchmo Strut, in which a one-off fee ($25) gains you entry into all the clubs along Frenchmen Street in the Faubourg, where scores of live bands play into the wee hours. Money goes to support nonprofit jazz outreach programme. See Ⓦwww.fqfi.org/satchmosummerfest.

September

Southern Decadence New Orleans' biggest gay extravaganza, held over six days on and around **Labor Day**, brings around 100,000 extrovert party animals to the gay bars and clubs of the French Quarter. Talent contests, club nights, karaoke and block parties abound, with an unruly costume parade of thousands on the Sunday afternoon. Many events are free, though the galas and big-name drag shows charge admission; clubs like *Oz* and *Parade* (see p.199) offer weekend passes. See Ⓦwww.southerndecadence.net.

Burlesque Festival Three days in **mid-to late September.** With its love of all things theatrical, sexy and witty, New Orleans has a meaningful place in the history of burlesque, which reached its heyday on Bourbon Street in the 1940s and 50s. This new festival takes the art form back to its glamorous postwar apogee, bringing in performers from around the US for a programme of exotic dancing, cabaret, variety and magic all performed to live jazz music. Venues include *Harrah's* casino, the *House of Blues*, and various French Quarter bars. See Ⓦwww.neworleansburlesquefest.com.

Ponderosa Stomp Two days in **late September.** Heaven on earth for rare record buffs and nostalgists, the Ponderosa Stomp, celebrating the unsung pioneers of rock and roll, r&b, country and soul music, is like the best roadhouse jukebox on earth come to life. Master-minded by local anaesthelogist Ira Padnos – known simply as Dr Ike – the Ponderosa Stomp places a special emphasis on Louisiana and Texas musicians, but extends its passion to all American roots music from rockabilly to Cajun. A combination of a three-day conference and two nights of concerts held during Jazz Fest, the Stomp quickly became a low-key counterpoint and complement to the bigger festival. In 2010 it took on a life of its own, extricated itself from the Fest, and shifted, in a slightly shorter version, to the fall. (Dates may change again in future years, so check the website for the latest news.) Previous artists have included rockabilly queen Wanda Jackson, gospel soulman Otis Clay, swamp pop maestro Phil Phillips and psychobilly pioneer "Legendary Stardust Cowboy" Norman Carl Odam. Concerts around $50. See ⓦ www.ponderosastomp.com.

Words and Music Superb four-day literary conference, held at **the end of September**, focusing on Southern and American writing, with panels, workshops, tutorial groups and readings, as well as music events and cocktail parties (sessions from $50, with various packages available). It's organized by Faulkner House Books (see p.188), whose Faulkner Society arranges a number of literary events throughout the year, all detailed on the festival website. See ⓦ www .wordsandmusic.org.

October

Art for Art's Sake New Orleans' official art season opens on the **first Saturday of October** with this high-profile event. Highlights include gallery receptions in the Arts District, along Magazine Street and in the French Quarter, a block party on Julia Street, and a closing gala at the CAC (see p.81). See ⓦ www.cacno.org.

New Orleans Film Festival Though it's no Sundance, this well-regarded festival, a week-long event held in **early or mid-October**, showcases big-name independent features and short experimental works. Screenings $9 each; six-film pass $48; All-Access pass to every screening, party, reception and related event $200. See ⓦ www.neworleans filmfest.com.

Voodoo Fest Held in City Park **on or around Halloween**, the three-day Voodoo Fest (officially "The Voodoo Experience") has in little more than a decade grown massively to become a top-league rock festival. Around 150 acts – from Eminem via The Pogues, REM, Duran Duran, Kiss and the New York Dolls, plus a refreshingly eclectic span of local acts including sissy rappers, artsy Bywater marching bands, old-school brass bands and sassy burlesque troupes – perform to a mixed, high-spirited, Halloween-costumed crowd.

Halloween Thanks to its long-held fascination with all things morbid, its campy sense of the ghoulish, and its passion for partying and costuming, New Orleans is the perfect place to celebrate Halloween (**October 31**). In addition to the massive Voodoo Fest (see above), pale-faced Goths start descending a week or so before the big day, attending their vampire conferences and covens; gruesome Haunted Houses pop up all along the outskirts of town, moonlit walking tours skulk through the cemeteries, and bars and clubs put on special gigs and costume balls. Other events, listed in the papers, include Second Lines and canine costume competitions. On the night itself major public events include the walking parade organized by *Molly's* bar in the Quarter (see p.147); the extravaganza hosted by Anne Rice's Vampire Lestat fan club (ⓦ www.vampirelestatfanclub.com); the thousands-strong masked fundraiser for Lazarus House, a local AIDS hospice (ⓦ halloweenneworleans.com), and the typically debauched party held by the alternative Mardi Gras krewe MOMS. You could also simply get dressed up and head to Lower Decatur Street in the Quarter and Frenchmen Street in the Faubourg, where you'll find the scariest street party in town. Mardi Gras impresario Blaine Kern's Krewe of Boo Parade, which winds its way from the Marigny via the French Quarter to the CBD, provides an early-evening, family-friendly alternative (ⓦ www.kreweofboo.org).

November

All Saints' Day and **All Souls' Day** New Orleans traditionally sets aside All Saints' Day – **Nov 1** – for remembering the ancestors, with locals tending family tombs in cemeteries citywide (see p.107). Nowadays it melds somewhat with All Souls', on **Nov 2** (when devout Catholics honour the souls of loved ones who have *not* been sainted). On both days you'll catch Gothy gigs and Second Lines paying respects to the dead – sinners and saints both.

Swampfest Terrific music festival held in Audubon Zoo over the **first weekend in November**. Celebrating the culture of southern Louisiana, it features big-name Cajun and zydeco bands, crafts demonstrations and some truly fantastic food stalls. Free with zoo entry. See ⓦwwww.audubon institute.org/swampfest.

New Orleans Po-boy Preservation Festival Tens of thousands of locals crowd head to Uptown to gorge on offerings from all the city's best neighbourhood po-boy vendors, voting on their favourites in half a dozen categories. See ⓦwww.poboyfest.com.

December

Tremé Creole Gumbo Festival A free weekend event in **early December**, featuring Tremé's best jazz, blues, gospel and brass bands, along with craft stalls and gumbo cooking demonstrations. It's held at the Jazz and Heritage Center, 1225 N Rampart St on the edge of Tremé, just a couple of blocks from the Quarter. See ⓦwww .tremegumbofest.com.

Christmas Though the entire city looks gorgeous during the festive season, garlanded with lights and beribboned wreaths, the French Quarter pulls out all the stops. Events include jazz masses at the cathedral; candlelit house tours; prix-fixe feasts, known as *reveillons*, put on by the finest Creole restaurants, and, following a tradition that dates back to the 1930s, the *Roosevelt* hotel lobby transforming itself into a block-long winter wonderland. City Park has its own festival of lights and an ice rink open for the season. See ⓦwww.frenchquarter festivals.org.

New Year's Eve New Orleans, which always throws a good party, is a fantastic New Year's destination. Festivities are concentrated around Jackson Square, with fireworks over the river and a whole lot of revelling throughout the French Quarter.

Shopping

Shopping in New Orleans, where mega-malls play second fiddle to small, stylish stores, can be a lot of fun. In a place where hanging out is a favourite pastime, most visitors spend a lot of time browsing and window-shopping, whether their budget extends to a framed WeeGee original or to one-of-a-kind crafts by local designers.

The **French Quarter** has its share of tacky tourist shops hawking bawdy T-shirts, ersatz voodoo gris-gris, ceramic Aunt Jemimas and cheap Mardi Gras masks – along with "galleries" displaying spectacularly ugly local art – but there are enough individualistic little places to buy gifts, clothes, books and music to fill a happy day or two's browsing. Post-Katrina must-haves, which you'll see everywhere from the cheapest Decatur Street emporia to the tasteful home furnishings stores on Chartres, include anything relating to fleur-de-lys, which became the city's de facto rebirth symbol after the storm, and designs based on New Orleans' distinctive iron water-meter covers, emblazoned with moon and stars, many of which were lost to the flood and to looting. Serious antique collectors will want to head for the grand old shops concentrated on Royal Street, the "Main Street" of the old Creole city.

On Saturdays, when the Quarter can get choked with tourists, you're best off heading for the antique shops, thrift stores and workshops along six-mile **Magazine Street**, which starts at Canal in the CBD and runs through the Warehouse and Garden Districts to Audubon Park. You could also spend a good few hours in the **Riverbend** area and around **Maple Street**, the studenty uptown district at the end of the streetcar line. If you've got serious money to spend on contemporary art, head for the galleries along Julia Street in the **Arts District** (see p.77).

Sadly, the fine old department stores that once graced **Canal Street** have all but disappeared; the elegant buildings are filled today with swanky hotels, questionable electrical stores, fast-food outlets and sportswear chains.

For details of Louisiana's **Tax-Free Shopping** scheme, whereby the city's nine percent sales tax is reimbursed to overseas visitors, see p.28.

Malls

Jackson Brewery (JAX) **600 Decatur St between Toulouse and St Peter** ☎566-7245, ⓦwww.jacksonbrewery.com. Daily 10am–6pm.
Housed in a restored 1891 brewery, JAX is struggling a bit nowadays, and is the least appealing of the downtown shopping centres. The only place of interest among the T-shirt and sunglasses stands is the Save Nola clothing store, whose profits go to post-Katrina rebuilding programmes (see p.189).

Riverwalk Marketplace **1 Poydras St, along the Mississippi** ☎522-1555, ⓦwww.riverwalkmarketplace.com. Mon–Sat 10am–7pm, Sun noon–6pm. Bustling, touristy mall running along the river from the Plaza d'España to the convention center. Its three storeys house more than a hundred shops and various stands and concessions, including, among the souvenir stores, chains such as Gap, Luggage Depot, and Footlocker. Of all the downtown shopping centres this one at least makes an effort to give a sense of place, with local music on the tannoy, New Orleans-related decor, and a not-bad food court dominated by local favourites (seafood, fried chicken, po-boys). The big Mardi Gras Madness store has an above-average selection of masks and fancy dress accoutrements; Crescent City Cooks!, meanwhile, is a good place for foodie gifts, including Tabasco lollies and roux spoons. There's even a branch of *Café du Monde* (see p.140); you can take your coffee and *beignets* to the riverwalk outside, which gives great views. For more on the mall, see p.60.

Shops at Canal Place **333 Canal St at N Peters** ☎522-9200, ⓦwww.theshopsatcanalplace.com. Mon–Sat 10am–7pm, Sun noon–6pm. A tranquil place to shop, with local stores RHINO (see p.194) and the shop of New Orleans jewellery designer Mignon Faget (p.190) joining standard upmarket national chains like Williams-Sonoma, Pottery Barn, Saks Fifth Avenue, L'Occitane, and Banana Republic. It also features a rep theatre (p.197), a gym, a five-screen cinema (p.197) and an utterly missable food court.

Antiques

Partly due to its strong links with Europe, especially France, and its crucial nineteenth-century role as a port, New Orleans remained a world-class **antiques** centre until the early 2000s. The double whammy of Katrina and the global recession hit the trade hard, but you'll still need serious money if you want to buy from the places on elegant **Royal Street**, some of which have been open since the late 1800s. If your budget doesn't stretch to Persian rugs or eighteenth-century armoires, check out the dusty old vintage stores along the 1100 and 1200 blocks of **Decatur Street**: great for bric-a-brac and funky retro furniture. Or go store-hopping along **Magazine Street**, where thrift and rummage stores sit alongside

The French Market, Farmers Market and Flea Market

New Orleans' **French Market**, extending along Decatur and North Peters streets downriver from Jackson Square, has been a marketplace since the 1700s. Today, along with the tourist shops selling T-shirts, Cajun and jazz CDs, cookbooks, Mardi Gras beads, masks, pralines and posters, there's a **Farmers Market**, which starts at the 1100 block of N Peters Street, selling fresh seasonal produce, sacks of beans and nuts, coffee, pyramids of spices and the like. The 1200 block is occupied by a **flea market**.

classy antiques warehouses. For rare and antique books, see p.187; for **vintage** clothes stores, see p.190.

French Quarter

Ida Manheim Antiques 409 Royal St at Conti
☎620-4114, ⓦidamanheimantiques.com.
Mon–Sat 9am–5pm. One of Royal Street's finest, in a handsome three-storey bank building designed by Benjamin Latrobe. They specialize in eighteenth- and nineteenth-century English pieces, including paintings, wooden furniture, clocks, tapestries and porcelain.

Keil's 325 Royal St at Conti ☎522-4552,
ⓦkeilsantiques.com. Mon–Sat 9am–5pm.
Keil's is a little piece of French Quarter history, trading since 1899, with an imposing double storefront opening onto a grand, three-storey showroom of eighteenth- and nineteenth-century French and English furniture, chandeliers and jewellery. Some good prices.

Lucullus 610 Chartres St at Wilkinson Row
☎528-9620, ⓦlucullusantiques.com. Mon–Sat 9am–5pm. Named for the Roman general who held notoriously lavish banquets, this is a splendid place for dining-related antiques. It's one of the less intimidating stores for casual shoppers, with a wide range of wares – copper saucepans, table linens, earthenware jars, cut-glass champagne flutes, oyster forks, candlesticks, wine racks

▲ Lucullus

grand dining tables – dating from the 1600s onwards.

Moss Antiques 411 Royal St at Conti
☎522-3981, ⓦmossantiques.com. Mon–Sat 9am–5pm. A favourite with serious buyers seeking out slightly smaller pieces of eighteenth- and nineteenth-century French and English furniture and decorative arts, including porcelain and Baccarat crystal. Also walking sticks and precious and semi-precious jewellery.

M.S. Rau 630 Royal St at Toulouse ☎523-5660,
ⓦrauantiques.com. Mon–Sat 9am–5.15pm. Exceptional, third-generation-owned store, specializing in rare nineteenth-century American antiques, with chandeliers, silver, ironwork, Cartier and Tiffany jewellery, early Edison phonographs and pieces by Prudent Mallard, New Orleans' foremost nineteenth-century cabinet maker. You may even find paintings from the likes of Renoir, Monet and Pissarro.

Quarter Past Time 606 Chartres St at Toulouse
☎410-0000. Mon, Tues & Thurs–Sun; hours vary. With more of the feel of a rummage store than an intimidating antiques emporium, this kooky old place focuses on clocks and watches, with a nice line in Art Deco timepieces. It also offers lamps, cocktail sets, Corgi toys and vintage Philco radios.

Royal Antiques 309 Royal St at Bienville
☎524-7033, ⓦwww.royalantiques.com. Mon–Sat 9am–5pm. More than 6000m of floor space in this tasteful nineteenth-century store, filled with English and French eighteenth- and nineteenth-century furniture, chandeliers, jewellery and silver. Also a good selection of Biedermeier pieces.

Vintage 429 429 Royal St at St Louis
☎529-2288, ⓦwww.vintage429.com. Daily 10am–5pm. The place for autographs – whether you're interested in Noel Coward, Barack Obama, Marilyn Monroe (whose autographed and framed photo will set you back $9000) or Thomas Jefferson (also $9000). You can also buy signed (new) guitars and first editions of Southern literary classics. More affordable are the 1950s cocktail sets, lunchboxes, cigarette cases and concert posters, plus pens and postcards.

Whisnant Galleries 229 Royal St at Iberville
☎524-9766, ⓦwhisnantgalleries.com.

Mon–Sat 9.30am–5.30pm, Sun 10am–5pm. This pricey store is unusual for the presence of African tribal art, sacred art from Asia, folk art and ethnic jewellery among the more usual European pieces

Magazine Street

Bush Antiques **2109 Magazine St** ☎581-3518, ⓦbushantiques.com. Mon–Sat 11am–5pm. Ravishing showroom that presents its inventory in twelve rooms, each styled as a themed vignette, evoking a decadent, jumbled elegance that is quintessentially New Orleans. The stunning pieces come from around the world, and can cost as little as a few hundred dollars.

Ann Koerner Antiques **4021 Magazine St** ☎899-2664, ⓦwww.annkoerner.com. Tues–Sat 10am–4pm. Including Scandinavian decorative art among the American regional and European pieces, this artistic store features lots of light eighteenth- and nineteenth-century Swedish furniture.

Neophobia **2855 Magazine St** ☎899-2444, ⓦwww.neophobia-nola.com. A rarity in New Orleans – mid-twentieth-century modern furnishings and accessories – and at very good prices. Come here for Tiki lounge paintings or Italian modernist vases, or splash out on a Mies Van der Rohe chair set.

Wirthmore Antiques **3727 Magazine St** ☎269-0660, ⓦwww.wirthmoreantiques.com. Tues–Fri 9am–5.30pm, Sat 10am–5.30pm. The homey front garden, tangled with wisteria, sets the tone for this friendly store that specializes in eighteenth- and nineteenth-century French and Italian provincial furniture. You'll find lots here, from lamps and linens to façence and armoires, with a selection of architectural antiques (flooring, mantels and the like) for good measure.

Art, prints and posters

There are scores of places to buy **art** in New Orleans, from the cheapest poster to the classiest Old Master. You have to be selective, though: although the Quarter, if anything, features more "local art galleries" than it ever did before Katrina, sadly, the bulk of them are filled with dispiritingly ugly tack. It also seems that every second shop in the Quarter, especially along Decatur and Royal, sells **posters** and **prints**. Best buys include official and unofficial Jazz Fest and Mardi Gras posters, reproduction historical prints, moody black-and-white photography and vintage maps. Don't overlook the artists who display their work in **Jackson Square**, either – along with portraits and caricatures, usually at very low prices, you'll find abstracts, quirky local scenes, and folk art. All works are originals.

If your budget for artworks runs to **fine oil paintings**, see the antiques stores detailed above. And if you're in the market for **cutting-edge works**, check the Arts District galleries listed on p.77. Places that sell one-off **arts and crafts**, including photography and paintings, are reviewed under the Gifts section on p.194.

Berta's and Mina's Antiquities **4138 Magazine St at Milan** ☎895-6201. Mon–Sat 10am–6pm, Sun 11am–5pm. Misleadingly named workshop/gallery/store crammed with the inventive folk art of Nicaraguan-born Nilo Lanzas, who started painting at the age of 63. His brash dioramas, many of them painted on old wooden windowframes, portray quirky biblical and rural scenes, or depict life in the imaginary town of Niloville, all of them daubed with witty, touching captions. They also sell outsider art by others, including Mina, Nilo's daughter.

A Gallery for Fine Photography **241 Chartres St at Bienville, French Quarter** ☎568-1313, ⓦwww.agallery.com. Thurs–Mon 10am–6pm. More of a gallery than a store, with superb antique and classic photographs to look at or to buy. Most prices reach four figures, and the rarest prints can go for as much as $100,000. Works date as far back as 1839 and include pictures by Julia Margaret Cameron, E.J. Bellocq, Edward S. Curtis, WeeGee, and Diane Arbus. Look out for Walker Evans' photos of the 1930s French Quarter, a host of jazz portraits, and

Clarence White's ghostly double-exposed images. The books section includes rare nineteenth-century titles.

Historic New Orleans Collection 533 Royal St at Toulouse, French Quarter ☎598-7147, ⓦwww .hnoc.org. Tues–Sat 9.30am–4.30pm, Sun 10.30am–4.30pm. Terrific, reasonably priced French Quarter museum store with a great collection of old reproduction maps and prints on subjects including New Orleans, the Civil War, Napoleon, and Audubon's "botanicals." Also postcards (early city plans, paintings of the Quarter in the 1930s and old photos), hand-crafted jewellery and new and used history books.

Photoworks New Orleans 521 St Ann St on Jackson Square, French Quarter ☎593-9090, ⓦwww.photoworksneworleans.com. Thurs–Tues 10am–5.30pm. The moody black-and-white photographs of Louis Sahuc capture the Quarter in all its romantic, quirky loveliness, from its balconies to its buskers to its grand old Creole restaurants. Prices from $300.

Vincent's 631 Decatur St at Wilkinson Row, French Quarter ☎522-2773. Mon–Fri 10am–5.30pm, Sat & Sun 10am–6pm. Good selection of mainstream prints and Mardi Gras and Jazz Fest posters, all at reasonable prices.

Beauty products

See also Fifi Mahony's (see p.192) and Ragin' Daisy (p.190) for make-up. For a list of **pharmacies**, see p.28.

Aidan Gill 2026 Magazine St at St Andrew ☎587-9090, ⓦwww.aidangill.com. Mon–Fri 10am–6pm, Sat 9am–5pm. Pampering for stylish gents: a beautiful, retro grooming store, with top-notch shaving gear (along with a few exquisite neckties and scarves) tastefully presented in huge oak cabinets. The main, appeal, however, is at the back, where you can settle into a comfy old-style barber's chair for a restyle ($35) or a luxurious hot-towel shave (30min; $40; followed by a local beer, a Guinness, or a wee dram). Appointments not necessary.

There's a second branch at 505 Fulton St, in the CBD near the casino.

Hové Parfumeur 824 Royal St at St Ann, French Quarter ☎525-7827, ⓦwww.hoveparfumeur .com. Mon–Sat 10am–5pm. There's a distinctly old-world ambience at this elegant, rose-pink-and-black parfumier, which has been around since the 1930s. Best seller is the Tea Olive scent, made from the sweet olive blossom common in New Orleans courtyards; sniff out too the Magnolia, Carnaval, and musky Rue Royale.

Books

New Orleans has captured the imaginations of writers and poets for generations, and the city remains a dream for bibliophiles. A huge number of beloved **neighbourhood stores** sell both new and secondhand books – used and rare books are particularly valued in this nostalgic, romantic city – and literary events, festivals and readings stud the city's social calendar. For **nonfiction**, try also the record stores (p.194) and the Historic New Orleans Collection (above).

The French Quarter, Faubourg Marigny and Bywater

Arcadian Bookshop 714 Orleans St at Royal, French Quarter ☎523-4138. Mon–Sat 10.30am–5.30pm. Hole-in-the-wall specializing in Louisiana, New Orleans and French history, with a number of French-language titles.

Beckham's Books 228 Decatur St at Iberville, French Quarter ☎296-2461. Daily 10am–5pm. Thousands of old editions, rare and out-of-print titles, and vintage magazines in a rambling, two-storey bookstore. With some unusual sections – typography, letter anthologies – it's particularly good for nonfiction, with politics, foreign affairs and lots of local titles including guidebooks. You could browse here all day.

Beth's Books 2700 Chartres St at Port, Bywater ℗948-0917. Daily 11am–6pm. Friendly, eclectic bookstore, closely associated with the splendid *Sound Café* next door (see p.142), selling local books and gifts. They have a few sidewalk tables.

Dauphine Street Books 410 Dauphine St at Conti, French Quarter ℗529-2333. Mon & Thurs–Sun 11am–6pm. A gem of a store: just one small room crammed with perilously high towers of used books, from saucy vintage pulp to academic tomes. It's a lovingly assembled collection, especially strong on local titles, history, African-American interest and Latin American translations, with lots of good inexpensive fiction. The helpful owner is happy to make recommendations.

Faubourg Marigny Art & Books 600 Frenchmen St at Chartres, Faubourg Marigny ℗947-3700. Daily noon–7pm or later. The city's oldest gay and lesbian bookstore, selling novels, art books, travel guides, regional titles, postcards, and calendars. They also host occasional readings and live music events.

Faulkner House Books 624 Pirate's Alley at Chartres, French Quarter ℗524-2940. Daily 10am–6pm. Tucked into the lemon yellow building where the novelist lived in 1925 while writing his first novel, *Soldiers' Pay*, this tiny, aesthetically pleasing bookstore is the literary hub of the Quarter, emphasizing Southern authors and local-interest titles, and cramming its ceiling-to-floor wooden cabinets with beautiful first editions, rare books, new writers, and poetry. The owners, who are a good source of information on local literary events, organize their own annual literary festival (see p.181).

Friends of the Cabildo Store 523 St Ann St on Jackson Square, French Quarter ℗524-9118. Tues–Sun 9.30am–4.30pm. Especially good for local-interest books, this is also a great, central place to pick up New Orleans-related engravings, prints, CDs, jewellery, gifts and cards.

Kitchen Witch 631 Toulouse St at Royal, French Quarter ℗528-8382, ℗www .kwcookbooks.com. Wed–Mon 10am–6pm, with an hour for lunch. Even if you're not a keen cook there's plenty to love about this characterful, very personal store, strung with fairy lights and spilling over with vintage junk and family mementoes. Among the toasters and parasols you'll find a treasure trove of rare and used cookbooks, many of which double as quirky social histories – if you're after a queer cookbook, African recipes from the 1930s, or tips on where to eat in the Ozarks, this is the place. They also have a good selection of jazz, blues, folk, and soul on vinyl.

Librairie Books 823 Chartres St at St Ann, French Quarter ℗525-4837. Daily 10am–5pm. In a handy location near Jackson Square, this battered old store sells used books at slashed rates, with a good selection of paperback mysteries and thrillers.

The Garden District and Uptown

Blue Cypress Books 8126 Oak St at Dublin, Uptown ℗352-0096, ℗www.bluecypress books.blogspot.com. Mon–Sat 10am–5.30pm, Sun 11am–4pm. This cheery Riverbend bookstore offers a healthy mix of new and used books, strong on contemporary literature and local-interest titles.

Garden District Bookshop The Rink, 2727 Prytania St at Washington ℗895-2266, ℗www.gardendistrictbookshop .com. Mon–Sat 10am–6pm, Sun 10am–4pm. Very cosy local literary headquarters, with a strong selection of New Orleans titles, new fiction, travel guides, limited editions, and autographed copies, plus regular author signings and literary events. It's also good for stationery, journals and posters.

Maple Street Book Shops 7523 Maple St at Cherokee ℗866-7059, and 7529 Maple St at Cherokee ℗866-4916, Uptown ℗www.maplestreetbookshop.com. Mon–Sat 9am–7pm, Sun 11am–5pm. Much-cherished Riverbend stores, stalwarts of the city's literary scene, housed in two neighbouring tumbledown cottages fronted by jasmine-filled gardens. No. 7523 sells used books, all at a third off the cover price, with many literary, scholarly titles. Next door, no. 7529 is the place for new titles, with lots of travel books, history and mythology. If you find it hard to tear yourself away, they've got a nice shady front porch where you can sit and read your purchases. Regular readings, signings and literary events.

Clothes and accessories

Though not famed as a fashion city, New Orleans is without doubt a stylish one. Locals adore dressing up, be it in haughty haute couture or flamboyant second-hand gladrags – **vintage clothes**, in particular, are a hit with a population that not only revels in nostalgia and drama, but also numbers many penniless musicians, students, and artists. In addition to the vintage stores reviewed on p.190, check the crop of warehouse-style rummage stores in the 1100 and 1200 blocks of Decatur, where you can pick up old Mardi Gras costumes and retro suits among the dusty antique mirrors, records and family mementoes.

Many of the clothes stores listed here also sell **jewellery**, shoes and other accessories. And if you crave a hep-cat hat to top that sharp suit we've picked out a couple of serious **hat stores**.

We've listed here mostly one-off, local stores; for **chain stores**, check the malls listed on p.184. There are also branches of Urban Outfitters and French Connection in the 400 block of North Peters Street, near the Shops at Canal Place, and an American Apparel at 3310 Magazine Street; Canal Street is the place for **sportswear**. Stylish **gents** on the hunt for clothes, used and new, should head for the 200 block of Magazine, where there are a rash of good menswear options.

French Quarter and around

Fleur de Paris 523 Royal St at Toulouse, French Quarter ☎525-1899, ⊛www.fleurdeparis.net. Daily 10am–6pm. Renowned for its ultra-glamorous window displays, Fleur de Paris specializes in flamboyant custom-made hats, uptown evening wear, and cocktail dresses. Prices are high (especially for their vintage-style dresses, which are better, and less expensive at Trashy Diva, see opposite), but then, this place is practically a work of art.

Meyer the Hatter 120 St Charles Ave at Canal, CBD ☎525-1048, ⊛www.meyerthehatter.com. Mon–Sat 10am–5.45pm. "Over 100 years of hats" at this traditional family business. Most of the space is taken up by Biltmores – the New Orleans jazzman's favourite – but you'll also find stetsons, baseball caps, Kangols, and much more.

Save Nola Jackson Brewery (JAX), 600 Decatur St between Toulouse and St Peter, French Quarter ☎558-1951, ⊛www .savenolanow.com. Daily 10am–6pm. If you're after a memento T-shirt or souvenir, be sure to get it from this friendly little store, where all proceeds fund organizations dedicated to rebuilding the city both physically and culturally. Well-made, simple and attractive casual wear – soft Ts, hoodies, sweatshirts – much of it made from recycled materials, incorporates the logos of save nola, Habitat for Humanity, and the Musicians' Clinic, among others, while

managing to look extremely stylish. Also pretty silver jewellery, bumper stickers, and small gifts.

Shushan's 536 St Peter St on Jackson Square, French Quarter ☎586-1188, ⊛www.shushans .com. Roughly Mon–Fri 10.30am–5.30pm, Sat 10am–6pm, Sun 11am–4pm. Look beyond the crawfish-emblazoned neckties and novelty socks and you'll find this is by far the best place in the Quarter for men to kit themselves out in New Orleans style, with stylish, authentic guayabera shirts and a great selection of hats – from straw Panamas to green felt bowlers – at very good prices.

Sole Starr 1222 Decatur St at Gov Nicholls, French Quarter ☎566-0777. Thurs–Mon 12.30–5.30pm. A riot of glitter, sequins and funky prints: inexpensive women's frocks, shoes, hats, wigs and accessories with edge, and a good line in men's shoes to boot. Flashy and fun.

Trashy Diva 829 Chartres St at Madison, French Quarter ☎581-4555. Daily noon–6pm. New Orleans' own Trashy Diva line uses retro prints and vintage dress patterns to create exquisite, feminine, and extremely flattering period-style clothes – perfect for steamy Southern debauchery on a wrought-iron balcony. Lines change seasonally, and there is lots of variety, whether you're after a simple 1940s-style cotton teadress or something in drop-dead-gorgeous 1930s satin. They also offer corsages and costume jewellery, while the

New Orleans has a superb selection of **thrift stores**, concentrated along Magazine Street and on Lower Decatur Street in the Quarter. While you can pick up fabulous vintage daywear at good prices, they also reap dividends when putting together a look for Mardi Gras, Halloween, or any other of the city's myriad excuses to dress up – many places sell readymade costumes alongside raggedy ball gowns, and at carnival time you'll find racks and racks of crazy pre-loved ensembles.

Buffalo Exchange 3312 Magazine St at Louisiana ℡891-7443, Ⓦwww.buffalo exchange.com. Mon–Sat 11am–7pm, Sun 11am–6pm. Local branch of the nation-wide clothes recycling store, offering right-on thrift store fashion at good prices.

Funky Monkey 3127 Magazine St at Ninth ℡899-5587. Mon–Wed 11am–6pm, Thurs–Sat 11am–7pm, Sun noon–6pm. Probably the best of Magazine Street's vintage stores, with the quirkiest selection and lowest prices. It's just the place to throw together a unique costume, with wigs, offbeat used clothing, costumes-in-a-pack, hats, bags, shoes and a nice line in men's suits. They also sell a small range of new, locally designed stuff.

Le Garage 1234 Decatur St at Barracks, French Quarter ℡522-6639. Tues–Sat noon–5pm. The biggest and by far the best of the rummage stores on this decadent stretch of Decatur. A barebones warehouse space contains old military uniforms, vintage Mardi Gras costumes, hats, suits and dresses, along with furniture and books and all manner of intriguing knick-knacks.

Ragin' Daisy 901 Chartres St at Dumaine, French Quarter, ℡544-5482, Ⓦwww .myspace.com/ragindaisy. Daily noon–6pm. Rock'n'roll glamour rules the roost at this friendly, eclectic little corner store, with vintage dresses and suits, burlesque get-ups, costume jewellery, neat little hats, beatnik accessories, bakelite bags and kinky boots. Plus gifts for the trashy style icon in your life, from offbeat design books and cocktail sets to funky magnets.

Reservoir 2045 Magazine St at Josephine (no phone). Mon–Sat 11am–6pm, Sun noon–5pm. A very good selection of used clothes, particularly men's, with a nice line in 1940s suits and dapper hats for as little as $8. Also lamps, cushions and all manner of intriguing junk.

lingerie store next door sells sexy antique corsets. The Trashy Diva shoe shop, a few doors down at no. 839, continues the theme with glamour girl courtshoes, pretty peeptoes, beaded flats, and retro wedges. There's another branch of the dress shop (Mon–Sat noon–6pm, Sun 1–5pm) at 2048 Magazine St.

Magazine Street

Dirty Coast 5704 Magazine St at Arabella ℡324-3745, Ⓦdirtycoast.com. Mon–Sat 11am–6pm, Sun noon–3pm. Bold, funky, graphic T-shirts, all with a New Orleans theme. References to current affairs and iconic local imagery range from the "Grey is Graffiti" dig at Fred Radtke, the "Grey Ghost" – who protests his dislike of graffiti and fliers by obliterating them with grey paint – to "Make Wetlands not War" and

psychedelic designs celebrating New Orleans' great piano hero Professor Longhair. Prices from $25.

Gogo 4222 Magazine St at Napoleon ℡304-8458, Ⓦwww.ilovegogojewelry.com. Daily 10am–5pm/6pm. Fresh and youthful jewellery – from a variety of artists, many of them local, and with a range of prices – displayed in a stylishly retro store.

Mignon Faget 3801 Magazine St at Peniston ℡891-2005, Ⓦwww .mignonfaget.com. Mon–Sat 10am–6pm. Classic, striking jewellery inspired by local nature, architecture and even foods (the gumbo necklace, a tangle of pearls, gemstones and silver seafood, is a delight) from local designer Mignon Faget, a stalwart on the New Orleans fashion scene since the 1960s. There is a second branch in The Shops at Canal Place (see p.184).

Thomas Mann 1812 Magazine St at Felicity ☎581-2113, ⓦ www .thomasmann.com. Mon–Sat 11am–5pm. Local artist Mann is best known for his "Techno-Romantic" jewellery – soft, quirky forms melded from burnished silver, brass and bronze and incorporating found objects – but all his work is modern, inventive and witty, taking inspiration from flowers, hearts and the natural world. New Orleanians love the cockroach pins, but you can also get beautifully crafted charm bracelets, broken-heart earrings and simple pendants; prices stretch from affordable to very expensive.

Winky's 2038 Magazine St at St Andrew ☎529-2441. Mon–Sat 11am–6pm, Sun noon–5pm. Fashionable store on the lower, slightly funkier end of Magazine Street. Selling hip clothes and accessories – mostly for women and kids – it's bright and fun, youthful and very slightly pricey. Head upstairs to the UP gallery (see p.194) for unique recycled home accessories.

Costumes, wigs and masks

New Orleanians love masking and costuming, and any visitor who wants to experience the city at its best really ought to join the fun. Scores of tourist shops in the French Quarter sell cheap feathered **masks**, boas and whacky hats to satisfy exhibitionist impulses – don't overlook these, for even at the cheapest places you can pick up eye-catching and disposable dress-up finds. For serious and more elegant **costuming**, though, at Mardi Gras, say, or Halloween, you'll want to combine a trawl through the **vintage stores** (see box opposite) with a visit to the specialist shops listed below. Even off-season, they are worth a browse, full of weird treasures.

See also Mardi Gras Madness in the Riverwalk Marketplace (see p.184) for cheap **basics**.

▲ Masks

🏃 **Decatur Street Costume Exchange** 1215 Decatur St at Gov Nichols, French Quarter ☏529-4387. Open during Mardi Gras only, roughly daily noon–5pm. If you can find it open, this inspired little place is your first French Quarter stop for used costumes – insane, traditional, sexy, funny, tatty or classy – along with unusual old wigs, masks and must-have props.

🏃 **Fifi Mahony's** 934 Royal St at Dumaine, French Quarter ☏525-4343. Mon–Fri & Sun noon–6pm, Sat noon–7pm. Fabulous wig store, staffed by gorgeous boys and girls with neon hair and glittering eyelids. In the back room you can try proper, expensive hairpieces – from Louise Brooks bobs to turquoise Marie Antoinette pompadours, priced between $50 and $200 – at a big, light bulb-edged mirror, while the front room offers all manner of cheaper party wigs, nail polish, hair mascara, make-up and eye jewels. They also have a small used clothes selection and a handful of offbeat accessories.

🏃 **Maskarade** 630 St Ann at Royal, French Quarter ☏568-1018, ⓦwww .themaskstore.com. Daily 10am–5.45pm. The Quarter's best mask store, with a refreshingly easy-going "Take photos, have fun" policy. The designer masks – creepy and beautiful, creative and unusual – are made from everything from leather to papier mache and run the gamut from Day of the Dead skulls to dragonflies. Prices from $30 for a simple black leather eyemask up to $350 for the most fantastical visions. **Serendipitous Masks** 831 Decatur St at Madison, French Quarter ☏522-9158, ⓦserendipitousmasks.com. Thurs–Mon

10am–6pm. Heaven or hell, depending on your persuasion: this quirky old store offers a weird and wonderful burst of the kitsch, the beautiful, the ugly, and the just plain strange in one feathery, sequiny, glittery explosion. Handmade and Venetian-style masks share every inch of space with baubles, Fabergé-style eggs, plates, dolls, velvet capes, sparkly flowers, headdresses and sceptres.

🏃 **Uptown Costume and Dancewear Company** 4326 Magazine St at Napoleon ☏895-7969. Mon–Fri 10am–5pm, Sat 10am–6pm. Cavernous fancy-dress store packed tight with wigs, masks, costumes, hats, shoes, accessories, and make-up. Staff are informative and helpful, even when rushed off their feet during Mardi Gras (when the place is milling with school marching bands and focused locals) and Halloween (stage make-up and hideous latex heads are particularly popular). Opening hours are extended during these busy periods.

🏃 **Vieux Carré Hair Shop** 8224 Maple St at Dante, Uptown ☏862-6936, ⓦwww .vieuxcarrehairshop. Mon–Fri 10am–5pm. Whether you're after a plastic pig face or Mickey Mouse hands, you'll find them in this friendly, family-owned theatrical supplier, somewhat incongruously set in a pretty Riverbend cottage. They take their business seriously here, as the ancient "yes we have warts!" sign will attest. Shelves of decrepit polystyrene heads sporting off-centre woollen wigs, beards, sideburns, and lashes share space with false bosoms and bottoms, stage make-up and feather boas, with a nice line in rubber masks and false noses.

Gifts, souvenirs and crafts

While you could buy souvenirs in many of the stores listed in this chapter – and, if you're after fridge magnets and ceramic masks, in a thousand places *not* listed in this chapter – there's also a host of shops specializing in quirky, well-made objects that make perfect **gifts**. The best finds, as ever, are in the Quarter (where you'll also encounter some overpriced tat) and along Magazine Street. See also the Historic New Orleans Collecion (p.187) and the clothes stores Ragin' Daisy (p.190) and Dirty Coast (p.190) for more ideas.

If you're after distinctive one-offs, head for the city's excellent **crafts** co-operatives. These sell locally made artworks from ceramics to photography – the best of it heavily referencing Katrina and local cultural eccentricities – that are easy to carry home. Look out for David Bergeron's frames and boxes, which, made from peeling wood reclaimed from storm-wrecked houses, pack an emotional punch, and ceramics from Joy Gauss, who uses street culture motifs, including the Skull and Bone gangs (see p.67), in her strange and original figurines.

Chateau de Vore 830 Chartres St at Madison, French Quarter ☎586-3881, ⓦwww .chateaudevore.com. Thurs–Mon 10am–6pm. Shabby chic, reclaimed and French-influenced home decorations and gifts – wooden crosses, fleur de lys candles, votive holders – in a shadowy, atmospheric room. A good range of prices.

Fun Rock'n 3109 Magazine St at Ninth (☎895-4102) and 1125 Decatur St at Gov Nicholls, French Quarter ☎524-1122. Sun–Thurs 11am–6pm, Fri & Sat 11am–7pm. This kitsch emporium is not just for kids, though the piles of tricks, novelties and games will keep the little ones happy. Meanwhile, young-at-heart hipsters will delight in the groovy plastic bags, vintage movie posters,

Elvis slippers and flashing heart-shaped spectacles, not to mention the South Park inflatable chairs.

Hazelnut 5515 Magazine St at Octavia ☎891-2424, ⓦwww.hazelnutneworleans.com. Mon–Sat 10am–5pm. Fancy home furnishings store part-owned by local boy Bryan Batt (of TV's *Mad Men*) and reflecting his eclectic, theatrical tastes; look out for the lovely New Orleans *toile* – from cushions to shower curtains – with retro-style images of the Quarter based on his original sketches.

Idea Factory 838 Chartres St at Madison, French Quarter ☎524-5195, ⓦwww.ideafactory neworleans.com. Wed–Sat & Mon 10am–6pm, Sun 10am–5pm. Lovely, warmly wood-fragranced little shop, a hit with all

Foodie gifts in the French Quarter

A glut of tourist stores in the Quarter do a rapid turnaround in easily transportable **foodie gifts**. There's little to choose between them, but a few are worth mentioning. If you want to recreate your New Orleans coffee ritual at home, then you may as well pick up the *beignet* mixes and cans of chicory coffee from the source, *Café du Monde* (see p.140), stopping for a cup of café au lait before you leave. Sweet-toothed tourists make a beeline for the hokily old-style **Aunt Sally's Creole Pralines**, nearby at 810 Decatur St in the French Market (Mon–Thurs 9am–5pm, Fri 9am–6pm, Sat & Sun 8am–7pm; ☎1-800/642-7257, ⓦwww.auntsallys.com). The sugary pecan candies are cooked on site in a big copper pot just as they have been since the nineteenth century, and they offer free samples of their speciality Creole, Creamy or Chewy (with added caramel) varieties. Another good place for Creole candy is **Leah's Pralines**, 714 St Louis St at Royal (Mon–Sat 10am–6pm, Sun noon–5pm; ☎523-5662, ⓦwww.leahspralines.com), a third-generation family business that also offers frosted almonds, pecan brittle, chocolate, and fudge, all hand-made (try the Cajun Mud, gooey layers of chocolate, caramel and pecans). If you're after **hot sauce**, the Farmers Market is a good bet, or the stores in the French Market – you'll find dozens of varieties, some of them emblazoned with flaming toilets, burning butts and such in an effort to seem hotter than the next. Anywhere that sells hot sauce will usually also stock the evil, inexplicably popular, make-your-own **Hurricane cocktail mixes** (see p.145), packed with sugar and artificial additives.

Other buys include red beans and rice mixes, filé (dried sassafras leaves) for gumbo, peppery crab-boil and jambalaya spices; you can get these at Decatur Street's **Central Grocery** while picking up one of its famed muffulettas (see p.143). If you're in a hurry and not in the mood to browse, stop at the Royal Street grocery store **Rouses** (see p.143), which sells ready-made spice mixes and seasonings at good prices. Do as the locals do and plump for Tony Chachere's range or those produced by celebrity chefs Emeril and Paul Prudhomme; if you like things really hot, try Slap Ya Mama or Joe's Hot Stuff. And if you're after **utensils** to help with your Louisiana-style blow-out back home, check out the Crescent City Cooks! cooking school in the Riverwalk Marketplace (see p.184).

For **picnic food**, head for the neighbourhood groceries and delis reviewed in the "Eating" chapter, on p.143, or the Farmers Market, covered on p.184.

ages, selling beautifully made woodcraft from around the nation. Prices are reasonable, whether you're after something tasteful (chopping boards, chopsticks, business-card holders), or eccentric (kinetic sculptures, mechanical toys).

La Maison d'Absinthe 823 Royal St at St Ann, French Quarter ☏1-877/737-2772, ⊛www .lamaisondabsinthe.com. You can skip the tiny absinthe museum at the back (the Southern Food and Beverage museum covers the subject better; see p.60) but the shop is worth a look for its intriguing French, Art Nouveau and absinthe-related gifts, from Piaf CDs and absinthe lollipops via French tin signs to a vintage absinthe fountain for $300.

Nadine Blake 1036 Royal St at St Philip, French Quarter ☏529-4913. Thurs–Mon 11am–6pm. Gorgeous stationery, art, design and fashion books, jewellery, cushions and home furnishings. Everything has a quirky European/New Orleans flair and is personally selected by the friendly husband-and-wife owners – she a local designer, he a British animator.

Papier Plume 842 Royal St at Dumaine, French Quarter ☏988-7265, ⊛www.papierplume.com. Daily 10am–6pm. Everything any aspiring wordsmith – inspired by these historic French Quarter streets – could desire: soft handmade leather notebooks, fountain pens, inkwells, calligraphy sets, sealing wax, and classy stationery sets.

Crafts

Artist's Market 1228 Decatur St/85 French Market Place, French Quarter ☏561-0046, ⊛www.artistsmarketnola.com. Daily 11am–6pm. Enormous Lower Decatur store showcasing the work of around seventy artists. There's a dramatically mixed range of stuff to suit most tastes – delicate fleur-de-lys jewellery, shabby chic ironware, handblown glass, handmade cards – so it's always worth a browse.

Dutch Alley Artists' Co Op 912 N Peters St at Dumaine, behind the French Market, French Quarter ☏412-9220, ⊛www .dutchalleyonline.com. Daily 10am–6pm. The arts and crafts at this co-op are a cut above. It's as touristy as you'd expect in this location, but with an excellent range including handmade hats, quilts, and pottery. Katrina art includes lovely bowls and chopping boards hewn from storm-felled trees, old tile mosaics, and affecting photos.

Louisiana Crafts Guild 608 Julia St at Camp, Warehouse District ☏558-6198, ⊛www.louisianacrafts.org. Tues–Sat 11am–5pm. Fine Southern crafts and folk art, most of which – metal work, wood, ceramics, outsider art and jewellery – has a strongly non-urban, rural emphasis. Some of it is very affordable; other pieces, like a gator made from beer bottle tops from big-name local artist Dr Bob, will set you back hundreds of dollars.

RHINO The Shops at Canal Place (see p.184), CBD ☏523-7945, ⊛www.rhinocrafts.com. Mon–Sat 10am–7pm, Sun noon–6pm. It may be in a slightly incongruous location, but the work from this local non-profit co-op ("Right Here In New Orleans") is invariably interesting and inspiring – fine filigree jewellery, ceramics, collages, greeting cards, textiles, hats, glassware, sculpture, salvaged woodwork, clothing. None of it comes cheap, but this is top-quality stuff.

UP 2038 Magazine St at St Andrew ☏ 529-2441, ⊛www.shopgreenneworleans.com. Mon–Sat 11am–6pm, Sun noon–5pm. Head upstairs at the clothes store Winky's (see p.191) to find a tiny cornucopia of funky, inexpensive, recycled art. Best buys include gaudy lampshades fashioned from melted-down Mardi Gras beads, desk tidies made from vintage tin cans, and clocks made from anything from lurex handbags to retro biscuit tins showing scenes of old New Orleans.

Music

Unsurprisingly, New Orleans has plenty of good places to buy **music**, with a heavy emphasis on local output and a handful of superb used record stores that have stayed afloat as the majors have dropped like flies. Most places sell rare and collectable stuff as well as current releases. For jazz and blues on vinyl, you should also stop by the Kitchen Witch bookshop (see p.188).

For a history of New Orleans music, plus **discography**, see p.234.

Jim Russell Records 1837 Magazine St at St Mary ℡ 522-2602, ⓦ www.jimrussellrecords .com. Mon–Sat 11am–5pm. Long-established Lower Magazine store offering a large collection of new and used CDs, along with rare vinyl, singles, and cassettes, specializing in local music, soul, R&B, rap and blues.

Louisiana Music Factory 210 Decatur St at Iberville, French Quarter ℡ 586-1094, ⓦ www.louisianamusicfactory.com. Mon–Sat 10am–7pm, Sun noon–6pm. A fantastic source of regional music at extremely competitive prices, with plenty of listening stations for jazz, R&B, gospel, Cajun, zydeco, blues, swamp pop, and roots music. They also deal in vinyl, along with hard-to-find used music books, plus posters, rare local-interest DVDs and box sets, and T-shirts. The expert staff organize frequent in-store performances (ⓦ www .youtube.com/user/lamusicfactory).

Peaches 408 N Peters St at Conti, French Quarter ℡ 282-3322, ⓦ peachesrecords neworleans.com. Mon–Sat 10am–8pm, Sun 11am–7pm. Katrina, along with the recession, has thrown up lots of anomalies like this in New Orleans – a colossal, prime-location space, which once hosted a bustling Tower Records but is now home to a family-owned local music store that's been operating (from different premises) since 1975. Though prices are a little higher than at the Louisiana Music Factory, Peaches is a particularly good place to buy hip-hop, rap and Bounce. Its original store in Gentilly was a hub for New Orleans rappers, including the Cash Money crew, and the emphasis remains on getting recognition for up-and-coming local artists – with a lot of vinyl and cassettes. Also soul, gospel and jazz, plus magazines and local-interest books and DVDs, and a smattering of folk art.

Skullyz 907 Bourbon St at Dumaine, French Quarter ℡ 592-4666, ⓦ www.myspace.com /skullyzrecordz. Sun & Mon noon–6pm, Thurs–Sat noon–8pm. Skinny boys in skinny jeans make a beeline for this friendly cupboard of a store specializing in rock, pop, punk, folk, noise and indie, national and local, with a selection of imports, used vinyl and collectables.

16

Theatre and the arts

D
espite the city's long association with the **performing arts** – from the earliest years of the French colony, when short dramas were performed in private drawing rooms, through to the nineteenth-century golden era, when theatres, ballrooms and the glorious French Opera House were packed every night – few visitors come to New Orleans for opera or the ballet. However, while the high-arts scene poses little competition for bigger, wealthier cities – arts funding is pitifully low – New Orleans does have respected operatic and orchestral companies, a small ballet company, a couple of rep theatres and a handful of places showcasing avant-garde and experimental works.

There's little in the way of **comedy**, but **spoken word** performances have a loyal following in local bars. The Sunday afternoon poetry reading series at the *Maple Leaf* (see p.61) is the oldest in the South, and features top-quality literary work; the *Gold Mine Saloon* in the French Quarter also hosts a well-received spoken word series on Thursday evenings (ⓌWwww.17poets.com).

Though America's first purpose-built movie house opened on Canal Street in 1896, it's long since been torn down. Nonetheless, the city does have its fair share of mainstream **cinemas** and a couple of places to catch independent and art-house films, as well as a respected festival, held in the fall (see p.181).

One of the best things about the high-art scene in New Orleans is the **Louisiana Philharmonic Orchestra** (Ⓦwww.lpomusic.com), owned by its musicians. Following Katrina, which lay waste to its permanent home, the *Orpheum Theater*, the Orchestra now performs a lively range of works, from light classics to modern pieces, in a variety of venues, including churches, high schools and outdoor stages. Tickets cost between $20 and $50 and can be booked through their website. The highly regarded **New Orleans Opera** (Ⓦwww.neworleansopera.org) and the **New Orleans Ballet Association** (Ⓦwww.nobadance.com) both stage short, well-received seasons at the *Mahalia Jackson Theater of the Performing Arts* and in smaller venues around town; tickets start at $20 for dance, $45 for opera.

To see what's happening on any particular night, check the **listings** in *Gambit* (Ⓦwww.bestofneworleans.com) or the *Lagniappe* supplement of the *Times-Picayune* (Ⓦwww.nola.com).

Theatres and performance venues

Contemporary Arts Center (CAC) 900 Camp St at St Joseph, Warehouse District Ⓦwww .cacno.org. Modern gallery and performance space in the heart of the Arts District, hosting art exhibitions, dance, performance art, video installations, indie movies, and experimental theatre. For more on the CAC, see p.81.

Le Chat Noir 715 St Charles Ave at Girod, CBD Ⓦwww.cabaretlechatnoir.com. The plush red velvet decor and upscale 1940s ambience in this elegant but relaxed supper-club-style venue provide the perfect environs for occasional cabaret and musical revues.

Mahalia Jackson Theater of the Performing Arts Louis Armstrong Park, Rampart St at St Ann ⓦ www.mahaliajacksontheater.com. Named after the New Orleans-born gospel singer, the *Mahalia* is a large setting for touring musicals, classical concerts, opera and ballet, ice spectaculars, boxing, and so on.

New Orleans Arena 1501 Girod St, adjacent to the Superdome, CBD ⓦ www.neworleansarena .com. In the shadow of its older sibling, the Superdome, the Arena seats about 20,000 for big-name rock and country concerts. It's also home to the city's basketball team, the Hornets.

NOCCA 2800 Chartres St at St Ferdinand, Bywater ⓦ www.nocca.com. The campus of the highly respected New Orleans Center for Creative Arts is extremely handsome, melding old cotton warehouses with cutting-edge design. It's occasionally open to the public for jazz, poetry and drama performances.

🏃 **Le Petit Théâtre du Vieux Carré 616 St Peter St at Chartres, French Quarter** ⓦ www.lepetittheatre.com. The Drawing Room Players, the nation's longest-running community theatre, formed in New Orleans in 1919. After three years treading the boards in private homes, they moved to this Spanish Colonial building in 1922, which remains their home base. On the corner of Jackson Square in the French Quarter, it's a friendly and genuinely charming setting for lively musicals, comedies and popular dramas.

🏃 **Southern Rep Theater The Shops at Canal Place, 333 Canal St at N Peters, CBD** ⓦ www.southernrep.com. Intimate professional theater in a conveniently situated mall (see p.184). The focus is on contemporary, bold work, much of it from Southern playwrights – up-and-coming and established – and performed by local actors. Small local theatre companies also stage productions during the "City Series" programme.

Superdome Sugar Bowl Drive, CBD ⓦ www .superdome.com. The vast stadium variously used for Saints' football games, Superbowl games, teeming trade shows and overblown rock concerts. For more on the building and its history, see p.82.

🏃 **Zeitgeist Multi-Disciplinary Arts Center 1724 Oretha Castle Haley Blvd at Terpsi- chore, Central City** ⓦ zeitgeisttheater.wordpress .com. Volunteer-run, non-profit arts centre in a bare-bones space with brick walls, concrete floor, and mismatched armchairs. One of the city's few truly alternative venues, it's a very friendly place, with an intriguing series of movies (lots of gay, lesbian, avant-garde, and world cinema), underground music, political poetry, performance art, theatre, lectures, workshops, and readings.

Cinemas

Though it has the usual multiplexes out in the suburbs, New Orleans is sadly lacking in purpose-built cinemas showing interesting movies. However, in addition to those listed below, the *Contemporary Arts Center* (see p.196) and *Zeitgeist* (above) host occasional movies. For details of the **New Orleans Film and Video Festival**, held each October, see p.181.

Landmark Cinemas The Shops at Canal Place, 333 Canal St at N Peters, CBD ⓦ www .landmarktheatres.com. Conveniently located five-screen cinema featuring mainstream, indie and world movies. Good gourmet snacks too.

🏃 **Prytania 5339 Prytania St at Leontine, Uptown** ⓦ www.theprytania.com. The only remaining single-screen cinema in the entire state of Louisiana, this lovely 1915 theatre shows arthouse, Hollywood, and independent movies. Screenings $5.25 before 6pm, $8 after.

Gay New Orleans

New Orleans is one of the most enjoyable cities in the United States for **gay travellers**. The French Quarter, in particular, has a sizeable gay community and a host of gay-owned restaurants, bars and businesses to serve it. In the anything-goes atmosphere of the Quarter, however, it can be hard to distinguish between gay-only and straight establishments – most places welcome everyone. The more residential Faubourg Marigny and Bywater also have a significant gay presence, with a lot of good local bars and clubs, and a number of gay-owned B&Bs and restaurants.

If you're after a wild time, plan your visit to coincide with one of New Orleans' **festivals** – especially those that involve dressing up, like Halloween (see p.181) and, of course, Mardi Gras (see p.163). The biggest gay festival, however, is the cross-dressing, heavy-drinking extravaganza known as **Southern Decadence** (see p.180), which peaks with a street parade in the Quarter on the Sunday of the Labor Day weekend. There's usually a **Gay Pride** parade or festival, too, but perhaps because there are so many other opportunities for gay celebration and expression – political activism tends to take second place to partying – it's neither as outrageous nor as well attended as Pride festivals in bigger cities.

Ambush, which hits the stands every other Tuesday, is New Orleans' major gay **listings paper**, available free from clubs, bars, cafés and record stores. Covering the Gulf South region, it's an entertainment paper first and foremost, heavy on juicy gossip and anecdote and low on political editorial. Its online arm, ⓦwww.ambushmag.com, includes a searchable database of back issues and links to other gay businesses and local web portals. Other useful **websites** include ⓦneworleansfruitloop.com, ⓦwww.gayneworleans.com, and ⓦwww.ambushonline.com, all of which have links to local gay publications, attractions, bars and clubs.

Gay accommodation

Although gay travellers will feel comfortable staying in most places in the city, the following **guesthouses**, concentrated in the French Quarter and Faubourg, are particularly welcoming.

B&W Courtyards 2425 Chartres St ⓦwww.bandwcourtyards.com; see p.121

Bon Maison 835 Bourbon St ⓦwww.bonmaison.com; see p.116

Chimes B&B 1146 Constantinople St ⓦwww.chimesneworleans.com; see p.119

The Frenchmen 417 Frenchmen St ⓦwww.frenchmenhotel.com; see p.121

New Orleans Guest House 1118 Ursulines St ⓦwww.neworleans.com/nogh/; see p.119

St Peter House Hotel 1005 St Peter St ⓦwww.stpeterhouse.com; see p.118

Ursuline Guest House 708 Ursulines St ⓦursulineguesthouse.com; see p.118

For flyers and current local information on the ground, head for the **gay bookstore** Faubourg Marigny Art & Books (p.188).

Gay bars and clubs

Many of New Orleans' **gay bars and clubs** are in the Quarter; if you want a quieter, more local scene, head for the neighbourhood joints in the Faubourg and the Bywater. Most venues are geared toward the boys, but nearly all welcome lesbians, and the ones along Bourbon Street at least are more than happy to serve straights. For a good mixed bar/club/restaurant in Bywater see also the *Country Club*, p.149.

The places reviewed below all feature a dizzying series of happy hours and special deals – these change regularly, so check the websites and the publications listed opposite.

The French Quarter

Bourbon Pub/Parade 801 Bourbon St at St Ann ☏529-2107, ⓦ www.bourbonpub.com. Daily 24hr. Crowded, long-established and always rowdy video-bar and club at the epicentre of the Quarter's gay nightlife scene. The heavy drinking, table dancing and videos happen downstairs, while upstairs offers regular theme nights from glam rock through "Singalong Sundays" to queer cabaret. Cover varies.

Café Lafitte in Exile and Balcony Bar 901 Bourbon St at Dumaine ☏522-8397, ⓦ www .lafittes.com. Daily 24hr. Operating on this spot since the 1950s, and for twenty years before that at the nearby *Lafitte's Blacksmith Shop* thus the name), this rambunctious, welcoming gay men's bar – once a haunt of Tennessee Williams – remains a much-loved favourite, with a balcony that becomes party central during the major festivals. Various promotions and happy hours, with naked pool tournaments, trash disco, and karaoke on Weds.

Golden Lantern 1239 Royal St at Gov Nicholls ☏529-2860. Daily 24hr. Established, extremely friendly neighbour-hood gay/drag bar – also known as *Tubby's* – usually full with a crowd of devoted regulars, old-timers, and faithful tourists. Their legendary Bloody Marys, packed with pickled green beans, okra, and green olives, are practically meals in themselves, and the Margaritas aren't bad, either. As the memorabilia makes very clear, it's the official home of Southern Decadence and the starting point for its parade.

Good Friends and Queen's Head Pub 740 Dauphine St at St Ann ☏566-7191, ⓦ www .goodfriendsbar.com. Daily 24hr. This good-natured bar has a cosy, neighbourhood feel, with a working fireplace and pool tables. It's also headquarters for the Mardi Gras Krewe of Barkus parade, when it fills with pooches in fancy dress (and their owners). The mock-English ambience at the *Queen's Head*, upstairs, extends to the much-used dartboard and a popular Sunday afternoon piano singalong (5–8pm).

Napoleon's Itch 734 Bourbon St at St Ann ☏371-5450, ⓦ www.napoleonsitch.com. Upscale – and unusually, smoke-free – dance club at the Bourbon/St Ann apex. Their annual Bourbon Street Extravaganza, a live street concert featuring drag queens and boy dancers, has become a Southern Decadence must-see. Cover varies.

Oz 800 Bourbon St at St Ann ☏593-9491, ⓦ www.ozneworleans.com. Daily 24hr. High-energy, high-tech gay dance club with a wild balcony. It's opposite the *Bourbon Pub* and *Napoleon's Itch*, and similarly lively, with drag nights, talent shows, and fabulous go-go boys. Cover varies.

Rawhide 2010 740 Burgundy St at St Ann ☏525-8106, ⓦ www.rawhide2010.com. Daily 1pm–5am. The Quarter's only leather-and-denim bar, *Rawhide 2010* is a little off the Bourbon Street circuit, with a loyal local clientele. Special events and promotions include crab boils, Shirtless Sundays, and monthly blackout parties, when all is in darkness.

Rubyfruit Jungle 1135 Decatur St at Gov Nicholls ☏571-1863, ⓦ www .rubyfruit-jungle.com. Wed &Thurs 5pm till, Fri

3pm till, Sat & Sun noon till. One of the few places geared primarily towards lesbians, this stylish three-storey bar/club offers a variety of events, with comedy, girl rappers and burlesque shows joining indie dance parties and movie nights.

Faubourg Marigny and Bywater

Big Daddy's 2513 Royal St at St Roch ☎948-6288. Daily 11am–2am. Non-sceney Marigny bar with occasional live revues on Friday nights and Sunday afternoons.
Cutter's 706 Franklin St at Royal ☎948-4200, ⓦwww.cuttersbar.biz. Daily 11am–3am. This friendly neighbourhood bear bar puts more

of an emphasis on community events – fundraisers, big game nights – than posing or cruising.
Friendly Bar 2301 Chartres St at Marigny ☎943-8929. Another of the low-key bars the Marigny specializes in; a place to drink and chat.
The Phoenix/Eagle 941 Elysian Fields Ave at N Rampart ☎945-9264, ⓦneworleans phoenix.com. Daily 24hr. *Phoenix* happy hour daily 2–7pm. The city's highest-profile Levi-leather bar, in an old two-storey Marigny house with a courtyard. Drinking and pool downstairs; DJs, cruising, and occasional impersonator shows upstairs at the *Eagle* (Tues–Sun).

Out of the City

Out of the City

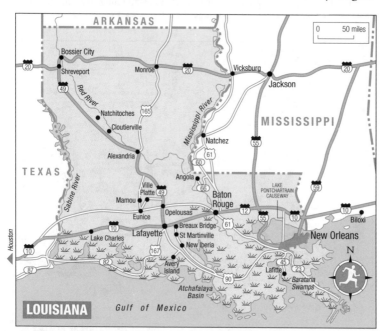

18

Out of the City

By far the most popular side trip from New Orleans is the drive along the **River Road**, which hugs the banks of the Mississippi all the way to Baton Rouge, seventy miles upriver. It's not a particularly eventful journey, winding through flat, fertile farmland, but a series of bridges and ferries allows you to crisscross the water, and you can stop off and tour several restored antebellum **plantation** homes along the way.

Alternatively, a thirty-minute drive south from New Orleans brings you to the remote fishing village of **Lafitte**, a trip that satisfies all sorts of adventurous urges. Not only can you travel to the end of the road, which simply gives up the ghost in the face of encroaching swamps and bayous, but you can also take a stroll or canoe-ride through the **Barataria Preserve**, a tangle of hardwood forest, cypress swamp and marsh that eventually dissolves into the Gulf of Mexico.

If you are in town in October or April, you could also join the thousands of locals who drive the long, lonely road to the maximum-security **Angola**

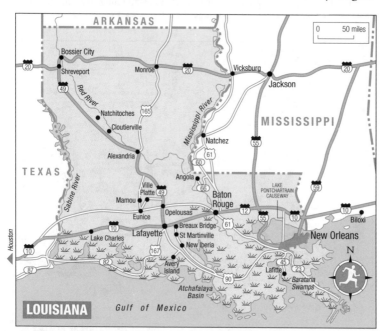

prison rodeo, an odd, only-in-America experience that is as unsettling as it is uplifting.

The River Road plantations

Before the Civil War, the spectacular homes strung along the **Mississippi River Road** were the focal points of the vast estates from where wealthy planters – or rather, their slaves – loaded cotton, sugar, or indigo onto steamboats berthed virtually at their front doors, ready to be transported to the markets in the city. Most of the **plantations** that you can visit today grew **sugar**, which from the earliest days of the colony was vital to the economy, protected by tariffs that blocked imports from the Caribbean. Though some sugar farms still exist, the era of the sugar baron was over by the 1930s, when many of the houses, too expensive to maintain, were abandoned. At the same time, the construction of the levee – a response to catastrophic flooding throughout the Mississippi valley in the 1920s – enabled ocean-going tankers to ply the river as far as Baton Rouge and heralded the era of the **petrochemical** companies.

Today, the levee runs the length of the banks, blocking the river from view, and though you'd never guess it from the tourist brochures – which romanticize the area as a magnolia-scented idyll swathed in azaleas and dreamy Spanish moss – it's the hulking chemical plants that dominate the River Road **landscape**. Almost as soon as you've crossed the soupy swamp that surrounds New Orleans you're confronted with a vista of grim refineries, whose colossal pipes, according to local environmental groups, annually spew out millions of pounds of toxins into the Mississippi. There are rural expanses, where wide sugarcane fields are interrupted only by vine-strewn, tumbledown shacks – the **prettiest stretches** are near the small town of Convent, on the east bank – but you'll more often find yourself driving through straggling communities of boarded-up lounge bars and laundromats, scarred by scrap piles, burnt-out cars and smokestacks.

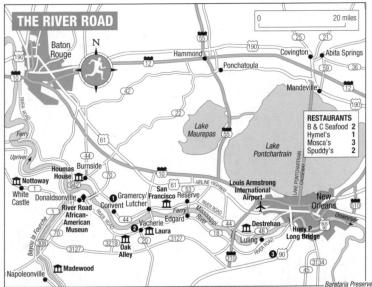

Plantation practicalities

To **drive to the River Road** from New Orleans, take I-10 west to exit 220, turn onto I-310 and follow it to Hwy-48 on the east bank (ie above the river on the map). It shortly becomes Hwy-44, or the River Road. For the west bank (below the river), cross Destrehan Bridge onto Hwy-18 rather than branching onto Hwy-48. Since signs for the plantations are poor, you should get hold of the detailed Louisiana River Road Plantation map, sold in bookstores around town (remember that the kinks in the river mean that distances are larger than they may appear). When timing your trip, it's best to get an early start and certainly to avoid the last tours of the day – not only do they tend to be the most hurried, but also you'll be hitting rush hour on the River Road. Tours last between 45 minutes and an hour.

For **food**, you can give the plantation restaurants a miss. You'll do far better at *Hymel's* (Tues & Wed 11am–2.30pm, Thurs & Fri 11am–2.30pm & 5–9pm, Sat 11.30am–10pm, Sun 11.30am–8pm; ☎225/562-7031), a simple, convivial place on the east bank, four miles downriver of the Sunshine Bridge on Hwy-44. The long menu includes delicious boiled and fried seafood, and the jukebox is a treat, playing Country & Western and Cajun music to a crowd of regulars. If you'd rather have a fried boudin ball or an alligator po-boy to go, head for the west bank and *B&C Seafood*, on Hwy-18 east of Laura plantation in Vacherie (Mon–Thurs 9am–6pm, Fri & Sat 9am–7pm; ☎225/265-8356) – they also serve delicious boiled crawfish in season. Very nearby, *Spuddy's* at 2644 Hwy-20 West (☎225/265-4013) is another friendly joint serving delicious local food, including home-made boudin and gumbo. In the evenings, it's well worth heading to *Mosca's*, 4137 Hwy-90 West, near Avondale on the west bank (Tues–Sat 5.30–9.30pm; ☎436-9942, ⓦwww.moscas restaurant.com; no credit cards). It's an institution among New Orleanians who make the twenty-minute drive out of town especially to feast on its fabulous Italian-Creole food – garlicky oysters Mosca, spaghetti and meatballs, and a delicious garlic chicken drenched in olive oil, rosemary and white wine – served "family-style" around big tables. The jukebox, with its Louis Prima and Sinatra, is a treat.

Oak Alley (p.208), Madewood (p.209) and Nottoway (p.210) offer **accommodation**. Each has its own style, but they all throw in a free house tour and a good breakfast.

A number of local **tour operators** offer bus trips from New Orleans to the plantations; turn to p.24 for details.

In the last few decades, some – but by no means all – of the neglected **plantation houses** have been given a reprieve as wealthy individuals, hoping to combat the local dependence on chemical industries, or PR-savvy oil companies, looking to clean up their image, have set about restoring them as tourist attractions. Generally speaking – the superb **Laura** plantation is an exception – **tours**, more often than not led by belles in bogus antebellum ball gowns, skimp on details about the estates as a whole, which included huge mills and vast complexes of slave quarters, presenting them instead as showcase museums filled with priceless antiques. The cumulative effect of these endless, ahistorical evocations of a long-lost "gracious" era can be stultifying, to say the least, making it a bad idea to try to visit too many homes in one day. Pick out just one or two, or perhaps reckon on spending the night. Many of the houses offer **B&B** rooms (rates often include tours), which as well as being rather luxurious places to sleep, allow you to absorb more of the atmosphere of the plantations than is possible on the walkthroughs. If you do stay overnight, make sure to get out on the River Road after dark – it's an extraordinary spectacle, with the refineries twinkling like alien cities in a post-apocalyptic gloom.

Destrehan

Destrehan (daily 9am–4pm; $15; ⓦ www.destrehanplantation.org), on the east bank, thirty minutes' drive from downtown New Orleans, is the oldest intact plantation house in the lower Mississippi valley, and a beautifully preserved example of Louisiana's early West Indies-style architecture (see p.40). Built in 1787, the house is named for Jean d'Estrehan, who, with his brother-in-law Etienne de Boré, invented the sugar granulation process that revolutionized New Orleans' nineteenth-century economy. D'Estrehan bought the house in 1792 and added two wings; it underwent further remodelling in the 1830s, when a number of Greek Revival features, including the eight thick Doric columns, were added.

In the 1970s the plantation was bought from oil giant Amoco by the nonprofit River Road Historical Society, whose restoration emphasizes the architectural features of the **main house**. Built using the *bousillage entre poteaux* technique (horse hair and Spanish moss, providing insulation, packed between steadying cypress pillars), it is raised a storey off the soggy ground to prevent flooding, and surrounded by double galleries to catch the breezes. In addition to house tours, they put on daily demonstrations of eighteenth-century crafts, including open-hearth cooking, indigo-dyeing, *bousillage* construction and the concoction of African-American herbal remedies.

It was at Destrehan, after the **slave rebellion** in January 1811 (see p.220), that a tribunal sentenced twenty slaves to death, ordering their heads to be exhibited on spikes strung out along the River Road.

San Francisco

Some twenty miles west of Destrehan, on one of the most industrial stretches of the River Road, **San Francisco** (daily: April–Oct 9.30am–4.30pm; Nov–March 9am–4pm; $15; ⓦ www.sanfranciscoplantation.org), two miles upriver of **Reserve** on Hwy-44, was built in 1856 by Creole planter Edmond Marmillion. Its fantastic combination of Italianate, Gothic Revival and gingerbread style was dubbed "Steamboat Gothic" by novelist Frances Parkinson Keyes (see p.45); painted in carousel shades of green, turquoise and peach, its rails, awnings, galleries and pillars were designed to recreate the ambience of a Mississippi showboat. San Francisco was a sugar estate until 1974, when the land was bought by a local oil company – their huge tanks now surround the place – which has funded its restoration. The house used to stand in more than one thousand feet of **gardens**, over half of which were swallowed up when the levee was built in the 1930s.

Tours of San Francisco focus on the gorgeous **interior** of the main house. Designed in the old Creole style, which was already out of fashion when it was built, its rooms open directly onto each other, with no hallway. The main rooms were on the top storey, decorated in bold colours and featuring cypress-panelled tongue-and-groove ceilings rather than plaster. Its exquisite ceilings, walls, blinds, mouldings and doors, a riot of pastoral trompe l'oeils, floral motifs and Italian cherubs, were the result of a redecoration masterminded by Marmillion's Bavarian daughter-in-law.

Incidentally, the **name** San Francisco is a corruption of the Creole "sans fruscin", or "without a penny" – a moniker coined by Marmillion's son, due to the colossal sum that went into decorating the place in 1860.

Laura

A bridge at Gramercy/Lutcher, a few miles beyond San Francisco on the east bank, crosses the river to Vacherie and the **Laura plantation** (ten tours daily 10am–4pm; $18; ⓦ www.lauraplantation.com), which offers something different to the rest of

▲ Laura plantation

the plantations along the River Road. Rather than dwelling lovingly on priceless antiques, **tours** here, which draw upon a wealth of recently discovered historical documents – from slave accounts and photographs to private diaries – sketch a vivid picture of day-to-day plantation life in multicultural Louisiana.

The earliest **inhabitants** of the Laura plantation were the local Colapissa tribe, who lived in huts behind the main house – built in 1804 by the slaves of a Frenchman, Guillaume DuParc – until around 1815. In the antebellum era, a multiracial mix of some five hundred people lived on the estate – two hundred of them slaves, whose quarters were strung along a three-mile road out into the fields.

DuParc died before the first sugar crop came in, and his wife Nanette ran the place for the next twenty years before handing it to her daughter, Elizabeth. The estate, which stretched eighteen miles inland from the river, was managed by the women of the family until 1891, when **Laura Locoul** – DuParc's great-granddaughter, for whom the plantation was renamed in 1874 – rejected the life carved out for her, sold the estate to the German Creole Waguespack family and moved to St Louis. It was bought in 1993 by a group of enthusiastic investors who embarked on an extensive restoration process that continues to this day.

The **house** looks largely as it did in 1905, during the Waguespacks' era: the original building would have been simpler, without the front door (Creoles believed front doors to be vulgar, used only by barn animals and Americans) and double steps. Built long before the construction of the levee, it stands facing the river to get the best of the breezes but high off the ground in order to safeguard it from flooding. Its columns, rooted 8ft into the silty earth, fan out underground to create a firm foundation. Guides chart the evolution of the building, emphasizing the craftsmanship of the slaves who built the place in just eleven days – after a full eleven months gathering the cypress and the bricks – and pointing out details such as the demi-portes, narrow doors which, designed to impede hoop-skirted women from entering, led to the men's privies. The facade, brightly coloured in red, blue, green and yellow, gives the place a distinctly Caribbean feel and identifies it as a Creole structure: Anglo-American planters preferred their homes to be snowy white.

Brimming with human-interest stories, tours of Laura reveal the hard-nosed realities of Creole **plantation management**. Traditionally, the business had to stay within the family – while the owner could hand it down to whichever child he or she wished, the recipient would have to have children themselves in order to inherit. Brutally, any family member not involved in the business had no right to live in the big house – even the doughty Nanette had to buy land from the estate in her declining years in order to build a home near her family, while in a climate of sibling squabbles and backbiting, the big house was subjected to a frenzy of wing-claiming and annex-building.

Laura also calls itself "the home of **Brer Rabbit**". Retold by the plantation's Senegalese slaves, the African folk tales of wily Compair Lapin were transcribed by a local Frenchman, Alcée Fortier, friend of author Joel Chandler Harris.

Oak Alley

The quintessential image of the antebellum plantation home, **Oak Alley** Mon–Fri 10am–4pm, Sat & Sun 10am–5pm; $15; ⓦ www.oakalleyplantation.com) is set in a wide expanse of sugar fields some nine miles upriver from Laura on the west bank. Though the house dates from 1839, the 28 monumental **live oaks** that form a magnificent canopy over the avenue from the front door to the river are 150 years older – and are expected to live another three hundred years.

Built on the site of an early Creole plantation, the splendid Greek Revival house, surrounded by fluted Doric columns – 28 of them, mirroring the number of live oaks – was originally called Beau Séjour. Abandoned in 1917, in the 1920s it was bought by the Stewarts, whose meticulous restoration set a trend for rescuing the old homes along the river. Today, 25 acres of the original estate are open to the public, while the remaining one thousand acres are leased out to sugar planters.

Oak Alley's famous live oaks are bare of the Spanish moss that drapes the greenery elsewhere in the region: Mrs Stewart thought that the ghostly gray wraiths were creepy and had them removed.

Supremely photogenic Oak Alley is one of the most touristed of the River Road plantations. The anecdotal **tours**, led by crinoline-garbed guides, are lively enough, though their version of events is somewhat sanitized; they're most interesting when pointing out domestic objects long since abandoned, such as the "rolling pin" headboard, with a detachable wooden pole to smooth out the lumpy Spanish moss- and horsehair-filled mattress.

Oak Alley's **restaurant** (daily 8.30am–10am & 11am–3pm) does decent, if overpriced, Creole standards, including gumbo, red beans and rice, and crawfish étouffé, but you'd do better to eat at one of the restaurants listed on p.205. You can also **stay** in pretty B&B cottages on the grounds; a relaxing setting once the house is closed in the evening (☎225/265-2151 or 1-800-44ALLEY; from $130).

River Road African American Museum

Also on the west bank, in the small town of **Donaldsonville** at 406 Charles St, the **River Road African American Museum** (Wed–Sat 10am–5pm, Sun 1–5pm; $4; ⓦ www.africanamericanmuseum.org) offers an alternative and welcome view of the region's history. Much of the museum, a hotchpotch of local memorabilia, old photographs and good intentions, is given over to the local experience of slavery – an 1858 inventory of slaves working on the Houmas House plantation (see opposite) represents just some of the 750 people, aged from two months to 68 years, owned by sugar magnate John Burnside. Along with potted histories of local black achievers (the nation's first African-American mayor, Pierre Caliste Landry, was formerly a slave at Houmas House), artists and jazz musicians, you'll see folk art, African masks and artefacts from River Road churches, farms and homes.

Houmas House

Flanked by colossal chemical plants, **Houmas House** (Mon & Tues 9am–5pm, Wed–Sun 9am–8pm; $20 house and gardens, $10 gardens and ground only; Ⓦhoumashouse.com), near the east bank settlement of Burnside on Hwy-942, is, in fact, two houses: the first, an early **Spanish colonial** structure, stands in the shadow of a far grander **antebellum** pile. In 1774 business partners Alexandre Latil and Maurice Conway snapped up 12,000 acres of land for 4¢ an acre from the local Houmas Indians, and proceeded to make their fortunes chopping down the forest of cypress around them. The simple, four-room house that they built was neither large nor ostentatious enough for the planters who lived here in the 1840s, who stuck a white, columned Greek Revival edifice in front of it.

In 1858 the plantation was bought for $1 million by Irishman **John Burnside**, the so-called "Prince of Sugar". Under his ownership it grew to become Louisiana's biggest sugar estate, its four mills and thousand slaves producing 9,000,000kg of the stuff per year – the largest volume in the nation. Though Burnside left no heirs, the plantation, which now covered twenty thousand acres, was eventually handed down to the son-in-law of one of his friends and continued to thrive until the Depression, when it fell into disuse. A decade later the house was bought by a doctor, who began a process of elegant restoration.

House tours start in the colonial building, where the kitchen, centering on a giant cypress table, displays racks of rustic domestic implements including a herb-filled spoon, which flavoured as it stirred, and a rudimentary fat-skimmer. A holy water cabinet on the wall attests to the Creoles' Catholic piety. The dining room is similarly plain, and very Spanish-looking, with its low, beamed ceilings and whitewashed walls. In contrast, the antebellum home, filled with a wealth of paintings and sculpture, reflects the golden era of the plantation. Unlike in the earlier house, where cypress predominates, here you'll see an abundance of marble, especially on the fireplaces and mantels. Even the richest families couldn't outwit the climate, however: the oppressive parlour, with its Victorian furniture overstuffed with Spanish moss, features a press to squeeze buckled and dampened books back into shape.

Two unusual hexagonal *garconnières* (see p.40) stand in the very pretty **grounds**, which are planted with a host of gorgeous exotics and local plantlife, including rose bushes and azaleas. The gnarled live oaks that form a shaded alley from the river to the main house are at least 150 years old – there used to be sixteen more until the construction of the levee in the 1930s swallowed up six acres of land.

Houmas House has a fancy **restaurant**, *Latil's Landing* (Wed–Sat 6–10pm, Sun 2–9pm; reservations essential; ☏225/473-9380), and the more casual *Café Burnside* (daily 11am–2pm) overlooking the pretty gardens, where you can eat seafood pasta, crabcakes or catfish with crawfish étouffé for around $15 per entrée.

Madewood

Taking a detour off the River Road south onto Hwy-308, which hugs Bayou La Fourche, brings you to the glorious Greek Revival **Madewood**, designed by eminent architect Henry Howard and now used as a **B&B** (☏504/369-7151, Ⓦwww.madewood.com; from $229 including wine and dinner for two). It took four years to gather enough cypress and brick to build the 21-room house, and another four years until construction was completed in 1850. The owner died two years later, leaving his wife to raise fourteen children and manage the estate until her death in 1896. Everything about Madewood is imposing, without being oppressive: the walls, between 46 and 61 cm thick, are made of solid brick covered with stucco and plaster, and the ceilings soar to 7.5m.

There are six huge rooms in the main building – most of them with balconies and giant four-posters, and all of them seeping a warm, faded grandeur – and two suites in a cottage on the grounds. Sleeping in these peaceful surroundings, with the freedom to pad around pretty much at will, is a great way to get the feel of the place. Evenings start with a wine and cheese reception; a candlelit dinner is served in the dining room, followed by brandy and coffee in the parlour. In the morning, you get a superb full breakfast.

Nottoway

Back on the River Road, **Nottoway** (daily 9am–4pm; $20, self-guided tours of the grounds $12; Ⓦwww.nottoway.com), the largest surviving antebellum plantation home in the South, lies eighteen miles south of Baton Rouge on the west bank. Built in 1859 as the main house on a seven-thousand-acre sugar estate, the 64-room white Italianate and Greek Revival edifice was designed by Henry Howard about a decade after his work on Madewood plantation. When it was built, its indoor plumbing, gas lighting and coal fireplaces were innovations, but today it's the sheer opulence of the place that is most striking – in particular in the columned ballroom, all white and gilt, with sparkling crystal chandeliers.

Nottoway has a classy **restaurant**, open daily for three meals, a more casual café (Tues–Sat 2–5pm) and nineteen luxurious **B&B** rooms (Ⓣ1-866/527-6884; from $190), in the main house and in buildings on the grounds, where rates include a welcome drink, full breakfast and a house tour.

The Barataria Preserve and Lafitte

The name **Barataria** (roughly translating as "dishonesty at sea") was first seen on eighteenth-century French maps of the swamp-choked delta of the Mississippi River. Through these labyrinths of barrier islands, shallow bays and secluded bayous the Lafittes and their band of privateers smuggled slaves and luxury goods from the Gulf to New Orleans; Native American shell middens dotted along the levees made ideal storehouses for their misbegotten booty. Today the area is protected by the **Barataria Preserve**, where you can walk a number of easy trails or paddle a canoe through the ghostly swamp, watching out for alligators and snakes, and listening for bird calls. Part of the rapidly vanishing Louisiana wetlands, the preserve has a number of land reclamation projects underway, attempting to undo some of the damage done by the building of canals through the swamps. If you are interested in volunteering to help, contact the visitor centre (see p.212).

Beyond the preserve, the road peters out altogether at the peaceful fishing community of **Lafitte**, where you can eat fresh seafood while gazing over the bayous; you're less than an hour from New Orleans, but you could be in another world. To **get here** from downtown, take Hwy-90 and cross the bridge over the mesh of oil refineries and scrappy suburbs to the west bank of the Mississippi. From there, Hwy-45 – also known as Barataria Boulevard – sweeps you south. As the woods on either side of the road get thicker, and the flooded forest of the swamp creeps nearer, you know you're approaching the preserve. If you don't have a car, see p.25 for a list of **swamp tour operators** that can provide transport from the city.

Since the beginning of the twentieth century, Louisiana has lost 2000 square miles of **wetland**, the marshy, swampy areas that fringe the coast. This drastic and rapid loss has catastrophic implications not only for local wildlife, much of which is endangered, but also, very literally, for human lives. Traditionally, wetlands provide protection from major storms sweeping in from the Gulf, and their erosion leaves coastal communities increasingly vulnerable. The fact that wetland erosion is largely a manmade phenomenon, and not just the result of natural erosion, however, has made the issue a political hot potato.

Left to behave naturally, rivers deposit sediment as they run to the sea, bolstering up the marshes and creating barrier islands – natural buffers against tropical storms. Periodic flooding is part of that process. Since the Flood Control Act of 1928, however, and the construction of the levees, the Mississippi has been prevented from following its natural course. Prior to Katrina, the wetlands were already disappearing; diminishing at a rate of 25 square miles per year, or one football field every forty minutes. Katrina itself destroyed eighty square miles in eight hours. Though substandard flood control measures are part of the problem, also significant are the navigation channels built by oil companies through the swamps to create shortcuts from their rigs in the Gulf. These channels allow seawater to flood in to the wetlands, which destroys the vegetation and literally washes the soil away, leaving the city more vulnerable to the storm surges that start out at sea. One such channel, the **Mississippi River Gulf Outlet** (Mr-Go), whose construction by the Corps of Engineers in the 1960s immediately wiped out 28,000 acres of wetland, funnelled catastrophic amounts of water into the city after Katrina (see p.59). After the storm, Congress set a 2008 deadline for the Corps to close Mr-Go and come up with a plan to restore the wetlands. Mr-Go was eventually closed to ships in 2009, but the corresponding restoration plan has yet to transpire.

Wetlands preservation organizations insist that the river be opened up to flow once again through the areas where it formerly flowed, and that bayous which have been blocked off in southern Louisiana be reopened in order to carry freshwater to the swamps to combat the saltwater erosion. While Congress assert that their hands are tied, and that the commitment to save the wetlands has to be a federal one, all along the coast, a number of small-scale but significant **volunteer programmes** offer replanting opportunities. For details, contact the following agencies:

Ⓦ**www.commongroundrelief.org** Grass-roots volunteer opportunities including bulrush-planting to restore the ground cover.

Ⓦ**mrgomustgo.org** Concise and clear action plans to start repairing the damage in the wetlands and in New Orleans.

Ⓦ**www.americaswetland.com** Raising awareness through education programmes, news bulletins and volunteer opportunities.

Ⓦ**healthygulf.org** Technical information, news, and networking opportunities.

Ⓦ**www.paceonline.org** Parishes Against Coastal Erosion; local strategies and news stories from the communities directly affected.

Ⓦ**www.restoreorretreat.org** Political lobbying for comprehensive coastal restoration and local solutions.

The Barataria Preserve

The **Barataria Preserve**, part of the scattered **Jean Lafitte National Historical Park and Preserve** – which has another site in the French Quarter (see p.41) and at the Chalmette Battlefield (p.61) – encompasses not only swamp, forest, marsh and bayous, but also many remnants of human habitation, from Native American settlements to nineteenth-century hunting and fishing camps. Most of the

animals here are shy and nocturnal, though you may see reptiles, armadillos and nutria; if you visit during summer you might even spot an **alligator** or two sunbathing on a log. **Birdlife** includes herons, egrets and ibis, and you will hear woodpeckers and red-shouldered hawks.

First stop should be the **Barataria Preserve Visitor Center** (daily 9am–5pm; ℡504/689-3690), 6588 Barataria Blvd in Marrero. Exhibits and a short film cover the ecology, wildlife and history of the preserve, detailing the devastating ecological effects of the vanishing wetlands, and there's also a series of **talks**, guided **hikes**, and **canoe treks** (some of which are moonlit). And they sell **mosquito repellent** wipes, which are absolutely essential, whatever time of year you visit.

Exploring the preserve

There are eight miles of **trails** in the preserve, varying from dirt paths to paved roads and boardwalks. Each takes you through a variety of habitats and landscapes, and each offers a slightly different experience. Note that the parking lots are open daily from 7am to 5pm, so if you'll be walking outside those times, park your car outside the lot. Try to time your trip to coincide with one of the **ranger-led walks** (daily: Sept–May 2pm; June–Aug 10am), when guides will point out flora and fauna lurking along the way: **snakes** slither in and out of grasses by the path, **alligators** bob in the murky water, and above your head **spiders** weave enormous silky webs. Watch out for the Crab-Like Spiny Orb Weaver, which floats in its invisible web like a starfish, and the Golden Silk Weaver, whose silk is the strongest natural fibre on earth, traditionally used by local Native American tribes to make nets and fishing lines.

Of the nine trails, the **Palmetto** trail (0.9 miles one way) takes you from the visitor centre to the Bayou Coquille trailhead, winding between the bayou's natural levee and the lower swamp, a virulent green from its carpet of plants. The **Bayou Coquille** trail (0.5 miles one way) starts at a Native American midden made of clam shells before weaving through forests of live oaks and red maple, past slopes of dense palmetto and into a liquid landscape of sodden baldcypress and pumpkin ash. The trail eventually emerges into a vast, treeless freshwater marsh, which stretches to the horizon. You can continue from here on the **Marsh Overlook** trail (0.4 miles one way), where in summer you're almost guaranteed to spot an alligator, or return to the visitor centre and set off on the **Ring Levee** trail (1.2-mile loop), which descends through dense forest and swamp. Keep your eyes open on this one for armadillos, turtles and otters.

Nine miles of **canoe routes** channel through the maze of narrow, silent canals into the heart of the swamp. You can almost picture the explorers and pirates of old, hacking their way through these impenetrable passages in search of adventure, or a new life. Check at the visitor centre for details of their **guided rides** (trips leave at 9.30am and last around 2hr, with sunset and moonlit options during the full moon). They can also advise about canoe rental.

Lafitte

South from the preserve, Hwy-45 takes you past a string of mobile homes, mansions and marinas to the fishing village of **Lafitte**. Dotted with fresh oyster and crab shacks, the road becomes less significant the further you go: most journeys around here are taken on the water. At 5134 Boutte St, *Boutte's* (Tues & Wed 11am–4pm, Thurs–Sun 11am–9pm; ℡504/689-3889) is a great spot for a fishy **lunch**, with a wooden deck overlooking the bayou. The seafood is fresh from the water, and very good value; the chicken gumbo is also delicious. Head south a little and you'll find the land simply stops and water takes over. This is the

end of the road, and – unless you have a boat, of course – there's nothing to do but turn back.

Angola Prison

Isolated at the end of the long and lonely Hwy-66, hemmed in by the Tunica foothills and the Mississippi River some sixty miles northwest of Baton Rouge, **Angola** – or "the farm" as it is commonly known – is the most famous maximum-security prison in the United States, its very name a byword for brutality and desperation. Famous inmates have included blues singer **Leadbelly**, who, as Huddy Ledbetter served here in the 1930s, and who, under the auspices of the musicologists John and Alan Lomax, recorded from his prison cell many of the songs that went to make up his Library of Congress recordings; New Orleans piano genius **James Booker**, who was held a short while for heroin possession; and the notorious **"Angola Three"**: black panthers Robert King, Herman Wallace and Albert Woodfox, who, after organizing within the prison, were each thrown into solitary confinement in 1971. King was released from solitary, and then from prison, after 29 years; Wallace and Woodfox, who had been implicated in the death of a prison guard, were finally, after 36 years, removed from solitary confinement in March 2008, and remain in Angola's maximum security wing pending an appeal. Today the prison holds about 5000 prisoners, 77 percent of whom are black. Most of the men are lifers, and around 100 of them are on Death Row.

Despite, or perhaps because of, its almost mythic status – never has a prison been the subject of so many blues songs – Warden Burl Cain is keen to present an image of a progressive prison. Thus, bizarrely, Angola is one of the most accessible prisons in the country for visitors. Outside the main gate, the **Angola Museum** (Tues–Fri 8am–4.30pm, Sat 9am–5pm, plus every Sun in Oct; free) offers a fascinating, if deeply uncomfortable, insight into this complex place. For $3 you can have your photo taken in a replica cell; you are not, however, encouraged to fool

▲ The Angola Prison rodeo

with Old Sparky, the electric chair used to execute 87 men and one woman between 1941 and 1991. Fading black-and-white photos and old newspapers reveal appalling prison conditions; the prodding sticks and belts used to beat convicts bring it a little closer to home. You can also see an array of prisoner-made weapons – a knife carved from a toothbrush, a blade made from a beef rib – used in the many attempted breakouts and uprisings. There's a **gift store** where you can buy CDs of prison spirituals, many of them sung by the prison choir, home-made jams, Louisiana State Pen hooded sweatshirts and even, should the urge take you, Angola dog collars. Pick up a free copy of the prison magazine **The Angolite**, an intriguing inmate-run publication filled with uncensored essays, poems and philosophical musings.

Since 1970, Angola has staged a **prisoner rodeo** every Sunday in October, an unsettling gladiatorial spectacle which draws thousands (there is also a two-day rodeo in April; both $10; reservations required; ℡225/655-2030, Ⓦangolarodeo .com). These are extraordinary affairs, the crowds baying while stripe-shirted lifers are flung, gored, and trampled in their struggle for dignity, glory, and a simple change of scene. Events include bust-outs and bulldogging, as well as a jawdropping game of convict poker, in which players attempt to play cards while being charged by a 900kg bull. Food booths manned by various inmate organizations serve dishes made from prison-grown produce – Angola is a working agricultural facility – from boudin balls to crawfish étouffé. You can also buy arts and "hobbycrafts" – carved sandalwood roses, jewellery, oil paintings – made by the prisoners, some of whom will serve you from behind a wire fence.

Contexts

Contexts

History

The history of New Orleans is inextricably tied up with that of the **Mississippi River**, which has been its **raison d'être**, the source of its fortunes and its potential destroyer. In 1543, **Hernando de Soto**, exploring the Gulf of Mexico as part of the relentless Spanish quest for gold in the Americas, encountered the river somewhere close to Natchez, in today's state of Mississippi. He died of a fever before he could establish any claim to the land, however, and more than a century passed before another expedition was dispatched to the Gulf. This time it was **France**, the most powerful nation in Europe, who hoped to establish a foothold on the shoreline, and thus form a link between French territories in Canada and the West Indies.

The French colony

In 1682, while France and England were grappling over the lucrative fur trade in the Mississippi valley, Robert Cavalier, **Sieur de la Salle**, journeyed down the Mississippi from Quebec. Reaching the mouth of the river, he planted a cross claiming the entire Mississippi valley for France and named it **Louisiana** in honour of his monarch, Louis XIV. La Salle returned to France a hero and was sent back two years later, hoping to build a city. He lost his way, however, landed on the Texas coast, and was eventually assassinated by his men as they headed overland toward Canada in a vain search for the river.

Under Québecois brothers Pierre le Moyne, **Sieur d'Iberville** and Jean-Baptiste le Moyne, **Sieur de Bienville**, the French in 1698 sent a second expedition to establish a colony from where they could trade with the Spanish in Mexico and block the westward expansion of the British. They settled along the coast, setting up inland trading posts at Natchez and Natchitoches; the capital was Biloxi, in present-day Mississippi.

In 1717, preoccupied with the war in Europe, Philippe, Duc d'Orléans – regent for the 5-year-old Louis XV – handed over responsibility for the development of Louisiana to Scottish financier **John Law**. Through a clever boosting campaign, Law's Company of the West engineered a major investment scam, in which shareholders were sold stakes in a promised gold- and silver-filled paradise peopled with friendly natives who would work for free. This so-called **Mississippi Bubble** burst in 1720, bankrupting many of its investors; by then many of them had already left Europe for Louisiana, only to be stranded without the wherewithal to return.

Meanwhile, Bienville, now governor of the colony, was ordered to establish a city near the mouth of the Mississippi. As it was almost impossible to navigate the treacherous lower reaches of the river, impeded by swamps, snags and sandbars, he chose a site some hundred miles upriver, on a portage that led to Lake Pontchartrain. Seeing the twin potential for defence and trade afforded by this convenient route between the river and the Gulf, Bienville had high hopes for his city, and named it **La Nouvelle Orléans** for the French regent.

Progress was slow for the early settlers, who, in the face of hurricanes and epidemics, painstakingly cleared the canebreak and set about building levees in an attempt to protect the banks from annual flooding. In 1721, engineer **Adrien de Pauger** laid out a military-style grid-plan on the morass – a layout that remains intact in the French Quarter. A year later, Bienville persuaded the French to shift the colonial capital from Biloxi to New Orleans; within five years or so the population doubled, more streets were built and drainage vastly improved.

The first **colonists** were a mixed bunch: convicts and aristocrats from France, French-Canadian adventurers and, between 1719 and 1730, a massive influx of **slaves** from Africa and the West Indies. These were joined by the **free people of colour**, educated and wealthy Francophones, most of whom were slave-owners from the West Indian colonies and who, unlike the enslaved blacks, held property rights and a limited amount of political power. Given the large slave population, in 1724 Bienville adopted the **Code Noir** as used by the French to govern Saint-Domingue (Haiti). The code laid out laws establishing the rights and responsibilities of both enslaved Africans and their owners, and while placing restrictions on slaves – including a ban on mixed marriages and property owner-ship – it also afforded them rights unknown in Anglo colonies. Crucially, as well as being allowed to sell their skills independently, New Orleans slaves were given Sundays off. Thus grew the Sunday gatherings in **Congo Square**, a patch of land behind the city where the slaves danced, drummed and traded in their thousands. The only place in the nation where slaves were permitted to gather freely, Congo Square was a breeding ground for jazz and for the spread of voodoo throughout the city. Although the Code Noir pronounced **Catholicism** to be the official religion, slaves used the gatherings to maintain and strengthen their own rituals and beliefs.

Due to internal wrangling, Bienville was recalled to France in 1725. Almost immediately, relations with the local Native Americans – with whom Bienville had been on reasonably good terms – deteriorated, climaxing in 1729 with an alliance between the Natchez and a group of slaves that led to a massacre at **Fort Rosalie**, some 150 miles upriver from New Orleans; 250 colonists were murdered and 450 women, children and slaves kidnapped before the French executed the rebels and virtually decimated the Natchez tribe.

Although he returned to govern in 1731, Bienville resigned for good in 1743 under pressure from his rivals, who held him personally responsible for the floods, droughts, epidemics and Native American uprisings that blighted the colony. His replacement, the Québecois **Marquis de Vaudreuil**, brought to this shabby outpost the fashions, customs and corruption of the French court. New Orleans' first theatrical production was staged soon after, and balls and musical performances filled the calendar. Meanwhile, as Bienville had predicted, the city steadily grew to become a major **market** for the lumber, bricks, tar, tobacco, indigo, hide and sugar being taken from the interior to the West Indies, the eastern seaboard and Europe, and the cargos of silk, wines, cocoa, spices and silver coming in from overseas.

The Spanish era

In 1754, the **French–Indian War** (which merged with what became known in Europe as the Seven Years' War) broke out between the French and English, grappling over their American colonies. After England seized Canada in 1760, Louis XV signed the secret **Treaty of Fontainebleau**, handing New Orleans and all Louisiana west of the Mississippi over to his cousin, Carlos III of Spain, for safekeeping. Carlos, for his part, was keen to establish a buffer between the encroaching British and his colony in Mexico. In 1763, the **Treaty of Paris**, which ended the Seven Years' War and effectively marked the end of France's involvement in North America, handed England all French territory east of the

Mississippi except New Orleans – which only then did Louis XV reveal he had already passed over to the Spanish.

The people of New Orleans were not happy with their new Spanish status. Some attempted to form a republic, calling for the overthrow of the first Spanish governor, **Antonio de Ulloa**. In October 1768, Ulloa fled to Cuba to be replaced by **Alexandro O'Reilly**, an Irish soldier of fortune who had worked his way up the Spanish ranks. Arriving with some three thousand troops, O'Reilly promptly executed the rebels in the Place d'Armes.

Despite early resistance, however, New Orleans benefited from its period as a Spanish colony. Sensibly, the governors maintained French as the official language and allowed French culture to remain intact. The Code Noir, however, was replaced by the Spanish system: slaves could now buy their freedom, and eventually thousands of slaves, mostly women and children, were **freed**. The Spanish also adopted an open **immigration** policy, which tripled the city's population. Newcomers included Anglo-Americans escaping the American revolution in the east, French Acadians banished by the British from Canada, and aristocrats fleeing revolution in France. New Orleans also became a haven in the 1790s for refugees – whites and free blacks, along with their slaves – escaping slave revolts against the French in **Saint-Domingue**.

As in the West Indies, the Spanish, French and free people of colour in New Orleans formed alliances to create a distinctive **Creole** culture, partly in an attempt to distinguish themselves from the newcomers. The Creoles, widely known for their love of the good life, were also busy amassing great fortunes and political power. After 1795, when local planter Etienne de Boré perfected the sugar granulation process, the **sugar plantations** boomed and their owners, the wealthiest men in the colony, came to dominate the political scene. Meanwhile, inspired by the events in Saint-Domingue, slaves instigated a revolt at Pointe Coupé, one hundred miles upriver from the city. Though its perpetrators were executed immediately, the Spanish were not able to rid the colony entirely of revolutionary ideas, and the threat of further **slave insurrection** was never far away.

In Europe, **Napoleon**, as part of his strategy to reassert French presence in the New World, offered the Spanish a kingdom in Tuscany in exchange for Louisiana. The Spanish, fearful of rendering vulnerable their territory in Mexico, agreed on the understanding that he would not turn it over to another power, and in 1800 the countries signed the secret **Treaty of San Ildefonso**. In 1803, however, Napoleon, fighting the British in Europe, realized that any attempt to hang on to his New World possessions required him to spread his armies too thinly. Imminent bankruptcy left him with no choice but to sell.

The Louisiana Purchase and "Americanization"

US President Thomas Jefferson, for his part, had been keeping his eye on New Orleans for some time, keen to control the length of the Mississippi River, which was fast developing as the nation's major commercial waterway. In 1803, under the terms of the **Louisiana Purchase**, he bought from Napoleon all French Louisiana, which stretched from the mouth of the river up to Canada and west to the Rocky Mountains, for $15 million – doubling the size of the United States and nearly bankrupting the nation in the process.

The Americans had bought a city of eight thousand people – a mixture of French, Spanish, Caribbean, Latin American, African and German settlers. More than four thousand were black slaves or free people of colour; half of the property in the French Quarter was owned by free blacks, many of them single women. After the purchase, demographics shifted again as traffic using the port doubled. Redneck boatmen – derided as "Kaintocks" by the Creoles – poured into the city on cumbersome flatboats, bringing goods from the interior to be traded or exported on great sea-going vessels, while fortune-seeking Anglo-Americans settled upriver from the French Quarter in what became known as the **American sector**. In 1804, fearing the spread of revolution from the West Indies – where the success of the Saint-Domingue slave revolts had led to the formation of the independent black state of Haiti – the Americans **banned the external slave trade**. Instead, slaves were bought from other states, literally "sold down the river" to New Orleans.

An exception was made in 1809 and 1810, however, when ten thousand French-speaking refugees from **Saint-Domingue** were invited, with their slaves, to settle in the city. Governor Claiborne's response to the subsequent doubling of New Orleans' **free black population** was to place numerous legal restrictions upon them, and many sold up and left for France or Mexico. Those who stayed continued to flourish, despite the efforts of the American administration, well into the antebellum era.

The arrival of the slaves, meanwhile, also gave **voodoo** a firmer foothold in New Orleans and led to another **revolt**. In January 1811, hundreds of slaves, led by Haitian Charles Deslondes, marched toward the city from forty miles upriver, razing plantations as they went. They were met eighteen miles out by US troops; most of the slaves were killed – some were beheaded and their heads displayed on spikes along the River Road.

In 1812, the same year that Louisiana achieved **statehood**, the United States declared war on the British. On January 8, 1815, the **Battle of New Orleans** was fought about two miles downriver of the city by General Andrew Jackson and a motley volunteer crew of Creoles, Anglo-Americans, free men of colour, Native Americans and pirates. The battle made Jackson a hero; soon afterward, however, news reached the city that the Americans had already won the war and that a peace treaty had been signed two weeks before the battle took place.

The year 1812 also saw the first **steamboat** puff its way down the Mississippi. This revolution in river traffic – steamers, able to travel both upriver and downriver, took days to travel distances that had taken flatboats months – marked the beginning of the city's greatest days as a port.

The antebellum years

The **antebellum years**, between 1820 and the onset of the Civil War, are known as New Orleans' golden era. In this period the city grew to become the major **slave-trading** centre in the South and its **port** boomed, exporting tobacco, grain, indigo, cotton and sugar and importing luxuries from Europe and the Caribbean. By the 1850s, commerce had made New Orleans the second largest city in the nation, bursting with a mix of Creoles, Anglo-Americans and ever more arrivals from Europe. Major **construction programmes** on massive Greek Revival edifices like the Mint and the Custom House reflected the city's self-importance and its resources.

It was also a time of great cultural and **recreational activity**. New Orleans was renowned for its theatres and ballrooms, many of which featured European-trained musicians and hosted the notorious **quadroon balls**, where, under a system known as **plaçage**, white men would take young quadroon girls (one-quarter black) as their mistresses, sometimes setting them up in homes of their own. And in the 1850s **Mardi Gras** took on a new, organized form with the appearance of a nighttime parade of Anglo-Americans calling themselves the "Mistick Krewe of Comus".

Not all was golden in the golden era, however. Though it's easy to exaggerate the **antipathy** between the Creoles and the Anglo-Americans, it is true that cultural and language barriers had led to bad feeling, and in the early 1800s the Creole-controlled city government had made conspicuously little effort to aid the progress of the new American districts. Thus, in 1836, the Americans called for a division of the city into three **municipalities** – the Vieux Carré, the American sector, and the outlying areas – each governed by its own council. The arrangement lasted until 1852, when the Anglo-Americans, who now dominated the legislature, called for reunification.

With so much invested in a smooth-running **slave economy**, government began to heap heavy restrictions upon slaves – who, by 1838, made up more than fifty percent of the population – and in 1852 manumission was finally deemed illegal. **Free blacks**, meanwhile, whose existence was seen as a threat to the economic system, continued to be stripped of rights they had enjoyed for generations: banks stopped selling stocks to these flourishing "fmcs", who were also banned from holding public meetings. In the 1700s, divisions in New Orleans had been largely based upon questions of class, money or education; now, under the Americans – who looked upon free blacks with the same disdain and fear as they did the slaves – colour became the crucial issue.

Meanwhile, the emergence in the 1850s of the fiercely anti-Catholic and anti-immigration "**Know Nothing**" party – so-called because of their covert and suspect methods – led to frequent **political violence** and even, in 1855, armed insurrection when the party attempted to topple the Democratic municipal government. The city also faced frequent hurricanes and drastic **floods**, which periodically wiped out entire plantations, along with countless fatal **epidemics** of yellow fever, typhoid and cholera – in the summer of 1853 alone some eight thousand people were felled by disease. Between June and November, those who could afford it left for the plantations or visited family in Europe, leaving the poor and the weak to die.

The Civil War, Reconstruction and Plessy vs Ferguson

By 1861, New Orleans was the largest **cotton** market in the world, and wholly dependent upon the slave economy. Louisiana joined the **Confederate states** on January 26; just three months later, New Orleans' General Pierre Gustave Beauregard ordered the first shots of the Civil War at **Fort Sumter** in Charleston Harbor.

By May 1861, the Union fleet had blockaded the mouth of the Mississippi and a year later the city was under **military rule**. White New Orleanians didn't react well to the occupation, and were particularly displeased with Major Benjamin **"Beast" Butler** (see p.79), notorious for his severe measures against those who remained loyal to the Confederacy. The slaves, however, joined forces with free men of colour to demand electoral and civil rights; in 1862 they started a Franco-phone newspaper, **L'Union**, which proposed full emancipation.

In April 1865, Lee's **surrender** at Appomattox ended the Civil War and the Thirteenth Amendment pronounced the emancipation of all slaves. While the Northern states embarked upon a period of industrialization and expansion, the defeated South was left to deal with a disintegrating social structure and a destroyed economy.

In 1867, the federal government passed the **Reconstruction** laws, placing the South under military rule until political stability was achieved. There followed in New Orleans an unprecedented period of violence when, as in the rest of the South, anyone working to transform the city came under attack as a "carpetbagger" (a Northern opportunist out for political and financial gain) or a "scalawag" (a Southern collaborator). Returned Confederates, having lost their property, were further humiliated by not being able to hold political office. Their former slaves, meanwhile, had new voting rights, were involved in government and played a central role in the new Metropolitan police force. Supremacist whites promptly formed militia such as the **White League**, who undertook brutal campaigns against the government and the newly integrated schools. Enraged by the seizure of a boatload of their weapons, they fought with the police at the **Battle of Liberty Place** (see p.74) in 1874 – just one in a string of race riots, street battles and large-scale massacres that devastated the city. In the face of systematic abuse, New Orleans' **black population**, backed by a few relatively liberal whites, eventually won more civil rights than anywhere else in the South. But they never achieved real power and when Reconstruction ended, in 1878, the previously free blacks of New Orleans were worse off than they had ever been.

The city faced serious economic decline in the late nineteenth century, due in part to the arrival of the **railroads**, which diminished river traffic, and to heavy debts incurred during the Civil War and Reconstruction. The death knell for the ideals of the post-Civil War government came in 1896, when the Supreme Court ruling in **Plessy vs Ferguson** upheld the conviction of Homer Plessy, a black New Orleanian, for attempting – as part of a wider civil disobedience campaign – to sit in a whites-only train carriage. Allowing for "separate but equal" facilities for blacks and whites, the ruling effectively took away the few civil rights that had been won during Reconstruction and legalized segregation throughout the South, a state of affairs that was to exist for more than sixty years.

The twentieth century

In the early years of the twentieth century New Orleans achieved a certain notoriety nationwide for its red-light district, **Storyville**, the spectacular parades and balls of **Mardi Gras** and its indigenous music, **jazz**. And although the **Depression** hit here as hard as it did in the rest of the country, it also heralded the resurgence of the French Quarter, which had disintegrated into a slum since the Civil War. Partly due to the energies of the many artists and writers who had moved in during the 1920s, the **Vieux Carré Commission** – the first organization of its type in the nation – was established to preserve the architecture of the old quarter, and under President Roosevelt's New Deal, the **Works Progress Administration** (WPA) restored a number of its most important buildings. Meanwhile, the local political arena was dominated by Roosevelt's avowed enemy, the quasi-fascist Governor **Huey Long**, whose radical "Share the Wealth" programmes were funded by strong-arm tactics, political patronage and financial corruption. Wildly popular with the state's share-croppers and despised by the old-guard elite, Long was assassinated outside the Baton Rouge capitol in September 1935.

By the 1950s a rash of **petrochemical** plants along the river had almost wiped out the old sugar plantations. Financial security, however, was hindered by the racial violence and fear that infected the American South during the **Civil Rights** era. Whites and middle-class blacks responded to desegregation by fleeing to the suburbs, leaving black communities downtown to be slashed and razed to make way for interstates and freeways. After **Hurricane Betsy** ripped through the city in 1965, New Orleans seemed to have little left to fight for. Salvation came, it seemed, with the 1970s **oil boom**, which saw a rash of corporate towers shoot up in the Central Business District. When the oil boom inevitably ended, however, in the mid-1980s, New Orleans faced one of the toughest periods in its history, with a lifeless economy, a crack cocaine plague and a sky-high crime rate, and, to cap it all, a notoriously corrupt police force.

Things shifted a decade later, however, with the election of Mayor **Marc Morial**, son of the city's first black mayor, "Dutch" Morial, in 1994. In the early years of the twenty-first century, New Orleans was enjoying a strong, popular, black-dominated city government and a relatively stable economy based upon tourism.

Katrina and the floods

New Orleans in the new millennium has been defined and shaped by the terrible events of August 2005. The city did not actually receive a direct hit when **Hurricane Katrina** came ashore on August 29, and in the first hours after the storm it seemed as though it had done relatively well, in light of the full-scale damage wrought along the Mississippi coast. By the end of that day, however, New Orleans' **levees** had breached in more than fifty places, and rising **floodwaters** covered 80 percent of the city, destroying much of it in their wake. Most damage was sustained by residential areas – whether in the suburban homes around the lakeside, from where most residents had evacuated, to the less affluent neighbourhoods of the east, like the **Ninth Ward** and Gentilly, where those too poor or ill or old to move were trapped in attics and on rooftops for days while a toxic soup, three metres deep, crept slowly upwards.

What followed was several days of sheer chaos. National Guard helicopters and boats, along with volunteer boatmen using their own vehicles to reach people stranded in their homes, executed desperate rescue missions. Thousands of evacuees were left for days without food and water in the stifling, overcrowded Superdome amid hysterical reports of lootings and murders (reports that have since been proved to be largely urban myths), while residents waded for miles through neck-high stagnant water, carrying children on their backs, to get to dry ground. Mayor Ray Nagin soon announced a mandatory evacuation of all remaining residents. This was impossible to enforce, however, and many people, terrified, paralysed and angry, refused to leave, remaining in a city with no infrastructure, no electricity, no sanitation, its law and order maintained by National Guard troops who enforced a curfew and claimed they would shoot on sight. For three weeks the city stood in a kind of terrified, queasy shock as the waters gradually drained away, leaving a silent, broken place cloaked in a ghostly grey. New Orleans' houses, once known for their beautiful ironwork balconies, sociable front stoops and elegant courtyards, had a new aesthetic style: dusty and colourless, the only embellishment provided by brown **tide-marks** – some of them well above head height – and brutal spray-painted crosses branding the houses that had been checked for bodies by first responders and indicating how many, if any, dead bodies had been found inside.

As the facts and figures emerged, it became clear that New Orleans had not been hit by a natural disaster. Rather, the city had been desperately let down by its man-made flood protection systems. Some floodwalls were not high enough; others, like those in the Industrial Canal abutting the Ninth Ward, and the 17th Street Canal in wealthier Lakeview, had not been built strong enough, and it was their sudden, explosive collapse that brought water rushing into the city with such violent force.

While it is estimated that 70,000 families were displaced after Katrina, it remains difficult to get accurate figures – and in particular for the final **death toll** in and around New Orleans. Rescue operations confirmed around 1500 dead, including those who died in hospitals or nursing homes in the days after the floods, but hundreds of other people were never found. It has been argued that a more realistic figure, taking into account those who died soon after the storm but outside the city, in temporary accommodation, or those who died of health issues caused or aggravated by the experience, is as much as four times that. What is clear is that while many people drowned, most deaths were a result of the city's total abandonment in the days after the flooding.

Recovery

Curiously, the success of **Mardi Gras** 2006 (see p.168) – as a healing process for locals, a signal to the rest of the world that the city wasn't done for, and as a springboard for other culturally and economic important festivals – was a small shoot of hope in an otherwise desperately bleak landscape. That same year, despite low turnout at the polls, **Mayor Ray Nagin** – who in a radio interview soon after the flood had famously cried in anger and frustration about the slow federal and state response to the emergency – was re-elected, despite misgivings about how city government was handling, or not handling, the recovery.

By 2007 shockingly little had changed. Many of those citizens lucky enough to have been granted a **FEMA trailer** were still living in them, trying to sort out complicated insurance claims and aid applications and attempting to dodge the fly-by-night swindlers who thrived in a city desperate for building contractors. Others, with nothing to return to, remained stranded in cities where they felt alienated and abandoned. The demographics of the city were changing – many African-Americans had been lost, while a new influx of **Mexican** workers flooded in to work in the construction and renovation industries. The **crime rate** soared, feeding off the rise in mental illness, untreated trauma, drug use, poverty and homelessness. Despite President Bush's declaration two years earlier, as he stood in Jackson Square two weeks after the floods, that government would do whatever it took to rebuild the city, New Orleans had been well and truly abandoned. Vast swathes of the Ninth Ward lay silent, overtaken by grass that grew to head height, while throughout the city only about half the schools and hospitals had reopened; roads lay pitted and unrepaired, traffic lights still not working. Unbelievably, with so many homeless, and so many unable to return, the decision was made to tear down some of the city's housing projects – despite voluble protests from their residents, and from those who had yet to return. The disappearance of so many low-income neighbourhoods, and of the people who lived there – the musicians and the hospitality industry workers and the schoolkids and the schoolteachers – began, in some quarters, to be seen almost as intentional, a kind of silent genocide. The **French Quarter**, meanwhile, which, as the oldest part of the city was built on the highest ground, was physically unhurt by the flooding, although the economic blow – not least the loss of a huge number of its work force – was tremendous. **Tourists** were still coming to New Orleans, and in particular to the Quarter, but numbers were still nowhere near their pre-Katrina levels.

However, as the years dragged on, and with the sustained help of grassroots organizations and **volunteers**, the city slowly began to take shape again. It is no cliché to assert that New Orleanians have a particularly intense attachment to their city, and that few other places inspire such a strong sense of home in the people who live there. In many ways it is a small town, where roots – and rituals, traditions, community, neighbourhood, family – certainly do run deep; it is a testament to the loyalty it inspires in its citizens that it has been able to survive. Even the **Ninth Ward** has gradually begun to repopulate, though the pioneers who have returned remain heroic figures in neighbourhoods that were once thriving.

Increasingly, however, Mayor Nagin was digging his own grave. Just as his administration revealed some of the more suspect deals made by Marc Morial's office, which had previously been seen as squeaky clean, many of his own private contracts in the years after Katrina were exposed as quite possibly corrupt. That, added to a famously injudicious, although well-meant, speech in which he claimed God was angry with the US for being in Iraq, and with black people for "not taking care of ourselves", and calling for New Orleans to return to being a **"chocolate city"** – a black majority city – led to Nagin being widely ridiculed and slowly disappearing from view. Meanwhile, with blame for the levee failures long having been shunted around between the Corps, local building contractors, and the levee boards responsible for the maintenance of the flood protection systems, in 2009 a Federal judge finally laid the blame for the flooding of the **Mr-Go navigation channel** at the hands of the Corps (see p.59), putting paid to the notion for once and for all that the flooding of New Orleans had been a natural disaster.

2010 and beyond

2010 was a crucial year for New Orleans. In February, right in the middle of Mardi Gras season, their football team, the beleaguered **Saints** – or Aints, as they had come to be known, for their famously dismal record – won the Superbowl against the Indianapolis Colts. Not only was this their first Superbowl win, it was the first time they had got anywhere near it, and fans were rewarded with a thrilling game that attracted the biggest TV audiences in the USA's history. The emergence of their team as winners bonded the city – from genteel Uptown belles to public school kids, drunken frat boys to jazz trumpeters – as nothing else could, and in the closing moments of the game the whole city literally erupted in emotion, the screams and tears and shellshock lasting just that bit longer than the usual post-win pandemonium. For a few days at least, New Orleans was no longer a loser; for a few days, New Orleans had finally recovered.

Meanwhile, in the feverish run up to the Superbowl, and on a big Mardi Gras weekend, there was also the small matter of a **mayoral election**. In a landslide that would have at any other time – and perhaps in any other city – made headline news, on February 6, 2010 Lieutenant Governor **Mitch Landrieu** was quietly elected to become the first white mayor of New Orleans since his father, Moon Landrieu, left office in 1978. Perhaps because of the game, or the Mardi Gras parades, or a general deep-seated distrust of politics and politicians – not helped by the high-profile conviction in November 2009 of Louisiana congressman **William J. Jefferson** for bribery and money-laundering – voting figures were very low (at around 90,000 lower even than in the first post-Katrina mayoral election in 2006).

Astonishingly, Landrieu won 66 percent of the vote, with majority support among both black and white voters; his closest rival, Troy Henry, an African-American businessman who famously called Landrieu "the leading black candidate", trailed behind with just 14 percent.

Landrieu, who had run against Marc Morial in 1998 and Nagin in 2006, comes from a local political dynasty – including his father and his sister Mary, a long-time Democratic senator for Louisiana. His campaign emphasized his political experience over the slick business credentials of Nagin – who had been a television executive before taking office – and his cronies. The extraordinary feat of not only winning an open mayoral race outright in the primary, but doing so as a white man in a majority black city, may well have had much to do with the legacy of his father. As mayor of the city from 1970 to 1978, Moon Landrieu was responsible for hiring a number of African-American officials in top city jobs, thus kickstarting the desegregation of the city's power base. Whether the election of Landrieu the younger heralds the beginning of a **post-racial era** in New Orleans politics, as many have opined, seems unlikely. What is indisputable is that he has a tough job ahead of him. Quite apart from the ongoing rebuilding issues – the population, at around 450,000, still remains twenty percent lower than pre-Katrina, and many of those who were able to return still face difficulty repairing their lives – he has City Hall infighting and corruption cases snapping at his heels, along with a stratospheric crime rate and a ravaged city budget to fix. Landrieu may have a lot on his plate, but as New Orleans enters the second decade of the twenty-first century, it looks in better shape, psychologically, than it has for a while. And as a place that has been dealt an unbelievably bad hand in the last few years, it certainly deserves an even break.

Books

ew cities in the United States have inspired as many stories as New Orleans. Since its earliest days, many of its greatest writers – Kate Chopin, George Washington Cable, Sherwood Anderson, Tennessee Williams et al – have been **outsiders**. Inspired by the stirring, sensual city, so unlike the rest of America, echoing with centuries of memories and ghosts, they composed some of their best work while living here. Others, locals like John Kennedy Toole and Anne Rice, captured the essence and spirit of their home town in a range of styles as diverse as the city itself.

Though a definitive modern **history** of New Orleans has yet to be written, many authors have dealt with its key themes, including the free people of colour, Reconstruction and Mardi Gras. Some of the liveliest histories available today were written in the 1930s, by figures such as Lyle Saxon and Robert Tallant, leading lights in the regeneration of the French Quarter, but these tend to be poor on black history. More recent accounts, many of them written since **Katrina**, are unafraid to examine the darker sides of New Orleans' history. The best attempt to unpick the complicated and mixed feelings that come with any true attempt to get to know the place, and can make uncomfortable, if illuminating reads. Those books below tagged with the 🏃 symbol are particularly recommended.

For details of New Orleans' **literary festivals**, see p.175. For **bookstore** listings, see p.187.

For details of New Orleans' **literary festivals**, see p.175. For **bookstore** listings, see p.187.

Fiction, poetry and drama

Brooke Bergan *Storyville: A Hidden Mirror*. Punctuated by E.J. Bellocq's haunting photo graphic plates of the prostitutes of Storyville, New Orleans' nineteenth-century red-light district, Bergan's lyrical quest to find truth, meaning and beauty in the past weaves together poetry, oral reminiscences and folklore.

James Lee Burke *The Tin Roof Blowdown*. Burke's 27th novel, written in the the immediate aftermath of Katrina, is a bleak, angry and miserable vision of the post-flood city, with Cajun cop Dave Robicheaux struggling to keep it together in an apocalyptic landscape of desperate lawlessness. Not always an easy read – and occasionally bordering on a careless casual racism – it ripples with the author's personal pain, and is all the more immediate for it.

🏃 **George Washington Cable** *The Grandissimes*. In the nineteenth century, Cable was regarded as one of the finest writers in America and *The Grandissimes* was his masterpiece. A labyrinthine saga of Creole family feuds, it's a superb evocation of the complex relations between the city's free men of colour and Creoles, its voodooists and slaves. Written during Reconstruction, but set in the years following the Louisiana Purchase in 1803, even at the time of publication it read like a nostalgic evocation of a lost era. One of Cable's chief aims, to represent without sentimentality the dying Creole culture, also informs the short stories of *Old Creole Days*, in which the patois can take some getting used to.

🏃 **Kate Chopin** *The Awakening*. Subversive story of a married Creole woman whose fight for independence ends in tragedy. Swampy New Orleans, around 1900, is portrayed as both a sensual hotbed for her sexual awakening and as her eventual nemesis.

William Faulkner *Mosquitoes*. Faulkner fans delight in the poetry, pace and vision of this satiric account of the wealthy bohemian set in the 1930s French Quarter; detractors dismiss it as a work of overblown hubris.

Ellen Gilchrist *In the Land of Dreamy Dreams*. Brittle, diamond-sharp stories spanning four decades of betrayal, lust and loss among New Orleans' uptown elite, penned by one of the modern city's finest chroniclers.

John Miller and Genevieve Anderson (eds) *New Orleans Stories*. Superb sampler of extracts from some of the city's classic chroniclers, including John James Audubon, Mark Twain, Lyle Saxon, Tennessee Williams, Ellen Gilchrist and Anne Rice.

Michael Ondaatje *Coming Through Slaughter*. Extraordinary, dream-like fictionalization of the life of doomed cornet player Buddy Bolden in 1931, written in a lyrical style that evokes the rhythms and pace of jazz improvisation.

Walker Percy *The Moviegoer*. Much-lauded 1961 novel in which movie buff Binx Bolling cracks under the strain of a privileged uptown upbringing. Profound tale of the search for meaning and redemption in an essentially empty world? Or an existentialist drone in which too little happens? Take your pick.

Anne Rice *Interview with the Vampire*; *The Witching Hour*; *Lasher*; *Memnoch the Devil* and many more. Rice's gothic tales of vampires, witches and evil spirits make good use of the city as a location; the vampire chronicles, featuring the brooding hero Lestat, are the most psychologically complex. Perhaps her finest novel, however, is the lesser-known *Feast of All Saints*, a fascinating historical saga set among the Creoles and free people of colour of antebellum New Orleans, dealing

sensitively and intelligently with issues of race, sexuality and gender.

Josh Russell *Yellow Jack*. Gothic portrayal, written in 1999, of the decline and fall of Claude Marchand, an ambitious daguerrotypist who perishes under the spell of voodoo and illicit desire in the decadent and death-plagued New Orleans of the 1840s.

Julie Smith *New Orleans Mourning*; *The Axeman's Jazz* and many more. Pacey detective novels featuring misfit New Orleans cop Skip Langdon sleuthing her way through the city's myriad social strata. The first in the series, Edgar Award-winning *New Orleans Mourning*, is by far the best, a tale of uptown murder set against a backdrop of carnival, corruption and cross-dressing.

John Kennedy Toole *A Confederacy of Dunces*. The quintessential New Orleans novel, published in 1980 – mainly through the efforts of his mother – eleven years after the author's suicide. A wildly funny anarchic black tragicomedy, in which the pompous and repulsive antihero Ignatius J. Reilly wreaks havoc through an insalubrious and surreal 1960s New Orleans, it became an immediate cult classic and went on to win the Pulitzer. Quite brilliant.

Tennessee Williams *A Streetcar Named Desire*; *Vieux Carré*. *Streetcar*, an overwrought tale of perverse desires and brutality in the sultry city, has become one of the seminal works in American drama. The film version (see p.244), though iconic in itself, doesn't do the play justice. Written thirty years later, *Vieux Carré*, a semiautobiographical account of Williams' early years in a dilapidated New Orleans boarding house, is as bleak in its vision as *Streetcar*, if somewhat lower-key.

Christine Wiltz *Glass House*. Pre-Katrina pageturner centring on the complex relationships between a rich white woman, her black maid, her maid's son and a host of multi-racial characters. Treading carefully through a slew of potential minefields, Wiltz deftly portrays the mistrust, violence and racism that plague early twenty-first-century New Orleans, while offering a hopeful vision of a future based on humanism and empathy.

History, travellers' tales and biography

Christopher Benfey *Degas in New Orleans*. A slightly misleading title for an engaging history that draws upon the novels of George Washington Cable and Kate Chopin, as well as the paintings of Edgar Degas – who stayed with family in the city in 1872 – to draw a memorable picture of the Creole experience during Reconstruction.

John W. Blassingame *Black New Orleans 1860–80*. Scholarly survey of the political and social life of blacks in the city during Reconstruction, covering both the experience of the educated, urban free men of colour and the newly freed plantation slaves.

Garry Boulard *Huey Long Invades New Orleans*. Gripping account of one of the most dramatic moments in New Orleans' twentieth-century history, when, in 1934, the "Kingfish", Louisiana's populist and notoriously corrupt governor, sent in troops to wrest control of the city from its old-money, old-guard elite.

John Churchill Chase *Frenchmen, Desire, Good Children and Other Streets of New Orleans*. Chatty, fast-paced and highly readable, if occasionally inaccurate, popular history of the city, originally written in 1949 (and updated in 1960) using its weird and wonderful street names as a lynchpin.

🏃 **Frank de Caro** (ed) *Louisiana Sojourns*. Chunky collection of travellers' tales put together in 1998; the chapters on the Mississippi River and New Orleans include extracts from Mark Twain, Frances Trollope and Simone de Beauvoir, among many others. Perfect background reading.

Mary Gehman *The Free People of Color of New Orleans*. Concise history of the city's free black population, from the first days of the colony, via the ravages of the Civil War and Reconstruction, up to the advent of "Jim Crow" segregation laws in the 1890s.

🏃 **William Ivy Hair** *Carnival of Fury*. This enthralling attempt to document the life of a black labourer who shot 27 whites in 1900 does a good job of illuminating the racial tensions that wracked post-Reconstruction New Orleans. Written in the 1970s, it was given a new introduction by Southern historian W. Fitzhugh Bundage in 2008.

🏃 **Ronald Lewis** *The House of Dance & Feathers*. The definitive written account of New Orleans' unique and deeply entrenched black street culture. The product of both the Neighborhood Story Project – an oral history programme– and Lewis, the man behind the eponymous Ninth Ward museum (see p.105), it's a large, lavishly illustrated volume that celebrates not only the history, traditions and practices of the city's Mardi Gras Indians and Social Aid and Pleasure clubs, but also its Skeletons, Baby Dolls and Second Liners. Using Lewis' words, oral histories and lashings of photographs, it's particularly rare and valuable for being compiled by the very people it describes.

Al Rose *Storyville*. Sizeable volume on New Orleans' notorious late nineteenth-century red-light district, packed full of photographs, newspaper reports and extracts from the famed "blue book", and scattered with oral accounts. Informative and fun, though the tone, at once prurient and puritanical, can be jarring.

Chris Rose *One Dead in Attic*. For eighteen months after Katrina – or the "Bitch" as he called it – Rose splayed his heart on his sleeve in his *Times-Picayune* columns, laying bare his gradual emotional and physical breakdown to a readership that knew exactly what he was going through. Much of it reads like a howl of pain and fury – the title piece, in which he obsessively revisits the city's devastated neighbourhoods and tries to make sense of those words spray-painted onto the exterior of a broken house, is heartbreaking – but there are also moments of hope, humour and even happiness in these stories of a city that, against the odds, survived.

Lyle Saxon *Fabulous New Orleans*. Evocative historical vignettes by one of the major lights in the renewal of the French Quarter in the 1930s. Folksy and romantic, rather than hard-hitting, they reveal as much about the time they were written as the times they recall: the account of a late nineteenth-century Mardi Gras, as seen through the eyes of the author as a young boy, is as fresh today as when it was written. Other works by Saxon include *Lafitte the Pirate*, a rollicking if somewhat sanitized biography of the buccaneer, and *Gumbo Ya-Ya*, a collection of Louisiana folk tales.

Billy Sothern *Down in New Orleans: Reflections from a Drowned City*. If you read just one modern history of the city make it this. A Brooklyn-born death penalty lawyer/activist who settled with his wife in New Orleans in 2001, Sothern writes with unparalleled passion, intelligence and anger about the horror and beauty of this heartbreaking, damaged place. His personal account of the storm is moving, but it is his uncompromising report of the

countless criminal injustices that the city has lived with for decades – the dirty secrets that the floods revealed to the world – that truly shock. Prisoners abandoned to slowly drown in their cells, dark-skinned citizens thrown into jail after rescuing their neighbours, police officers shooting evacuees – that Sothern manages to imbue the horror with such humanism and hope is one of the miracles of this powerful, important book.

J. Mark Souther *New Orleans on Parade*. An intriguing history of the twentieth-century city, framing it in terms of its need to package and parade itself for tourists, and the impact that has had on everything from racial politics to preservation policies to the music scene.

Ned Sublette *The Year Before the Flood*. Musician and historian Sublette lived in New Orleans for nearly a year in 2004, leaving soon before Katrina. The first half of this book, which weaves biography (the author spent much of his childhood in a small Louisiana town in the 1950s), musicology and social history, provides a solid context for the second part, in which Sublette and his wife struggle to come to terms with the complexities of life in contemporary New Orleans, at once seduced, inspired and horrified by it. The author's *The World That Made New Orleans* (2009), a superbly researched, detailed history of the early city, with particular emphasis on the African population, the musicians, and the Spanish colonists, is an essential companion piece – slightly less personal but just as lively.

Mark Twain *Life on the Mississippi*. America's wittiest and wisest chronicler turns his attention to New Orleans in chapters 41 to 50 of this marvellous travel book. Bringing to life as only he can the bustling nineteenth-century waterfront, the steamboat men and the river, Twain also dwells on the city's intriguing death customs and its cemeteries, and on the oddity of Mardi Gras and the Southern accent, taking in some tasty fish dinners along the way.

Christina Vella *Intimate Enemies: The Two Worlds of the Baroness Pontalba.* Sprightly biography of one of the colonial city's most fascinating figures. The saga of the baroness' eventful life, divided between New Orleans and France, makes gripping reading.

Samuel Wilson Jr, Patricia Brady and Lynn D. Adams (eds) *Queen of the South: New Orleans in the Age of Thomas K. Wharton, 1853–1862.* Wharton, one of the major architects of antebellum New Orleans, kept detailed diaries of his life in the rapidly expanding city. Edited and reproduced here, backed with fine illustrations,

they form a fascinating account, with much discussion on architecture, but also covering epidemics, political violence, race relations, social life and the weather.

Christine Wiltz *The Last Madam: A Life in the New Orleans Underworld.* Wiltz's biography of Norma Wallace, the last of the city's "landladies", who presided over a French Quarter prostitution empire for more than forty years, is a vivid evocation of the Quarter in its sleazy, low-living heyday. Smart, glamorous and above all powerful, Wallace makes a great subject, and this is a lively read, drawing upon testimonies from movie stars, gangsters, crooked cops, hardheaded prostitutes and political bigwigs, as well as Wallace's own memoirs, tape-recorded two years before her suicide in 1974.

Mardi Gras

For the definitive title on **Mardi Gras Indians**, see *The House of Dance & Feathers*, on p.229.

James Gill *Lords of Misrule.* Excellent, informed exploration of the role of Mardi Gras in maintaining racial divisions in New Orleans, beginning with carnival's earliest days and closing with detailed accounts of the furious city council debates over desegregation of the krewes in the early 1990s.

Reid Mitchell *All on a Mardi Gras Day.* Like Gill's book (see above), this is a first-rate cultural study of New Orleans carnival, tracing its long history as a political battleground. Well written, vivid and accessible,

with chapters on race, gender and class.

Henri Schindler *Mardi Gras New Orleans.* Exquisite coffee-table book from the art director of many of the old krewe parades. Nostalgic for what he calls the lost era of Mardi Gras artistry, Schindler covers carnival from its Creole days up until the 1950s, illustrating the period with rare photos and vintage designs. His equally beautiful *Mardi Gras Treasures: Invitations of the Golden Age* focuses on the elaborate invitations and dance cards designed between 1870 and 1930.

Architecture

Randolph Delehanty *Ultimate Guide to New Orleans*. A dozen architectural tours of the city, written in a lively and personal style. The same author's *New Orleans: Elegance and Decadence*, with photographs by Richard Sexton, is a plush coffee-table book filled with desirable pictures of gorgeous residences and gardens, from the shabby to the palatial, that demonstrate the city's very particular, and very seductive, arty/bohemian aesthetic.

Malcolm Heard *French Quarter Manual*. Outstanding volume, packed with old photos, plans and literary extracts. Not only an illuminating guide to the baffling array of styles that make up the French Quarter's vernacular architecture, but also a good read.

S. Frederick Starr *Southern Comfort*. Beautifully illustrated coffee-table book surveying the development of the Garden District in the nineteenth century and telling the stories of its developers, architects, craftsmen and residents.

Music

Danny Barker and Allyn Shipton *Buddy Bolden and the Last Days of Storyville*. Highly entertaining, anecdotal stories of New Orleans' early jazz scene. The much-loved jazz banjoist Barker, who rekindled the city's brass band traditions and died in 1994, was well known for his chatty style, which perfectly encapsulates the spirit of the music he played, and makes for a rollicking read.

Joshua Berrett (ed) *The Louis Armstrong Companion: Eight Decades of Commentary*. Broad selection of essays, interviews, letters, reviews and autobiography, revealing one of the world's most influential musicians in all his complexity. It's a fine introduction to the subject, featuring lots of previously unpublished material: standouts include Armstrong's own lament about defeatism and negativity in his fellow black men.

🏃 **Jason Berry, Jonathan Foose and Tad Jones** *Up from the Cradle of Jazz*. Copious, fascinating account of the genesis and the heyday of New Orleans R&B in the years following World War II. Originally written in the 1980s, it was updated in 2009, with a chapter about the effect of Katrina on the music scene and a lament for the struggles many musicians still face.

🏃 **Thomas Brothers** *Louis Armstrong's New Orleans*. Published in 2006, this is the best of the single volumes on Armstrong, a vivid account not only of the wildly talented trumpeter but also of his contemporaries and the context in which he was able to flourish. A brilliant evocation of the cradle of jazz and the exciting hotbed of creativity that fired the early twentieth-century city.

Mick Burns *Keeping the Beat on the Street*. Compiled just before Katrina, this collection of interviews and personal accounts provides a detailed insight into the renaissance of New Orleans' brass bands and their relation to the city's street culture. Setting off with Danny Barker and the Fairview Baptist Band, the book talks to all the major players, pundits and neighbourhood stars, giving lots of space to old-timers who have gained a new popularity in recent years.

Samuel Charters *New Orleans: Playing a Jazz Chorus*. Prolific writer, producer and musicologist Charters first wrote about the city and its musicians in the 1950s, when Dixieland jazz was undergoing a huge surge in popularity. He returned in December 2005 to explore his old haunts and uncover traces of the city he knew half a century earlier, commenting on new traditions and new musicians with the eye of experience.

Nik Cohn *Triksta: Life and Death and New Orleans Rap*. From the stunning opener, in which well-heeled, middle-aged, white music journalist Cohn finds himself compelled by some wild impulse to wander through the Iberville housing projects in January 2000, this memoir offers a compelling outsider-insider's look at the local rap scene. On the face of it, this is Cohn's story, a personal account of his wilful attempts to enter, despite his lack of experience, the closed world of New Orleans rap by transforming himself into a lyricist/talent-spotter/producer. However, this self-deprecating, funny, disarmingly honest rites-of-passage tale illustrates much more than a mid-life crisis, giving a rare insight into an aspect of the city – and many of its citizens – that have been woefully under-represented in the mainstream.

Jeff Hannusch *I Hear You Knocking: The Sound of New Orleans Rhythm and Blues*. Although it suffers a little now from being written in the 1980s, this delightful mixture of anecdote and scholarship still holds its own as one of the best books there is about New Orleans R&B. Short chapters outline the careers of the stars of the 1950s and 1960s, with sections on piano players, producers, blues singers and female artists. Accessible, brimming with enthusiasm and a rocking good read to boot.

Art, Aaron, Charles and Cyril Neville with David Ritz *The Brothers Neville*. Readable autobiography from New Orleans' favourite musical brothers. Telling their own stories, each Neville comes across with a distinctive voice, and although most of the book concentrates on the 1950s and 1960s, their testimonies paint a vivid picture of the music industry – particularly its racism – and life on the mean streets of New Orleans over the second half of the twentieth century.

Mac Rebennack (Dr John) with Jack Rummel *Under a Hoodoo Moon*. Addled but very readable and often funny autobiography from New Orleans' inimitable "Night Tripper", maestro of the city's distinctive piano funk styling. His prelude, which calls the book "a testament to funksterators, tricknologists, mu-jicians, who got music burning in their brains and no holes in their souls", sets the tone.

Tom Sancton *Song for My Fathers: A New Orleans Story in Black and White*. Sancton's memoir of growing up as an Uptown white boy in 1950s New Orleans, where, encouraged by his novelist father, he learned to play clarinet at the foot of famed black jazz musicians including George Lewis, trumpeter Punch Miller and banjoist George Guesnon before joining Harold Dejan's esteemed Olympia Brass Band. Both a poignant testimony to the power of music to break down boundaries in a racially riven city and a loving appreciation of the different men who raised him.

Satchmo *My Life In New Orleans*. Published originally in 1954, and written in Armstrong's distinctive hep-cat style, this is a great evocation of what life was like for a poor, talented and ambitious young man trying to hit the big time in New Orleans, starting with his birth and ending with his departure to Chicago to play with his idol Kid Oliver.

Charles Suhor *Jazz in New Orleans*. Concentrating on a neglected period in the city's jazz history – the years from the end of World War II to the 1970s – these articles, written by a local music writer and drummer, are particularly strong in their coverage of individuals who were central in the re-emergence of Dixieland jazz.

New Orleans music

T he high-spirited, soulful **music** of New Orleans has had an impact on North America and the world out of all proportion to the city's size. Though no single reason can explain why New Orleans gave birth to jazz a century ago, no other city was so ideally situated to synthesize the traditions of the Old World and the New. Not only did it pass from French, to Spanish and into American hands, but it was home from its earliest years to large populations of both African slaves and free people of colour. As an international port, it was also exposed to the manifold rhythms of Latin America and the Caribbean.

Thanks to the Code Noir, adopted in Louisiana in 1724 (see p.218), New Orleans was the only city in the United States in which slaves, including first-generation arrivals from Africa and Haiti, congregated freely together. Right up until the mid-1800s, at weekly gatherings in **Congo Square** (see p.218), slaves would sing in African languages, play African instruments and perform African dances. As well as being joined by free people of colour and local Houmas tribes, they became a tourist attraction for whites, watched by crowds of Anglo-American New Orleanians and visitors from further afield. The Yankee architect Benjamin Latrobe, for example, in 1819 commented on the dancing, the drums and a "curious…stringed instrument which no doubt was imported from Africa", which sounds like a forerunner of the banjo.

An even more direct influence on the emergence of jazz, however, was **brass band** music. New Orleans' first brass parade took place in 1787, to celebrate a meeting between Governor Miro and the Houmas. By 1820, each ethnic group had its favourite ensembles, who competed in occasional "battles of the bands". In 1838, the *Picayune* observed "a real mania in this city for horn and trumpet playing". That mania only increased, with marching bands featuring prominently in **Mardi Gras parades** and being hired for public occasions of all kinds – including, famously, funerals.

Meanwhile, from the early nineteenth century onward, formal, classically trained **orchestras** would play the latest European dance tunes in the ballrooms, and the city also boasted a thriving opera house. The cultural links between Louisiana and France remained strong, and many musicians completed their schooling in Europe.

After the **Civil War**, brass band music grew ever more popular throughout the United States, spurred by a craze for the rousing tunes of bandmaster John Philip Sousa. The voices of newly freed slaves were now also being heard, albeit largely at first in bowdlerized minstrel and vaudeville shows. In New Orleans, the merging of musical traditions was hastened by an influx of former slaves from rural Louisiana, as well as migrants from the North, and immigrants from Germany and Italy. In addition, in the bitter aftermath of **Reconstruction**, the city's extraordinarily complex system of social and racial gradations, based on subtle differences in skin tone and degrees of European, Caribbean or African ancestry, became eroded. As a result of the Supreme Court ruling in the Plessy vs Ferguson case (see p.222), which led to the legal categorization of all people of colour as "negroes", mixed-race Creoles and black musicians found themselves competing for work and, inevitably, playing together.

Jazz takes root

Toward the end of the nineteenth century, the music that became known as **"jazz"** developed out of the incorporation of African and Caribbean rhythms into both brass band and popular dance music. This was often a very literal process, as young, unschooled musicians from the "spasm" bands who played home-made instruments for tips on the streets would graduate into formally constituted brass bands. Increasingly, in turn, brass band musicians joined the adhoc groups who were now providing the entertainment in the clubs and dance halls. In part because they supplied the sheer volume essential in crowded indoor venues, trumpets, cornets, trombones and clarinets swiftly replaced the violin as lead instruments, playing above a rhythm section of perhaps guitar, bass, drums and piano.

Legend has it that the defining moment in jazz history came in 1897 when the smooth, sophisticated sound of Creole multi-instrumentalist **John Robichaux** was rendered passé by the "hot" new sound of the anarchic, flamboyant cornet player **Buddy Bolden**. In fact there's no evidence that Robichaux, whose band thrived for at least two decades and featured many of the seminal figures of early jazz, was any less talented or popular than Bolden. Bolden did, however, provide the archetype of the tortured jazz genius: he was declared insane following his erratic behaviour during a Labor Day parade in 1906 and never played again.

Another crucial turning point was New Year's Eve, 1912, when the 11-year-old **Louis Armstrong** was arrested for firing a pistol into the air at Rampart and Perdido streets, and sent to the Colored Waif's Home on the city outskirts. There he received his first formal tuition as a cornet player, and learned to read music.

Few jazz groups seem to have played in the brothels of **Storyville**, New Orleans' red-light district, which flourished between 1897 and 1917 (see p.65). Most brothels employed solo pianists, often known as professors. Storyville was not so much the "birthplace" of jazz as the incubator for a particular kind of jazz – piano-based, ragtime-derived and Caribbean-influenced. Its most famous exponent, **Jelly Roll Morton**, was later to claim, "I myself happened to be the creator of jazz in 1902".

In the absence of the fabled Edison cylinder said to have been cut by Buddy Bolden around 1900, no one now knows what the first jazz bands sounded like. New Orleans musicians were responsible for the earliest jazz **recordings**, twenty years later, but by then the music had expanded far beyond the city. Following the closure of Storyville, which coincided with a clampdown on live entertainment throughout the city, there was a mass exodus of musicians to Chicago and then New York, where they helped start the Jazz Age of the 1920s.

Freddie Keppard, whose band took Chicago by storm in 1914, refused to be recorded on the grounds that other musicians would copy his style. Instead, the first jazz band to make a record, in New York in 1917, was a group of white New Orleanians called the **Original Dixieland Jazz Band**. Their million-selling Dixie Jass Band One-Step inspired black New Orleans bands such as those of **Edward "Kid" Ory** (in California) and **Joe "King" Oliver** (in Chicago) to try their hands. Oliver's Creole Jazz Band cut the first definitive jazz classics in 1923, then broke up acrimoniously, but Louis Armstrong, his second trumpeter, went on to form the Hot Fives – which occasionally grew to become the Hot Sevens – in New York. Jelly Roll Morton was also in Chicago by 1923, and reached his creative peak recording there with the Red Hot Peppers in 1926.

New Orleans itself soon came to be seen as a backwater, far from the cutting edge of jazz, and even those New Orleans musicians who had achieved success elsewhere found it hard to adapt in the Big Band and swing era of the 1930s. Several jazz pioneers dropped into obscurity and despair – Oliver, for example, died as a janitor in Savannah in 1938 – while those who managed to crest the incoming wave, such as Armstrong and the saxophonist Sidney Bechet, displayed a marked reluctance to return home to the South.

As academic interest in jazz grew, however, New Orleans came to be seen as a repository of "authentic" jazz. Hence the excitement over the "rediscovery" of a former Oliver and Armstrong sideman, trumpeter **Bunk Johnson**, in the early 1940s. Dental problems had precluded Johnson from playing for ten years, so the well-wishers who paid for his teeth to be fixed felt that he could not have been corrupted by modern styles. His re-emergence did him little long-term good, but the jazz revival continues to this day, with the New Orleans, or **Dixieland**, style being regarded as "traditional".

Rhythm and blues

In the late 1940s, New Orleans once again spearheaded the creation of a radical new form of popular music. While the blues had never been a major force in the city, its electrified cousin, **rhythm and blues**, certainly was. In collaboration with the bandleader and producer **Dave Bartholomew**, a shy young bar-room pianist, **Antoine "Fats" Domino**, announced himself as *The Fat Man* in 1949. Together they went on to sell a hundred million records worldwide, with hits including *Ain't It a Shame* and *Blueberry Hill*. Domino's sound changed little over the years, but its crossover appeal with young audiences meant that he came to be regarded as a rock'n'roll – rather than an R&B – star.

Thanks to Fats Domino's huge international success, New Orleans became a major **recording centre**. Cosimo Matassa's studio at Rampart and Dumaine churned out a stream of hits, not only from Domino himself but by emulators such as Lloyd "*Lawdy Miss Clawdy*" Price, and even Little Richard from Georgia, all of whose greatest material was recorded in New Orleans. However, the most influential figure within the city itself was Henry Roeland Byrd. A former tapdancer and boxer who reinvented himself in 1949 as pianist **Professor Longhair**, "Fess" was a one-man synthesis of all that made New Orleans funky. One bandmate defined his style as "a Caribbean left hand and a boogie woogie right hand", Jerry Wexler of Atlantic Records hailed him as "the Picasso of keyboard funk", and the Professor himself said his music consisted of "offbeat Spanish beats and Calypso downbeats". His genius remained unrecognized and unrewarded for most of his life, but his legacy includes three of New Orleans' greatest party records: *Tipitina*, which gave its name to the uptown club where he gave his final performances before his death in 1980, the carnival anthem *Go to the Mardi Gras* and the extraordinary, intoxicating *Big Chief*.

During the early 1960s, New Orleans churned out an almost inexhaustible stream of R&B and pop hits, thanks largely to composer-producer-pianist **Allen Toussaint**, who was responsible for Jessie Hill's *Ooh Poo Pah Doo*, Ernie K-Doe's *Mother-in-Law*, former boxing champion Lee Dorsey's *Working in a Coalmine* and *Holy Cow*, and the young Irma Thomas' *It's Raining* and *Ruler of My Heart*. Toussaint went on to achieve fame as a solo artist and continues to work regularly in the city, making occasional live appearances and releasing CDs such as 2009's magnificent *The Bright Mississippi*.

The 1960s to the present

The city's music scene all but collapsed in the mid-1960s, however, as recording studios went broke and clubs closed down. Some blame a "clean-up" operation by district attorney Jim Garrison – certainly the city government has never truly championed its music heritage – others say it was the advent of rock music that delivered the hammer blow. Among musicians who left town was session man Mac Rebennack, who, while working for Sonny and Cher in California, developed a musical persona based on the nineteenth-century voodoo man **Dr John**.

Failing to find anyone willing to play the part, he took on the role of the "Night Tripper" himself. Though albums from 1967's Gris-Gris onward may have gone overboard on depicting New Orleans as a mysterious, voodoo-riddled and other-worldly realm, he was scrupulous about honouring the city's musical heritage, working with Professor Longhair and employing such prime talent as troubled keyboard wizard **James Booker**.

From the 1970s onwards, however, spurred in part by the growth of Jazz Fest (see p.175), New Orleans music regained its vigour. The process was kicked off by the international success of the Neville brothers. The eldest, Art Neville, recorded *Mardi Gras Mambo* with the Hawkettes in 1954 and was also (as he remains) a member of the Meters – nowadays known as the funky Meters – while the pure-voiced Aaron cut an all-time **soul** classic in 1967's *Tell It Like It Is*. They only came together as a group with brothers Charles and Cyril for the Wild Tchoupitoulas album in 1972. A critical if not a financial triumph, that superb tribute to the music of the **Mardi Gras Indians** (see p.166) resulted in the formation of the **Neville Brothers**, still the city's best-known band.

New Orleans has also continued to produce major-league jazz performers, even if most of them swiftly move on to the international arena. The extended **Marsalis** family – especially trumpeter Wynton, the virtuoso classicist, and the funkier saxophonist Branford – were the great success story of the 1980s (since when the younger trombonist/producer Delfeayo and drummer Jason have also made waves), while stars to emerge since then – many of them graduates of the city's esteemed **NOCCA**, or New Orleans Center for Creative Arts – include smooth trumpeters **Nicholas Payton** and **Irvin Mayfield**, young heartthrob trombonist/trumpeter **Troy Andrews** (also known as Trombone Shorty, a name he picked up as a talented street urchin busking for tips), and virtuoso clarinettist **Dr Michael White**.

The 1990s saw the emergence of a new breed of young **brass bands** whose raw energy was surely a match for the spasm bands of a century earlier, and who continue to pump the lifeblood through much of the city's party scene and street parades. Inspired by jazz banjoist and educator **Danny Barker**, who in the 1970s reached out to the younger generation and made it cool once more for kids to learn how to play music, many young musicians – Leroy Jones and Dr Michael White among them, both of whom are key players today – went on to create their own styles, while others joined older, established bands. Some youngsters, meanwhile, formed their own, hipper brass bands. The subsequent wild success of the **Dirty Dozen Brass Band**, who started out as a kazoo band, inspired a host of youngsters to take up a brass instrument, cutting their teeth in school and church bands and refining their chops on the street. The Dirty Dozen are now the grand-daddies of the scene, regulars on the national and international touring circuit. Hot on their heels are the **ReBirth Brass Band**, who invariably bring the house down with their exciting, raucous party sound that extends from traditional standards to Michael Jackson covers. The ubiquitous, charismatic trumpeter **Kermit Ruffins** – who, like his friendly rival Irvin Mayfield, is something of a cultural ambassador for the city – started his days in the ReBirth before becoming a solo jazz star with his Barbecue Swingers band. In their wake came younger brass bands like the very cool, hugely popular **Soul Rebels**, the edgy Coolbone, the New Birth and the Lil Rascals, and more recent arrivals the **Stooges**, **TBC** and the (unusually) all-female **Pinettes**.

Although it operates off the radar of many visitors, the most commercially successful of all New Orleans genres in the last couple of decades has been the city's flourishing **rap** scene. Rooted in the call-and-response African/Indian chants of so much New Orleans music, and with a heavy emphasis on neighbourhood shout-outs, the jittery hip-hop style known as **Bounce** burgeoned during the 1990s. Though this was a local style, honed on the streets, it had a huge influence on national rap and crunk acts, and local labels **No Limit** – run by multimillionaire home boy **Master P** and featuring such artists as **Mystikal** – and **Cash Money**, home to the **Hot Boys**, achieved mind-boggling success. Having long since moved beyond Bounce, former Hot Boys **Juvenile** and, especially, **Lil Wayne** now rank among the world's best-selling artists, while Bounce as street music has undergone a renaissance since Katrina, most notably in the form of the city's so-called **"sissy Bounce"**, as performed by gay/transvestite artists like **Katey Red**, **Big Freedia** and **Sissy Nobby**. Though these performers may seem unique in the homophobic, testosterone-fuelled world of gangsta rap and hip-hop, they in fact continue a quintessentially New Orleans tradition of cross-dressing and theatrical transgression that dates back to the burlesque/drag shows of many black clubs in the 1940s and 50s, and which featured popular cross-dressing R&B stars like Bobby Marchan and Patsy Vidalia.

After Katrina

Fears in the aftermath of **Katrina** that the deluge might have dealt a fatal blow to New Orleans' musical traditions have largely, if slowly, been allayed. Though the city's infrastructure is still fragile, and getting gigs in an economically and physically diminished city is more difficult than it once was, the great majority of its performers have returned, and those who have not been able to are still working here as frequently as they can – in 2010 members of the Soul Rebels, for example, were still commuting 700 miles a week to make their long-standing Thursday-night gig at *Le Bon Temps* from their post-storm exile in Houston. In some ways the floods, and the dispersal of so many of the city's musicians in their wake, afforded New Orleans music more visibility, and its bands more touring opportunities, than they had previously. Perhaps even more importantly, new generations of musicians are once more being trained in the city's schools, and a number of nonprofit organizations (see p.154) are devoted to maintaining the city's cultural heritage by funding education programmes and providing new instruments.

Nonetheless, the musical landscape, inevitably, continues to change: older performers disappear from the scene, while younger ones, not necessarily schooled in New Orleans traditions, but inspired by its musical history, its musical community, and its way of life, move in. Fashions, like anywhere, shift, and so while jazz and black music still form the city's backbone, **rock** in general, and **indie** in particular, have become more prominent in recent years. The best new bands have a distinctly New Orleans flavour – from the **Zydepunks**, who offer a boozy, melodic, and utterly mongrel blend of Balkan, zydeco, Spanish and Irish raucousness, to the theatrical **New Orleans Bingo! Show**, spearheaded by skewed genius and master musician Clint Maedgen. Perhaps one of the most characteristically eclectic melding of New Orleans tradition old and new is offered by the young, generally white, groups of travelling **"hobo"** musicians, who tinge their old-time folk-acoustic repertoire with trad jazz and swing, and who, like the brass bands before them, perform both as ragtag street buskers and in the clubs.

For more on the current music scene and its major players, see the **Live Music** chapter, which starts on p.153. For reviews of the best **books** about New Orleans music, see p.232.

Discography

This is a highly selective list, and thus all the following recordings warrant the ⅍symbol.

Various Artists *Crescent City Soul: The Sound of New Orleans 1947–1974* (EMI). None of the dozens of compilations of New Orleans R&B is perfect – there's just too much material to choose from – but this four-CD set is as close as any, including essentials such as *The Fat Man* (Fats Domino), *Mother-in-Law* (Ernie K-Doe) and *Ooh Poo Pah Doo* (Jessie Hill), plus another 116 cuts besides.

Louis Armstrong *The Hot Fives (and Sevens) Volumes 1–3* (Columbia). Definitive collection of the 1925–28 recordings whereby New Orleans' greatest son brought jazz onto the world stage.

James Booker *Resurrection of the Bayou Maharajah* (Rounder). Culled from his legendary solo gigs at the *Maple Leaf* bar between 1977 and 1982, this cornucopia of electrifying keyboard genius features extended medleys, improvisations and rambling, intro-spective interludes. There is no better example of Booker's flurrying New Orleans triplets and his unfailing R&B instinct.

Coolbone *Brass-Hop* (Hollywood Records). This funky, hard-hitting 1997 experiment in rap-brass fusion benefits from a slick LA production job; if you prefer a rougher sound, try the **Soul Rebels'** *Let Your Mind be Free* (Mardi Gras Records).

Doc Cheatham and Nicholas Payton *Doc Cheatham and Nicholas Payton* (Verve). Two great trumpeters breathe fresh life into jazz standards, in a gloriously elegiac meeting that was recorded in 1996 when Cheatham, who has since died, was 91 and Payton was just 23.

Dr John *Goin' Back To New Orleans* (Warner Brothers). Accompanied by a fabulous roster of postwar greats, Dr John takes a vibrant, inspirational journey through a century of New Orleans music. Still the best intro-duction to Mac's fabulous body of work.

Dr John and the Lower 911 *City that Care Forgot* (429 Records). This uncompromising, angry post-Katrina album, which features Eric Clapton, Willie Nelson, Terence Blanchard, Ani DiFranco and Terrance Simien, won a Grammy for best contempo-rary blues album in 2008. Not all the tracks quite hit the mark, but the pain the Doctor feels in response to the city's flagrant neglect, and its long, difficult recovery, seep out of songs like *My People Need a Second Line* and *We Gettin' There*. An emotional, powerful ride.

Fats Domino *My Blue Heaven: The Best of Fats Domino* (EMI). You'd need a box set to do the Fat Man full justice, but this twenty-track anthology has the major hits.

Jelly Roll Morton *The Chicago Years* (Louisiana Red Hot Records). The Red Hot Peppers' finest moments, recorded between 1926 and 1928, and lovingly restored to near-pristine condition.

The Neville Brothers *Treacherous: A History of the Neville Brothers* (Rhino). This exciting, eclectic compilation of Nevilles' highlights stops in 1985, but it takes in Art's 1954 *Mardi Gras Mambo*, Aaron's sweet soul ballad *Tell It Like It Is* from 1967 and two stand-out tracks from *The Wild Tchoupitoulas* 1972 album of Mardi Gras Indian music.

The New Orleans Bingo! Show
Volume II: For A Life Ever Bright
(The New Orleans Bingo! Show).
There's no better way to spend a
New Orleans night than at the high-
energy *Bingo!* show, a sexy indie
cabaret featuring bingo games, a host
of characters including the evil Mr
Turk, a mysterious theremin player
and the ubiquitous, super-talented
saxophonist/songwriter Clint
Maedgen. As this CD proves, *Bingo!*
is far more than a live act, however,
with songs like *New Orleans,* a
drunken homage to the "most interesting city you ever did see"; *Mid
City Baby*, a modern take on classic
New Orleans R&B; and the heartbreakingly lovely *Something in Her
Shows* bearing repeated listening.

Preservation Hall Jazz Band *Preservation* (Sony Red). Live 2010 recording
from the venerable band, with guest
performances from a host of musicians
– the Blind Boys of Alabama, Richie
Havens, Terence Blanchard, Tom
Waits, Jim James, Pete Seeger, Dr John,
Steve Earle, Merle Haggard, Paolo
Nutini, Ani DiFranco among them –
paying homage to New Orleans jazz.
Proceeds go to Preservation Hall and
its music outreach programme. If you
prefer your trad jazz a little more trad,
try the PHJB's *New Orleans Preservation
Vol. 1* from 2009, a lively collection
featuring PHJB showstoppers like
Short-Dressed Gal and the rollicking
Wish I could Shimmy Like My Siser Kate,
along with jazz dirges, Mardi Gras
Indian songs, and a few new composi-
tions (and stunning vocals) from young
turk Clint Maedgen.

Professor Longhair *Fess: The Professor
Longhair Story* (Rhino). Sumptuous
two-CD selection of the best of Fess,
worth the price for 1964's *Big Chief –
Part 2* alone.

ReBirth Brass Band *The Main Event:
Live at the Maple Leaf* (Louisiana Red
Hot Records). The ReBirth's raucous,
uplifting brass rearrangements and
Second Line stomps make the *Maple
Leaf* the place to be on a Tuesday
night (see p.161). This CD is the next
best thing, blasting the boys' inspired
improvisational genius into your own
front room.

Kermit Ruffins *Live at Vaughan's*
(Basin Street Records). The hardest-
working musician in New Orleans,
versatile trumpeter Kermit Ruffins is
in peak, convivial form on this 2007
live CD, which ranges from traditional
brass to swing, and features lots of
racket from the audience and a cute
cameo from his young daughter on
*Do You Know What It Means to Miss
New Orleans. The Barbecue Swingers
Live*, from ten years earlier, is another
good bet, with giving off a youthful
optimism and hip-hoppy verve.

Irma Thomas *Time Is On My Side:
The Best of Irma Thomas* (EMI). The
young Irma Thomas sings her heart
out on stunning songs like *Time Is On
My Side*, *Ruler of My Heart*, and *It's
Raining*, recorded in collaboration with
producer Allen Toussaint in the 1960s.

Allen Toussaint *The Bright Mississippi* (Nonesuch Records). Veteran
Toussaint is on dazzling form on this
largely instrumental, coolly stylish
2009 homage to the musical heritage
of the Big Muddy.

Dr Michael White *Dancing In The Sky*
(Basin Street Records). While firmly
rooted in the legacy of the greats, to
call this 2004 collection from New
Orleans' finest clarinettist "traditional"
does little justice to the freshness and
beauty of tracks like *Gypsy Second Line*.
Blue Crescent, produced in 2008, is
another masterpiece, reflecting on the
devastation of Katrina and featuring
a host of fabulous performers –
Nicholas Payton, Jason Marsalis, and
trombonist Lucien Barbarin, among
others. The standout, *Katrina*, a piece
of mournful beauty which starts with
the sound of an imminent storm, is
intensely powerful, while, in the best
jazz funeral tradition, sadness gives

way to joyful celebration in tracks like *King of the Second Line* and *St Louis Blues*.

Wild Magnolias *Life Is a Carnival* (Metro Blue). Mardi Gras Indian funk at its most accessible, with guest appearances from Dr John, Cyril Neville, Russell Battiste and Allen Toussaint, and a host of other local luminaries.

The Zydepunks *Finisterre* (Nine Mile Records). A wonderful 2008 collection of songs from one of New Orleans' most exhilarating live acts. Despite the name, the accordion- and fiddle-based Zydepunks play as much klezmer, folk, Celtic, Spanish and Balkan as they do zydeco and hobo-punk, and this album gives you the best of their range. Highlights include *Dear Molly*, one of the sweetest, saddest eulogies to the lost city you will ever hear, tinged with Irish lament, and the equally melancholy, if somewhat more theatrical, *La Vie est Courte et Cruelle*.

Greg Ward

New Orleans on film

N ew Orleans has captured the imagination of filmmakers since 1918, when the first Tarzan movie, *Tarzan of the Apes*, was filmed in the nearby swamps with members of the New Orleans Athletic Club swinging through the trees in ape costumes. It's a supremely photogenic city, particularly in the French Quarter, which lends itself perfectly to steamy, noirish visions and haunting Gothic nightmares. On top of that, its countless romantic associations – Mardi Gras, the Mississippi River, the lost culture of the Creoles, the pirates, the prostitutes, the voodoo queens – offer rich pickings for storytellers. Since Katrina, of course, a number of films have replayed some of the less appealing images now associated with the city, in an attempt to come to terms with the tragedy.

All the King's Men (Robert Rossen, 1949). Thinly veiled biopic of 1930s Governor Huey Long – popularly known as the "Kingfish" for his catch-phrase "Every man a king" – whose hard-nosed radical politics, bully-boy tactics, and blatant corruption led to his murder in 1936. A gripping insight into Louisiana's notoriously corrupt political system.

Always for Pleasure (Les Blank, 1978). Outstanding, impressionistic documentary whirl through New Orleans' street parades, jazz funerals and Mardi Gras festivities. Perform-ances include turns by Professor Longhair and the Wild Tchoupitoulas Mardi Gras Indians.

Bad Lieutenant: Port of Call New Orleans (Werner Herzog, 2009). Very dark, wildly surreal black comedy that is not, apparently, based on Abel Ferrara's movie from 1992, though there are obvious similarities in the emphasis on the shadowier side of crimefighting. Local boy Nicolas Cage gives one of his more skewed perform-ances as the cop-on-the-brink in the out-of-control post-Katrina city. Not an easy ride, the film's dark brutality does a good job of evoking the crazi-ness of that time, for better or worse – light relief, of a sort, is provided by the singing lizards.

The Big Easy (Jim McBride, 1986). Dennis Quaid shot to fame as the maverick New Orleans cop who plays cat-and-mouse in the French Quarter with uptight assistant DA Ellen Barkin. Great fun, not least for Quaid's preposterous Cajun accent.

Blaze (Ron Shelton, 1989). Inspired by the autobiography of 1950s stripper Blaze Starr, who had an affair with Earl Long – younger brother of Huey, and, like his brother before him, another maverick Louisiana governor – this movie palls occasionally, despite its juicy material. It's an intriguing curio, though, with very watchable performances from Paul Newman as the unstable governor and Lolita Davidovitch as the tart-with-a-heart he falls for.

The Buccaneer (Cecil B. de Mille, 1938). Based on Lyle Saxon's book *Lafitte the Pirate*, this riproaring swash-buckler, starring Fredric March, shamelessly romanticizes the role of Lafitte in Andrew Jackson's victory against the British in the 1815 Battle of New Orleans.

Down by Law (Jim Jarmusch, 1986). From its moody opening shots, panning across decrepit street-scapes, to the stylish soundtrack from Tom Waits and John Lurie, Jarmusch's monochrome hymn to New Orleans lowlife is a treat. Waits and Lurie are the jaded jailbirds making a bid for freedom, led by their *faux-naïf* cellmate, Roberto Benigni in an early American role. New Orleans is shown at its dissipated best, populated by pimps, corrupt policemen and tear-stained lushes.

Easy Rider (Dennis Hopper, 1969). Hippy anthem to life on the road, with hirsute bikers Dennis Hopper and Peter Fonda riding their Harleys cross-country in search of freedom. New Orleans, where they pick up a couple of hookers and freak out in St Louis No. 1 Cemetery, represents the death blow to their dreams. For all the acid-trip posturing, the New Orleans scenes do give an oddly true-to-life impression of the city's decadence and decay, and, in particular, the sheer weirdness of carnival.

The Flame of New Orleans (René Clair, 1941). Marlene Dietrich is fabulous as a Russian émigré posing as an heiress in this romantic drama set on the Mississippi steamboats and in the gambling dens and barrelhouses of nineteenth-century New Orleans.

Interview with the Vampire (Neil Jordan, 1994). Movie version of Anne Rice's first vampire novel, with Tom Cruise as the malevolent Lestat, and the puffy-faced Brad Pitt playing against type as his victim/consort Louis. The complexities of the novel don't quite make it onto the screen, though Kirsten Dunst as the tragic child vampire Claudia is undeniably affecting.

Jezebel (William Wyler, 1938). Classic melodrama set in antebellum New Orleans. Bette Davis shines as the rebellious heroine – the sort who wears scarlet dresses to society balls – who must lose the man she loves (Henry Fonda, suitably lily-livered in the role) to yellow fever.

JFK (Oliver Stone, 1991). Three hours of Stone's conspiracy theory paranoia can be a bit much, and Kevin Costner is dull as New Orleans DA Jim Garrison, investigating the Kennedy assassination, but the supporting cast – including Gary Oldman as Oswald – put in some polished performances, and there are some great location shots.

King Creole (Michael Curtiz, 1958). Elvis is at his darkest, pouting best as a hustler in this drama of gangsters, sleazy nightclubs and doomed love. The black-and-white city looks great, and the songs, including the title number and *I'm Evil,* are among the King's finest.

My Forbidden Past (Robert Stevenson, 1951). Passions run high in 1890s New Orleans, when bad-to-the-bone heiress Ava Gardner schemes to seduce a lazily sexy Robert Mitchum away from his wife.

Panic in the Streets (Elia Kazan, 1950). Pacey film noir, in which bubonic plague-carrying murderer Jack Palance is hunted down along New Orleans' seedy waterfront.

Piano Players Rarely Ever Play Together (J. Palfi Stevenson, 1982). Magnificent documentary which brings three generations of piano maestros – Tuts Washington, Professor Longhair and Allen Toussaint – to play together for the first time. Their interaction in the build-up to the performance, and the interplay of their different musical styles, are fascinating in themselves, but Longhair's sudden death during filming, and the footage of his jazz funeral, serve to make it an even more poignant document. And the music is, of course, fantastic.

Pretty Baby (Louis Malle, 1977). Seductive portrayal of the Storyville bordellos of the early 1900s, seen through the eyes of a virgin prostitute (Brooke Shields) and tortured photographer E.J. Bellocq (Keith Carradine). Filmed on location at the *Columns Hotel* (see p.120).

The Princess and the Frog (Ron Clements and John Musker, 2009). Though audience numbers were not as high as predicted (it hadn't occurred to anyone that boys just wouldn't go and see a movie with the word "Princess" in the title), this Disney production was much lauded not only for its return to traditional animation over CGI but also for being the first cartoon to feature a black heroine, and for its spirited depiction of New Orleans in the 1920s. Local boy Randy Newman's typically witty score adds to the appeal.

A Streetcar Named Desire (Elia Kazan, 1951). In a tortuous attempt to comply with the Production Code, which controlled censorship in Hollywood, Tennessee Williams' drama about nymphomania, hysteria and homosexuality loses something in the film version. Still fabulous, though, with fine performances from Method actors Marlon Brando and Kim Hunter, and from Vivien Leigh, all rolling eyes and wilting feather boas as the troubled Blanche Dubois. New Orleans – the little you see of it outside Stanley and Stella's shabby apartment – is suitably steamy.

Tightrope (Richard Tuggle, 1984). Clint Eastwood plays an uncharacteristically sexually explicit role as the troubled New Orleans detective hunting down a serial killer in a dark and seedy city. Geneviève Bujold co-stars as the femme fatale.

Tootie's Last Suit (Lisa Katzman, 2009). A moving independent documentary about Tootie Montana, the Mardi Gras Indian chief who masked Indian for more than fifty years and was afforded the honorary title "Chief of Chiefs" by his contemporaries. Following him as he plans to make one last "suit" and parade one last time, the film reveals the personal and political struggles entailed in keeping the cultural heritage alive, and ends in the kind of tragedy that typifies the difficulty of living as a poor black man in New Orleans.

Trouble the Water (Carl Deal and Tia Lessin, 2008). The aerial images of New Orleans residents stranded on their rooftops are all too horribly familiar today. This movie, which relies heavily on personal footage taken on a DVD camera by Ninth Ward residents Kimberly and Scott Roberts, shows us instead what it was like to be in those homes – on those rooftops, in those attics – and follows the couple as they are evacuated to Memphis only to return to the only place they can call home. At times almost unbearably painful – the recordings of stranded people calling emergency services to be told there was no one left in the city to save them, for example – but with glimpses of hope and redemption, this is a beautifully immediate, emotional ride.

When the Levees Broke (Spike Lee, 2006). No one does righteous anger like Spike Lee, and this powerful, stunning documentary – the full four hours of it – was the first to ram the point home that the catastrophe that hit New Orleans in 2005 was not a natural disaster, but a man-made, entirely preventable event. Telling the story via news footage, interviews, home movies and punditry, using a variety of voices and points of view, and with a haunting soundtrack from local musician and frequent Lee collaborator Terence Blanchard, this is an intense, important and brave film that pays homage to not only the city that was lost but also the people who were abandoned during and after the federal flood. Essential viewing.

Wild at Heart (David Lynch, 1990). At the time of its release, Lynch's surreal, dark style was all the rage; with hindsight, however, the self-conscious bizarreness can seem a little pretentious, if delightfully skewed. Nicolas Cage and Laura Dern ham it up as the passion-crazy lovers fleeing Dern's evil mother; New Orleans, a nightmare of violet shadows and lacy iron balconies, is just one stop on their demented roadtrip through the Deep South.

Glossary

t's not only the architecture, the music, the food and the street culture that give New Orleans its distinctive style. Add to this the city's lively **vernacular**, peppered with words and phrases from as far away as Paris and Haiti, and its distinctive **accent** – a melding of French, Spanish, Irish, Sicilian, and African that, bizarrely, sounds more like Brooklynese than a Deep South drawl – and you may have to pinch yourself to remind yourself you're in the United States. The following widely used terms will help you find your feet.

Banquette Sidewalk.

Cajun Rural, French-speaking people living in the bayous and plains of southern Louisiana. Cajun music is based around the fiddle and the accordion, with lilting lyrics sung in French.

Creole From the Spanish *criollo*, or native; the term literally refers to a free (unslaved) person born to Spanish or French settlers in the nineteenth-century colony. It has since come to refer to anyone born in the city, including the free black people of mixed heritage who made up the city's "gens de couleur libres" (see below).

Fais-do-do Cajun dance.

Free people of colour/fmcs/Gens de couleur libres Educated, often wealthy, black Francophones, most of whom were slave owners from the West Indian colonies, and who, unlike the enslaved blacks, owned property and held some political power in the colonial city.

Gris-gris ("gree-gree") Voodoo term for a spell or totem.

Krewe Carnival club.

Lagniappe A little extra, given for free.

Make groceries To go shopping.

Neutral ground Median (a word that is *never* used in New Orleans).

Parish County; New Orleans is in Orleans parish.

Quadroon Nineteenth-century term to define somebody who was one-quarter black.

Quadroon balls Nineteenth-century dances, held in the Creole city (today's French Quarter); see p.220.

Quarters The French Quarter.

Second Line Literally, the line of mourners that dances behind the brass band in a jazz funeral, often swirling frilly umbrellas; more broadly, the motley group of followers who spontaneously attach themselves to any street parade. For more, see p.68.

Vieux Carré ("voo carray") Another name for the French Quarter; French for "Old Square."

Where y'at? How you doing? Traditional answer: "Aw'rite".

Yeah you right Term of agreement, pronounced as one word.

Zydeco Black Cajun music played fast and hard.

Architectural terms

Bousillage entre poteaux Building technique in which horsehair and Spanish moss is packed between cypress pillars, providing insulation.

Briquete entre poteaux Architectural process commonly used in the

construction of eighteenth-century New Orleans houses; soft brick is set between steadying, hand-hewn cypress beams.

Colonnette Narrow iron pillar holding up the gallery of a Creole townhouse.

Creole cottage Typical French Quarter residence, raised from the ground above a closed, ventilated "crawl space," and with a high gabled roof. Doors open straight from the street into the living quarters, and are indistinguishable from the outside from the shuttered ceiling-to-floor windows.

Creole townhouse Multistorey version of the Creole cottage.

Gallery Outside porch, often supported on *colonnettes*, and extending over the sidewalk.

Garçonnière Small apartment in the courtyard of a Creole residence, where the sons of the house would live after reaching adolescence.

Shotgun cottage Long, narrow clapboard structures, built in the late 1800s, with a single row of rooms opening onto each other. Usually painted in bright or ice cream colours, they're also notable for their decorative wooden gingerbread details.

Food and drink

Andouille ("on-*doo*-we") Spicy, smoked Cajun pork sausage, often used in gumbo and jambalaya.

Bananas Foster Flamboyant dessert invented at *Brennan's* restaurant in 1951. Sliced bananas, doused in rum and banana liqueur, are added to a mountain of brown sugar and set alight at your table to create the ultimate in boozy comfort food.

Barbecue shrimp Not BBQ as we know it; the huge, whole shrimp are baked in their shells and served in a hot buttery, garlicky, herby sauce.

Beignets ("*ben-yay*") Deep-fried, square doughnuts without a hole, served hot and smothered in powdered sugar.

Biscuits Sourmilk scones, traditionally eaten at breakfast – a Southern tradition, not limited to Louisiana.

Boudin Spicy Cajun sausage, traditionally made with pork liver – sometimes adding pig blood (*boudin noir*) – and hefted up with "dirty" rice (see below). Known as Cajun fast food, it's available in a variety of forms, including shrimp, crawfish, and alligator.

Bread pudding Gooey dessert, made with French bread and raisins, and usually drenched in sweet, liquor-filled custard.

Café brûlot Dark, spicy coffee flavoured with brandy, orange liqueur, orange peel, and spices, set alight before serving.

Calas Creole rice fritters with their roots in West African cooking, traditionally sold by the city's free women of colour and served for breakfast.

Chaurice Cajun sausage, similar to and probably with its origins in, Spanish chorizo.

Chicory Related to endive; a roasted, ground root traditionally used to flavour New Orleans coffee.

Chitlins Smoked, savoury pig intestines – found in Southern soul food restaurants, but not in those that serve Creole soul food.

Cochon du lait Marinated, pit-roasted suckling pig; a Cajun speciality.

Daube Beef stew.

Debris Juicy meat leftovers, usually from slow-cooked roast beef or pork, often served in a sloppy po-boy.

Dirty rice Rice cooked with chicken livers, giblets, onions, peppers, and spices.

Dressed (when referring to a po-boy) Served with shredded lettuce, tomatoes, pickles and mayonnaise.

Étouffé Literally "smothered" in Creole sauce (a roux with tomato, onion and spices), usually served over shrimp or crawfish on a bed of rice.

Filé Dried sassafras, formerly ground by the local Native Americans to thicken soups, and still often added to gumbo.

Grillades ("*gree-yards*") Sliced veal or beef served in a rich gravy, usually with grits, often for breakfast.

Grits Southern breakfast staple of mushy ground corn boiled and traditionally served with a dollop of butter, maple syrup, or gravy. Contemporary restaurants may add cheese and/or shrimp.

Gumbo Thick soup-cum-stew made with any kind of meat you can imagine – seafood, chicken, rabbit, duck, or sausage – and often served over rice. The name is generally agreed to come from *gombo*, the Bantu word for okra, which can be used as a thickening agent. There are as many varieties of gumbo as there are cooks – some start with a roux, others swear by the okra – but it remains the definitive Louisiana dish.

Gumbo z'herbes Vegetarian gumbo, full of greens, created by African slaves for Lent. It's also served on Good Friday, traditionally a Catholic day of fasting.

Hurricane New Orleans' most famous cocktail (see p.145).

Hush puppies Fried cornmeal balls eaten as a side dish throughout the South.

Jambalaya Spicy rice jumbled together with seafood, sausage, chicken, tomatoes, garlic, bell peppers, celery, and onion. Its origins are in both African (joliof rice) and Spanish cooking (paella), and its name is thought to come from the Spanish or French words for ham (*jamon* and *jambon*), tacked onto the Spanish word *paella*.

King Cake A ring of sweet, cinammon-infused brioche, iced in the carnival colours of gold, green, and purple, eaten throughout Mardi Gras season. The tradition of adding a fava bean (nowadays a plastic baby) to the cake – whoever finds it must buy the next King Cake – dates as far back as the pre-Christian European feast of Saturn.

Loaf An older name for a po-boy, still used to describe overstuffed French bread sandwiches in some restaurants.

Macque choux Creamy, piquant stew of corn, tomatoes, onion and peppers.

Mirliton Squash.

Muffuletta Italian sandwich; a large, round sesame-seed bun stuffed with aromatic meats and cheeses, dripping with olive and garlic dressing. Traditionally bought from the *Central Grocery* (see p.143) or the *Napoleon House* (see p.129).

Oysters Rockefeller Concocted at *Antoine's* restaurant around 1900, and named for the oil magnate. These days most versions come baked in a creamy spinach sauce, but *Antoine's* secret recipe uses greens.

Pain perdu French toast ("lost bread").

Panéed Lightly breaded and fried in butter.

Po-boy Long sandwich crammed with oysters, shrimp, roast beef, or almost anything else edible. It was created by two local bakers in 1929, who handed them out free to striking streetcar drivers ("poor boys"). Though they are often described as French bread sandwiches, po-boys are not actually made from baguettes, but from special loaves with soft, powdery insides, a thin, brittle crust, and squared ends. Locals tend to have them "dressed" – served with mayonnaise, salad and pickle.

Praline ("*praw-leen*") Incredibly sweet candy discs, usually brittle, made from caramelized brown sugar, melted butter, and pecans ("pi-*cons*").

Ramos Gin Fizz Locally invented cocktail, traditionally served at the *Sazerac Bar*. See p.145 for more.

Ravigote Piquant mix of mayonnaise and capers, usually served with cold shellfish.

Rémoulade Chilled spicy sauce made with garlic, spring onion, horseradish, mustard, and lemon, and slathered over cold shrimp.

Roux French thickener for many Creole and Cajun dishes, made from butter and flour heated together.

Sazerac Another classic New Orleans cocktail, this one whisky-based. See p.145 for more.

Tasso Lean, spicy, dried and smoked pork used in small quantities as a flavouring agent.

Ya-ka-mein (or yet-ka mein, yakamein, yakamay, yakameat and countless other variations) Clear, salty broth with beef, egg, noodles and spring onions. Generally sold in soul food and Black Creole restaurants, Asian groceries, catering trucks, or on Second Line parades. Its origins are obscure: it's believed either to have been brought over by nineteenth-century Chinese railroad workers or by GIs returning from Korea.

Travel store

Travel

Andorra The Pyrenees, Pyrenees & Andorra Map, Spain
Antigua The Caribbean
Argentina Argentina, Argentina Map, Buenos Aires, South America on a Budget
Aruba The Caribbean
Australia Australia, Australia Map, East Coast Australia, Melbourne, Sydney, Tasmania
Austria Austria, Europe on a Budget, Vienna
Bahamas The Bahamas, The Caribbean
Barbados Barbados DIR, The Caribbean
Belgium Belgium & Luxembourg, Bruges DIR, Brussels, Brussels Map, Europe on a Budget
Belize Belize, Central America on a Budget, Guatemala & Belize Map
Benin West Africa
Bolivia Bolivia, South America on a Budget
Brazil Brazil, Rio, South America on a Budget
British Virgin Islands The Caribbean
Brunei Malaysia, Singapore & Brunei [1 title], Southeast Asia on a Budget
Bulgaria Bulgaria, Europe on a Budget
Burkina Faso West Africa
Cambodia Cambodia, Southeast Asia on a Budget, Vietnam, Laos & Cambodia Map [1 Map]
Cameroon West Africa
Canada Canada, Pacific Northwest, Toronto, Toronto Map, Vancouver
Cape Verde West Africa
Cayman Islands The Caribbean
Chile Chile, Chile Map, South America on a Budget
China Beijing, China,

Hong Kong & Macau, Hong Kong & Macau DIR, Shanghai
Colombia South America on a Budget
Costa Rica Central America on a Budget, Costa Rica, Costa Rica & Panama Map
Croatia Croatia, Croatia Map, Europe on a Budget
Cuba Cuba, Cuba Map, The Caribbean, Havana
Cyprus Cyprus, Cyprus Map
Czech Republic The Czech Republic, Czech & Slovak Republics, Europe on a Budget, Prague, Prague DIR, Prague Map
Denmark Copenhagen, Denmark, Europe on a Budget, Scandinavia
Dominica The Caribbean
Dominican Republic Dominican Republic, The Caribbean
Ecuador Ecuador, South America on a Budget
Egypt Egypt, Egypt Map
El Salvador Central America on a Budget
England Britain, Camping in Britain, Devon & Cornwall, Dorset, Hampshire and The Isle of Wight [1 title], England, Europe on a Budget, The Lake District, London, London DIR, London Map, London Mini Guide, Walks In London & Southeast England
Estonia The Baltic States, Europe on a Budget
Fiji Fiji
Finland Europe on a Budget, Finland, Scandinavia
France Brittany & Normandy, Corsica, Corsica Map, The Dordogne & the Lot, Europe on a Budget, France, France Map, Languedoc & Roussillon, The Loire, Paris, Paris DIR,

Paris Map, Paris Mini Guide, Provence & the Côte d'Azur, The Pyrenees, Pyrenees & Andorra Map
French Guiana South America on a Budget
Gambia The Gambia, West Africa
Germany Berlin, Berlin Map, Europe on a Budget, Germany, Germany Map
Ghana West Africa
Gibraltar Spain
Greece Athens Map, Crete, Crete Map, Europe on a Budget, Greece, Greece Map, Greek Islands, Ionian Islands
Guadeloupe The Caribbean
Guatemala Central America on a Budget, Guatemala, Guatemala & Belize Map
Guinea West Africa
Guinea-Bissau West Africa
Guyana South America on a Budget
Holland see The Netherlands
Honduras Central America on a Budget
Hungary Budapest, Europe on a Budget, Hungary
Iceland Iceland, Iceland Map
India Goa, India, India Map, Kerala, Rajasthan, Delhi & Agra [1 title], South India, South India Map
Indonesia Bali & Lombok, Southeast Asia on a Budget
Ireland Dublin DIR, Dublin Map, Europe on a Budget, Ireland, Ireland Map
Israel Jerusalem
Italy Europe on a Budget, Florence DIR, Florence & Siena Map, Florence & the best of Tuscany, Italy, The Italian Lakes, Naples & the Amalfi Coast, Rome, Rome DIR, Rome Map, Sardinia, Sicily, Sicily Map, Tuscany & Umbria, Tuscany Map,

Venice, Venice DIR, Venice Map
Jamaica Jamaica, The Caribbean
Japan Japan, Tokyo
Jordan Jordan
Kenya Kenya, Kenya Map
Korea Korea
Laos Laos, Southeast Asia on a Budget, Vietnam, Laos & Cambodia Map [1 Map]
Latvia The Baltic States, Europe on a Budget
Lithuania The Baltic States, Europe on a Budget
Luxembourg Belgium & Luxembourg, Europe on a Budget
Malaysia Malaysia Map, Malaysia, Singapore & Brunei [1 title], Southeast Asia on a Budget
Mali West Africa
Malta Malta & Gozo DIR
Martinique The Caribbean
Mauritania West Africa
Mexico Baja California, Baja California, Cancún & Cozumel DIR, Mexico, Mexico Map, Yucatán, Yucatán Peninsula Map
Monaco France, Provence & the Côte d'Azur
Montenegro Montenegro
Morocco Europe on a Budget, Marrakesh DIR, Marrakesh Map, Morocco, Morocco Map,
Nepal Nepal
Netherlands Amsterdam, Amsterdam DIR, Amsterdam Map, Europe on a Budget, The Netherlands
Netherlands Antilles The Caribbean
New Zealand New Zealand, New Zealand Map

DIR: Rough Guide DIRECTIONS for short breaks

Available from all good bookstores

Nicaragua Central America on a Budget
Niger West Africa
Nigeria West Africa
Norway Europe on a Budget, Norway, Scandinavia
Panama Central America on a Budget, Costa Rica & Panama Map, Panama
Paraguay South America on a Budget
Peru Peru, Peru Map, South America on a Budget
Philippines The Philippines, Southeast Asia on a Budget,
Poland Europe on a Budget, Poland
Portugal Algarve DIR, The Algarve Map, Europe on a Budget, Lisbon DIR, Lisbon Map, Madeira DIR, Portugal, Portugal Map, Spain & Portugal Map
Puerto Rico The Caribbean, Puerto Rico
Romania Europe on a Budget, Romania
Russia Europe on a Budget, Moscow, St Petersburg
St Kitts & Nevis The Caribbean
St Lucia The Caribbean
St Vincent & the Grenadines The Caribbean
Scotland Britain, Camping in Britain, Edinburgh DIR, Europe on a Budget, Scotland, Scottish Highlands & Islands
Senegal West Africa
Serbia Montenegro Europe on a Budget
Sierra Leone West Africa
Singapore Malaysia, Singapore & Brunei [1 title], Singapore, Singapore DIR, Southeast Asia on a Budget
Slovakia Czech & Slovak Republics, Europe on a Budget
Slovenia Europe on a Budget, Slovenia
South Africa Cape Town & the Garden Route, South Africa, South Africa Map

Spain Andalucía, Andalucía Map, Barcelona, Barcelona DIR, Barcelona Map, Europe on a Budget, Ibiza & Formentera DIR, Gran Canaria DIR, Madrid DIR, Lanzarote & Fuerteventura DIR Madrid Map, Mallorca & Menorca, Mallorca DIR, Mallorca Map, The Pyrenees, Pyrenees & Andorra Map, Spain, Spain & Portugal Map, Tenerife & La Gomera DIR
Sri Lanka Sri Lanka, Sri Lanka Map
Suriname South America on a Budget
Sweden Europe on a Budget, Scandinavia, Sweden
Switzerland Europe on a Budget, Switzerland
Taiwan Taiwan
Tanzania Tanzania, Zanzibar
Thailand Bangkok, Southeast Asia on a Budget, Thailand, Thailand Map, Thailand Beaches & Islands
Togo West Africa
Trinidad & Tobago The Caribbean, Trinidad & Tobago
Tunisia Tunisia, Tunisia Map
Turkey Europe on a Budget, Istanbul, Turkey, Turkey Map
Turks and Caicos Islands The Bahamas, The Caribbean
United Arab Emirates Dubai DIR, Dubai & UAE Map [1 title]
United Kingdom Britain, Devon & Cornwall, Edinburgh DIR England, Europe on a Budget, The Lake District, London, London DIR, London Map, London Mini Guide, Scotland, Scottish Highlands

& Islands, Wales, Walks In London & Southeast England
United States Alaska, Boston, California, California Map, Chicago, Colorado, Florida, Florida Map, The Grand Canyon, Hawaii, Los Angeles, Los Angeles Map, Los Angeles and Southern California, Maui DIR, Miami & South Florida, New England, New England Map, New Orleans & Cajun Country, New Orleans DIR, New York City, NYC DIR, NYC Map, New York City Mini Guide, Oregon & Washington, Orlando & Walt Disney World® DIR, San Francisco, San Francisco DIR, San Francisco Map, Seattle, Southwest USA, USA, Washington DC, Yellowstone & the Grand Tetons National Park, Yosemite National Park
Uruguay South America on a Budget
US Virgin Islands The Bahamas, The Caribbean
Venezuela South America on a Budget
Vietnam Southeast Asia on a Budget, Vietnam, Vietnam, Laos & Cambodia Map [1 Map],
Wales Britain, Camping in Britain, Europe on a Budget, Wales
First-Time Series FT Africa, FT Around the World, FT Asia, FT Europe, FT Latin America
Inspirational guides Earthbound, Clean Breaks, Make the Most of Your Time on Earth, Ultimate Adventures, World Party
Travel Specials Camping in Britain, Travel with Babies & Young Children, Walks in London & SE England

For more information go to www.roughguides.com

ROUGH GUIDES

www.roughguides.com
nformation on over 25,000 destinations around the world

- **Read** Rough Guides' trusted travel info
- **Access** exclusive articles from Rough Guides authors
- **Update** yourself on new books, maps, CDs and other products
- **Enter** our competitions and win travel prizes
- **Share** ideas, journals, photos & travel advice with other users
- **Earn** points every time you contribute to the Rough Guide community and get rewards

Small print and

Index

A Rough Guide to Rough Guides

Published in 1982, the first Rough Guide – to Greece – was a student scheme that became a publishing phenomenon. Mark Ellingham, a recent graduate in English from Bristol University, had been travelling in Greece the previous summer and couldn't find the right guidebook. With a small group of friends he wrote his own guide, combining a highly contemporary, journalistic style with a thoroughly practical approach to travellers' needs.

The immediate success of the book spawned a series that rapidly covered dozens of destinations. And, in addition to impecunious backpackers, Rough Guides soon acquired a much broader and older readership that relished the guides' wit and inquisitiveness as much as their enthusiastic, critical approach and value-for-money ethos.

These days, Rough Guides include recommendations from shoestring to luxury and cover more than 200 destinations around the globe, including almost every country in the Americas and Europe, more than half of Africa and most of Asia and Australasia. Our ever-growing team of authors and photographers is spread all over the world, particularly in Europe, the US and Australia.

In the early 1990s, Rough Guides branched out of travel, with the publication of Rough Guides to World Music, Classical Music and the Internet. All three have become benchmark titles in their fields, spearheading the publication of a wide range of books under the Rough Guide name.

Including the travel series, Rough Guides now number more than 350 titles, covering: phrasebooks, waterproof maps, music guides from Opera to Heavy Metal, reference works as diverse as Conspiracy Theories and Shakespeare, and popular culture books from iPods to Poker. Rough Guides also produce a series of more than 120 World Music CDs in partnership with World Music Network.

Visit www.roughguides.com to see our latest publications.

Rough Guide credits

Text editor: Steven Horak
Layout: Umesh Aggarwal
Cartography: Deshpal Dabas
Picture editor: Mark Thomas
Production: Rebecca Short
Proofreader: Serena Stephenson
Cover design: Dan May, Chloë Roberts
Photographer: Greg Ward
Editorial: **London** Andy Turner, Keith Drew, Edward Aves, Alice Park, Lucy White, Jo Kirby, James Smart, Natasha Foges, Róisín Cameron, James Rice, Lara Kavanagh, Emma Traynor, Emma Gibbs, Kathryn Lane, Monica Woods, Mani Ramaswamy, Harry Wilson, Lucy Cowie, Alison Roberts, Joe Staines, Matthew Milton, Tracy Hopkins, Ruth Tidball; **Delhi** Madhavi Singh, Lubna Shaheen, Jalpreen Kaur Chhatwal
Design & Pictures: **London** Scott Stickland, Dan May, Diana Jarvis, Nicole Newman, Sarah Cummins, Emily Taylor; **Delhi** Ajay Verma, Jessica Subramanian, Ankur Guha, Pradeep Thapliyal, Sachin Tanwar, Anita Singh, Nikhil Agarwal, Sachin Gupta

Production: Liz Cherry
Cartography: **London** Ed Wright, Katie Lloyd-Jones; **Delhi** Rajesh Chhibber, Ashutosh Bharti, Rajesh Mishra, Animesh Pathak, Jasbir Sandhu, Karobi Gogoi, Alakananda Roy, Swati Handoo
Online: **London** Faye Hellon, Jeanette Angell, Fergus Day, Justine Bright, Clare Bryson, Aine Fearon, Adrian Low, Ezgi Celebi; **Delhi** Amit Verma, Rahul Kumar, Narender Kumar, Ravi Yadav, Debojit Borah, Rakesh Kumar, Ganesh Sharma, Shisir Basumatari
Marketing & Publicity: **London** Liz Statham, Jess Carter, Vivienne Watton, Anna Paynton, Rachel Sprackett, Laura Vipond; **New York** Katy Ball, Judi Powers; **Delhi** Ragini Govind
Digital Travel Publisher: Peter Buckley
Reference Director: Andrew Lockett
Operations Assistant: Becky Doyle
Operations Manager: Helen Atkinson
Publishing Director (Travel): Clare Currie
Commercial Manager: Gino Magnotta
Managing Director: John Duhigg

Publishing information

This first edition published September 2010 by
Rough Guides Ltd,
80 Strand, London WC2R 0RL
11 Local Shopping Centre, Panchsheel Park, New Delhi 110017, India
Distributed by the Penguin Group
Penguin Books Ltd,
80 Strand, London WC2R 0RL
Penguin Group (USA) .
375 Hudson Street, NY 10014, USA
Penguin Group (Australia)
250 Camberwell Road, Camberwell, Victoria 3124, Australia
Penguin Group (Canada)
195 Harry Walker Parkway N, Newmarket, ON, L3Y 7B3 Canada
Penguin Group (NZ)
67 Apollo Drive, Mairangi Bay, Auckland 1310, New Zealand
Cover concept by Peter Dyer.

Typeset in Bembo and Helvetica to an original design by Henry Iles.
Printed in Singapore
© Samantha Cook 2010
Maps © Rough Guides
No part of this book may be reproduced in any form without permission from the publisher except for the quotation of brief passages in reviews.
264pp includes index
A catalogue record for this book is available from the British Library
ISBN: 978-1-85828-659-4
The publishers and authors have done their best to ensure the accuracy and currency of all the information in **The Rough Guide to New Orleans**, however, they can accept no responsibility for any loss, injury, or inconvenience sustained by any traveller as a result of information or advice contained in the guide.

1 3 5 7 9 8 6 4 2

Help us update

We've gone to a lot of effort to ensure that the first edition of **The Rough Guide to New Orleans** is accurate and up-to-date. However, things change – places get "discovered", opening hours are notoriously fickle, restaurants and rooms raise prices or lower standards. If you feel we've got it wrong or left something out, we'd like to know, and if you can remember the address, the price, the hours, the phone number, so much the better.

Please send your comments with the subject line "**Rough Guide New Orleans Update**" to ✉ mail@roughguides.com. We'll credit all contributions and send a copy of the next edition (or any other Rough Guide if you prefer) for the very best emails.

Have your questions answered and tell others about your trip at ⊕ www.roughguides.com

Acknowledgements

In New Orleans, huge thanks are due to Christine de Cuir; Sal and Vivien Impastato, Maria, Janey and all the team at 500 Chartres; Paul Gustings; and Larone Hudson. A hearty thank you also to the Rough Guides team, including Andrew Rosenberg, Mani Ramaswamy and Monica Woods for guiding the project from commission to fruition; Deshpal, Katie and Ed Wright for tireless work on the maps; Mark Thomas for fun picture meetings; Umesh Aggarwal for adroit typesetting; and, especially, to editor Steven Horak, for being such a pleasure to work with and for his enthusiasm and patience throughout the project. At home, big love to Pam Cook, a New Orleanian at heart, whom I still hope will join us for a drink in the Napoleon House sometime soon; to Jim Cook and Ulli Sieglohr for their interest and enthusiasm, and for listening so patiently to the endless stories; and of course to my very dear Greg Ward, for sharing all this, and so much more – and without whom this book, and so many other good things, just wouldn't have happened. Above all this book was written for the people of New Orleans: those who remain, those who have passed and those who have yet to return.

Photo credits

Index

Map entries are in colour.

C

258

INDEX

INDEX

259

Map symbols

maps are listed in the full index using coloured text

State boundary

Chapter boundary

US interstate highway

US highway

State highway

Motorway

Major road

Minor road

Steps

Railway

Coastline/river

Ferry

Bridge

Arch

Place of interest

Information office

Post office

Parking

Airport

Garden

Plantation home

Museum

Swamp

One-way arrow

Church

Building

Stadium

Cemetery

Park

So now we've told you about the things not to miss, the best places to stay, the top restaurants, the liveliest bars and the most spectacular sights, it only seems fair to tell you about the best travel insurance around

✦ WorldNomads.com
keep travelling safely

Recommended by Rough Guides

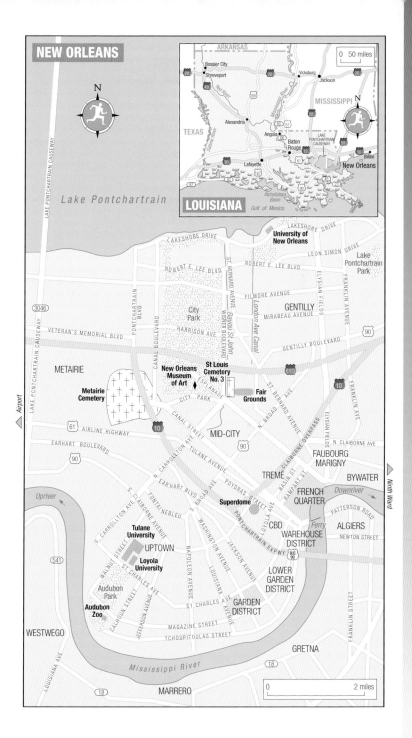

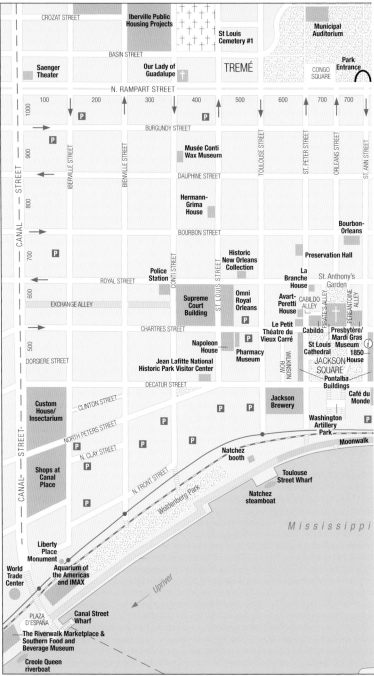

CROZAT STREET

Iberville Public
Housing Projects

St Louis
Cemetery #1

Municipal
Auditorium

BASIN STREET

Saenger
Theater

Our Lady of
Guadalupe

TREMÉ

Park
Entrance

CONGO
SQUARE

N. RAMPART STREET

100   200   300   400   500   600   700   700

1000

BURGUNDY STREET

900

IBERVILLE STREET

BIENVILLE STREET

Musée Conti
Wax Museum

TOULOUSE STREET

ST. PETER STREET

ORLEANS STREET

ST. ANN STREET

DAUPHINE STREET

CANAL — — STREET

800

Hermann-
Grima
House

BOURBON STREET

Bourbon-
Orleans

700

Historic
New Orleans
Collection

Preservation Hall

Police
Station

CONTI STREET

ST. LOUIS STREET

La
Branche
House

St. Anthony's
Garden

ROYAL STREET

600

EXCHANGE ALLEY

Supreme
Court
Building

Omni
Royal
Orleans

Avart-
Peretti
House

CABILDO
ALLEY

PIRATE'S ALLEY

PERE ANTOINE ALLEY

CHARTRES STREET

Le Petit
Théatre du
Vieux Carré

Cabildo

Presbytère/
Mardi Gras
Museum

500

DORSIERE STREET

Napoleon
House

Pharmacy
Museum

WILKINSON ROW

St Louis
Cathedral

1850
House

Jean Lafitte National
Historic Park Visitor Center

JACKSON
SQUARE

DECATUR STREET

Pontalba
Buildings

Custom
House/
Insectarium

CLINTON STREET

Jackson
Brewery

Café du
Monde

STREET-

NORTH PETERS STREET

Washington
Artillery
Park

N. CLAY STREET

Moonwalk

CANAL — — STREET

Shops at
Canal
Place

N. FRONT STREET

Natchez
booth

Woldenberg Park

Toulouse
Street Wharf

Natchez
steamboat

Mississippi

Liberty
Place
Monument

World
Trade
Center

Aquarium of
the Americas
and IMAX

Upriver

PLAZA
D'ESPAÑA

Canal Street
Wharf

The Riverwalk Marketplace &
Southern Food and
Beverage Museum

Creole Queen
riverboat

Algiers

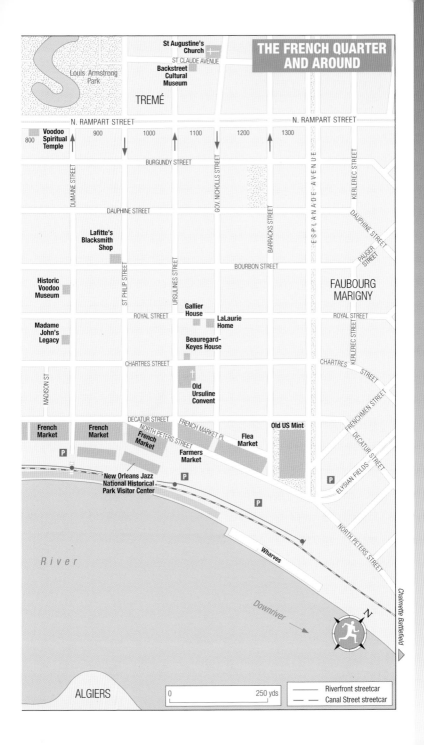

THE FRENCH QUARTER
AND AROUND

St Augustine's
Church

ST CLAUDE AVENUE

Backstreet
Cultural
Museum

Louis Armstrong
Park

TREMÉ

N. RAMPART STREET

N. RAMPART STREET

800 Voodoo
Spiritual
Temple

900   1000   1100   1200   1300

BURGUNDY STREET

DUMAINE STREET

GOV. NICHOLLS STREET

ESPLANADE AVENUE

KERLEREC STREET

DAUPHINE STREET

DAUPHINE STREET

Lafitte's
Blacksmith
Shop

ST PHILIP STREET

BARRACKS STREET

PAUGER STREET

URSULINES STREET

BOURBON STREET

FAUBOURG
MARIGNY

Historic
Voodoo
Museum

Gallier
House

ROYAL STREET

ROYAL STREET

LaLaurie
Home

Madame
John's
Legacy

Beauregard-
Keyes House

KERLEREC STREET

CHARTRES STREET

CHARTRES

STREET

MADISON ST

Old
Ursuline
Convent

FRENCHMEN STREET

DECATUR STREET

Old US Mint

French
Market

French
Market

NORTH PETERS STREET

FRENCH MARKET PL

French
Market

FRENCH MARKET PL

Flea
Market

DECATUR STREET

P

Farmers
Market

New Orleans Jazz
National Historical
Park Visitor Center

P

ELYSIAN FIELDS

P

P

NORTH PETERS STREET

River

Wharves

Downriver

N

Chalmette Battlefield

ALGIERS

0   250 yds

—— Riverfront streetcar
- - - Canal Street streetcar

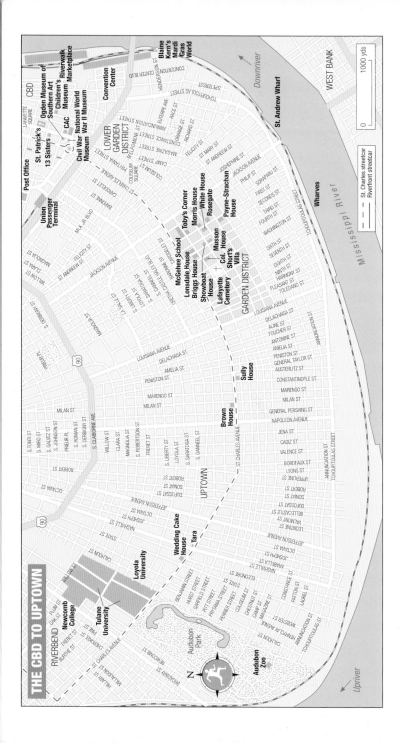

THE CBD TO UPTOWN

CBD

Post Office
St. Patrick's
13 Sisters

Ogden Museum of
Southern Art
Children's
Museum
CAC

LAFAYETTE
SQUARE

Riverwalk
Marketplace

Civil War National World
Museum War II Museum

Convention
Center

Blaine
Kern's
Mardi
Gras
World

Union
Passenger
Terminal

LOWER
GARDEN
DISTRICT

Toby's Corner
Morris House
White House
Rosegate

St. Andrew Wharf

McGehee School
Lonsdale House
Briggs House
Showboat
House
Lafayette
Cemetery

Col.
Short's
Villa

Musson
House

Payne-Strachan
House

Downriver

GARDEN DISTRICT

Sully
House

Brown
House

UPTOWN

Wedding Cake
House
Tara

RIVERBEND

Newcomb
College

Tulane
University

Loyola
University

Wharves

Mississippi River

WEST BANK

Audubon
Park

Audubon
Zoo

N

Upriver

- - - St. Charles streetcar
— — — Riverfront streetcar

0   1000 yds